Critical Essays on E.E. Cummings

D0205435

Critical Essays on E.E. Cummings

Guy Rotella

G.K. Hall & Co. • Boston, Massachusetts

Library of Congress Cataloging in Publication Data
Main entry under title:

Critical essays on E.E. Cummings.

(Critical essays on American literature)
Includes index.
1. Cummings, E. E. (Edward Estlin), 1894–1962— Criticism and interpretation—Addresses, essays, lectures. I. Rotella, Guy L. II. Series.
PS3505.U334Z57   1984   811'.52   83-12668
ISBN 0-8161-8677-4

CRITICAL ESSAYS ON AMERICAN LITERATURE

This series seeks to anthologize the most important criticism on a wide variety of topics and writers in American literature. Our readers will find in various volumes not only a generous selection of reprinted articles and reviews but original essays, bibliographies, manuscript sections, and other materials brought to public attention for the first time. Guy Rotella's book on E.E. Cummings is a welcome addition to our list in that it is the most comprehensive collection of scholarship on this writer yet assembled. Among the thirty-nine essays are reprinted articles and reviews by John Peale Bishop, Edmund Wilson, Allen Tate, Kenneth Burke, R.P. Blackmur, John Berryman, Helen Vendler, Malcolm Cowley, and L.S. Dembo. In addition, there is an extensive introduction that surveys the history of scholarship, a revised essay by Norman Friedman, and an original article by Professor Rotella. We are confident that this collection will make a permanent and significant contribution to American literary study.

JAMES NAGEL, GENERAL EDITOR

Northeastern University

For my parents

CONTENTS

INTRODUCTION

Two days after E.E. Cummings' death, the *New York Times* carried a story about a coffee shop waitress who mourned the poet's passing and who, when questioned, turned out to own two of his books.[1] This charming, if sentimental, anecdote is a good index to Cummings' popular reputation, one matched in this century only by Robert Frost's. It is less easy to indicate Cummings' critical reputation, however, which at times seems complicated by his very popularity. In fact, a rather detailed survey of Cummings scholarship is required if the critical response to his work is to be made clear.

Critical comment on Cummings in the 1922 to 1977 period reflects a more or less continuous and intensifying scholarly interest in his work.[2] It also reflects a tendency for his reputation and for critical interest in him to rise and fall concurrently with developments in the history of American literary scholarship. In the twenties, Cummings published several of his important works: the autobiographical World War I novel *The Enormous Room* (1922); four collections of poems, *Tulips and Chimneys* (1923), *&* (1925), *XLI Poems* (1925), and *is 5* (1926); and the play *Him* (1927). Not surprisingly, the Cummings criticism of the decade is dominated by reviews. Those of *The Enormous Room* typically veer to extremes of praise or condemnation, the choice seemingly determined by a given reviewer's attitude toward the literary avant-garde or toward Cummings' unconventional judgments of war, governments, and value systems. Perhaps the most important review is John Peale Bishop's, with its anticipation of later explorations of the novel's pilgrimage conversion motifs.[3] Also significant is Edward Cummings' (the poet's father's) introduction to *The Enormous Room*;[4] it reprints letters and telegrams involved in securing Cummings' release from La Ferté-Macé, the French prison setting of the novel.

The reviews of Cummings' poetry of the twenties are typically "mixed." His "eccentric" typography is the despair of some reviewers; it enchants others, but most express high praise for his themes and serious doubts about the legitimacy of his technical experiments. This ambivalence eventually led to what became for a time a cliché of Cummings

1

criticism (especially that by "non-specialists"), the idea that he is a profoundly traditional, even conventional, poet in spite of his modernist, experimental surfaces. Important reviews are those by Slater Brown—with
whom Cummings was imprisoned in France ("B" in *The Enormous
Room*)—and Edmund Wilson. Brown emphasizes the influence of painting on Cummings' poetic techniques.[5] Wilson charges Cummings with
immaturity.[6] Other reviewers note Cummings' use of improvisation and
of the techniques of such seventeenth-century poets as Marvell and
Herrick.

Reviews of Cummings' first play, *Him*, tend to excess: it revitalizes a
moribund theatre; it is empty and boring. More temperate responses
register delight in the play's verbal and dramatic innovations and distress
at its lack of concern for "produceability" and clarity of meaning. Of
special interest is Gilbert Seldes' pamphlet *"him" and the Critics*, a collection of excerpts from twenty-seven newspaper reviews of the Provincetown Playhouse production.[7] In any case, it would be some time before
commentary on *Him* got much beyond assertion, summary, or description.

In addition to reviews of specific works, Cummings criticism in the
twenties did produce three important more general studies. The best of
these is Gorham B. Munson's "Syrinx."[8] Munson affords Cummings'
poetry the sort of careful analytic attention to technique that would not
become typical of the scholarship for many years. His argument, that
Cummings' use of experimental methods for the expression of traditional
lyric themes marries form and content rather than divorces them,
represents an important repudiation of those who would separate Cummings' techniques from his themes. Furthermore, Munson demonstrates
that Cummings' punctuation and typography are *"active instruments for
literary expression,"* that their intention and achievement is the renewal
of antique themes. A similar point is made in an extensive section on
Cummings' orthographic and punctuational devices in Robert Graves'
and Laura Riding's *A Survey of Modernist Poetry*.[9] Also of interest is Paul
Rosenfeld's observation, in his *Men Seen*, of Cummings' connection to the
"old Puritanic stem" of New England literature.[10] All of these arguments
and suggestions are expanded on by later scholars.

Reviews again dominate Cummings criticism in the thirties,
although there is a slight increase in the number of general studies
devoted to his work. Books receiving significant attention from the
reviewers are Cummings' experimental account of his journey to the
Soviet Union, *Eimi* (1933), and three volumes of poetry, *ViVa* (1931), *No
Thanks* (1935), and *Collected Poems* (1938). His minor works of the
decade, such as the ballet scenario *Tom* or the translation of Louis
Aragon's revolutionary poem, *The Red Front*, receive perfunctory attention at most. Judgments of *Eimi* are wide-ranging; for example, it is
variously described as a comic masterpiece, a work of exhibitionistic
obscurantism, a witty but affected book, a radical defense of individual

and artist against the collectivist threat, a brilliant experiment in poetic prose, and a willful confusion of poetry with prose. Most intriguing are reviews by pro-Soviet avant-gardists who perceive Cummings' critique of Communist Russia as a betrayal of the revolution by an erstwhile ally; they augur the difficulties certain "liberal" critics would have from the thirties onward in dealing with Cummings' increasingly conservative political stance.

The major development in the reviews of the poetry of the thirties is the recognition of the intensified use of satire in the poems, a recognition that leads to the common division of Cummings' verse into lyric and satiric categories. The most significant reviews of *ViVa* are those by Horace Gregory and Allen Tate. Each makes a charge that, whether repeated or refuted, remains a staple of Cummings scholarship. Gregory asserts that Cummings' poetry is static, without development.[11] Tate charges that Cummings' work is so personal as to be private.[12] Reviews of *No Thanks* and *Collected Poems* make similar complaints or defend Cummings against them.

Of the significant essays on Cummings in the thirties, John Peale Bishop's "The Poems and Prose of E.E. Cummings" is an attempt to place him as an artist and modernist,[13] while John Finch's "New England Prodigal"[14] and Paul Rosenfeld's "The Enormous Cummings"[15] relate the poet to the traditions of literary transcendentalism. The most important essay of the period, however, is R.P. Blackmur's "Notes on E.E. Cummings' Language."[16] Blackmur charges that Cummings' anti-intellectual, romantic-egoistical poetry, with its private vocabulary, is imprecise, and even unintelligible. In part because of the force with which he presents it, in part because of the portion of truth it contains, Blackmur's argument has had enormous weight. For the next several decades commentators on Cummings would have, directly or indirectly, to respond to it. Yet Blackmur's damning essay contains the seeds of its own refutation in its suggestion that continued practice of Cummings' private notation might eventually "produce a set of well-ordered conventions susceptible of general use." Just such a view is taken by many later critics when they attempt to counter Blackmur's strictures, and it is the basis for Blackmur's own modification of his earlier judgment in his 1941 review of *50 Poems*.[17]

In the thirties, Blackmur and others established the terms of what is a continuing controversy about Cummings' artistic merit: at one pole is praise for his transcending individualism, his social criticism, his technical innovations, and his refurbishing of worn conventions; at the other pole is condemnation for uncontrolled egoism, for an anachronistic conservatism, for "false" experimentalism and anti-intellectualism, for imprecision and unintelligibility, and for a lack of thematic and technical development.

Cummings' minor works of the forties, such as the plays *Anthropos* and *Santa Claus*, received scant critical attention, but his two major volumes, the collections *50 Poems* (1940) and *1 x 1* (1944), were reviewed by influential critics in influential publications. Cummings' work claimed serious attention. Nevertheless, that attention continued to produce complex and qualified results. Blackmur's review of *50 Poems*, mentioned above, is the major review of the decade. It presents a balanced response, admiring Cummings' immediacy and energy and decrying his too general vocabulary. Furthermore, in it Blackmur expands his suggestion that Cummings' private notation, used continuously, might attain a usable precision. The expansion results from Blackmur's attending to the poems' "use of prepositions, pronouns, and the auxiliary verbs in the guise of substances, and of words ordinarily rhetorical . . . for the things of actual experience." The approach this suggests is employed by many later critics. If Blackmur's review of *50 Poems* is a balanced one, most other contemporary reviews are rather harshly negative, often on the grounds that Cummings had failed to develop as an artist.

The reception of *1 x 1* nearly reverses that of *50 Poems*. Most of the reviews are positive, yet a major one is negative. In it, F.O. Matthiessen insists that the static quality of Cummings' themes and techniques flatly contradicts his constant concern with growth.[18] Clearly, the question of Cummings' development remains crucial in the criticism of the forties.

As the stature of his reviewers indicates Cummings' own stature in the forties, so, too, does a small number of general essays and—the most important event of Cummings' criticism in the decade—the publication in 1946 of the Cummings number of the *Harvard Wake*.[19] The issue contains comment on Cummings by important writers and critics, among them, Jacques Barzun, John Dos Passos, Harry Levin, Marianne Moore, Karl Shapiro, Allen Tate, Lionel Trilling, and William Carlos Williams. The special issue also has significant essays by Lloyd Frankenberg, on Cummings' thematic praise of an aristocracy based not on rank but aliveness, by Paul Rosenfeld, on *Eimi*, and by Theodore Spencer, on Cummings' techniques for replacing the time content of language with simultaneity. Also of interest is Fairfield Porter's brief comment on Cummings as a painter, an aspect of his creative life receiving little further attention until Rushworth M. Kidder's essays of the seventies.

One additional aspect of Cummings scholarship in the forties merits mention here. In 1938 the first edition of Cleanth Brooks' and Robert Penn Warren's *Understanding Poetry* had appeared, containing an explication of "Buffalo Bill's."[20] This exemplar of the New Critical technique of close textual analysis signaled what would become a major method of subsequent Cummings scholarship. Several explications of Cummings poems appeared in the forties. However, these were but a predictive rumble to the eruption of such criticism in the fifties and sixties. At the same time, though, the doctrines of the New Criticism would as often impede as encourage attention to Cummings' particular aesthetic virtues.

The fifties and sixties witnessed a remarkable growth in American literary scholarship; the Cummings criticism of the period reflects that growth. The number of items in the fifties considering him and his work more than doubles the number in the forties. If not quite an industry, Cummings scholarship was a thriving small business. This expanded attention to Cummings is characterized by still more extensive reviews of his major works, by more frequent and fuller considerations of him than before in literary and period "histories," by a great increase in essays offering "close readings" of individual poems, by the earliest extensive bibliographical and biographical attention to him, by the first dissertations to take him as their subject, and, most significantly, by several lengthy scholarly articles. These last continue to examine the by-then determined issues of Cummings criticism (the relationship of his techniques to his themes, his growth or lack of it), but they do so more maturely than earlier commentary, offering evidence as well as assertion; frequently they push beyond those issues.

Cummings' important works of the fifties are *Xaipe* (1950), *i: Six Nonlectures* (1953), *Poems 1923–1954* (1954), and *95 Poems* (1958). On the whole, the reviews are "respectful" and indicate that Cummings has become an established, if hardly an establishment, writer. Among the significant reviews of *Xaipe*, some continue the controversy over Cummings' development, others affirm the expressiveness of his experimental techniques and their appropriateness to the expression of his themes. Other important reviews, among them Randall Jarrell's,[21] make a new charge against Cummings: the absence of the tragic element in his work trivializes both its lyric joy and satiric outrage. *i: Six Nonlectures* collects the talks Cummings gave while Norton Professor of Poetry at Harvard in 1952–1953. Reviews of it tend to summarize those talks or to describe their occasions, their autobiographical content, or their characteristically peculiar style. A few emphasize the concern of the "non-lectures" with the individual in a mass society, their revelation of Cummings' relationships to strains of transcendental thought, and their reflection of the poet's tendency to sentimentalism.

The publication in 1954 of the retrospective collection *Poems 1923–1954* occasioned several essay-reviews reconsidering Cummings' poetic career. Some are enthusiastic, others echo earlier complaints, but most are "mixed" and are of interest for their attempts to locate Cummings on the map of modern poetry. Perhaps of most interest is Randall Jarrell's assessment in the *New York Times Book Review*.[22] He finds Cummings' collection a "formidable" one, but complains of its monotony and its too pure split between lyric affirmation and satiric negation. In this, as in his distress at Cummings' alleged lack of a tragic dimension, Jarrell reveals the New Critical bias which sometimes distorted the scholarly response to Cummings in the fifties. In contrast to the many thoughtful reviews of *Poems 1923–1954*, those of *95 Poems* are often perfunctory, issuing conventional praise or repeating old charges. There are exceptions, a few of which find the collection below Cummings' usual standard.

Another sign of the increased critical attention paid Cummings in the fifties is the appearance of many close analyses of individual poems, the bulk of them published in the *Explicator*. However paradoxically, these, too, are the result of New Critical emphases. They are most important for their typical insistence on and demonstration of the unity of Cummings' techniques with his themes. Related indicators of increased attention are Paul Lauter's initial work in primary and secondary bibliography[23] and the four doctoral dissertations taking Cummings as their subject. A more dramatic sign than these is the publication in the fifties of the first book on Cummings. Charles Norman's biography, *The Magic-Maker: E.E. Cummings*,[24] is more appreciative than it is scholarly or critical. Nevertheless, it makes available much factual, anecdotal, and "atmospheric" information on the poet's life, works, and residences, and, for whatever this is worth, it bears Cummings' imprimatur.

The most important development in Cummings criticism in the fifties, though, is the number of serious scholarly essays devoted to him, several of which appeared in some of the more influential literary journals of the period, among them, *PMLA*, *The Kenyon Review*, and *American Literature*. Summaries of the most significant essays follow. They outline the course of Cummings scholarship in the decade. In "::2:1 The World and E.E. Cummings," George Haines, IV returns to what had become by the thirties a cliché of the criticism: the ease with which Cummings' poetry can be divided into and contained by lyric and satiric categories. However, Haines pushes well beyond that cliché in his attempt to resolve the paradox that Cummings loathes abtraction and expresses his loathing concretely, while his love of the concrete is often only expressed abstractly.[25] In "The Poetic Mask of E.E. Cummings: Character and Thought of the Speaker," Norman Friedman—who became and remains Cummings' most insightful and prolific critic—argues that the informing characteristic of Cummings' persona is the elevation of "freshness of response and accuracy in its expression" over the chief obstacle to such response and expression, submission to mass life.[26] Related points are made by Ralph J. Mills in "The Poetry of Innocence: Notes on E.E. Cummings"[27] and by Barbara Watson in "The Dangers of Security: E.E. Cummings' Revolt Against the Future."[28] According to Mills, Cummings uses his appraisal of being and becoming to oppose " 'civilized' scientific method." Watson places Cummings' themes in historical context by stressing his rejection of the devitalizing factors enabling the growth of mass societies.

S.V. Baum's "E.E. Cummings: The Technique of Immediacy" considers Cummings' devices of simultaneous presentation, as those devices work against the sequential nature of syntax.[29] In " 'Only to Grow': Change in the Poetry of E.E. Cummings," Rudolph Von Abele rebuts the charge that Cummings' poetry lacks development by demonstrating its technical and thematic progress through three distinct periods.[30] Eleanor M. Sickels' "The Unworld of E.E. Cummings" alleges the degeneration of Cummings' satiric verse from effective propaganda and art into a nihilism that is the *reductio ad absurdum* of his radical individualism.[31] Essays on Cummings' language by Norman Friedman ("Diction, Voice, and Tone: The Poetic Language of E.E. Cummings")[32] and Robert E. Maurer ("Latter-Day Notes on E.E. Cummings' Language")[33] make detailed refutations of R.P. Blackmur's earlier strictures. Louis C. Rus's "Structural Ambiguity" prepares the way for later linguistics approaches to the poetry.[34]

Cummings' drama and prose also receive attention in essays of the fifties. In "*Him* (1927)," Eric Bentley and Theodore Hoffman replace what had been mere controversy about the play with more objective analysis,[35] as does Robert E. Maurer in "E.E. Cummings' *Him*."[36] Kingsley Widmer's "Timeless Prose" gives similar serious attention to *The Enormous Room* and, more briefly, to *Eimi*.[37]

It is clear that Cummings' critical reputation improved in the fifties. By-then conventional questions about his artistic growth and the relationship of his techniques to his themes were asked objectively and pursued analytically. They were typically answered in his favor. Nevertheless, in quantity and in level of critical approval, Cummings scholarship never reached the levels accorded such of his contemporaries as Frost, Hemingway, Eliot, Faulkner, and Stevens. (There was, for instance, still no critical book on Cummings.) In part, this is explained by the fact that many critics found—and find—Cummings' breadth and depth of subject, theme, and technique less than fully major. However, it is also in part explained by the fact that Cummings' personal, lyrical, anti-analytical, "anti-intellectual," "simple," and unallusive poetry was (or seemed) out of step with the period's literary and critical fashion for impersonal, dramatic, analytical, intellectual, complex, and allusive art. In the sixties and seventies the fashion would change and in some ways come closer to making demands Cummings' verse might meet. Cummings' reputation in the next two decades would benefit from this change, however partially or indirectly.

Reviews played a minor role in the Cummings scholarship of the sixties; only *73 Poems* (1963) received significant notice. Not surprisingly in responses to a posthumous volume (Cummings died in 1962), the reviews are typically respectful in tone. Few of them make any critical contribution; some, even when respectful, continue to charge Cummings with insufficient development and ineffective techniques. The latter charge, although now made less often and less vigorously than in previous decades, continues to be rebutted—as it was in the fifties—by a large number (nearly twice that in the previous decade) of close analyses of individual poems. Repeatedly these studies demonstrate the unity of Cummings' themes and techniques. And their weight increases as the number of poems receiving such analysis mounts. In fact, by the early sixties it was generally accepted that Cummings is a serious craftsman whose techniques, however eccentric, are integral to his thematic expression—as some critics, of course, had long insisted. These explications, as well as Cummings' continuing appearance as the subject of dissertations, indicate that the thoughtful attention which typified Cummings scholarship in the fifties was consolidated and expanded in the sixties. This is further indicated by the many major essays on Cummings—more than in any previous period, by the appearance of significant treatments of Cummings in parts of books, and by the several books taking him as their subject. These dominate the Cummings criticism of the period.

Many of the essays on Cummings published in the sixties fall into the same categories as do those of the fifties. The classification showing most growth is that including the essays employing a linguistics approach to the poems. This is not surprising; Cummings' frequent violations of the principles of conventional grammar and syntax make him a prime subject for the then developing use of the tools of linguistics for literary analysis. But although these essays are of interest as early examples of what would become an increasingly significant critical method, most of them are of little importance to Cummings scholarship, for they are more interested in using Cummings' poetry as a means to illuminate linguistics study than the reverse. An exception to this (an exception that in its inversion of those emphases will become more typical of linguistics studies of Cummings in the seventies) is Irene R. Fairley's "Syntax as Style," which discusses syntactic deviance as an expressive device in three Cummings poems.[38]

Among the general Cummings essays of the decade, John Logan's "The Organ-Grinder and the Cockatoo" is particularly illuminating in its discussion of Cummings' thematic and technical paradigms, love and language, respectively.[39] The major thematic essay of the sixties is Patricia Buchanan Tal-Mason Cline's discussion of Cummings' demand for an "holistic experience of life" in her "The Whole E.E. Cummings."[40] The most significant essay of the sixties on Cummings' technique is Haskell S. Springer's "The Poetics of E.E. Cummings," with its emphasis on Cummings' frequent (and frequently concealed) use of "traditional prosodic principles."[41] In other important contributions in essays, Bernard Benstock, in "All the World a Stage," discusses the elements of drama—especially of dramatic characterization—in Cummings' poems;[42] James P. Dougherty, in "Language as a Reality in E.E. Cummings," argues that Cummings avoids the pitfalls of abstraction not by grounding his work in phenomenological particulars, as most of his contemporaries do, but by reference to the "tangibility of language itself";[43] and Sister Mary David Babcock, O.S.B., in "Cummings' Typography: An Ideogrammic Style," suggests that Cummings' use of typography to capture "aliveness" has connections with the Chinese ideogram.[44] Other essays of the sixties also provide context for Cummings and his works. For instance, John Clendenning's "Cummings, Comedy, and Criticism" locates him in the American humor tradition.[45] More significant is Norman Friedman's attempt to define Cummings' place within (and without) the modernist tradition in his "E.E. Cummings and the Modernist Movement" (reprinted here with a "Post Script" written especially for this volume).[46]

As in the fifties, some of Cummings' individual works also receive attention from essayists in the sixties. Three essays analyze *The Enormous Room*: David E. Smith's "*The Enormous Room* and *The Pilgrim's Progress*,"[47] Marilyn Gaull's particularly fine "Language and Identity: A Study of E.E. Cummings' *The Enormous Room*,"[48] and James P. Dougherty's "E.E. Cummings: *The Enormous Room*."[49] Two critics treat *Him*: Katherine J. Worth in her "The Poets in the American Theatre,"[50] and Manuel L. Grossman in his "*Him* and the Modern Theatre."[51] In a break with the usual course of Cummings criticism, Charles Stetler devotes an entire essay to a single volume of Cummings' poems. "E.E. Cummings' *73 Poems*: With Life's Eye" explores the book as an impressive final stage in Cummings' career-long growth as an artist. The essay is typical of much Cummings scholarship of the sixties in its implicit rejection of earlier accusations of non-development.[52]

The essays summarized above fall more or less clearly into categories established in the previous decade. A few others break relatively new ground. Sister Joan Marie Lechner, O.S.U., considers Cummings as a "nature poet" in "E.E. Cummings and Mother Nature";[53] Fred E.H. Schroeder discusses his use of obscenity in "Obscenity and its Function in the Poetry of E.E. Cummings";[54] and Mick Gidley examines Cummings' "poempictures" in "Picture and Poem: E.E. Cummings in Perspective."[55] Richard S. Kennedy's biographical essay, "Edward Cummings, the Father of the Poet," suggests the influence of the poet's father's world view on the poet.[56]

So far, this survey of work on Cummings in the sixties indicates a strongly positive response to his achievement. The indicator is accurate, but two significant essays complicate the picture. Carl Bode's "E.E. Cummings and Exploded Verse," while it admires some of the experimental love songs and the energy of Cummings' indignation and irreverence, concludes that an obsessive quest for novelty causes much of his work to fail.[57] In "An Instrument to Measure Spring With," Clive James notes that Cummings' ideas, put into practice, would bring an end to civilization.[58]

In addition to the sustained importance of critical essays as a component of Cummings criticism in the sixties, treatments of Cummings in parts of books make significant contributions to the scholarship for the first time in those years. One of the most important of these is the section on Cummings from L.S. Dembo's *Conceptions of Reality in Modern American Poetry*.[59] Other significant treatments in parts of books are in David R. Weimer's *The City as Metaphor*,[60] in George Wickes' *Americans in Paris*,[61] and in two important surveys of the history of American poetry. In his *American Poets from the Puritans to the Present*, Hyatt H. Waggoner, through examination of Cummings' metaphysics, connects him with Emerson. They share an intuitive epistemology, an organic aesthetic, and a kind of "mystical antinomianism." Unfortunately, only a percentage of Cummings' poems successfully express his ideas; too often his techniques are unimaginative and repetitive.[62] Roy Harvey Pearce, in *The Continuity of American Poetry*, concentrates on the personal element in the poems and finds that Cummings' redemption of language from deadening abstraction is successful but that his "self-transcendence" is often merely "self-realization."[63]

If all of these signal Cummings' increased critical stature in the sixties, this is signaled more strongly still by the several books in the period devoted entirely to him and his works. F.W. Dupee and George Stade edited *Selected Letters of E.E. Cummings*,[64] George J. Firmage published his descriptive bibliography of primary works, *E.E. Cummings: A Bibliography*,[65] and Charles Norman brought out an updated version of his biography, entitled *E.E. Cummings: A Biography*.[66] Moreover, five critical books and one pamphlet on Cummings also appeared in the sixties. The first of these, and still the best study of Cummings' poetry, is Norman Friedman's *e.e. cummings: the art of his poetry*.[67] The book is an overview of Cummings' poetry through *95 Poems*. Successive chapters take up, in sophisticated detail, Cummings' major themes, the stances of his speakers, his "neutral," reverential, and burlesque styles, and his technical devices. Later chapters examine Cummings' craft (through a rare glimpse of manuscript versions of a Cummings poem) and argue that although his development has not been by crisis or reversal his poetry does reveal significant growth in thought, expression, form, and technique. A second edition of the book, in 1967, adds a lengthy listing of critical responses to Cummings published from 1922 to 1965. Friedman's concern with Cummings' artistic development is more central still in his second book on the poet, *e.e. cummings: The Growth of a Writer*.[68] After laying technical and thematic groundwork, this more introductory but nonetheless illuminating study examines—in order by genre and chronologically by decade—each of Cummings' published works preceding the posthumous *73 Poems*.

Another book on Cummings published in the sixties is S.V. Baum's *EΣTI: eec E.E. Cummings and the Critics*, which reprints twenty-six reviews of and essays on Cummings' work as well as primary and secondary bibliographies and a useful introductory essay tracing the development of Cummings' reputation.[69] Somewhat less significant are Robert E. Wegner's *The Poetry and Prose of E.E. Cummings*, an intelligent overview, accurately described by its author as an "appreciation,"[70] and Eve Triem's pamphlet, *E.E. Cummings*, which is necessarily brief and general but often pointed in its insights.[71] More valuable than these is Barry A. Marks' excellent *E.E. Cummings*.[72] Especially important are its often striking analyses of a few specific poems and its detailed theoretical and analytical treatment of matters often ignored or merely noted by other critics: Cummings' "child vision"; his thematic use of sex; his relationship to characteristic aesthetic principles of his age; his relationship to formalist concepts of the poet as craftsmanlike maker and creator of order; his sharing and critique of such American traits as optimism, intensity of spirit, and millenial drive for perfection; and the religious quality of much of his writing.

The serious interpretive and research scholarship marking Cummings studies in the fifties and sixties continued and increased in the early and middle seventies. And the period maintained the more or less accepted estimate of Cummings as a kind of minor-major poet, modernist in style and traditional in theme. (Nagging doubts about the value of his experiments and about his growth as a writer also persist, despite the arguments of Friedman and others.) In any case, the major development of Cummings criticism in the early and middle seventies is not any dramatic reversal or even revision of his reputation, but an increased focusing on more and more specific subjects and critical questions. Reviews, of course, play a small role in the commentary of these years. *Selected Letters of E.E. Cummings* (1969) and *Complete Poems 1913–1962* (1972) received relatively little attention, perhaps because of their "retrospective" quality. An exception to this is Helen Vendler's major review of *Complete Poems*.[73] Her conclusions: that Cummings' optimism excludes too much and that he is a "great aborted talent" "abysmally short on ideas," may result in part from her New Critical bias in favor of ironic, polyvalent art with a tragic cast, but they are also the thoughtful judgments of one of our finest critical intelligences. As such, they can serve to remind us that, despite the defenses and praises of Cummings specialists, many generalists—who, after all, may have a better perspective on the matter—maintain serious reservations about the relative quality and stature of Cummings' art. To an extent, for all the scholarly work, his reputation remains unresolved.

However this may be, critical attention to Cummings in the early and middle seventies does increase. This is shown in the fourteen dissertations considering him (these, by the way, continue to appear at a rough rate of one or two a year), but more significantly in the number of major articles on Cummings. It is in these that the movement of the scholarship toward greater specificity is most evident. Nonetheless, two of the essays do take a general approach. Malcolm Cowley's "Cummings: One Man Alone" combines biographical and critical comment;[74] William Heyen's "In Consideration of Cummings" finds much of the poetry a response and resistance to "the blunt fact of death" and argues that many of the poems have more depth of irony and duplicity in them than is usually noticed.[75] The other essays of the period are more narrowly focused. Joseph W.

Mahoney's "E.E. Cummings Today" is a bibliographical survey; it finds that Cummings scholarship moves between seeing him, on the one hand, as an anti-cultural, anti-intellectual writer and seeing him, on the other, as an ingenious interpreter of his culture who makes new demands on the intellect.[76] Richard S. Kennedy's "E.E. Cummings at Harvard: Studies"[77] and "E.E. Cummings at Harvard: Verse, Friends, Rebellion"[78] explore the aspects of Cummings' life indicated by their titles. John W. Crowley's "Visual-Aural Poetry" examines Cummings' typography.[79] Linguistics approaches to Cummings continue in essays by Jan Aarts, Richard Gunter, and Tanya Reinhart.[80]

More important than these are several essays extending the sixties' attention to Cummings' major prose and dramatic works, *The Enormous Room* and *Him*. James F. Smith, Jr.'s "A Stereotyped Archetype: E.E. Cummings' Jean leNègre" considers the character from *The Enormous Room* as an archetype of individual humanity confronting government inhumanity.[81] Harold T. McCarthy examines Cummings' anomalous responses to the experiences recorded in the novel in terms of Cummings' American-patrician heritage in "E.E. Cummings: Eros and Cambridge, Mass."[82] The title defines the focus of George S. Peek's "The Narrator as Artist and the Artist as Narrator: A Study of E.E. Cummings' *The Enormous Room*."[83] Jeffrey Walsh describes the experience of *The Enormous Room* as catalyzing Cummings' social vision.[84] Essays on *Him* are William I. Oliver's "*Him*—A Director's Note," which considers the play as a complex of surrealism, realism, and expressionism,[85] and Marjorie S.C. Smelstor's " 'Damn Everything but the Circus,' " which explores *Him* in the context of the popular arts of the twenties.[86]

An area of Cummings' work which had been largely ignored, his paintings and drawings, receives significant attention in the middle seventies. Rushworth M. Kidder examines and provides intellectual background for Cummings' career as a painter in "E.E. Cummings, Painter."[87] Cummings' graphics for *The Dial* are the subject of Kidder's " 'Author of Pictures.' "[88] The same drawings are discussed—as complements to Cummings poems—in Robert Tucker's "E.E. Cummings as an Artist."[89]

As in the sixties, some Cummings essays of the early and middle seventies place him in larger contexts. Allan A. Metcalf notes some similarities between Cummings' work and Dante's;[90] James E. Tanner compares Cummings' experimental style to William Burroughs'.[91] Mary Ellen Solt notes Cummings' influence on "concrete poetry,"[92] while Paul Fort locates him within the dialectic struggle between aestheticism and energy typical of modern American poetry,[93] and Renzo S. Crivelli traces Cummings' connections with movements in modern art and music.[94]

Despite their increased specificity, most of the essays of the seventies summarized so far fall into categories established by the earlier criticism. However, as the decline of New Critical domination had earlier enabled reexamination and reevaluation of Cummings' work, so the development of critical modes and approaches to replace, supplement, or complement those of the New Criticism generated some new areas of Cummings scholarship in the early and middle seventies. Of course, linguistics approaches to Cummings had begun earlier. Other new approaches are reflected in the attention to elements of popular culture in Cummings in the essay by Marjorie S.C. Smelstor mentioned above and in Patrick B. Mullen's "E.E. Cummings and Popular Culture."[95] Eleanor Hombitzer presents a structuralist interpretation of "a wind has blown the rain away and blown,"[96] and John M. Lipski uses topology, a branch of mathematics concerned with spatial properties, to examine "disconnectedness" in Cummings' poems.[97] A more traditional development is the beginning use by scholars—particularly Richard S. Kennedy and Rushworth M. Kidder—of the materials in the Cummings collection of Harvard University's Houghton Library.

Of treatments of Cummings in parts of books in the early and middle seventies only one is crucial: Dickran Tashjian's examination of Cummings' relationships to Dadaism in his *Skyscraper Primitives: Dada and the American Avant-Garde 1910–1925*.[98] Also significant is Richard S. Kennedy's introduction to George James Firmage's edition of the original manuscript of *Tulips & Chimneys*.[99] The introduction is important in its own right for its definition of Cummings' "Apollonian, Satyric, and Hephaestian" styles, and also because it inaugurates Liveright's continuing series of "typescript editions" of Cummings' works, about which more in a moment.

The books on Cummings in the early and middle seventies reflect the pattern of Cummings essays in the period. One is a general treatment; two are more narrowly focused. A fourth is a collection of essays. *E.E. Cummings: A Remembrance of Miracles*, by Bethany K. Dumas, is comprehensive, a workmanlike introduction with chapters on the life, the early poems, the later poems, the prose, and the plays.[100] Gary Lane's *I Am: A Study of E.E. Cummings' Poems* analyzes individual poems to demonstrate the development (over Cummings' career) from motifs to major themes of five "ideas": seduction, the individual and individualistic heroism, the transcendent unification of life and death, death-in-life, and love as the means to and end of transcendence.[101] Still more specifically focused is Irene R. Fairley's *E.E. Cummings and Ungrammar*.[102] Applying the methods of linguistics, Fairley treats Cummings' grammatical irregularities in detail, relating them to his themes. She concludes that he uses "ungrammar" not only for the creation of particular effects in individual lines, but also for the creation of larger structural patterns which become a major source of cohesiveness in his work. Fairley finds Cummings to be a "conservative revolutionary"—in his syntactic deviance as well as in his other techniques and in his themes.

In addition to these books, two pamphlets on Cummings appeared in the years under survey. Both are by Wilton Eckley. One is a selective check-list, the other an introductory sketch.[103] They are of minor importance. Of major importance is Norman Friedman's *E.E. Cummings: A Collection of Critical Essays.*[104]

In the years since the middle seventies, Cummings has continued to receive serious critical attention. Major contributions have been made in books and essays, as well as in one not so obviously scholarly area, exhibitions of Cummings' paintings and drawings. The most significant contribution in this period (roughly 1977 to 1982) is Richard S. Kennedy's *Dreams in the Mirror: A Biography of E.E. Cummings.*[105] A thoughtfully written and superbly researched life of the poet (it makes wide use of the Cummings materials at Houghton Library, at the Humanities Research Center of the University of Texas, and elsewhere), *Dreams in the Mirror* covers in detail all the important personal and artistic events of Cummings' life. Where appropriate the facts are further illuminated by sensitive literary analysis, including superb insights into the development of Cummings' innovative style. Kennedy's biography is definitive. It will be a starting point for all future work on the poet's life and art.

Second in importance only to *Dreams in the Mirror* is Rushworth M. Kidder's *E.E. Cummings: An Introduction to the Poetry*, a volume in the Columbia Introductions to Twentieth-Century Poetry series.[106] As its subtitle announces, the book is introductory, and it gives the expected basic information on Cummings' life, works, themes, techniques, and on the development of his art. However, the book is introductory in a rather more particular sense, and in this sense it makes an especially significant contribution to Cummings scholarship. As early as the forties, close analyses of Cummings' poems appeared rather frequently, and in the fifties and sixties their number greatly increased. Even so, however, most of these analyses were devoted to relatively few poems. Thus, they did not provide the close attention to large numbers of poems that is needed if Cummings' artistic quality is to be more precisely and convincingly evaluated, if continuing doubts about the effectiveness of his techniques, about the relationships of those techniques to his themes, and about his poetic development are to be resolved. Kidder's *E.E. Cummings* goes far toward fulfilling this need, for (combined with information on the sources, allusions, and so on of particular poems) close analyses—arranged chronologically by volume—make up the bulk of the book. Furthermore, Kidder's readings are likely to engender significant responses, refinements, and rebuttals. In any case, the appearance of Kennedy's biography, of Kidder's introduction, and of my own *E.E. Cummings: A Reference Guide*, all indicate strong continuing scholarly interest in Cummings and his work. (So, too, does Southern Illinois University Press's 1980 Arcturus paperback reissue of Friedman's *e.e. cummings: The Growth of a Writer.*)

Another such indication is the devoting to Cummings of an entire issue of the prestigious *Journal of Modern Literature*, under the special editorship of Richard S. Kennedy.[107] Comments on some of the more significant entries in the issue, and a listing of the contents, appear below. *Linguistics in Literature* has also announced plans for a special Cummings number, edited by Bethany K. Dumas and Phillip J. Gibson. As of this writing, the issue has not appeared; however, its table of contents is available and reads as follows: Norman Friedman, "Recent Developments in Cummings Criticism: 1976–1980"; Linda B. Funkhouser and Daniel C. O'Connell, "Cummings Reads Cummings"; Bethany K. Dumas and Phillip J. Gibson, "Parenthetical Remarks"; William Van Peer, "Top-Down and Bottom-Up: Interpretative Strategies in the Reading of E.E. Cummings"; Irene R. Fairley, "Syntax for Seduction: A Reading of Cummings' 'since feeling is first' "; Regis L. Welch, "The Linguistic Paintings of E.E. Cummings, Painter-Poet."

Another important development of recent Cummings scholarship is the continuing appearance of volumes in Liveright's series of Cummings Typescript Editions. Inaugurated in 1976 with the edition of *Tulips & Chimneys*, the series of published and unpublished writings is based on Cummings' typed and autographed manuscripts in the Houghton Library, the Barrett Library of the University of Virginia, the Humanities Research Center of the University of Texas, and the Beinecke Rare Book and Manuscript Library of Yale University. The editor of the series is George James Firmage. Since *Tulips & Chimneys*, four additional volumes have appeared: *The Enormous Room* and *No Thanks* in 1978; *Xaîpe* and *ViVa* in 1979. The first two have introductory essays by Richard S. Kennedy; they provide biographical and interpretive background for the respective works. All four volumes have afterwords by George James Firmage which give information on manuscript sources, variants, and other matters of publication. In living up to its intention "to present the texts of the poet's works exactly as he created them, in versions that are faithful to the letter as well as the spirit of his originals," the Cummings Typescript Editions promise eventual availability of definitive editions for all of Cummings' works. In Liveright's immediate plans are *Etcetera: The Unpublished Poems of E.E. Cummings* and a companion volume, largely of juvenilia, tentatively titled *For the Record*, both edited by George James Firmage and Richard S. Kennedy. In addition, a Norton Critical Edition of *The Enormous Room*, edited by Kennedy, is planned for 1984. Independent of these projects, work on a computer-assisted concordance is underway as well.

In addition to these many signs of continuing scholarly interest in Cummings is a large number of critical essays. Two of the most important of these appear in the Cummings issue of the *Journal of Modern Literature*. They are Rushworth M. Kidder's superb and well-illustrated "Cummings and Cubism: The Influence of the Visual Arts on Cummings' Early Poetry" and Norman Friedman's "Cummings Posthumous," which gives detailed consideration to those works of Cummings published since his death, thus completing the survey begun in *e.e. cummings: The Growth of a Writer*. Also included in the special issue are a particularly illuminating section of Kennedy's biography, "E.E. Cummings: The Emergent Styles, 1916," Irene R. Fairley's "Cummings' Love Lyrics: Some Notes of a Female Linguist," Linda Bradley Funkhouser's "Acoustical Rhythms in 'Buffalo Bill's,' " Edith Everson's "E.E. Cummings' Concept of Death" (on *Santa Claus*), Valerie Meliotes Arms' "A Catholic Reading of Cummings' 'Morsel Miraculous,' " and Artem Lozynsky's "An Annotated Bibliography of Works on Cummings," as well as some previously unpublished poems and other documents. Broadly speaking, these essays continue the trends of the scholarship of the sixties and the early and middle seventies: increased attention to particular works and issues and a shifting away from New Critical approaches both toward such more traditional ones as attempts to place the artist and his works in biographical, historical, and cultural contexts, and toward such more non-traditional and often quite specialized ones as linguistics or acoustical analysis. Recent essays published outside the special issues follow a similar pattern.

Close readings of Cummings persist, of course, as in William V. Davis's " 'A Remembrance of Miracles': e.e. cummings' 'un / der fog' "[108] and Laurence Perrine's "E.E. Cummings' 'what if a much of a which of a wind,' "[109] More typical, though, are several recent essays which provide various sorts of context for Cummings' work. Susan Gates's "E.E. Cummings' Spectatorial View" argues that Cummings' World War I prison experience caused his aesthetic vision to intensify and his spiritual vision to become more transcendental.[110] Gary A. Boire reconsiders the novel which resulted from that prison experience in " 'An Incredible Vastness': Re-reading E.E. Cummings's *The Enormous Room*." Boire calls Cummings a "moralistic visionary" who examines the "fundamental structure of his broken world" in order to discover "the means by which one might achieve a personal harmony, a viable reintegration of the self." He places *The Enormous Room* in the genre of spiritual autobiography and relates it to such works as Augustine's *Confessions*, Defoe's *Robinson Crusoe*, and Wordsworth's *The Prelude*.[111]

Religious versions of literary context are offered by Samuel Pickering's "E.E. Cummings' *Pilgrim's Progress*"[112] and by Noam Flinker's "Biblical Sexuality as Literary Convention: The Song of Songs in E.E. Cummings' 'Orientale.' "[113] Also of interest are Robert K. Martin's "Cummings, Crane, and *The Bridge*," which considers Crane's debt to Cummings,[114] and Jo Brans's interview with John Cheever, "Stories to Comprehend Life," in which Cheever notes his debt to Cummings' work.[115] A more specialized piece, one useful for measuring an aspect of Cummings' emergence as a significant figure for scholarly study, is Richard H. Crowder's history of

Cummings bibliography, " 'he's free into the beauty of the truth': A Review Essay."[116]

Of the essays and other materials outside the special issues, the most important of those with a traditional cast are biographical in their concerns. Often intimate glimpses of the poet are given by his long-"estranged" daughter, Nancy Cummings de Forêt, in her *Charon's Daughter: A Passion of Identity*.[117] Robert K. Martin discusses Cummings' life and work in connection with the Paris of the twenties in his Cummings entry in the *Dictionary of Literary Biography*.[118] And Norman Friedman recounts his personal relations with Cummings in "Knowing and Remembering Cummings."[119] Also significant are two review essays occasioned by the publication of Kennedy's biography, for they provide important comment on Cummings' life and reputation and on influences on his work. They are Guy Davenport's "Satyr and Transcendentalist"[120] and John Bayley's "Mothermonsters and Fatherfigures."[121] The latter is especially useful for providing a contemporary British estimate of Cummings.

An essay traditional in its analytical precision and in its provision of intellectual and other contexts, but verging toward more experimental approaches in its interdisciplinary method is Rushworth M. Kidder's " 'Twin Obsessions': The Poetry and Paintings of E.E. Cummings."[122] A related but more narrowly focused piece is Kidder's "Picture into Poem: The Genesis of Cummings' 'i am a little church.' "[123] These last two essays, which continue Kidder's important work on the interlocking of Cummings' dual roles of poet and painter, are related to other materials and events signaling the renewed interest of recent years in Cummings as a painter. An exhibit of Cummings' paintings and drawings was held at the Hirshhorn Museum in Washington, D.C., from December 2, 1976, to February 6, 1977. The catalog, *E.E. Cummings: The Poet as Artist*, by Frank Gettings, reproduces sixty-eight works.[124] Other exhibits have been mounted at the Gotham Book Mart in New York, from January 25 to February 26, 1982, and at the Dryden Galleries in Providence, Rhode Island, from November 7 through 24, 1982. An exhibit is planned for February of 1983 at the Nielsen Gallery in Boston. Perhaps the most significant recent exhibit is that arranged by Milton A. Cohen, "E.E. Cummings' *Paintings*: The Hidden Career," at the University of Texas at Dallas from September 8 to October 12, 1982, and at the Dallas Public Library from October 18 to November 27, 1982. The exhibition catalog, titled as the exhibit, and also by Milton A. Cohen, contains a useful history and evaluation of Cummings' career as a painter, as well as reproductions, many of them in color, of twenty of his works.[125]

Much other recent work on Cummings employs more experimental approaches. Not surprisingly, the majority of these apply linguistics analysis to the works. A listing of some of them will indicate their nature and scope: Richard D. Cureton, "E.E. Cummings: A Study of Deviant Morphology";[126] Richard D. Cureton, " 'he danced his did': An Analysis" (a detailed study of the linguistically famous line from "anyone lived in a pretty how town");[127] Eleanor Cotton, "Linguistic Design in a Poem by Cummings" (an analysis of "if everything");[128] Dorith Orfi-Schelps, "E.E. Cummings: A Paradox of Non-Difficulty" (linguistics and other analysis of "quick i the death of thing");[129] W.G. Regier, "E.E. Cummings: Redundancy as Poetic Process."[130] Related to these is Thomas M. Linehan's analysis of the "stylistic voices" in Cummings' novel, "Style and Individuality in E.E. Cummings' *The Enormous Room.*"[131] A structuralist approach informs Nomi Tamir-Chez's "Binary Oppositions and Thematic Decoding in E.E. Cummings and Eudora Welty."[132]

Several other critical approaches have also been applied to Cummings in recent years. Reader response theory is the concern of Irene R. Fairley's "Experimental Approaches to Language in Literature: Reader Response to Poems."[133] Fairley uses readers' reactions to "quick i the death of thing" to demonstrate empirically that such reactions need not be wholly idiosyncratic and subjective, that they may show substantive agreement on matters of structure and meaning. Quantification and frequency of appearance charts are the stuff of two essays by Judith A. Vanderbok, "The Nature of E.E. Cummings' Sonnet Forms: A Quantitative Approach"[134] and "Growth Patterns in E.E. Cummings' Sonnets: A Quantitative Approach."[135]

Quite different from such methods are the psychological ones employed in two recent Cummings studies. Renzo S. Crivelli, in *"The Enormous Room* e la visione del pellegrino," presents a psychoanalytical reading of the novel, discovering in it a pilgrimage from an aseptic modern world to one of saving, if sometimes septic, contact with the self and with others. The pilgrimage is effected through the mediating metaphor of the novel's "excremental vision."[136] In "E.E. Cummings and the Thoughts That Lie Too Deep for Tears," David V. Forrest, M.D., presents an insightful and informative study of the poet and his works through discussion of such psychiatric topics as denial, merging, heterostasis, and "mature," "immature," "neurotic," and "narcissistic" defenses.[137] Forrest is also responsible for the quirky and informal *Spring: The Journal of The E.E. Cummings Society*, initiated in 1980 and published quarterly since then.

As this survey of criticism indicates, by the early eighties, Cummings scholarship has reached maturity. The major texts are established and available; minor and unpublished materials are being brought out. There is a full-dress critical biography; there are relatively complete primary and secondary bibliographies; there are several book-length critical studies of real quality. Furthermore, the many essays devoted to Cummings show constant and continuing interest in his work. Moreover, he remains a lightning rod for energetic new approaches to literary study. Nonetheless, Cummings' critical reputation (as opposed, of course, to his "popular" one) remains in doubt. It will be a major task of future Cummings scholarship to work towards resolving that doubt, to evaluate and judge as well as to analyze and codify his work, to locate him as precisely as possible within modern, national, and other literary traditions as well as to consider him as an independent figure.

Considerations guiding the selection of materials for inclusion in this collection are several and, admittedly, sometimes conflicting. First of all, I felt that the book should function as an eclectic but representative introduction to the man and his work as well as to the criticism. Thus it would have to (and does) include at least one largely biographical essay, essays covering the major works, essays reflecting some of the major critical approaches that have been applied to those works, and materials representing the different periods of Cummings criticism. This last requirement suggests an historical function for the volume, one relevant not only to the essays but also, in fact, especially, to the reviews. The reviews reprinted here were chosen for coverage (thus, there is at least one for each of Cummings' major works), for their demonstration, where appropriate, of controversy or conflict in reviewers' responses (so that not only are negative as well as positive reactions included, but also—in some of the cases where important critics differed in their assessments—positive and negative reactions to the same work), and, finally, for their critical value in illuminating Cummings' work or in helping to define his reputation and/or the questions crucial to determining that reputation.

The essays, too, were chosen for coverage, for their places in the history of Cummings criticism (that is, for their places in the development of his reputation and/or for their indications of new areas of scholarly interest in Cummings or of the applications of new or different scholarly methods to his work), for their roles in critical controversies about the nature or quality of Cummings' achievement (as in the various essays from different periods on Cummings' language or on the question of his development), and, again, for their power to illuminate.

Of course, even in a work of this length, the considerations noted must finally define an ideal more precisely than they do an actuality. It was necessary to exclude much that is both representative and illuminating. My first decision was to exclude the most easily available material. Therefore, I reprint no sections from the many fine books on Cummings' life and art, and, with a few significant exceptions which I will note in a moment, no essays already reprinted in previous collections. Of course, no serious student of Cummings can afford to ignore those sources. I also decided to exclude specific analyses of individual poems, for the obvious reason that they are too narrow for a volume of this sort. One other exclusion requires more detailed explanation. I have frequently noted the many linguistics analyses of Cummings in the last twenty-five or so years, and my exclusion of them from this study will seem strange. The reasons for this are two. First, the linguistics essays are often extremely specialized; several focus on a single line. Furthermore, they are often more interested in using Cummings as a test or sample case than in illuminating his work. Second, because in Irene R. Fairley's *E.E. Cummings and Ungrammar*—the one linguistics study of Cummings which is broad in scope and which also uses linguistics analysis to illuminate Cummings rather than the reverse—the individual chapters are so interdependent as to make effective excerption impossible. Had it been possible, I should have violated my decision not to reprint parts of books on Cummings in order to include a section from Fairley's.

It remains for me to comment briefly on the relationships of this collection to the two previous volumes reprinting Cummings criticism. S.V. Baum's *EΣTI: eec E.E. Cummings and the Critics* appeared in 1962. It reprints fifteen reviews and eleven essays. The current collection includes seven of those reviews, most of them of Cummings' earlier works. This overlapping results from the fact that relatively few of the early reviews are of lasting importance. Baum chose astutely, and in several instances I can only follow him. The overlapping is qualified as well as justified, however, since here the reviews also in Baum are typically paired with others offering alternative views. Of Baum's eleven essays, two reappear here: R.P. Blackmur's "Notes on E.E. Cummings' Language" and John Peale Bishop's "The Poems and Prose of E.E. Cummings." Both are historically and critically crucial and belong in a collection that hopes to be comprehensive. Of course, the major distinction between this book and Baum's is simply chronological. Several of the reviews included here and more than two-thirds of the essays appeared after Baum's work was published. Finally, with twenty-four reviews and fourteen essays, this book differs from Baum's in the amount of important material it is able to include.

Similar points can be made about this book and the remaining collection of Cummings materials, Norman Friedman's *E.E. Cummings: A Collection of Critical Essays*, published in 1972 as a volume in Prentice-Hall's Twentieth Century Views series. One review included in Friedman is also reprinted here, R.P. Blackmur's of *50 Poems*. I repeat it because I believe it should be considered in tandem with Blackmur's "Notes on E.E. Cummings' Language," which it partially modifies. I also include one of the essays in Friedman, Robert E. Maurer's "Latter-Day Notes on E.E. Cummings' Language," because it is a direct and compelling rejoinder to Blackmur's essay.

Although less so than from Baum's this collection also differs from Friedman's in its chronological coverage. Of Friedman's reprinted essays, all but two—both from the 1946 Cummings issue of the *Harvard Wake*—are from the fifties and sixties; of the reviews, one is from the thirties, one from the forties, and the other two from the fifties. Friedman simply does not seek the historical coverage the present volume does. Furthermore, ten years have elapsed since publication of Friedman's collection, and more than one-third of the essays in this book are drawn from those years. Finally, this volume differs from Friedman's in the amount of material included; where Friedman reprints fourteen pieces (ten essays and four reviews), this collection reprints thirty-seven; it also includes an essay written especially for it on "uses of nature" in Cummings' later poems. I do not mean to suggest that the present collection supersedes the previous ones; the relative lack of overlap between them demonstrates that they are complementary. I do mean to suggest that, by, as it were, adding to and by bringing up to date the other collections, *Critical Essays on E.E. Cummings* claims a place for itself.

A project of this kind involves the assistance of many persons and institutions. I owe a major debt to Cummings' bibliographers, especially to Richard Crowder of *American Literary Scholarship*; the work of those scholars facilitated the research for this book. Thanks are also due to the authors, journal editors, publishers, and permissions managers who made possible the reprinting of the materials included here, and to Irene R. Fairley, Rushworth M. Kidder, Richard S. Kennedy, and Norman Friedman, who made available important materials I could not otherwise have obtained. I am especially grateful to Norman Friedman for contributing the "Post Script" to his "E.E. Cummings and the Modernist Movement." Acknowledgment is also due to the libraries and library staffs of Boston College, of Brandeis, Boston, Harvard, Tufts and Northeastern universities, and of the Boston Public Library. Special thanks to Francis Cox, Edward Doctoroff, and Jon Lanham of Widener Library. Finally, I thank my editor, James Nagel, who made this volume possible, and my wife, Mary Jane, who assisted in every stage of its preparation.

Guy Rotella
December, 1982

NOTES

1. "Waitress Mourns Poet: 'Beautiful Person' Died," *New York Times*, 4 Sept. 1962, p. 33.

2. Because the history of Cummings' critical reception from 1922 to 1977 is described at length in the introduction to my *E.E. Cummings: A Reference Guide* (Boston: G.K. Hall, 1979), pp. vii–xxxii, this introduction condenses and summarizes the description given there. Discussion of Cummings scholarship in the years since the period covered by the reference guide follows the summary.

3. John Peale Bishop, "Incorrect English," *Vanity Fair*, July 1922, p. 20.

4. Edward Cummings, "Introduction," in *The Enormous Room*, by E.E. Cummings (New York: Boni & Liveright, 1922), pp. i–vi.

5. Slater Brown, rev. of *Tulips and Chimneys*, *Broom*, 6 (1924), 26–28.

6. Edmund Wilson, "Wallace Stevens and E.E. Cummings," *New Republic*, 19 Mar. 1924, pp. 102–103.

7. Gilbert Seldes, *"him" and the Critics: A Collection of Opinions on E.E. Cummings' Play at the Provincetown Playhouse* (New York: The Provincetown Playhouse, 1928).

8. Gorham B. Munson, "Syrinx," *Secession*, No. 5 (1923), pp. 2–11.

9. Laura Riding and Robert Graves, On Cummings, in their *A Survey of Modernist Poetry* (London: Heinemann, 1927), pp. 9–34, 59–64.

10. Paul Rosenfeld, "E.E. Cummings," in his *Men Seen: Twenty-Four Modern Authors* (New York: The Dial Press, 1925), pp. 191–200.

11. Horace Gregory, "An Adolescent Songster," *New York Herald-Tribune Books*, 13 Dec. 1931, p. 22.

12. Allen Tate, "E.E. Cummings," *Poetry*, 39 (1932), 332–37.

13. John Peale Bishop, "The Poems and Prose of E.E. Cummings," *Southern Review*, 4 (1938), 173–86.

14. John Finch, "New England Prodigal," *New England Quarterly*, 12 (1938), 643–53.

15. Paul Rosenfeld, "The Enormous Cummings," *Twice a Year*, 3–4 (1939–1940), 271–80.

16. R.P. Blackmur, "Notes on E.E. Cummings' Language," *Hound & Horn*, 4 (1931), 163–92.

17. R.P. Blackmur, rev. of *50 Poems*, *Southern Review*, 7 (1941), 201–05.

18. F.O. Matthiessen, rev. of *1 x 1*, *Kenyon Review*, 6 (1944), 688–90.

19. Special Cummings Issue, *Harvard Wake*, No. 5 (1946), pp. 20–76.

20. Cleanth Brooks and Robert Penn Warren, Analysis of "Buffalo Bill's," in their *Understanding Poetry* (New York: Holt, 1938), pp. 296–98.

21. Randall Jarrell, rev. of *Xaipe*, *Partisan Review*, 17 (1950), 728–30.

22. Randall Jarrell, "A Poet's Own Way," *New York Times Book Review*, 31 Oct. 1954, p. 6.

23. Paul Lauter, *E.E. Cummings: Index to First Lines and Bibliography of Works By and About the Poet* (Denver: Alan Swallow, 1955).

24. Charles Norman, *The Magic-Maker: E.E. Cummings* (New York: Macmillan, 1958).

25. George Haines, IV, "::2:1 The World and E.E. Cummings," *Sewanee Review*, 59 (1951), 206–27.

26. Norman Friedman, "The Poetic Mask of E.E. Cummings: Character and Thought of the Speaker," *Literary Review*, 2 (1958), 124–44.

27. Ralph J. Mills, "The Poetry of Innocence: Notes on E.E. Cummings," *English Journal*, 48 (1959), 433–42.

28. Barbara Watson, "The Dangers of Security: E.E. Cummings' Revolt Against the Future," *Kenyon Review*, 18 (1956), 519–37.

29. S.V. Baum, "E.E. Cummings: The Technique of Immediacy," *South Atlantic Quarterly*, 53 (1954), 70–88.

30. Rudolph Von Abele, " 'Only to Grow': Change in the Poetry of E.E. Cummings," *PMLA*, 70 (1955), 913–33.

31. Eleanor M. Sickels, "The Unworld of E.E. Cummings," *American Literature*, 26 (1954), 223–38.

32. Norman Friedman, "Diction, Voice, and Tone: The Poetic Language of E.E. Cummings," *PMLA*, 72 (1957), 1036–59.

33. Robert E. Maurer, "Latter-Day Notes on E.E. Cummings' Language," *Bucknell Review*, 5 (1955), 1–23.

34. Louis C. Rus, "Structural Ambiguity: A Note on Meaning and the Linguistic

Analysis of Literature with Illustrations from E.E. Cummings," *Language Learning*, 6 (1955), 62–67.

35. Eric Bentley and Theodore Hoffman, "Him (1927)," in *From the Modern Repertoire: Series Two*, ed. Eric Bentley (Denver: Univ. of Denver Press, 1952), pp. 485–94.

36. Robert E. Maurer, "E.E. Cummings' *Him*," *Bucknell Review*, 6 (1956), 1–27.

37. Kingsley Widmer, "Timeless Prose," *Twentieth Century Literature*, 4 (1958), 3–8.

38. Irene R. Fairley, "Syntax as Style: An Analysis of Three Cummings Poems," in *Studies Presented to Professor Roman Jakobson by His Students* (Cambridge: Slavica Publishers, 1968), pp. 105–11.

39. John Logan, "The Organ-Grinder and the Cockatoo: An Introduction to E.E. Cummings," *Critic*, 20 (1961), 39–40, 42–43.

40. Patricia Buchanan Tal-Mason [Cline], "The Whole E.E. Cummings," *Twentieth Century Literature*, 14 (1968), 90–97.

41. Haskell S. Springer, "The Poetics of E.E. Cummings," *South Atlantic Bulletin*, 32 (1967), 8–10.

42. Bernard Benstock, "All the World a Stage: The Elements of Drama in the Poetry of E.E. Cummings," in *Studies in American Literature*, Louisiana State Univ. Studies, Humanities Series, No. 8, ed. Waldo McNeir and Leo B. Levy (Baton Rouge: Louisiana State Univ. Press, 1960), pp. 104–31.

43. James P. Dougherty, "Language as a Reality in E.E. Cummings," *Bucknell Review*, 16 (1968), 112–22.

44. Sister Mary David Babcock, O.S.B., "Cummings' Typography: An Ideogrammic Style," *Renascence*, 15 (1963), 115–23.

45. John Clendenning, "Cummings, Comedy, and Criticism," *Colorado Quarterly*, 12 (1963), 44–53.

46. Norman Friedman, "E.E. Cummings and the Modernist Movement," *Forum*, 3 (1962), 39–46.

47. David E. Smith, "*The Enormous Room* and *The Pilgrim's Progress*," *Twentieth Century Literature*, 2 (1965), 67–75.

48. Marilyn Gaull, "Language and Identity: A Study of E.E. Cummings' *The Enormous Room*," *American Quarterly*, 19 (1967), 645–62.

49. James P. Dougherty, "E.E. Cummings: *The Enormous Room*," in *Landmarks of American Writing*, ed. Hennig Cohen (New York: Basic Books, 1969), pp. 288–302.

50. Katherine J. Worth, "The Poets in the American Theatre," in *American Theatre*, Stratford-Upon-Avon Studies, No. 10, ed. John Russell Brown and Bernard Harris (London: Edward Arnold, 1967), pp. 102–07.

51. Manuel L. Grossman, "*Him* and the Modern Theatre," *Quarterly Journal of Speech*, 54 (1968), 212–19.

52. Charles Stetler, "E.E. Cummings' *73 Poems*: With Life's Eye," *Xavier University Studies*, 7 (1968), 5–16.

53. Sister Joan Marie Lechner, O.S.U., "E.E. Cummings and Mother Nature," *Renascence*, 12 (1960), 182–91.

54. Fred E.H. Schroeder, "Obscenity and its Function in the Poetry of E.E. Cummings," *Sewanee Review*, 73 (1965), 469–78.

55. Mick Gidley, "Picture and Poem: E.E. Cummings in Perspective," *The Poetry Review*, 59 (1968), 179, 181–95.

56. Richard S. Kennedy, "Edward Cummings, the Father of the Poet," *Bulletin of the New York Public Library*, 70 (1966), 437–49.

57. Carl Bode, "E.E. Cummings and Exploded Verse," in his *The Great Experiment in American Literature* (New York: Praeger, 1961), pp. 81–100.

58. Clive James, "An Instrument to Measure Spring With," *The Review*, No. 2 (1969), pp. 38–48.

59. L.S. Dembo, "E.E. Cummings: The Now Man," in his *Conceptions of Reality in Modern American Poetry* (Berkeley: Univ. of California Press, 1966), pp. 118–28.

60. David R. Weimer, "Grassblades Assassinated: E.E. Cummings," in his *The City as Metaphor*, Random House Studies in Language and Literature, No. 8, ed. Paul Fussell, Jr. (New York: Random House, 1966), pp. 78–87.

61. George Wickes, "E.E. Cummings and the Great War," in his *Americans in Paris*, Paris Review Editions (Garden City, New York: Doubleday, 1969), pp. 69–118.

62. Hyatt H. Waggoner, "The Transcendental and Extraordinary: E.E. Cummings," in his *American Poets from the Puritans to the Present* (Boston: Houghton Mifflin, 1968), pp. 511–25.

63. Roy Harvey Pearce, "Cummings," in his *The Continuity of American Poetry* (Princeton: Princeton Univ. Press, 1961), pp. 359–66.

64. *Selected Letters of E.E. Cummings*, ed. F.W. Dupee and George Stade (New York: Harcourt, Brace & World, 1969).

65. George J. Firmage, *E.E. Cummings: A Bibliography* (Middletown, Conn.: Wesleyan Univ. Press, 1960).

66. Charles Norman, *E.E. Cummings: A Biography*, 2d ed. (New York: Dutton, 1967).

67. Norman Friedman, *e.e. cummings: the art of his poetry* (Baltimore: The Johns Hopkins Press, 1960).

68. Norman Friedman, *e.e. cummings: The Growth of a Writer* (Carbondale: Southern Illinois Univ. Press, 1964).

69. S.V. Baum, *EΣTI: eec E.E. Cummings and the Critics* (East Lansing: Michigan State Univ. Press, 1962).

70. Robert E. Wegner, *The Poetry and Prose of E.E. Cummings* (New York: Harcourt, Brace & World, 1965).

71. Eve Triem, *E.E. Cummings*, Univ. of Minnesota Pamphlets on American Writers, No. 87 (Minneapolis: Univ. of Minnesota Press, 1969).

72. Barry A. Marks, *E.E. Cummings*, Twayne's United States Authors Series, No. 46 (New York: Twayne, 1964).

73. Helen Vendler, rev. of *Complete Poems, 1913-1962*, *Yale Review*, 62 (1973), 412–19.

74. Malcolm Cowley, "Cummings: One Man Alone," *Yale Review*, 62 (1973), 332–54.

75. William Heyen, "In Consideration of Cummings," *Southern Humanities Review*, 7 (1973), 131–42.

76. Joseph W. Mahoney, "E.E. Cummings Today: A Bibliographical Survey," *Literatur in Wissenschaft und Unterricht*, 6 (1973), 188–201.

77. Richard S. Kennedy, "E.E. Cummings at Harvard: Studies," *Harvard Library Bulletin*, 24 (1976), 267–97.

78. Richard S. Kennedy, "E.E. Cummings at Harvard: Verse, Friends, Rebellion," *Harvard Library Bulletin*, 25 (1977), 253–91.

79. John W. Crowley, "Visual-Aural Poetry: The Typography of E.E. Cummings," *Concerning Poetry*, 5 (1972), 51–54.

80. Jan Aarts, "A Note on the Interpretation of 'he danced his did'," *Journal of Linguistics*, 7 (1971), 71–73; Richard Gunter, "Sentence and Poem," *Style*, 5 (1971), 26–36; and Tanya Reinhart, "Patterns, Intuitions, and the Sense of Nonsense: An Analysis of Cummings' 'anyone lived in a pretty how town,' " *PTL: A Journal for Descriptive Poetics and Theory*, 1 (1976), 85–103.

81. James F. Smith, Jr., "A Stereotyped Archetype: E.E. Cummings' Jean le Nègre," *Studies in American Fiction*, 1 (1973), 24–34.

82. Harold T. McCarthy, "E.E. Cummings: Eros and Cambridge, Mass." in his *The Expatriate Perspective: American Novelists and the Idea of America* (Rutherford, N.J.: Fairleigh Dickinson Univ. Press, 1974), pp. 123–35.

83. George S. Peek, "The Narrator as Artist and the Artist as Narrator: A Study of E.E. Cummings' *The Enormous Room*," *Ball State University Forum*, 17 (1976), 50–60.

84. Jeffrey Walsh, "The Painful Process of Unthinking: E.E. Cummings' Social Vision in *The Enormous Room*," in *The First World War in Fiction: A Collection of Critical Essays*, ed. Holger Klein (London: Macmillan, 1976), pp. 32–42.

85. William I. Oliver, "*Him*—A Director's Note," *Educational Theatre Journal*, 26 (1974), 327–41.

86. Marjorie S.C. Smelstor, " 'Damn Everything but the Circus': Popular Art in the Twenties and *him*," *Modern Drama*, 17 (1974), 43–45.

87. Rushworth M. Kidder, "E.E. Cummings, Painter," *Harvard Library Bulletin*, 23 (1975), 117–38.

88. Rushworth M. Kidder, " 'Author of Pictures': A Study of Cummings' Line Drawings in *The Dial*," *Contemporary Literature*, 17 (1976), 470–505.

89. Robert Tucker, "E.E. Cummings as an Artist: *The Dial* Drawings," *Massachusetts Review*, 26 (1975), 329–53.

90. Allan A. Metcalf, "Dante and E.E. Cummings," *Comparative Literature Studies*, 7 (1970), 374–86.

91. James E. Tanner, "Experimental Styles Compared: E.E. Cummings and William Burroughs," *Style*, 10 (1976), 1–27.

92. Mary Ellen Solt, On Cummings, in her *Concrete Poetry: A World View* (Bloomington: Indiana Univ. Press, 1970), p. 47.

93. Paul Fort, "From 'l inga' to 'unders of dream': E.E. Cummings' Growth and Twentieth Century American Poetry," *Revue des Langues Vivantes / Tijdschrift voor Levende Talen*, U.S. Bicentennial Issue (1976), pp. 121–41.

94. Renzo S. Crivelli, "E.E. Cummings: La Poetica del Movimento," *Studi Americani*, 18 (1972), 313–43.

95. Patrick B. Mullen, "E.E. Cummings and Popular Culture," *Journal of Popular Culture*, 5 (1971), 503–20.

96. Eleanore Hombitzer, "E.E. Cummings: 'a wind has bown the rain away . . .': Versuch einer Strukturalistischen Deutung," *Der Fremdsprachliche Unterricht*, 27 (1973), 25–40.

97. John M. Lipski, "Connectedness in Poetry: Toward a Topological Analysis of E.E. Cummings," *Language and Style*, 9 (1976), 143–63.

98. Dickran Tashjian, "E.E. Cummings and Dada Formalism," in his *Skyscraper Primitives: Dada and the American Avant-Garde 1910–1925* (Middletown, Conn.: Wesleyan Univ. Press, 1975), pp. 165–87.

99. Richard S. Kennedy, "Introduction," in *Tulips & Chimneys*, by E.E. Cummings, ed. George James Firmage (New York: Liveright, 1976), pp. ix–xv.

100. Bethany K. Dumas, *E.E. Cummings: A Remembrance of Miracles* (New York: Barnes & Noble Books, 1974).

101. Gary Lane, *I Am: A Study of E.E. Cummings' Poems* (Lawrence: The Univ. Press of Kansas, 1976).

102. Irene R. Fairley, *E.E. Cummings and Ungrammar: A Study of Syntactic Deviance in His Poems* (Searington, New York: Watermill Publishers, 1975).

103. Wilton Eckley, *The Merrill Checklist to e.e. cummings*, Charles E. Merrill Checklists, ed. Matthew J. Bruccoli and Joseph Katz (Columbus, Ohio: Charles E. Merrill,

1970) and Wilton Eckley, *The Merrill Guide to e.e. cummings*, Charles E. Merrill Guide, ed. Matthew J. Bruccoli and Joseph Katz (Columbus, Ohio: Charles E. Merrill, 1970).

104. Norman Friedman, *E.E. Cummings: A Collection of Critical Essays*, Twentieth Century Views (Englewood Cliffs, N.J.: Prentice-Hall, 1972).

105. Richard S. Kennedy, *Dreams in the Mirror: A Biography of E.E. Cummings* (New York: Liveright, 1980).

106. Rushworth M. Kidder, *E.E. Cummings: An Introduction to the Poetry* (New York: Columbia Univ. Press, 1979).

107. E.E. Cummings Special Number, *Journal of Modern Literature*, 7 (1979), 175–393.

108. William V. Davis, " 'A Remembrance of Miracles': e.e. cummings' 'un / der fog,' " *Notes on Modern American Literature*, 1 (1977), Item 30.

109. Laurence Perrine, "E.E. Cummings' 'what of a much of a which of a wind,' " *Notes on Modern American Literature*, 4 (1980), Item 12.

110. Susan Gates, "E.E. Cummings' Spectatorial View," *Lost Generation Journal*, 5 (1978), 9, 19.

111. Gary A. Boire, " 'An Incredible Vastness': Rereading E.E. Cummings's *The Enormous Room*," *English Studies in Canada*, 4 (1978), 330–40.

112. Samuel Pickering, "E.E. Cummings' *Pilgrim's Progress*," *Christianity and Literature*, 28 (1978), 17–31.

113. Noam Flinker, "Biblical Sexuality as Literary Convention: The Song of Songs in E.E. Cummings' 'Orientale,' " *Papers on Language and Literature*, 16 (1980), 184–200.

114. Robert K. Martin, "Cummings, Crane, and *The Bridge*," *Books at Brown*, 27 (1979), 47–63.

115. John Cheever, "Stories to Comprehend Life," [Interview with Jo Brans], *Southwest Review*, 65 (1980), 337–45.

116. Richard H. Crowder, " 'he's free into the beauty of the truth': A Review Essay," *Analytical and Enumerative Bibliography*, 3 (1979), 268–83.

117. Nancy Cummings de Forêt, *Charon's Daughter: A Passion of Identity* (New York: Liveright, 1977).

118. Robert K. Martin, "E.E. Cummings," in *American Writers in Paris, 1920–1939*, Dictionary of Literary Biography, 4, ed. Karen Lane Rood (Detroit: Gale Research, 1980), pp. 105–11.

119. Norman Friedman, "Knowing and Remembering Cummings," *Harvard Library Bulletin*, 29 (1981), 117–34.

120. Guy Davenport, "Satyr and Transcendentalist," *Parnassus*, 8, No. 2 (1980), 42–50.

121. John Bayley, "Mothermonsters and Fatherfigures," *TLS*, 5 Mar. 1982, pp. 235–36.

122. Rushworth M. Kidder, " 'Twin Obsessions': The Poetry and Paintings of E.E. Cummings," *Georgia Review*, 32 (1978), 342–68.

123. Rushworth M. Kidder, "Picture into Poem: The Genesis of Cummings' 'i am a little church,' " *Contemporary Literature*, 21 (1980), 315–30.

124. Frank Gettings, *E.E. Cummings: The Poet as Artist* (Washington, D.C.: Smithsonian Institution Press, 1976).

125. Milton A. Cohen, *E.E. Cummings' "Paintings": The Hidden Career* (Dallas: Univ. of Texas at Dallas and Dallas Public Library, 1982).

126. Richard D. Cureton, "E.E. Cummings: A Study of Deviant Morphology," *Poetics Today*, 1 (1979), 213–44.

127. Richard D. Cureton, " 'he danced his did': An Analysis," *Journal of Linguistics*, 16 (1980), 245–62.

128. Eleanor Cotton, "Linguistic Design in a Poem by Cummings," *Style*, 14 (1980), 274–86.

129. Dorith Orfi-Schelps, "E.E. Cummings: A Paradox of Non-Difficulty," *Studi Americani*, 23–24 (1980), 323–43.

130. W.G. Regier, "E.E. Cummings: Redundancy as Poetic Process," in *Papers from the 1979 Mid-America Linguistics Conference, November 2–3, 1980*, ed. Robert S. Haller (Lincoln: Univ. of Nebraska, 1980), pp. 414–21.

131. Thomas M. Linehan, "Style and Individuality in E.E. Cummings' *The Enormous Room*," *Style*, 13 (1979), 45–59.

132. Nomi Tamir-Chez, "Binary Oppositions and Thematic Decoding in E.E. Cummings and Eudora Welty," *PTL: A Journal for Descriptive Poetics and Theory*, 3 (1978), 235–48.

133. Irene R. Fairley, "Experimental Approaches to Language in Literature: Reader Response to Poems," *Style*, 13 (1979), 335–64.

134. Judith A. Vanderbok, "The Nature of E.E. Cummings' Sonnet Forms: A Quantitative Approach," *Revue*, No. 2 (1977), pp. 29–51.

135. Judith A. Vanderbok, "Growth Patterns in E.E. Cummings' Sonnets: A Quantitative Approach," *Association for Literary and Linguistics Computing Bulletin*, 6 (1978), 42–52.

136. Renzo S. Crivelli, "*The Enormous Room* e la visione del pellegrino," *Studi Americani*, 21–22 (1978), 153–99.

137. David V. Forrest, M.D., "E.E. Cummings and the Thoughts That Lie Too Deep for Tears," *Psychiatry*, 43 (1980), 13–42.

REVIEWS

Incorrect English

John Peale Bishop*

"The supreme test of a book," Ezra Pound says somewhere, "is that we should feel some unusual intelligence working behind the words. I have expressly written here not 'intellect' but 'intelligence'. There is no intelligence without emotion." And the first thing which one would like to say of *The Enormous Room* of E. E. Cummings is that it is intelligent. Behind the disordered, elaborated and frequently beautiful play and interplay of words, one is conscious of a sensitive, pitying and ironic mind, and of varied and intensely felt emotions. In bare outline, the book is the record of three months spent in a French prison for political spies and suspects; but, though one cannot well doubt a single related fact, so evident is the necessity for honesty, *The Enormous Room* is hardly to be taken as a document, another account of indignities and injustices endured and now to be told. It is rather a presentation of emotions, the tale of "the long and difficult way" through which a young man had to come before he could discover the richness of life at its poorest. A loose analogy with the Pilgrim's Progress is preserved, and at the end are the Delectable Mountains who are none other than a gypsy, a negro thief, a none too honest Pole, and a poor abject creature named Surplice.

NERVOUS RAGE

The simple facts are these: Cummings and his friend B were in October, 1917, serving with the Norton Harjes Ambulance as members of a Sanitary Section affiliated with the French Army. An overzealous French censor decided that B's letters betrayed dangerous if not revolutionary opinions; Cummings and his friend were arrested as suspicious characters and despatched to a miserable and unspeakably filthy detention camp there to await at the autumn's end the commission which was to send B. to Précigne for the duration of the war and to allow Cummings his liberty. I will leave it to others to comment on the justice and wisdom of this

*First published in *Vanity Fair*, 18 (1922), 20. Reprinted from *The Collected Essays of John Peale Bishop*. Copyright 1948 by Charles Scribner's Sons; copyright renewed. Reprinted with the permission of Charles Scribner's Sons.

31

arrangement. It need only be said that Cummings never permits himself either a shriek or a whine throughout the length of the book. What he has to say concerning the greatness and goodness of the French Government in permitting him to live at La Ferté is spoken very quietly, now with a gentle contempt and now with a terrible controlled indignation. There are moments of self pity when he looks firmly at his fellow prisoners to stem his own misery; there are times when his very gentleness seems the effort of a mind trembling upon hysteria.

"And his ghastly and toylike wizened and minute arm would try to make a pass at their lofty lives," he says, speaking of a crippled, impotently indignant little Belgian, whom with an irony perhaps not unconscious, he calls the Machine-Fixer—for his talk with the little man is almost always on those machines by which peoples are governed. Then follows this passage which will indicate as well as any this vein beautifully incisive and ironic of Cummings.

"O gouvernement français, I think it was not very clever of you to put this terrible doll in La Ferté; I should have left him in Belgium with his little doll-wife if I had been you; for when governments are found dead there is always a little doll on top of them, pulling and tweaking with his little hands to get back the microscopic knife which sticks firmly in the quiet meat of their hearts."

The emotional and visual memory are closely balanced; Mr. Cummings can recall with a full nervous exactitude the look and feel of the scene; he can elaborate with precision the emotions of a given moment. To be able to do both these things is rarer than it would seem and to show how the sensuous and emotional are fused in his mind I cite those sentences in which The Wanderer is introduced.

UNRULY OVERTONES

Not that he always succeeds in bringing out his effects; there are passages enough where the main thought is out-thundered by the overtones, where adjectives and nouns break from his control in a verbal Bedlam. Yet when the subject is one of essential importance to his narration he can and does build up a scene, character intensely and imaginatively alive. Celina confronting le Directeur, the chapters named for Jean le Nègre, The Wanderer and Surplice represent Cummings at his best and that best seems to me to give him a definite claim to be considered among the important living American writers. I doubt if any other could have informed physical squalor, beastliness and degradation with so splendid a spiritual irradiance.

So far as I am concerned, the trouble with The Enormous Room is exactly that which is to be found in practically all the experimental prose in America, which is simply that not enough time has been taken to bring the form to completion.

The Enormous Room is written in a gamey personal idiom which moves in one direction toward a highly organized, rhythmic prose, and in the other toward the last crudities of the vernacular. His vocabulary shows equally the dustiness of the dictionary and the muck of the street. His interest in extending the limits of prose is obvious. He is quite willing to employ an adverb to modify a noun—"three very formerly and even once bonnets" or another noun—"softnesses eyes" and he has not hesitated to use words not commonly accepted in print. If Cummings needs a defence for having done so, it is provided for him in Havelock Ellis's essay on Zola in *Affirmations*. I have neither the desire nor the ability to add anything to what is said there.

Off the Shoals

John Dos Passos*

When the American Chicle Company brings out gum of a new shape and unfamiliar flavour gumchewers are delighted and miss their subway trains in rush hour and step on each other's heels crowding round slot machines in their haste to submit to a new sensation. Frequenters of cabarets and jazzpalaces shimmy themselves into St Vitus dance with delight over a new noise in the band or a novel squirm in the rhythm. People mortgage their houses to be seen in the newest and most bizarre models of autos. Women hock their jewels and their husbands' insurance policies to acquire an unaccustomed shade in hair or *crêpe de chine*. Why then is it that when any one commits anything novel in the arts he should be always greeted by this same peevish howl of pain and surprise? One is led to suspect that the interest people show in these much talked of commodities, painting, music, and writing, cannot be very deep or very genuine when they wince so under any unexpected impact.

The man who invented Eskimo Pie made a million dollars, so one is told, but E. E. Cummings, whose verse has been appearing off and on for three years now, and whose experiments should not be more appalling to those interested in poetry than the experiment of surrounding ice-cream with a layer of chocolate was to those interested in soda fountains, has hardly made a dent in the doughy minds of our so-called poetry-lovers. Yet one might have thought that the cadences of

> Or with thy mind against my mind, to hear
> nearing our hearts' irrevocable play—
> through the mysterious high futile day
> an enormous stride

*Reprinted from *The Dial*, 73 (1922), 97–102. Reprinted by permission of Mrs. John Dos Passos.

                    (and drawing thy mouth toward

        my mouth, steer our lost bodies carefully downward)

would have melted with as brittle freshness on the senses of the readers of
The Dial as melted the brown-encrusted oblongs of ice-cream in the
mouths of tired stenographers and their beaux. Can it be that people like
ice-cream and only pretend to like poetry?

Therefore it is very fortunate that this book of E. E. Cummings' has
come out under the disguise of prose. The average reader is less self-
conscious and more open to direct impressions when reading prose than
verse; the idea that prose is *Art* will have closed the minds of only a few
over-educated people. Here at last is an opportunity to taste without over-
much prejudice a form, an individual's focus on existence, a gesture un-
foreseen in American writing. The attempt to obscure the issue, on the
paper cover blurb and in the preface, will fool no one who reads beyond
the first page. It's not as an account of a war atrocity or as an attack on
France or the holy Allies timely to the Genoa Conference that *The Enormous Room* is important, but as a distinct conscious creation separate
from anything else under heaven.

Here's a book that has been conceived unashamedly and directly
without a thought either of the columnists or the book trade or Mr Sumner,
or of fitting into any one of the neatly labelled pigeon-holes of novel, play,
essay, history, travel book, a book that exists because the author was so
moved, excited, amused by a certain slice of his existence that things happened freely and cantankerously on paper. And he had the nerve to let
things happen. In this pattern-cut generation, most writers are too afraid of
losing their private reputations as red-blooded clear-eyed hundred-
percenters, well-dressed, well-mannered and thoroughly disinfected
fashion plates, to make any attempt to feel and express directly the life
about them and in them. They walk in daily fear that someone will call
them morbid, and insulate themselves from their work with the rubber
raincoat of fiction. *The Enormous Room* seems to me to be the book that
has nearest approached the mood of reckless adventure in which men will
reach the white heat of imagination needed to fuse the soggy disjointed
complexity of the industrial life about us into seething fluid of creation.
There can be no more playing safe. Like the old steamboat captains on the
Mississippi we'll have to forget the hissing of the safety-valve and stoke like
beavers if we are to get off the sticky shoals into the deeper reaches beyond.
And many an old tub will blow sky high with all hands before someone
makes the course. *The Enormous Room* for one seems to me at least to
have cleared the shoals.

Along with Sandburg and Sherwood Anderson, E. E. Cummings
takes the rhythms of our American speech as the material of his prose as of
his verse. It is writing created in the ear and lips and jotted down. For ac-

curacy in noting the halting cadences of talk and making music of it, I don't know anything that comes up to these two passages. This is a poem that came out in *The Dial*:

> Buffalo Bill's
> defunct
>> who used to
>> ride a watersmooth-silver
>>> stallion
> and break onetwothreefourfive pigeonsjustlikethat
>>>> Jesus
>> he was a handsome man
>>> and what i want to know is
>> how do you like your blueeyed boy
>> Mister Death

This from *The Enormous Room*:

> Sunday: green murmurs in coldness. Surplice fiercely fearful, praying on his bony both knees, crossing himself. . . . The Fake French Soldier, alias Garibaldi, beside him, a little face filled with terror . . . the Bell cranks the sharp-nosed priest on his knees . . . titter from bench of whores—
> And that reminds me of a Sunday afternoon on our backs spent with the wholeness of a hill in Chevancourt, discovering a great apple pie, B. and Jean Stahl and Maurice le Menusier and myself; and the sun falling roundly before us.
> —And then one *Dimanche* a new high old man with a sharp violet face and green hair—'You are free my children, to achieve immortality—*Songez, songez, donc—L'Eternité est une existence sans durée—Toujours le Paradis, toujours l'Enfer*' (to the silently roaring whores) 'Heaven is made for you'—and the Belgian ten-foot farmer spat three times and wiped them with his foot, his nose dripping; and the nigger shot a white oyster into a far-off scarlet handkerchief—and the priest's strings came untied and he sidled crablike down the steps—the two candles wiggle a strenuous softness . . .
> In another chapter I will tell you about the nigger.
> And another Sunday I saw three tiny old females stumble forward, three very formerly and even once bonnets perched upon three wizened skulls, and flop clumsily before the priest, and take the wafer hungrily into their leathery faces.

This sort of thing knocks literature into a cocked hat. It has the raucous directness of a song and dance act in cheap vaudeville, the willingness to go the limit in expression and emotion of a negro dancing. And in this mode, nearer the conventions of speech than those of books, in a style infinitely swift and crisply flexible, an individual not ashamed of his loves and hates, great or trivial, has expressed a bit of the underside of History with indelible vividness.

The material itself, of course, is superb. The Concentration Camp at

La Ferté-Macé was one of those many fantastic crossroads of men's lives where one lingered for unforgetable moments, reaching them one hardly knew how, shoved away from them as mysteriously by some movement of the pawns on the chessboard, during the fearfully actual nightmare of war. A desperate recklessness in the air made every moment, every intonation snatched from the fates of absolute importance. In The Wanderer and Jean le Negre and Surplice and Mexique and Apollyon and the Machine Fixer and in those grotesque incidents of the fight with the stovepipes and Celina's defiance we have that intense momentary flare in which lifetimes, generations are made manifest. To have made those moments permanent on a printed page is no common achievement.

For some reason there is a crispness and accuracy about these transcripts of the smell and taste and shiver of that great room full of huddled prisoners that makes me think of Defoe. In *The Journal of the Plague Year* or in the description of a night spent among enormous bones and skeletons in the desert journey in *Captain Singleton* one finds passages of a dry definiteness that somehow give the sort of impression that gives this hotly imaged picture of a road-side crucifix:

> I banged forward with bigger and bigger feet. A bird, scared, swooped almost into my face. Occasionally some night-noise pricked a futile, minute hole in the enormous curtain of soggy darkness. Uphill now. Every muscle thoroughly aching, head spinning, I half-straightened my no longer obedient body; and jumped: face to face with a little wooden man hanging all by itself in a grove of low trees.
>
> —The wooden body, clumsy with pain, burst into fragile legs with absurdly large feet and funny writhing toes; its little stiff arms made abrupt cruel equal angles with the road. About its stunted loins clung a ponderous and jocular fragment of drapery. On one terribly brittle shoulder the droll lump of its neckless head ridiculously lived. There was in this complete silent doll a gruesome truth of instinct, a success of uncanny poignancy, an unearthly ferocity of rectangular emotion.
>
> For perhaps a minute the almost obliterated face and mine eyed one another in the silence of intolerable autumn.

Perhaps one thinks of Defoe because of the unashamed directness with which every twitch of the individual's fibres, stung or caressed by the world's flowing past outside, is noted down. There is no straining through the standard literary sieve.

Of the English eighteenth century too is the fine tang of high adventure along roads among grotesque companions that comes to the surface in passages like this:

> The highroad won, all of us relaxed considerably. The *sac* full of suspicious letters which I bore on my shoulder was not so light as I had thought, but the kick of the Briouse *pinard* thrust me forward at a good clip. The road was absolutely deserted; the night hung loosely around it, here and there tattered by attempting moonbeams. I was somewhat sorry

to find the way hilly, and in places bad underfoot, yet the unknown adventure lying before me, and the delicious silence of the night (in which our words rattled queerly like tin soldiers in a plush-lined box) boosted me into a condition of mysterious happiness. We talked, the older and I, of strange subjects. As I suspected he had not always been a *gendarme*. He had seen service among the Arabs.

and the first description of The Wanderer:

B. called my attention to a figure squatting in the middle of the *cour* with his broad back against one of the more miserable trees. This figure was clothed in a remarkably picturesque manner; it wore a dark sombrero-like hat with a large drooping brim, a bright red gipsy shirt of some remarkably fine material with huge sleeves loosely falling, and baggy corduroy trousers whence escaped two brown, shapely, naked feet. On moving a little I discovered a face—perhaps the handsomest face that I have ever seen, of a gold brown color, framed in an amazingly large and beautiful black beard. The features were finely formed and almost fluent, the eyes soft and extraordinarily sensitive, the mouth delicate and firm beneath a black moustache which fused with the silky and wonderful darkness falling upon the breast. The face contained a beauty and dignity which, as I first saw it, annihilated the surrounding tumult without an effort. Around the carefully formed nostrils there was something almost of contempt. The cheeks had known suns of which I might not think. The feet had travelled nakedly in countries not easily imagined. Seated gravely in the mud and noise of the *cour* under the pitiful and scraggly *pommier* . . . behind the eyes lived a world of complete strangeness and silence. The composure of the body was graceful and Jovelike. This being might have been a prophet come out of a country nearer to the sun. Perhaps a god who had lost his road and allowed himself to be taken prisoner by *le gouvernement français*. At least a prince of a dark and desirable country, a king over a gold-skinned people who would return when he wished to his fountains and his houris. I learned upon inquiry that he travelled in various countries with a horse and cart and his wife and children, selling bright colors to the women and men of these countries. As it turned out he was one of the Delectable Mountains; to discover which I had come a long and difficult way. Wherefore I shall tell you no more about him for the present, except that his name was Joseph Demestre.

We called him The Wanderer.

There is about this sort of writing a gusto, an intense sensitiveness to men and women and colours and stenches and anger and love that, like the face of Joseph Demestre, "annihilates the surrounding tumult without an effort." When a book like *The Enormous Room* manages to emerge from the morass of print that we flounder in, it is time to take off your new straw hat and jump on it.

[Review of *Tulips and Chimneys*]

Slater Brown*

Modern art gets much less explanation than it deserves. The artist is too busy pioneering, the intransigent critic too busy fighting his own battles. Nor does any explanation come from the critics of the older school. They have a fear of tasting anything which they cannot recognize at a glance, they refuse to understand anything which is disturbingly new. But since they are house-broken only in their own traditions and would inevitably make a mess of themselves if they wandered afield, it is perhaps fortunate for the world that they make no attempt to understand the underlying aesthetic upon which these crisp and brilliant poems of E. E. Cummings are built.

For Cummings is not only a poet but a painter. His knowledge of word value is as profound as his knowledge of color, and it is largely for this reason, because he has carried over the eye and method of art into the field of poetry, that the fresh, living, glamorous forms he has created seem so intangible. To many of those who do not understand this fact, this translation of one art into the technic of another, the poems of E. E. Cummings seem nothing more than verbal and typographical mannerism.

But it is not unapparent in his work that Cummings' approach to poetry has been quite definitely through painting. The spatial organization of color has become the durational organization of words, the technical problem that of tempo. Words, like planes in abstract painting, function not as units in a logical structure, but as units functioning in a vital and organic structure of time. Logic and all its attributes of grammar, spelling and punctuation, become subservient to the imperial demands of form. The words must come at the *moment juste*, the spark perfectly timed must ignite them at their fullest incipient power.

> while in the battered
> bodies the odd unlovely
> souls struggle   slowly   and   writhe
> like caught.brave:flies;

In this quotation the verbal units fall, almost as if by fate, into a sharp relentless tempo that drives each into the highest incandescence of its meaning. There is no waste, the skilful orchestration of tempo forces each word to the final limit of its stress.

But Cummings not only derives his technical organization from painting. The sudden and glaring accuracies of description with which his poetry abounds, are those of an amazingly adept draughtsman who has for the moment exchanged his own medium for that of words. In some cases this pictorial accuracy is that of a photograph taken with a lens of

*Reprinted from *Broom*, 6 (1924), 26–28. Reprinted by permission of Slater Brown.

ice, brutally clear. But in many of his more recent poems, of which there are all too few examples in the present volume, this accuracy, deepened and sharpened by satire, cuts both ways. These poems, particularly the one published in the fourth number of *Secession*, have all the quality of Daumier plus that formal significance which Daumier never attained. It is a satire both in form and import far beyond the timid and retiring ironies of T. S. Eliot; a satire which reveals Cummings as completely innoculated against that galloping stagnation which seems to carry off so many of our younger American poets.

Of the grace of Cummings' poetry much has been written. But grace is an emanation, the residue or by-product of a means which has utterly realized its aesthetic or extra-aesthetic purpose. It is an ease which springs from the perfect economy of method. But since it cannot be its own purpose, since it can only be attained by way of a technic whose purpose is not grace itself, it necessarily extends beyond the reaches of analysis. Nevertheless it may be touched by a consideration of that purpose from which it emanates, and though I may be leading myself by the nose into a very doubtful territory of assumptions, I should say that the formal grace (one might as well say beauty and be done with it) of Cummings' work is largely due to the fact that the lines of his poems are built for speed. Their beauty is that of all swift things seen at rest.

In his best work this speed is evident; there exists in them an organized direction toward which each verbal unit functions at its highest velocity. Cummings seldom attempts to achieve momentum through the utilization of mass, the violent and often painful impact of his poems is the active manifestation of speed; their formal beauty has that quality common to racing cars, aeroplanes, and to those birds surviving because of their swift wings.

But it is this speed, this sudden impact of his poems which turns so many people against them. Men do not like to be knocked down, particularly by some quality they admire. But if art is to have any of the contemporary virtues it must have speed, and though it is perhaps more pleasant to be softly overturned by the witching waves of Amy Lowell, or knocked slowly numb by the water droppings of Georgian poetasters, it is certainly more exhilarating to experience the sharp, the living, the swift, the brilliant tempos of E.E. Cummings. And though the selection of poems in this volume is neither a sensitive nor a comprehensive one, though it contains poems of questionable value, it nevertheless stands as the most important work of poetry yet published in America.

Flare and Blare

Harriet Monroe*

Mr. Cummings' first book opens with a fanfare—there is a flourish of trumpets and a crash of cymbals in the resounding music of *Epithalamion*, a certain splendor of sound carried just to that point of blare which should match an exaggerated and half-satiric magnificence of mood. "Go to, ye classic bards," he seems to say, "I will show you what I can do with iambic pentameter, and a rhyme-patterned stanza, with high-sounding processional adjectives, long simile-embroidered sentences, and *O-thou* invocations of all the gods!" And lo and behold, this modernist does very well with them—Picasso and the rest, turning from the chaos of cubism to the cold symmetry of Ingres, must not get ahead of him! He will be in the fashion, or a leap or two ahead of it—and the muse shall not outrun him!

Listen to two separate stanzas from this glorified and richly patterned spring-song, this earth-and-sky-inspired *Epithalamion*:

> And still the mad magnificent herald Spring
> Assembles beauty from forgetfulness
> With the wild trump of April: witchery
> Of sound and odor drives the wingless thing,
> Man, forth into bright air; for now the red
> Leaps in the maple's cheek, and suddenly
> By shining hordes, in sweet unserious dress,
> Ascends the golden crocus from the dead.

> . . . .

> O still miraculous May! O shining girl
> Of time untarnished! O small intimate
> Gently primeval hands, frivolous feet
> Divine! O singular and breathless pearl!
> O indefinable frail ultimate pose!
> O visible beatitude—sweet sweet
> Intolerable! Silence immaculate
> Of God's evasive audible great rose!

(Right here is due a parenthetical apology. Mr. Cummings has an eccentric system of typography which, in our opinion, has nothing to do with the poem, but intrudes itself irritatingly, like scratched or blurred spectacles, between it and the reader's mind. In quoting him, therefore, we are trying the experiment of printing him almost like anybody else, with the usual quantity of periods, commas, capital letters, and other generally accepted conventions of the printer's art.)

In a more or less grandiloquent mood the poet swaggers and riots

*Reprinted from *Poetry*, 23 (1924), 211–15. Copyright 1924 by The Modern Poetry Association. Reprinted by permission of Henry S. Monroe and the editor of *Poetry*.

through his book, carrying off Beauty in his arms as tempestuously as ever Petruchio his shrew. The important thing, of course, is that he does capture her—she is recognizable even when the poet, like Petruchio, laughs at her, tumbles her up-to-date raiment, sometimes almost murders her as he sweeps her along.

She drops swift phrases in passing:

> . . . Between
> Your thoughts more white than wool
> My thought is sorrowful.
>
> Across the harvest whitely peer,
> Empty of surprise,
> Death's faultless eyes.
>
> Softer be they than slippered sleep.
>
> Thy fingers make early flowers of
> All things.
>
> And all the while my heart shall be
> With the bulge and nuzzle of the sea.
>
> Thy forehead is a flight of flowers.
>
> The green-greeting pale-departing irrevocable sea.
>
> The body of
> The queen of queens is
> More transparent
> Than water—she is softer than birds.
>
> The serious steep darkness.
>
> Death's clever enormous voice [in war].
>
> The Cambridge ladies who live in furnished souls. . . .
> They believe in Christ and Longfellow, both dead.

Some poems guffaw into grotesques leering with tragic or comic significance. The *Portraits* are mostly of this kind, and certain of the *Impressions*. Here the poet is often too nimble—he tires the reader with intricate intellectual acrobatics which scarcely repay one for puzzling out their motive over the slippery typographical stepping-stones. But even here the fault is one of exuberance—the poet always seems to be having a glorious time with himself and his world even when the reader loses his breath in the effort to share it. He is as agile and outrageous as a faun, and as full of delight over the beauties and monstrosities of this brilliant and grimy old planet. There is a grand gusto in him, and that is rare enough to be welcomed in any age of a world too full of puling pettifoggers and picayunes.

One might quote many poems in proof of this poet's varied joys. We shall have to be satisfied with two. The first is number one of the *Chansons Innocentes*:

> In just-
> Spring, when the world is mud-
> luscious, the little
> lame balloon-man
>
> whistles   far   and wee.
>
> And Eddie-and-Bill come
> running from marbles and
> piracies, and it's
> spring,
>
> when the world is puddle-wonderful.
>
> The queer
> old balloon-man whistles
> far   and   wee.
>
> And Betty-and-Isbel come dancing
> from hop-scotch and jump-rope, and
>
> it's
> spring,
> and
>   the
>   goat-footed
> balloon-man whistles
> far
> and
> wee.

The second of our quotations is number two of the *Orientale* series:

> I spoke to thee
> with a smile, and thou didst not
> answer:
> thy mouth is as
> a chord of crimson music.
>   Come hither—
> O thou, is life not a smile?
>
> I spoke to thee with
> a song, and thou
> didst not listen:
> thine eyes are as a vase
> of divine silence.
>   Come hither—
>
> O thou, is life not a song?

I spoke
to thee with a soul, and
thou didst not wonder:
thy face is as a dream locked
in white fragrance.

Come hither—

O thou, is life not love?

I speak to
thee with a sword,
and thou art silent:
thy breast is as a tomb
softer than flowers.

Come hither—

O thou, is love not death?

Altogether a mettlesome high-spirited poet salutes us in this volume. But beware his imitators!

Wallace Stevens and E.E. Cummings

Edmund Wilson*

Mr. Wallace Stevens is the master of a style: that is the most remarkable thing about him. His gift for combining words is fantastic but sure: even when you do not know what he is saying, you know that he is saying it well. He derives plainly from several French sources of the last fifty years but he never—except for a fleeting phrase or two—really sounds like any of them. You could not mistake even a title by Wallace Stevens for a title by anyone else: Invective Against Swans, Hibiscus on the Sleeping Shores, A High-Toned Old Christian Woman, The Emperor of Ice-Cream, Exposition of the Contents of a Cab, The Bird with the Coppery Keen Claws, Two Figures in Dense Violet Night, Hymn from a Watermelon Pavilion, and Frogs Eat Butterflies. Snakes Eat Frogs. Hogs Eat Snakes. Men Eat Hogs.

These titles also represent Mr. Steven's curious ironic imagination at its very best. The poems themselves—ingenious, charming and sometimes beautiful as they are—do not always quite satisfy the expectation aroused by the titles. When you read a few poems of Mr. Stevens, you get the impression from the richness of his verbal imagination that he is a poet of

*First published in the New Republic, 38 (1924), 102–03. Reprinted by permission of Farrar, Straus and Giroux, Inc. "Wallace Stevens and E.E. Cummings" from Shores of Light: A Literary Chronicle of the 1920s and 1930s by Edmund Wilson. Copyright 1952 by Edmund Wilson. Copyright renewed © 1980 by Helen Miranda Wilson.

rich personality, but when you come to read the whole volume through you are struck by a sort of aridity. Mr. Stevens, who is so observant and has so distinguished a fancy, seems to have emotion neither in abundance nor in intensity. He is ironic a little in Mr. Eliot's manner; but he is not poignantly, not tragically ironic. Emotion seems to emerge only furtively in the cryptic images of his poetry, as if it had been driven, as he seems to hint, into the remotest crannies of sleep or disposed of by being dexterously turned into exquisite amusing words. Nothing could be more perfect in its tone and nothing by itself could be more satisfactory than such a thing as Last Looks at the Lilacs. But when we have gone all through Mr. Stevens, we find ourselves putting to him the same question which he, in the last poem of his book, puts To a Roaring Wind:

> What syllable are you seeking,
> Vocallissimus,
> In the distances of sleep?
> Speak it.

Mr. E. E. Cummings, on the other hand, is not, like Mr. Stevens, a master in a peculiar vein; a master is precisely what he is not. Cummings's style is an eternal adolescent, as fresh and often as winning but as half-baked as boyhood. A poet with a genuine gift for language, for a melting music a little like Shelley's which sighs and rhapsodizes in soft light vowels disembarrassed of their baggage, of consonants, he strikes often on aetherial measures of a singular purity and charm—his best poems seem to dissolve on the mind like the flakes of a lyric dew; but he seems never to know when he is writing badly and when he is writing well. He has apparently no faculty for self-criticism. One imagines him giving off his poems as spontaneously as perspiration and with as little application of the intellect. One imagines him chuckling with the delight of a school-boy when he has invented an adverb like "sayingly" or hit upon the idea of writing capitals in the middles of words instead of at the beginnings. One imagines him just as proud to have written

> last   we
> on the groaning flame of neat huge
> trudging kiss moistly climbing hideously with
> large
> minute
> hips, O
>   .press

as:

> On such a night the sea through her blind miles
> of crumbling silence

or the sonnet about the little dancer

> absatively posolutely dead,
> like Coney Island in winter.

And there is really, it seems to me, a certain amateurishness about the better of these specimens of his style as well as about the worse. Just as in the first example he takes one of the lines of least resistance with a difficult sensation by setting down indiscriminately all the ideas it suggests to him without ever really taking pains to focus it for the reader, so in the second he succumbs to an over-indulgence in the beautiful English long i which from "I arise from dreams of thee" to Mr. T. S. Eliot's nightingale filling "all the desert with inviolable voice" has been reserved for effects of especial brightness or purity but which Mr. Cummings has cheapened a little by pounding on it too much. One or two accurately placed long i's, if combined with other long vowels, are usually enough by themselves to illuminate a poem, but Mr. Cummings is addicted to long i's, he has got into the habit of using them uncritically, and he insists upon turning them on all over until his poems are lit up like Christmas trees.

Mr. Cummings's eccentric punctuation is, I think, typical of his immaturity as an artist. It is not merely a question of unconventional punctuation: unconventional punctuation very often gains its effect. But I must contend, after a sincere effort to appreciate it and after having had it explained to me by a friend of Mr. Cummings, that Mr. Cummings's does not gain its effect. It is Mr. Cummings's theory that punctuation marks, capitalization and arrangement on the page should be used not as mere conventional indications of structure which make it easier for the reader to pay attention to the meaning conveyed by the words themselves but as independent instruments of expression susceptible of infinite variation. Thus he refuses to make use of capitals for the purposes for which they were invented—to indicate the beginnings of sentences and the occurrence of proper names—but insists upon pressing them into service for purposes of emphasis; and he even demotes the first person singular of the pronoun by a small i, only printing it as a capital when he desires to give it special salience—not, apparently, realizing that for readers accustomed to seeing it the other way it calls ten times as much attention to "I" to write it as a small letter than to print it in the ordinary fashion. But the really serious case against Mr. Cummings's punctuation is that the results which it yields are ugly. His poems are hideous on the page. He insists upon shattering even the most conventional and harmless of his productions, which if they had their deserts would appear in neat little boxes like the innocuous correct prose poems of Mr. Logan Pearsall Smith, into an explosive system of fragments which, so far from making the cadences easier to follow only involves us in a jig-saw puzzle of putting them together again. In the long run, I think it may be said that words have to carry their own cadence and emphasis through the order in which they are written. The extent to which punctuation and typography can help out is really very limited.

Behind this formidable barrier of punctuation for which Mr. Cummings seems unfortunately to have achieved most celebrity, his emotions are conventional and simple in the extreme. They even verge occasionally on the banal. You have the adoration of young love and the delight in the coming of spring and you have the reflection that all flesh must die and all "roses" turn to "ashes." But this is perhaps precisely where Mr. Cummings has an advantage over Mr. Stevens. Whatever Cummings is he is not chilled; he is not impervious to life. He responds eagerly and unconstrainedly to all that the world has to offer. His poetry constitutes an expression—and for the most part a charming expression—of a kind very rare in America—it is the record of a temperament which loves and enjoys, which responds readily with mockery or tenderness, entirely without the inhibitions from which so much of American writing is merely the anguish to escape. He is one of the only American authors living who is not reacting against something. And for this example of the good life—and for the fact that, after all, he is a poet at a time when there is a great deal of writing of verse and very little real poetic feeling—Mr. Cummings deserves well of the public.

People Stare Carefully

Marianne Moore*

One has in Mr. Cummings' work, a sense of the best dancing and of the best horticulture. From his Forty-One Poems and lest one seem to stutter, seventy-nine, emerge the seasons, childhood, humanity selectly and unselectly congregated, war, death, *l'amour* with a touch of love, music, painting, books, and a fine note of scorn. In finding Picasso a sculptor among "uninteresting landscapes made interesting by earTHQuake," Mr. Cummings is fanciful, yet faithful to that verisimilitude of eye and of rhetoric which is so important in poetry.

Settling like a man-of-war bird or the retarded, somnambulistic athlete of the speedograph, he shapes the progress of poems as if it were substance; he has "a trick of syncopation Europe has," determining the pauses slowly, with glides and tight-rope acrobatics, ensuring the ictus by a space instead of a period, or a semi-colon in the middle of a word, seeming to have placed adjectives systematically one word in advance of the words they modify, or one word behind, with most pleasing exactness.

In being printed phonetically, although decorously spelled, these poems constitute a kind of verbal topiary-work; not however, in the manner of the somewhat too literal typographic wine-glasses, columns, keys,

*First published in the *Dial*, 80 (1926), 49–52. Reprinted by permission of Clive E. Driver, literary executor of the estate of Marianne C. Moore.

and roses approved by Elizabethan poets and their predecessors. We have, not a replica of the title, but a more potent thing, a replica of the rhythm—a kind of second tempo, uninterfering like a shadow, in the manner of the author's beautiful if somewhat self-centred, gigantic filiform ampersand of symbolical "and by itself plus itself with itself." The physique of the poems recalls the corkscrew twists, the infinitude of dots, the sumptuous perpendicular appearance of Kufic script; and the principle of the embedded rhyme has produced in Post Impression XI and Portrait III of And, in the big A, the big N, and the big D, which mark respectively each third of the book, some sublimely Mohammedan effects. TUMTITUMTIDDLE THE BLACK CAT WITH THE YELLOW EYES AND THE VIOLIN, advances metronomically through the rest of the poem and

> ta
> ppin
> g
> toe
>
> hip
> popot
> amus Back
>
> gen
> teel-ly
> lugu-
> bri ous

descends the page "as fathandsbangrag."

    There is in these poems, a touch of love perceived in allusions to unconscious things—horses' ears and mice's meals. Also, there is a more egotistic and less kind emotion which has the look of being in its author's eyes, his most certain self. One wishes that it weren't. Love is terrible—even in the East where the Prince who wished to find a perfectly beautiful woman, commissioned the Arabs rather than the nobility to find the girl, convinced that "the quickest and best judges of a man or a woman are the very same persons who are the best judges of a horse or a cow." But when love is presented under the banner of Watteau, as a philtre, not to say the menu, it is not terrible; it is merely circumstantial, or at most phenomenal. An admirer of the dead languages—"an Oxford Scholar in a scarlet gown" let us say, who reads no Latin but Petronius—lacks certitude. That the academy-tinctured, modern books of a western poet, should preserve no more than the devouring, in the sense that it is the destroying passion of master for slave, robs testimony, even poet's testimony, of its terror.

    If there is not much love in these pages, however, there is glamour—verbal as figurative:

> . . . horses of gold
> delicately crouching beneath silver
> youths   the leaneyed
>
> Caesars borne neatly through enormous
> twilight . . .
>
> . . . while the infinite processions
> move like moths and like boys and
> like incense and like sunlight

There is Spring like a

> Hand in a window
> (carefully to
> and fro moving New and
> Old things,while
> people stare carefully
> moving a perhaps
> fraction of flower here placing
> an inch of air there)and
>
> without breaking anything.

The Woolworth building becomes "the firm tumult of exquisitely insecure sharp algebraic music." "SNO" falls:

> tiny,angels sharpen:themselves
>
> (on
>   air)
> don't speak . . .

There is verbal excitement in the renaissance of certain important words—of marvellous, of perfect, of beautiful, or wonderful:

> And if, somebody hears
> what i say—let him be pitiful:
> because i've travelled all alone
> through the forest of wonderful,
> and that my feet have surely known
> the furious ways and the peaceful,
>
> and because she is beautiful

If we have not Karnak and the pyramids, we have in these pages, a kind of engineering which includes within it, the jewellery of Egypt and the panting sense of those who wore it. We have the spryness of Vienna—the spun glass miniature object, porcupine or angel-fish—and we have an object from Crete.

There is in the art museum at Eighty-Second Street and Fifth Avenue, a late Minoan ivory leaper. Suspended by a thread, the man swims down with the classic aspect of the frog. As a frog startled, palpitating, and inconsequential, would seem in the ivory man to have become classic, so Mr. Cummings has in these poems, created from inconvenient emotions, what one is sure is poetry. There is here, the Artificiall Changling of John Bulwer's Anthropometamorphosis—"the mad and cruell Gallantry, foolish Bravery, ridiculous Beauty, filthly Finenesse . . . of most Nations."

The Poetry of E.E. Cummings

Maurice Lesemann*

The only way, of course, to form even a temporary judgment of art as experimental as Mr. Cummings', is to subject it to the severe test of familiarity. After these two books have been read a second and a third time, returned to at odd moments and read aloud to friends (the most rigorous test of all), their novelty wears off completely. They assume a certain stature; and after a time they begin to tell about themselves.

One of the most surprising things they reveal is that Mr. Cummings writes poetry of two entirely separate species. All through his work—as far back as *Tulips and Chimneys*, the first book—there is a distinct line of cleavage. The poems group themselves in fairly equal numbers on the two sides.

One species is concerned with the external world. The poems relate to our own time. They pick out specific objects, persons, street-corners and anecdotes, and present these either without comment or with the mingled scorn and laughter of satire. Often an incident or a person (not a "character" but a person as object) is presented in the manner of James Joyce—the reader sitting with the author in the seat of consciousness, the poem impinging upon the consciousness exactly like the raw sense-impressions of experience. When followed strictly, this most difficult of literary methods is a little unrewarding in verse. In prose it may become very significant. The dimensions of prose may afford the reader sufficient data to do his own relating and generalizing. But in short poems the scheme allows for no other meaning than the simplest largest meanings of objects. A tree or stone presented in this fashion is almost as real as in life, and reading the poem is like passing by the stone or the tree. One is thoroughly convinced of its existence, but thinks nothing more about it.

It seems to me that Cummings does about as well with this method as anyone can in verse. It offers him free play for his brilliant gift of description. For example, in the very Cummingesque sonnet entitled *Mame*, from *is 5*, his latest volume:

*Reprinted from *Poetry*, 29 (1926), 164–69. Copyright 1926 by The Modern Poetry Association. Reprinted by permission of Marjorie H. Lesemann and the editor of *Poetry*.

she puts down the handmirror. "Look at" arranging
before me a mellifluous idiot grin
(with what was nose upwrinkled into nothing
earthly, while the slippery eyes drown
in surging flesh). A thumblike index down-
dragging yanks back skin "see" (i, seeing, ceased
to breathe). The plump left fist opening
"wisdom." Flicker of gold. "Yep. No gas. Flynn"

the words drizzle untidily from released
cheeks "I'll tell duh woild; some noive all right.
Ain't much on looks but how dat baby ached."

and when I timidly hinted "novacaine?"
the eyes outstart, curl, bloat, are newly baked

and swaggering cookies of indignant light

Clearly the chief pleasure to be got from this kind of poem is in its skill and in the bold vigor of its portraiture. Not all the poems in this group, however, are so wholly objective. In this latest book, especially, they escape from plain description by adding satire. Take this from one of the very biting poems concerning the war:

my little darlings, let us now
passionately remember how—
braving the worst, of peril heedless,
each braver than the other, each
(a typewriter within his reach)
upon his fearless derrière
sturdily seated—Colonel Needless
To Name and General You Know who
a string of pretty medals drew

(while messrs jack james john and jim
in token of their country's love
received my dears the order of
The Artificial Arm and Limb)

There are a number of poems in *is* 5 which are delightful for sheer appalling cleverness, but the two quotations pretty well set the bounds of this part of Mr. Cummings' work—the part that deals with the external world. It is notable that in all this group, taking the various volumes together, there are scarcely a dozen poems which imply any emotion other than laughter. They are full of boisterous energy, and seem to have been written with great gusto, but they are external, clear of all comment, all overtones, save laughter, the most external of the emotions. Often they communicate no intensity but that of the writer working excitedly with his words. This poet never reveals his inward emotional self while he is aware of the present century. The picture he gives of his own time is invariably vivid, and almost invariably unpleasant. He goes out to it with all the energy of his mind, but his inner self withdraws and preserves itself remote and immune. As in the later work of Joyce, there is a strenuous effort to meet all manifestations of externality without flinching; an effort to say yes to the world without establishing a profound inner connection. The resultant world-of-the-poems is a lurid place inhabited by thugs, policemen, Greek restauranteurs, pimps and prostitutes, drug addicts, crooked politicians, and an occasional stupid business man. This cast of characters has certainly not been chosen for its startling effect. The most startling character Mr. Cummings could offer at the present moment of American literature would be an intelligent and likable business man, who has no urge to be an artist. Perhaps the building of a peculiarly selected poem-world is necessary to poets nowadays, to form a callus upon their spirits and protect them from empirical harshness.

All this is no indictment of the poet's work itself. An artist does not need to reflect the life of his time, though often he gains power when he learns to do so. Edgar Lee Masters is a striking example. A poet need not imply in his work a background woven of the life about him, but somewhere, somehow, he must reflect his own inner life warmly and movingly. This I think Mr. Cummings does in his second species of poetry. Here is a sonnet from *XLI Poems*:

> when learned darkness from our searched world
>
> wrestest the rare unwisdom of thy eyes,
> if thy two hands flowers of silence curled
>
> upon a thought, to rapture should surprise
> my soul slowly which on thy beauty dreamest
> —proud through the cold perfect night whisperless
>
> to mark, how that asleep whitely thou seemest
>
> (whose lips the whole of life almost do guess)
>
> if god should send the morning; and before
> my doubting window leaves softly to stir,
> of thoughtful trees whom night hath pondered o'er
> —and frailties of dimension to occur
>
> about us
>   and birds known, scarcely to sing
>
> (heart, shalt thou bear the marvel of this thing?)

It seems to me that anyone who reads this poem, and rereads it, cannot fail to respond to it, in spite of its dubious grammar. He will want to hunt out further poems of Mr. Cummings for himself. He will discover that in many poems the lines, instead of being broken according to their organic rhythm, are broken in a new way—to give emphasis to images and to set off words by idea-clusters. He may believe, as I do, that the plan seems more important to Mr. Cummings, with his strong sense for the graphic arts, than the literary result justifies. The theory is plausible, but the effect is often an irrelevant intrusion of graphic technique into an art that is essentially linear. A poem moves in a single line past the point of consciousness; and along that line the reader's ideas and images are formed at moments that are quite incalculable by the artist. Cummings' attempts to reinforce these moments can rarely synchronize with the reader's own processes. He is hindered and confused. In the poems that are merely light and clever this does not matter, of course. In fact, it might be noted that the poet has only begun to exploit the graphic possibilities of verse. He could go much farther—line-artist that he is—and escape the limitations and associations of type altogether by hand-lettering each poem. He could print in as many colors as his publisher would permit.

But the typography of the poems is of little concern one way or the other, once the reader has grown familiar with it and has learned to find the rhythms by ear rather than by eye. And, as in the poem last quoted, he will discover, alongside the modern Cummings of the incurable externalism, a Renaissance Cummings, an entirely different personality, delighted by archaic usages, elaborate imagery and involved metaphor, easily stirred by far-away symbols, a poet of almost frail delicacy—one with an Elizabethan genius for song-rhythms and for lyrical adoration of his lady. His other kind of verse is stimulating; this kind, for all its romantic embroidery, is esthetically satisfying.

In is 5, the latest volume, there are signs that the two may merge. Gradually the poet's inner world is getting into communication with the world of the present. If this continues Mr. Cummings may begin to amaze us all over again.

Drama in Extremis

John Hyde Preston*

Mr. Cummings is not the first to have an overpowering care for words—for words above all things—for their sound, color, and their most minute expressionism. Pater, Flaubert, Keats, and God knows how many others, have been concerned with words as words, but only insofar as they could be made precise, accurate, and perfect mirrors of the sense behind them. But Cummings, a reckless grandchild of the Symbolists, throwing their riches about improvidently, has little regard for meaning and sense, and belabors himself, on the contrary, to suggest, to create sudden im-

*Reprinted from the Saturday Review of Literature, 4 (1927), 453. Copyright 1927 by Saturday Review. All rights reserved. Reprinted by permission.

pressions, and to hint at sense through the medium of sound (and fury). Another man might do this kind of thing admirably. But Cummings, smart-alecky, and burdened by his artistic immaturity and bad taste, has yet to learn that, to be clearly understood, he must not speak with his mouth full—little difference whether it be full of mush or precious stones.

Yet Cummings has an extraordinary genius for language, as is only too perfectly brought out in his poetry, from the splendid "Tulips and Chimneys" down to the much inferior "Is 5." It has the characteristics of a genius as fine as Keats's or Rimbaud's; but unlike theirs, it is undisciplined, affected, and is now growing maudlin. And this new play (which is not a play at all, but a mess of formless talk with a not very clear idea behind it) is the *reductio ad absurdum* of his talents and his highly modernistic Symbolism. Cummings knows no more about play-writing than I know about Hungarian wild-flowers; and it evidently pleases him to think that comprehensibility is the first of the Seven Deadly Virtues. Take this stage-direction, for example:

> *A Plainclothesman, his entire being focussed on something just offstage to the audience's left, stalks this invisible something minutely.*

I suppose I am obliged to consider this as delicate comedy; but if I were a stage manager I think I should have some difficulty in explaining to the Plainsclothesman just what he is expected to do! Or take this speech (at random) from the text:

> Horseradish will not produce consequences unless cowslips which is unlikely so be not daunted tho' affairs go badly since all will be well. The cards say and the leaves admit that enough is as good as a feast which will cause you some flatulence which you will not mind as long as Gipsy continues to remain a diurnal watering pot but beware of a woman called Metope who is in the pay of Triglyph disguised as either an insurance agent or I forget which it doesn't matter and whenever a stuffed platitude hits you in the exaggerated omplalos respond with a three-fisted aphorism to the precise casazza.

You will have to draw your own conclusions. But if you can make any suggestions as to the possible significance of the foregoing, it may help matters out considerably. I rather fancy that Mr. Cummings, also, would be interested to know what it means, since he sacrifices himself thus bravely so as not to sacrifice his precious subconscious.

If you like complexes run riot, you will find pages that are fairly side-splitting here (such as I quoted), but side-splitting after the manner of a raging old drunk. And as for the essential idea (whatever little of it there is here), Calderon treated it, centuries ago, with considerable more intelligence and dramatic force, in "Life Is a Dream." In "Him" life is something of a nightmare, with a quantity of excellent horse-play and large doses of bad taste (*vide* especially Act II, Scene VIII, which is no better than cheap, tenth-rate vulgarity).

So much for the man who once had the promise of an American Keats. Symbolism simply took hold of his mind; and, true to his nature, he had no idea of when to stop; he gave it the free rein and it bolted with his gifts. You will probably think him mad, and he would enjoy your thinking so; but he is just a prep-school boy flaunting his smartness in your face. For, after all, only a man almost abnormally sane could imagine and set down such deliberately crazy stuff.

Cummings' *Him*

S. Foster Damon*

In a recent account of E. E. Cummings's play "Him," the baffled reviewer, while admitting several of Cummings's excellences, asks for suggestions as to "possible" significances. May I utilize some of your space to take up his challenge?

In my opinion, the chief characters, "Him" and "Me," represent respectively those twin aspects of the mind known to psychiatrists as the "Persona" and the "Anima," and named by Blake over a century ago the "Spectre" and the "Emanation." The drop-scene represents the outer Consciousness, where the Anima is being anaesthetized by the doctor (or "Censor"). The three Fates—rather commonplace persons—sit about, ignoring the tragedy enacted before their eyes while they chatter their usual nonsense, in which a canary assumes the proportions of a hippopotamus.

The rising of this curtain is lifting the lid of a skull; therein one beholds the bitter, grotesque dream-life of an American in love with snow and skyscrapers. There are two persons in a room with a mirror. One of them cannot sleep. Nothing happens, except love and death and hunger and dreams. The audience itself is the mirror at first; then the room revolves. Los woos Enitharmon with a series of phantasmagoria, some side-splitting, some indecent, some terrible. It is the awful, circular drift of the dust of reality in one skull.

Historically, "Him" belongs in the tradition started by Strindberg's "Dream Play," adapted by Joyce for the Hell scene in "Ulysses," and again remodeled for the "Beggar on Horseback" and Dos Passos's unappreciated "Garbage Man;" yet so many other elements impinge (Dada and O'Neill, I believe), and the auctorial personality is so strong, that the result is wholly new. One could discuss the play as another manifestation of the Literature of Nerves, established by T. S. Eliot's "Waste Land." But no one of any of these ancestors contains at once the raucous laughter, the realism brutal to the height of lyricism, the shameless and unexcused

*Reprinted from the *Saturday Review of Literature*, 4 (1928), 522. Copyright 1928 by *Saturday Review*. All rights reserved. Reprinted by permission.

bawdry, the sudden symbolic vistas, and the profound poignancy of some scenes—especially the scene with the pistol and the other one after the balked love affair.

So many people seem to have been puzzled by this play that I offer these suggestions; but they are suggestions only, and nothing more. As for the reviewer's last remark: "So much for the man who once had the promise of an American Keats," I can merely add that one Keats is enough. He was so very great that his ghost has haunted poets now for a century, scaring them all into feeble imitation. It is ridiculous to compete with a genius on his own chosen field. That Cummings has staked out another field for himself is greatly to his credit, whatever crop it may bear.

Personal Convention

Allen Tate*

The occasion of this review is unfortunately a single book by Mr. Cummings, and the opportunity for generalization about his work as a whole is slight. But it is an opportunity that must be seized, if the reviewer intends to say anything at all: the quality of *Viva*, being quite uniform with that of its predecessors, imposes upon the reviewer no obligation to announce to the public important changes, in Mr. Cummings' work, of style, composition, or point of view. This fact alone is, of course, of no significance, but it brings to the reviewer a grateful feeling of relief; it permits him to write with a full sense of the merit of the three previous books of verse by this poet, a sense that corrects, as it should, a feeling of disappointment in the quality of *Viva*.

It is not that the quality has "fallen off." Cummings' faults are well-known, I believe, if not generally defined, and they are still essentially the faults of *Tulips and Chimneys*. In that volume it was not easy to distinguish his own quality, and thus his limitations, from the influence of other poets, Keats and Swinburne; but this influence has disappeared. The special quality of his talent stands forth without the misleading features of an unformed style. He has refined his talent, perhaps not to the point of which it is ideally capable, but at least to the point at which he is able to convey the particular kind of meaning that very properly obsesses any poet in contact with his medium. From first to last his work has shown the growth of a uniform quality, and a progressive tendency to define that quality with a certain degree of purity.

His uniformity is not uniformity of style. The point could be labored, but I think it is sufficient to refer the reader of Cummings to the three

*Reprinted from *Poetry*, 39 (1932), 332–37. Copyright 1932 by The Modern Poetry Association. Reprinted by permission of Helen H. Tate and the editor of *Poetry*.

distinct styles of poems *XVIII*, *LI*, and *LVII* in *Viva*. He has a great many styles, and having these he has none at all—a defect concealed by his famous mechanism of distorted word and line. For a style is that indestructible quality of a piece of writing which may be distinguished from its communicable content but which in no sense can be subtracted from it: the typographical device can be seen so subtracted by simple alteration either in the direction of conventional pattern or in the direction of greater distortion. The typography is distinct from style, something superimposed and external to the poem, a mechanical system of variety and a formula of surprise; it is—and this is its function—a pseudo-dynamic feature that galvanizes the imagery with the look of movement, of freedom, of fresh perception, a kind of stylization which is a substitute for a living relation among the images themselves, in the lack of a living relation between the images and the sensibility of the poet. Mr. Cummings' imagery reaches the page still-born.

This characteristic of his verse has been brilliantly analyzed by Mr. R. P. Blackmur, in his *Notes on E. E. Cummings' Language (The Hound and Horn*, January, 1931). To that essay I refer the reader for a discussion of Cummings' replacement of stock poetic conventions with an equally limited set of conventions of his own. "By denying the dead intelligence and putting on the heresy of unintelligence," says Mr. Blackmur, "the poet only succeeds in substituting one set of unnourished conventions for another." Again: "As if sensation could be anything more than the idea of sensation . . . without being attached to some central body of experience, genuinely understood and *formed* in the mind." And Mr. Blackmur summarizes his view: "So long as he is content to remain in his private mind, he is unknowable, impenetrable, and sentimental."

These statements reach to the center of Cummings' defects, but I believe that Mr. Blackmur takes too seriously the "heresy of unintelligence"; it is rather the heresy of supposing that personality, as such, outside the terms of something that is not personality, can ever be made known. Now in addition to the typographical mechanism there is another that grows out of it—the mechanism of emotionally private words that are constantly overcharged into pseudo-symbols. This has two aspects. There is the repetition of single words (Mr. Blackmur, in his comprehensive study, examines in detail the personal *clichés*: flower, petal, bloom, etc.); and there is the headlong series of miscellaneous words that attempt to imitate the simultaneity and shock of fresh sensation. Mr. Blackmur shows that the weight of the series cancels the sensory value of its single items. Both this device and the distorted line probably proceed from the poet's sense of the insufficiency of his style: there is something wrong, something obscure that demands a superimposed heightening for effect.

Without this external variety we get, in Cummings, the uniformity that I have mentioned, but it is rather a uniformity of meaning, of reference, than of conception. No single poem introduces the reader to an implicit body of idea beneath its surface, a realm of free play detached once and for all from the poet. We are led to the next poem, and from the aggregate of Mr. Cummings' poems we return to the image of his personality: like all poets he seems to say "more" than the explicit terms convey, but this "more" lies in the origin of the poem, not in the interplay of its own terms. From *To His Coy Mistress* we derive no clue to the existence of such a person as "Andrew Marvell"; from *Viva* we get only the evidence of personality. And this is what Cummings' poetry "means." It is a kind of meaning very common at present; Mr. Cummings is the original head of an easily imitable school. This does not mean that he has ever been *successfully* imitated; no one else has written "personal" poetry as well as Mr. Cummings writes it. It is rather that he has shown the possibility of making personal conventions whose origin and limit are personality. It is a kind of convention that, given "talent," can make of anyone a poet. It requires a certain interest in oneself, which permits one to ascribe to one's "feeling-tone" for words an objective meaning, a comprehensible meaning, to the relations existing among those words. This stanza, by no means an extreme example of pure "feeling-tone," illustrates the process:

> your slightest look easily will unclose me
> though I have closed myself as fingers,
> you open always petal by petal myself as Spring opens
> (touching skilfully, mysteriously) her first rose

There is sententiousness in excess of the occasion, which remains "unknowable," and we are brought back to the poet who becomes the only conceivable reference of an emotion in excess of what is said. But "Cummings" in that sense is an empty abstraction, and the fact that the poet Cummings leads us there, away from the poem itself, explains Mr. Blackmur's remark that the poetry exists only in terms of something that is "impenetrable" and "sentimental." It fails to implicate the reader with the terms of a *formed* body of experience. The poet asks us at last not to attend to the poem as poetry, but to its interesting origin, who, the publisher assures us, has a "cheerful disdain for the approval of pundits and poetasters."

In Mr. Cummings' work there is much to amuse and entertain, and much that one admires. A rigorous selection from his four books would give us some of the best poetry of the age. In *&* the magnificent sonnet on death and the love sonnet ending "an inch of nothing for your soul," though projected in Mr. Cummings' personal imagery, achieve a measure of objective validity by reference to the traditional imagery of such poetry, which he inverts, but by implication leans upon. His best verse is that in which he succeeds, perhaps unintentionally, in escaping from his own personality into a world of meaning that not even the "heresy of unintelligence" can let him ignore. For this reason he cannot forever be immune to the heavy hand of the pundits. If he finds such pretension tiresome, it is the fate of interesting personalities to be continually bored.

When We Were Very Young

Francis Fergusson*

Mr. Cummings' diary of his visit to Russia in 1931, first published in 1933 and long unavailable, has now been reissued. This should be good news to readers of various kinds. The passage of time has confirmed and documented Cummings' essential vision of the "unworld" of Marxian totalitarianism, without dimming the brilliance of the people, cities, railways, buildings that he perceived and recorded with unique immediacy in the shabby grey expanse of Russia under the Revolution. He sees Soviet Russia as the dim Hades of antiquity, peopled by throngs of shades who have lost what makes life valuable to him; he sees it as the end of all that Paris in the 'twenties, "Paris in the spring," meant to his generation of Americans, in their perennially youthful quest for life and freedom. The contrast between his "world" and that of the Soviets reveals both with a richness and intensity, a seriousness and realism (for all its lightness of manner), which makes most of the statistical and doctrinaire accounts of the Soviets look frivolous and second-hand. EIMI is thus a travel-book in the grand manner. Like *The American Scene*, for instance, it is the intimate record of the impingement of an alien way of life upon a very acute, candid, and individual sensibility. The publishers are to be congratulated for bringing it out again; it is required reading for all who wish to understand our recent intellectual history, especially our fumbling efforts to grasp the meaning of totalitarian revolution.

As William Troy pointed out when the book first appeared, Cummings' style, with its impressionistically distorted syntax and typography, is difficult, especially in a long work. "The instantaneous alone is his concern," Mr. Troy wrote; ". . . typography is made to perform a dynamic function by approximating visually the actual thought, object, sensation being rendered. . . . The objection is simply that the reader's powers of instantaneous response become exhausted before he gets through very many of the 432 pages of this particular 'book.' " This diagnosis is accurate. The reader should not attempt to read EIMI as a narrative, which it isn't, or to seek *any* form in the work as a whole, for he will be thwarted and disappointed if he does. It should be read (again like *The American*

*Reprinted from the *Kenyon Review*, 12 (1950), 701–05. Copyright 1950 by Kenyon College. Reprinted by permission of Francis Fergusson and the *Kenyon Review*. Editor's note: This review of the reissue of *Eimi* is printed here to indicate the actual place of *Eimi* (1933) in the chronology of Cummings' work.

Scene) in small doses: as a series of sharp sensations, overheard conversations, glimpsed faces, each of which may be turned over in the mind as one mulls over one's own undigested memories of significant moments. If one reads EIMI in this way, it provides endless food for the imagination and understanding.

The easiest parts of the book are those "instantaneous" shots of people talking, arguing, explaining, when Comrade Kemminks' own voice gives place to the voices he heard—and which the reader hears again, like dead Caruso in a gramophone. Cummings is a superb mimic, and he has preserved a nightmarish gallery of journalists, misfit adolescents, fellow-travelling tourists, and Russian people (usually seen and heard but not understood), all washed in the colorless light of doctrine, and hustled in the tide of mass-movement. Among the best of these snapshots is that of "Virgil," his first guide and mentor in Moscow, a professor-journalist-fellow-travelling theatre-critic from Cambridge, Mass. Or there is the dentist and his wife who had taken the Intourist trip and emerged sold on the regime; or there is the cynical American soldier of fortune he meets in Odessa just before he escapes. Cummings himself seldom indulges in theory, but he gives many varieties of Marxian rationalizing in the very words of the rationalizers. The effect is like that of an old newsreel: quaintly alive in its old-fashioned clothes, but more disturbing than contemporary life, because of the historic and symbolic significance which the passage of time has quietly added.

When "Kemminks" speaks in his own voice, and in the style which Mr. Troy described, he is much harder reading; but here again the reader should take the book as a series of little units, like the author's own lyrics. Sometimes a change in the weather, rain, or an unusual light at evening, will induce a memory of the freer world outside, and we get a passage having to do with stars, flowers and tenderness, like Cummings' love-poems. These musical passages gain greatly by contrast with the dreary scene in which they occur. Sometimes he will employ all his linguistic resources to mimic or evoke an image of the Soviet "unman," or mass. The best of these is probably the visit, in a huge silent crowd, to Lenin's megalithic mausoleum, which begins like a sleepwalking death-rite:

```
facefacefaceface
     hand-
          fin-
                claw
     foot-
          hoof
     (tovarich)
                es to number of numberless ( un
—smiling)
     with dirt's dirt dirtier with others' dirt with dirt of themselves dirtiest
```

waistband dirtily never smile shufflebudge dirty pausehalt
   Smilingless.

The book as a whole has, as I remarked, no form beyond the mere haphazard temporal sequence of the author's journey into Russia and out again. The essence of Cummings' method is to obey his immediate vision and feeling, at the expense of all thinking *about* his material, even as much as would be required to arrange it in a larger poem. The play, *him*, is I think Cummings' only effort (and very interesting it is) to make a considered composition out of the fragmentary responses of the sensibility which constitute the life of the "poet." In EIMI he attempts no such ordering or composition. But we are always being addressed by "Comrade Kemminks," and this voice, or mask, or Poundian *persona* is itself a sort of persistent form, giving the book such unity as it possesses.

Any reader of any bit of Cummings is familiar with this *persona*, this mask which feels and sees and sings. It "is" (to use Cummings' favorite word) the basic postulate of his famous style, with its ceaseless lyricism, its "instantaneousness," as though there were no past but in feeling, no future for which thought may be taken; it underlies his habit of vaudevillian improvizing with whatever comes to hand, flowers and junk, the coy parentheses of the type-setter, the vulgarities of the modern street, and remembered bits of Homer's Greek or Dante's Italian. This persona *is* also a creature of American Paris and of Rive Gauche Greenwich Village in their more youthful and glamorous 'twenties. In this medium (which already seems remote) Kemminks feels most alive; he is its creature, native to that element. One must remember that Paris between the wars nourished many vagabonds of genius, Pound and Joyce among them, and there is a kinship between Cummings' style and the style of Pound's *Cantos* (pastiche plus voice) and even the style of *Finnegans Wake*, which appears to be a sort of dissolved and digested pastiche.

Because Comrade Kemminks was formed in Paris, Paris in those between-wars days, he represents the western world in Russia in a very special way: not as its advocate, for he mistrusts the pillars of society at home only a shade less than he does the Marxian dogma, but as one of its most lively and intransigent creatures. In short, his encounter with the Revolution is not in terms of creed or theory at all, but at the level of "being," as the existentialists put it, or, as I should prefer to say, at the sharp point of momentary actuality. The substance of the book is what Kemminks sees, feels, hears, sings, moment by moment. For this reason it would be beside the point to complain that the book dates. It is true that its very life is that of a time which is past, for who, nowadays, would attempt to resurrect Greenwich Village Bohemianism? And how seriously can one take the "persona" itself, with its sometimes annoying archness, the perverse defenselessness of an undergraduate François Villon with clean underwear? One may *judge* the life of the book as one will, but the life is there; it is, paradoxically, in the pathetic and comic transience of its materials.

A re-reading of EIMI reminds one how auspicious a *genre* the travel-book may prove in our time. It allows one to by-pass the more difficult problems of form and meaning, to make sketches (which even in the hands of masters may be livelier than the finished work). It preserves the raw material which the poetic intelligence reveals. And it gives the writer something to write *about*. Cummings benefited to the full from these properties of the travel-book, making his singing-mask significant by contrast, offering a thousand undigested sights and insights upon which the imagination of the reader may feed. His success is clearer now than it was seventeen years ago. We are ready, I think, or at least readier than we were, to think over, to try to grasp imaginatively, the divided world or unworld which EIMI evokes, caught in its unacting act, in many poignant flashes.

Two Kinds of Against

Kenneth Burke*

Despite superficial differences, E. E. Cummings' "No thanks" and Kenneth Fearing's "Poems" have important ingredients in common. Both poets have an exceptional gift for the satirically picturesque. Both specialize in rhetorical devices that keep their pages vivacious almost to the extent of the feverish. Both are practised at suggesting the subjective through the objective. And both seem driven by attitudes for which there is no completely adequate remedy in the realm of the practical (with Cummings, a sense of isolation—with Fearing, an obsession with death).

Cummings has more range, which is not always a virtue in his case, as much of his wider scope is devoted to cryptic naughtiness of an immature sort, a somewhat infantile delight in the sexual parts, alembicated confessions that seem unnecessarily shy and coy (material which, I suspect, Cummings would have abandoned long before now, had he not discovered a few processes of stylistic chemistry for extracting the last bit of ore). And like the chronic invalid who comes to identify his doctor with his disease, hating them interchangeably, he is dissatisfied not only with the current political and economic texture, but also with the "famous fatheads" and "folks with missians" (vindictively mis-spelled) who would attempt its radical cure. Fearing can be buoyed up with the thought of a situation wherein "millions of voices become one voice" and "millions of hands . . . move as one." But Cummings sees the process from the other

*Reprinted from the *New Republic*, 83 (1935), 198–99. Reprinted by permission of Kenneth Burke.

side, as he strikes at those "worshipping Same," says they "got athlete's mouth jumping on & off bandwaggons," and in not very loving verse lambastes the "kumrads" for being deficient in love.

But even a lone wolf cannot feel wholly content without allies. Hence, as with belligerent capitalist states, his occasional nondescript alliance with anyone who will serve (witness his scattering of somewhat shamefacedly anti-Semitic aphorisms, usually consigned to cryptogram, but still "nonsufficiently inunderstood"). As we read "No thanks" carefully, the following picture emerges: For delights, there is sexual dalliance, into which the poet sometimes reads cosmic implications (though a communicative emphasis is lacking). For politics, an abrupt willingness to let the whole thing go smash. For character building, the rigors of the proud and lonely, eventually crystallizing in rapt adulation of the single star, which is big, bright, deep, near, soft, calm, alone and holy—"Who (holy alone) holy (alone holy) alone."

Cummings' resistance to man-made institutions of any kind serves to stimulate a romantic sense of communion with nature (even the mercurial must have *some* locus of constancy); and the best work in the volume is unquestionably his natural description: the hush of snow falling or fallen; the solemn times when "emptied. hills. listen."; a bird in flight; the "mOOn Over tOwns mOOn"; rain that can "move deeply," with life and sex burgeoning in response; the bursting forth of a "white with madness wind" that tears "mountains from their sockets" and makes "writhing alive skies"; Poe's version of the jangling and tintinnabulation of the bells, bells, bells, brought up to date; the spread of "twilight's vastness"; and an elegiac piece, an account of the poet ascending a hill by the sea

> at dusk
>   just when
>   the Light is filled with birds—

a poem so intense, and so well sustained, that we greatly resent the few spots where his mannerisms threaten to undo the mood.

We might say that Cummings' biology is good, but his history is too bad. As historian, at the best he must niggle:

> little
> mr Big
> notbusy
> Busi
> ness notman.

And at the worst, he must attack in the lump:

> news alimony blackmail whathavewe
> and propaganda

—an attitude too non-negotiable for a society to run a going concern on.

Fearing's clearly formed philosophy of history gives his work much better coördination and direction as satire. Cummings the antinomian symbolizes refusal as the little boy that won't play. Fearing, the poet as politician, can offer a take-it-or-leave-it basis of collaboration, a platform, a communist set of values that makes for an unambiguous alignment of forces and a definite indication of purpose. He has a frame of reference by which to locate his satire. Whereas Cummings as satirist is driven by his historical amorphousness into *personal moods* as the last court of appeal, Fearing can attack with the big guns of a *social framework*. He can pronounce moral judgments; and remembering Juvenal or Swift we realize what an advantage this is, for any invective, implicit or explicit, is strongest when the inveigher is appealing to a rigorous code of likes and dislikes. Whereas both poets are alive to the discordant clutter about us, Cummings tends to be jumpy, shifty, look-for-me-here-and-you'll-find-me-there. (After reading him for an hour or so, I show the tetanic symptoms of a cocaine addict.) Fearing is better able to take on something of the heavy oratorical swell, which he manages by an exceptional fusion of ecclesiastic intonations (the lamentation) and contemporary cant (slang, business English, the imagery of pulp fiction, syndicated editorials and advertising).

An inverted Whitman, Fearing scans the country with a statistical eye; but where Whitman sought to pile up a dithyrambic catalogue of *glories*, Fearing gives us a satirically seasoned catalogue of *burdens*. Whitman, the humanitarian, could look upon a national real-estate boom and see there a mystical reaching out of hands. Fearing conversely would remark upon the "profitable smile," the "purpose that lay beneath the merchant's warmth." This method leads at times to the mechanical device of indictments held together by a slightly varied refrain, but for the most part the poet is as ingenious as he is sincere. I know of no better patent, for instance, than this way of saying (in "1933") that the official pronouncements are crooked and that the organization to reenforce the crookedness is terrifyingly efficient:

> You heard the gentleman, with automatic precision,
> > speak the truth.
> Cheers. Triumph.
> And then mechanically it followed the gentleman lied.
> Deafening applause. Flashlights, cameras, microphones.
> Floral tribute. Cheers.

His "Dirge" to the average man winds up superbly by the use of slang interjections:

> And wow he died as wow he lived,
> > going whop to the office and blooie home to sleep and
> > > biff got married and bam had children and oof got
> > > fired,
> > zowie did he live and zowie did he die . . .

It is harder in limited space to illustrate Fearing than Cummings, as Fearing does not get his effects so succinctly. But I might give one more instance of his skill. Readers will recall the often cited remark of Eliot's wherein he characterizes his "general point of view" as "classicist in literature, royalist in politics and anglo-catholic in religion." One may greatly respect Eliot for his important attainments, and still enjoy the deftness of Fearing's reference to

> That genius, that litterateur, Theodore True,
> St. Louis boy who made good as an Englishman in
>   theory, a deacon in vaudeville, a cipher in politics,
> undesirable in large numbers in any community.

Through the volume, Fearing's discerning hatred of all that the "fetishism of commodities" has done for us, as regards the somewhat prospering as well as the destitute, is brilliantly conveyed, along with a quality of reverie, of fears and yearnings that delve far deeper than the contemporary.

Two Views of Cummings

Philip Horton and Sherry Mangan*

I

It would be nice to have all of Cummings' published verse collected in one volume, arranged chronologically and printed in its original form and order. This would have the statistical virtues of a complete and orderly docket whereby to review the pros and cons of his claims on poetry. It would be even nicer—not to say more valuable to have a selection of the very best of his work arranged in some kind of descending scale of categories (Sonnets, Satires, Sexires, and Whimsies alliterates to mind.) Aside from genuine literary value such a volume would have the virtues of economy:—clarity, efficiency, and paucity—and the greatest of these, perhaps, would be paucity. It would probably be about one fourth the size of the present fat collection. But the book at hand is neither of these: it is not a complete collection, nor is it by any conceivably acceptable standards a selection. To my mind its best description is to call it mostfully an unbook.

In the first place it includes most, but not all and sometimes not even the best, of the poetry from *Tulips and Chimneys, &, XLI Poems, Is 5,*

*Reprinted from *Partisan Review*, 4 (1938), 58–63, by permission of *Partisan Review*.

Viva, and *No Thanks*, as well as a score of new poems. Two of the best poems in his early traditional manner, "Epithalamion" and "Puella Mea" are omitted, and many of his best sonnets; the list is too long to be specific. In the second place, it is almost impossible to find a given poem without leafing through pages of trivial eccentricities and getting the typographical jitters. The poems are simply numbered 1–315. There is no index of first lines, nor is there any convenient division by subject matter as was often used in the original editions. True, the table of contents lists the poems chronologically by volumes; thus *Tulips and Chimneys* is represented by poems 1–47. But if you want to find the poem on Picasso, for instance, which originally appeared as one of the "Portraits" in *Tulips and Chimneys*, you will now discover it among *XLI Poems* as number 103. Another of the "Portraits" comes to light as poem 51. Likewise, two of the "La Guerre" poems, originally in *Tulips and Chimneys*, are now numbered 69 and 101 under & and *XLI Poems* respectively. Apparently *Unsinn* is the appropriate active principle in the making of this unbook.

As regards the poetry, the most general statement to be made is that it shows no technical improvement or intellectual development over a period of fifteen years. The *enfant terrible* of 1923 has become the professional *vieux gaillard* of today—a poet distinctly *manqué*. The poetry gives one an apparently inexhaustible repetition, not of ideas or even emotions, but of moods, whimsies, attitudes, prejudices—in short all the effluvia of personality; and the personality is one that has been a familiar museum-piece in the whatnots of literary parlours for the last decade. Perhaps it is the untimely resurrection of this famous *poupée* that outrages the sensibilities and leaves one after reading the book with the feeling of having been party to an indecency. Surely the baroque antiquity of such a quip as poem 299 (one of the "New Poems!")—

> Q:dwo
> we know of anything which can
> be as dull as one englishman
> A:to

should be locked under glass in the corner cuddy. The same is true of the notorious typography: its only virtue today lies in its quaint persistence as a historical curiosity. As for the sexires, they have multiplied, like the whimsies and typography, unchanged in kind and quality. All that needs to be said of them, once and for all, is that they are not very good on any level. They are inferior in both technique and spirit to such ballads as "Down In The Lehigh Valley" on the one hand, and on the other to popular songs like "My Handy Man." Compare, for instance, the prurient emasculation of poem 250: "may i feel said he (i'll squeal said she" to the epic sweep of: "The grass was gone for miles around Where Lil's white arse had bumped the ground"; or the hackneyed double entendre of poem 134 (the breaking in of a new car) with the rich imagery and invention of

"My Handy Man." Even the serious sex poems are corrupted by prurience, sicklied o'er with sentimentality. They stem not from the great stream of the tradition, but from the minor tributary of cheap burlesque; they are more concerned with exhibition than enjoyment—like the strip-teaser with one eye on the censors and the cops in the back row.

The satires, which together with the sex poems are largely responsible for Cummings' popular reputation, very rarely deserve the name. They are more often bits of sarcasm, fancy invective, and nose-thumbings. The real fun we get from reading the best of them is derived not from their success as poems, but from the exhibition of a clever (and potentially serious) poet deliberately pointing his sophistications with vulgarities, his poetic language with gutter slang. It is the bald trick of in-congruity—a popular one in burlesque, and is supported by many of the common devices. This one, for example, of the censored rhyme (cf. the ballad "Sweet Violets"):

> every kumrad is a bit
> of quite unmitigated hate

or the elaborate pun:

> a myth is as good as a smile . . .
> . . . entitled a wraith's
> progress or mainly awash while chiefly submerged

or for closing lines the classic anti-climax of nonsense:

> it isn't snowing snow you know
> it's snowing buttercups

and

> for a bad cigar is a woman
> but a gland is only a gland)

Now there is no possible objection to either nonsense or doggerel when given and taken as such, though one may well dislike to have it sand-wiched in with serious poems. The trouble here lies in the ambiguity. Apparently Cummings has cultivated the confusion of incongruities for so long that he himself is rarely certain to what degree or in what kind he wants to be serious. Similarly, he slips so easily into the jargon of newspaper, stage and street that he perfectly blunts the edge of what was meant to be indignation or bitterness. Thus, in one of his best and serious satires, the lines

> obey says toc, submit says tic
> Eternity's a Five Year Plan

give the effect of cant. The same triviality results in poem 214, a love ballad after the manner of Villon, which almost succeeds in overcoming its defects. In this case the jargon is that of musical comedy lyrics after Cole Porter or Kaufman.

> i am a birdcage without any bird
> a collar looking for a dog, a kiss
> without lips; a prayer lacking any knees

and again

> . . . a hand's impression in an empty glove
> a soon forgotten tune, a house for lease.

This mingling of the trivial and serious, and the general confusion of values throughout Cummings' work, is by no means accidental. It is a result of his deliberate rejection of knowledge, whether of himself or of life at large.

> that you should ever think, may god forbid . . .
> for that way knowledge lies, the foetal grave
> called progress and negation's dead undoom.

This from the last poem in the volume. The consequences of Cummings' anti-intellectualism have been so carefully analyzed by R. P. Blackmur in his *Double Agent* that there is little else to be said to it. The *Collected Poems* merely confirms Blackmur's remarks. In the Introduction, for instance, Cummings writes: "Life, for eternal us, is now; and now is much too busy being a little more than everything to seem anything, catastrophic included." This is a typical Cummings statement, for while appearing to embrace and affirm, it actually reduces to negation and rejection. Likewise, the more he tries in the later poems to define his beliefs, the more he resorts to negatives. He likes to describe the philistine norms by the negative prefix: "unselves," "unlives," "unhearts," "unminds," etc.; but the trick merely shows up his own impoverished and fuzzy affirmations. He praises the "whyless-soul," the "general looseness of doom," the "mystery of growing," and life—"the one undiscoverable guess." But he himself does not grow in his poetry. Having rejected knowledge, the chiefest instrument of evaluation and the essential means to maturity, he can hardly be expected to offer more than the scattered impulses of an immature personality. The most revealing of his negative statements, which strikes one with the impact and illumination of an absolute truth, are the lines in poem 214:

> so that my life (which liked the sun and moon)
> resembles something that has not occurred

Substituting "poetry" for "life," the statement would have had even greater pertinency. As Mr. Blackmur has pointed out, his poetry offers notes and materials for poems rather than actually achieved poems. To give Cummings his due, he has written a handful of really good love sonnets and poems, which still deserve publication in a modest volume of their own. Excepting them, nothing much in the way of poetry has occurred.

II

To the predictable exasperation of all right-thinking critics, the special miracle of Cummings, even under the severe strain of a collected edition, blithely persists, viable, inextinguishable, a fact. The indignation of our literary theologians is comprehensible enough: Cummings's faults stand right out—indeed, what Eliotellus in eight years has not, for his graduation piece, permanently annihilated him? Yet his poetry lives easily through such attack; for his faults are inseparably the faults of his virtues, and in those virtues—gusto, abundance, magniloquence—he is nearly unique.

Of course much of the critical animus against Cummings derives from American critics' ignorance of or dislike for the restless development of French poetry. Although René Taupin has perhaps oversharp eyes in seeing so much influence of Gourmont and Rimbaud in Cummings's work (Apollinaire's *Calligrammes* are admittedly more evident), it is nevertheless true that Cummings is more in the French than in the English stream. By and large, our poetry stems from French, our criticism from English influences; and since before Poe, there has been this exasperation of the Anglophile cataloguers that French poetry would neither stay put itself nor refrain from stimulating the poetry of other languages.

But apart from this, what essentially is the case usually brought against Cummings? Failure in exact communication, pretentiousness, execrable taste, and limitation of subject.

The poet whose primary interest is to communicate either fails entirely or, if he succeeds, does so on a abysmal level, for which prose would have served. The poet whose primary interest is, within the fair limits of language (private and secret Humpty-Dumpty use of words strictly barred), to express with the maximal accuracy, depth, and vividness his experience, by succeeding in that expression, succeeds in communication, i.e., the perfect recreation of that experience in the reader. It is simply this paradox which Luis Cardoza y Aragón crystallizes in his brilliant dictum: "where there is no miracle, there is no poetry."

Now the miracle of Cummings is indubitably heretical, conceivably satanic. His words do not, by limiting one another, construct an exact and unmistakable impression; each word, on the contrary, explosively releases in the reader as much of its total content of meanings and emotivity as the reader is capable of supporting. Hence the poem in Cummings's mind and in the reader's mind are two quite different variants of the poem, not in any wise identical but both of great potency. It is principally for this reason that his poems practically defy paraphrase into prose. The glaring non-sequitur of our theologians is to argue that, since the miracle is heretical, there is no miracle. To attempt to argue out of existence the notorious fact of Cummings's poetic power merely by (quite correctly) alleging that it is not canonical, is a petulant absurdity.

Similarly self-deceptive is the contention that Cummings is discredited by his pretentiousness. That timidity of opinion of which *New-Yorker*ism is the perfect flower may chidingly deprecate as bumptious the classic poetic quality of iactantia; but, whether one likes it or not, "exegi monumentum" happens to have proved itself a historically correct statement. It would not wholly amaze, though it might equally displease, if

> the harder the wind blows the
> taller i am

proved equally so.

Cummings's taste is more difficult to defend; indeed, it is often quite indefensible. The retention of, for example, 43, "it may not always be so; and i say . . .", is certainly a triumph more of courage than of prudence, though one cannot but admire the honest temerity of a récolte that is truly a collection, and not a selection; and in 47, "notice the convulsed orange inch of moon . . .", the bathos of the last line is all too characteristic. These are not merely youthful lapses: examples could be multiplied from the poems, and the Introduction's self-identification with the aging Renoir faintly and fraily stinks. Yet the basic antithesis of today is less that of good *v* bad taste than that of taste *v* no-taste. Cummings, like the Italians, has, admirably, *a lot of* taste; it is merely regrettable that some of it is bad. But the bad is quite compensated for by a complete absence of the fashionable "perfect gray."

The accusation of undue limitation of subject, however, begins, by 1938, to carry much more weight. True enough, spring, love and death are large and universal subjects; but to make them a complete universe of discourse begins to suggest, after some sixteen years, a certain lack of sensibility, imagination, and courage. Especially in the bulk of a collected volume, there becomes apparent a cloying quality, a monotony of mere lusciousness, however spectacularly successful. It is yet somewhat early to assume, however, that Cummings's interests will never as consciously expand beyond this frame as they have to date been deliberately confined within it. One's *Collected Poems* often signalize the termination of a period. If at his present age he does not break through this eggshell into the world, he will remain, regrettably, a magnificent but minor singer; it is not impertinent to hope, however, that his present maturity will produce, with the impact of broader (and, after all, somewhat more interesting) experience upon this alert, sinewed and lusty talent, some further and deeper conclusion, beyond love-is-enough.

[Review of 50 Poems]

R.P. Blackmur*

Mr. Cummings' poems depend entirely upon what they create in process, only incidentally upon what their preliminary materials or intentions may have been. Thus, above all, there is a prevalent quality of uncertainty, of uncompleted possibility, both in the items and in the fusion of the items which make up the poems; but there is also the persistent elementary eloquence of intension—of things struggling, as one says crying, to be together, and to make something of their togetherness which they could never exhibit separately or in mere series. The words, the meanings in the words, and also the nebula of meaning and sound and pun around the words, are all put into an enlivening relation to each other. There is, to employ a word which appealed to Hart Crane in similar contexts, a sense of synergy in all the successful poems of Mr. Cummings: synergy is the condition of working together with an emphasis on the notion of energy in the working, and energy in the positive sense, so that one might say here that Mr. Cummings' words were energetic. The poems are, therefore, eminently beyond paraphrase, not because they have no logical content—for they do, usually very simple—but because so much of the activity is apart from that of logical relationships, is indeed in associations free of, though not alien to, logical associations. In short, they create their objects.

Now there has been a good deal of catcalling at Mr. Cummings, and lately there has been a good deal of indifference, general indifference which is meaningless and also the indifference of some of his admirers who have taken him scot-free of attention: all good, all operative, all part of the canon, and this indifference is the worst injustice of all. There is, for the poet, no discipline like the justified reservations of his admirers, and this should be especially the case with a poet so deliberately idiosyncratic as Mr. Cummings. I have been one of his admirers for twenty-one years since I first saw his poetry in the *Dial*; and it may be that my admiration has gone up and down so many hills that it is a little fagged and comes up to judgment with entirely too many reservations. Yet I must make them, and hope only that the admiration comes through.

First, there is the big reservation that, contrary to the general belief and contrary to what apparently he thinks himself, Mr. Cummings is not—in his meters, in the shapes of his lines, in the typographical cast of his poems on the page—an experimental poet at all. In his "peculiar" poetry he does one of two things. He either reports a speech rhythm and the fragments of meaning punctuated by the rhythm so as to heighten and make it permanent in the reader's ear—as famously in "Buffalo Bill," but

*Reprinted from the *Southern Review*, 7 (1941), 201–05, by permission of the *Southern Review*.

just as accurately elsewhere as, for example, in poem 27 in this volume—or in trying to do so he makes such a hash of it that the reader's ear is left conclusively deaf to the poem. I assume he is attempting to heighten sound in the failures as well as the successes; if he is not, if he is trying to write a poetry in symbols which have no audible equivalents—a mere eye poetry—then he is committing the sin against the Holy Ghost. My belief is that the high percentage of failures comes from his lack of a standard from which to conduct experiments, and without which experiment in any true sense is impossible; so that in fact many of his oddities are merely the oddities of spontaneous play, nonsense of the casual, self-defeating order, not nonsense of the rash, intensive order. There is no reason he should not play, but it is too bad that he should print the products, for print sheds a serenity of value, or at least of "authority" upon the most miserable productions which are very deceptive to the innocent.

It should be emphasized in connection with this that Mr. Cummings is an abler experimenter than most poets with rhythm and cadence and epithet; and that these experiments come off best when he is not engaged in false experiments with meter—when he is writing either heightened prose as in "Buffalo Bill," or when he is writing straightway meter of four or five iambic feet. Which is what one would expect.

My second reservation is less significant for most readers but more important for his best readers, and has to do with his vocabulary, which seems to me at many crucial points so vastly over-generalized as to prevent any effective mastery over the connotations they are meant to set up as the substance of his poems. I do not mean it is just hard to say, which is of little importance, but that it is hard to *know*, which is very important, where you are at in poems which juggle fifty to a hundred words so many times and oft together that they lose all their edges, corners, and boundary lines till they cannot lie otherwise than in a heap. But this reservation, formerly held to an extreme, does not now need to be; it is now but a cautionary reservation and applies to no more than half the new poems; for Mr. Cummings' practice has improved with his increasing interest, as it seems, in persuading his readers of the accuracy of the relationships which his words divulge.

My third reservation is minor, and has to do with the small boy writing privy inscriptions on the wall; a reservation which merely to state is sufficiently to expound. Some of the dirt perhaps comes under the head of the poetry of gesture, and some perhaps is only the brutality of disgust. My complaint is meant to be technical; most of the dirt is not well enough managed to reach the level of either gesture or disgust, but remains, let us say, coprophiliac which is not a technical quality.

Beyond these reservations, which in this book of fifty leave ten poems free, Mr. Cummings' work is sufficiently admirable to allow for any amount of good will and concession and full assent to method, all warranted by the substance we are thus permitted to reach. Special attention should be called to the development of fresh conventions in the use of prepositions, pronouns, and the auxiliary verbs in the guise of substances, and in general the rich use of words ordinarily rhetorical—mere connectives or means of transition in their ordinary usage—for the things of actual experience. There are questions which may be asked of which the answers will only come later when the familiarity of a generation or so will have put the data in an intimately understandable order. How much of the richness depends on mere novelty of usage, the gag-line quality? How much depends on the close relationship to the everyday vernacular, the tongue in which Who and Why and How and No and Yes and Am, for example, are of supreme resort, and are capable of infinite diversity of shading? How much depends perhaps on Mr. Cummings' sense of the directional nubs, and the nubs of agency and of being, in his chosen words; a sense that resembles, say, the dative and ablative inflections in Latin? How much, finally, depends on the infinite proliferating multiplicity of available meanings in his absolute commonplaces made suddenly to do precise work? The questions would not be worth asking did not each furnish a possible suggestion as to the capacity for meaning and flavor of his usage; nor would they be worth asking if there were not a major residue of his verse, as standard as death, which his oddities only illuminate without damaging.

I quote the first stanza of poem 34;

> my father moved through dooms of love
> through sames of am through haves of give,
> singing each morning out of each night
> my father moved through depths of height.

To Be

Peter DeVries*

The trouble with reviewing Cummings is that when you do so you are uncomfortably aware of engaging in something he has, once again, been briskly and diligently reproving, namely analyzing it instead of eating it. "Art is a mystery" is a point he has made often in one way or another—he made it again in the foreword to the catalogue for the recent New York exhibition of his paintings—and anybody with a yardstick is a fool and a public enemy. He has so convincingly hated the "why or because or although" of rational scrutiny, in so many of his books, as against the virginity of experience celebrated in all of them, that when one has just closed another the last thing he wants to do is be caught hang-

*Reprinted from *Poetry*, 64 (1944), 158–64. Copyright 1944 by The Modern Poetry Association. Reprinted by permission of Peter DeVries and the editor of *Poetry*.

ing around analysis, certainly not by Cummings himself. Poking the stiff scholastic finger into his sentences, serving up examples of instances, picking the tissues of his writing apart to prove that it is literature, is not something that reading it exactly leaves you in the mood to do. He himself, you are sure, would much rather you just set your glass down and said Thanks, that was good.

His impatience with analysis—literary it is felt as well as scientific—is not too hard to understand, and the explanation does not altogether lie in his temperament: one to which, so to speak, flowers are of a lot more interest than botany. Criticism is at times quite capable of a desiccating effect, especially when concerned with those intricate and solemn scrutinies of the obvious through which we are sometimes conducted. I forget the name of the old-time gramophone comedian with the monologue about his father, which told how the old man would pick up things in the street and take them home to see what they were. Well so one time he picked up something and as usual took it home, where, examining it closely, he discovered what it was—an armful of kindling wood. Criticism is often fully as thorough as that, and has at times some of the other attributes of over-intellectual preoccupation Cummings has always disliked. And yet it has been in sophisticated criticism that his poetry has encountered its fullest appreciation, rather than in the straightforward relish of the more average reader; which is a paradox for it would seem that the clear-springing emotional line, the fresh rill of lyric utterance, the forthright and innocent belief, would make it the other way round.

Resistance to unfamiliar technique probably accounts for it, still. It seems unfortunate but there are still those who see only the broken bones of syntax, typographical "eccentricity," stanzas punctuated with a pepper shaker, and all that. Besides these, there is a fair-sized group of strong admirers in whose affections he is firmly rooted, a surprising number of whom seem to have called on him in New York and will tell you how nice he was; there is the respect of his fellow-practitioners, no small thing; and finally the doubtfulness of wide numbers who have read a poem or lines and images here and there that struck them, or who have found the fun in his poetry and can't quite take it seriously, or look at it askance and don't know quite what to think about it but suppose his significance lies at a not exactly determined point somewhere between the Elizabethan lyric and bubble gum.

The most familiar of his liberties with the "laws of grammar"—shifting the parts of speech at will—has reached a point in this new book where it occurs constantly, almost on every page, till his readers probably no longer even notice it, have simply accepted it as his natural kind of vocabulary. Practically every poem has instances: "turn men's see to stare"; "forests of ago"; "we'll move away still further: into now"; "true lovers in each happening of their hearts/ live longer than all which and every who"; "if time should ask into his was/ all shall, their eyes would never miss a yes." . . . And so on. The view of this as merely novel or tricky is discredited by his continued success with it. Instead of wearing thin, which it would certainly long ago have done if it were only a trick, it seems more natural and right for him than ever. It is not a trick; it is speech.

The view of his vocabulary as that of a mere "connoisseur of words" is equally wrong. The most conspicuous precedent for thus shifting the grammatical function of words that comes to mind, is folk speech itself. "Upping" the price, "horsing" around, "booking" a guy, "nosing" around, "flooring" somebody, "railroading" something, are all examples of the same thing. The other day somebody asked me to "nutshell" something for him (an article which was already in *The Reader's Digest*, so I guess we are in a hurry all right). I cannot profess to having given the matter any profound or extended thought, but in comparing the examples that have suggested themselves, I notice an interesting difference between the grammatical interchanges of Cummings and those of the man in the street or garage or A&P. It is already illustrated in the respective instances given. The man in the street or garage or A&P seems to want in every case a verb, and when there isn't any, or he can't think of one, or those there are don't suit him, makes it out of whatever noun there is handy, while Cummings seems to want a noun and makes it out of every other part of speech in the language. The former resorts to his invention to express action, the latter to express existence. There is a kind of key to Cummings in it.

This way with words enables them best to reveal his essential vision, best to express what is to him the most mysterious and beautiful fact of all, the reality of existence itself, the fact and experience of *being*. All the realities that we may experience while "mythical guests of Is" he posits in terms of the noun, to express their *substantive* quality, to use a word which may reassure troubled grammarians. *To be*, is what he wants man most to be; the pure, deep identity, the wonderful one times one, is the beautiful mystery he celebrates. Hence the nouns: a noun is for what *is*.

> such a sky and such a sun
> i never knew and neither did you
> and everybody never breathed
> quite so many kinds of yes

Love, which he so constantly sings, is not an illusion, but the intensest form of aliveness—of being.

Next to the bright clear lyric note, what we find most often in him is bitter satire and lampoon, and there is some of that again in *One Times One*. It is a familiar and understandable contrast, that of the sensitive nature lashing out at what outrages it, recreating in ugliest lineaments the pomp and pretense and vulgarity that twist and befoul the life it loves.

This time there is perhaps more, relatively, of the familiar Cummings distaste for "reason" and the scientific and analytical solvents of experience. When he tells the scholar to go fly a kite, he means it:

> o by the by
> has anybody seen
> little you-i
> who stood on a green
> hill and threw
> his wish at blue
>
> with a swoop and a dart
> out flew his wish
> (it dived like a fish
> but it climbed like a dream)
> throbbing like a heart
> singing like a flame
>
> blue took it my
> far beyond far
> and high beyond high
> bluer took it your
> but bluest took it our
> away beyond where
>
> what a wonderful thing
> is the end of a string
> (murmurs little you-i
> as the hill becomes nil)
> and will somebody tell
> me why people let go

Ditching botany to go pick flowers is all very well, and feeding the pigeons on the grass, seed, a lot better than sticking them in the holes in rolltop desks. But there seems a point at which this emphasis is fruitless, and unfortunate from the point of view of poetry as well as science. Artists inveighing, according to their lights, against elements in their time is a common and perfectly valid thing; but resisting a force that is so obviously going to have an enormous effect on the direction and outlook of man, and which can and should be absorbed into his vision, is another matter. The artist who can absorb this force in an integrated vision of the onward movement of the race would seem more adequately to be directing the human imagination. I have a feeling I may be finding implications not intended in such lines as

> given the scalpel they dissect a kiss;
> or, sold the reason, they undream a dream

and

> anything's righter
> than books
> could plan

and

> buds know better
> than books
> don't grow

and

> the mightiest meditations of mankind
> cancelled are by one merely opening leaf

and

> when man determined to destroy
> himself he picked the was
> of shall and finding only why
> smashed it into because

but coming across them as incessantly as one does gives one the impression that somebody has got something in his craw. It becomes at times disquieting for those who cherish his writing but believe the unfortunate cleavage posed between science and poetry to be somewhat exaggerated. Science itself operates among wonders that need be no bar to imagination, and neither the poet nor anyone else who respects the imagination need dream any dreams the less. With or without the scalpel, may not "only the impossible happen" still, and may we still not breathe as many kinds of yes? And yet things like "Peace is the inefficiency of science" and "War is the science of inefficiency" contain dreadful truths that ought to be brought home to all those who regard the war as an interruption after which we can once more pursue the vision of Progress through Prosperity, our destinies turned over, once again, to Congressmen purring like refrigerators.

Cummings' poetry with its celebration of the individual human identity is particularly nourishing and reassuring today when that identity is either destroyed by mass violence or submerged in the mass disciplines that shall save it. He remains a pure voice to hear, and he embodies a healing faith; at his best level he is himself like that sunbeam of his which is always truthful. He has his one bird and his ten thousand stars, and we know the bird will still always teach him how to sing, and none teach the stars how not to dance. His counsel runs clear as a stream; that old counsel of his which is really so simple and yet as hard as Relax—to eat flowers and not to be afraid.

[Review of *1 x 1*]

F.O. Matthiessen*

Cummings, whom Winters has long since rejected as showing "little comprehension of poetry," is still the experimentalist of one experiment. Ten years ago, following Blackmur's dissection of his language as a species of unvaried babytalk, he seemed likely to drop from the concern of a decade whose attention was upon social issues. But the turn of fashion's wheel has brought a renewed popularity to Cummings' belief that "the single secret will still be man," and Spencer, among others, has recently argued that we can now see that "the emphasis on social issues, from which Cummings was so far removed, produced little good poetry." That strikes me as a superficial view. Not only does it overlook that the best work so far of Auden's generation has sprung from such emphasis, but it also seems to confuse social issues with radical opinions, and to forget that a deepening preoccupation with society was what added stature to such different poets as Wallace Stevens and Eliot.

The fascinating thing about Cummings is that he is always talking about growth, and always remains the same. *1x1* finds him still against all his old enemies of the past quarter century, against advertisers ("a salesman is an it that stinks to please"), against war, against intellect, against "unwish," "unself," "undream," "unhe," against "manunkind" and all the "prodigies of un." "Mostpeople" are still "snobs," whereas "the most who die, the more we live," and "there's nothing as something as one."

Cummings is as concerned with and as incapable of the organic principle as Emerson was, and for surprisingly similar reasons. He insists that man and his work must continue to unfold and grow. He has rephrased here Emerson's doctrine of "all in each": "so isn't small one littlest why." But he too is the son of a New England clergyman for whom "life" consists entirely of inspired moments, and is thus without the basic requirement for growth—continuity. The mystery is how he has managed to defy nature by not changing and still keeping alive. The explanation lies again in Emerson's vein, in his capacity for exuberant renewal of the moment. In Cummings' case the phenomenon may best be described in linguistic terms, since his work is all a gay logomachy. As a romantic anarchist, a poem consists for him in a moment's breaking through the laws of syntax. He is against nouns ("dull all nouns"), but even worse than nouns are probing conjunctions, since doubting can turn men's "faith to how, their joy to why." The sole principle of life is in the verb: the great I AM. And so the moment can be created only by the glory of the present indicative,

*Reprinted from the *Kenyon Review*, 6 (1944), 688–90. Copyright 1944 by Kenyon College. Reprinted by permission of the *Kenyon Review* and Yale University.

and in one of his most brilliant displacements the poet deplores the centuries of "original soon."

But a poem cannot be written entirely by conjugating the verb to be, and, consequently, the device on which Cummings rings every possible change to increase expectancy is the comparative: "beauty is more now than dying's when." Sometimes his special use might be termed the extending comparative, since it loops beyond one quality to another: "heart was big/as the world ain't square." At others, the continuing comparative:

> love is a spring at which
> crazy they drink who've climbed
> steeper than hopes are fears. . . .

There "steeper" continues from the hill to the hopes and fears in order to bring us closer to the unique essence. But always the comparative aspires to be the superlative: "purest than fear's obscener." And why not, since "beautiful most is now"?

But the perpetually unique soon becomes solipsistic. Worse still, for Cummings' values, it becomes expected. It might almost be said that from the moment when he turned his first noun into a verb ("but if a look should april me") he has been writing the same poem. It is probably the first time on record that a complicated technique has been devised to say anything so basically simple. The pay-off is, unfortunately, monotony. After half a dozen electric shocks in the penny arcade you begin to wonder why the first was so thrilling. You are also not quite so sure that it's most people who are snobs. But if Cummings' circus act was once good enough to make people sit up, it is still just as "wonderful one times one." . . . The poems . . . still display his remarkable playful joy that eludes any analysis.

[Review of Xaîpe]

Randall Jarrell*

During the early '20's E. E. Cummings's reputation was at its highest point: at one moment, a sort of false dawn, he was more imitated, better regarded, than Eliot himself. But as people came to demand that poets, and the very chairs they sat in, be socially conscious, Mr. Cummings slowly came to seem an irrelevant and unaccountable anachronism; when poets read his verse, as it pushed on into the heart of that last undiscovered continent, e. e. cummings, they thought of this moral im-

*Reprinted from *Partisan Review*, 17 (1950), 728–30, by permission of *Partisan Review*.

possibility, this living fossil, with a sort of awed revulsion. Later, as the fortunes of unengaged art improved, as novels by E. M. Forster replaced novels about strikes, as Mr. Cummings approached a certain age—that age at which literary survivors come to the king's row, and are accepted as Fathers of the Tribe—most of his reputation returned, and he now seems one more dean of American poets. He had a sort of underground popularity even during the darkest '30's—many a good party-member had a guilty taste for Cummings or Sherlock Holmes; I think that he will remain popular for a long time, for several reasons. He is one of the most individual poets who ever lived—and, though it sometimes seems so, it is not just his vices and exaggerations, the defects of his qualities, that make a writer popular. But, primarily, Mr. Cummings's poems are loved because they are full of sentimentality, of sex, of more or less improper jokes, of elementary lyric insistence—they are the popular songs of American intellectuals. (I hope the reader won't think this a joke, but will seriously consider the similarities between the two.) That the poems are extravagantly, professedly modernist, experimental, *avant-garde*, is an additional attraction: the reader of modern poetry—especially the inexperienced or unwilling reader—feels toward them the same gratitude that the gallery-goer feels when, his eyes blurred with corridors of analytical cubism, he comes into a little room full of the Pink and Blue periods of Picasso. Even the poems' difficulties are of an undemanding, unaccusing sort—that of puzzles: a poem that looks like the ruins of a type-casting establishment will not elicit from the editors of the *Saturday Review of Literature* a fraction of the indignation with which they see, in Eliot, some random quotation from Pausanias.

Rilke, in his wonderful "Archaic Statue of Apollo," ends his description of the statue, the poem itself, by saying without transition or explanation: *You must change your life.* He needs no explanation. We know from many experiences that this is what the work of art does: its life—in which we have shared the alien existences both of this world and of that different world to which the work of art alone gives us access—unwillingly accuses our lives. But Mr. Cummings's poems say to us something very different: that we and the poet are so superior to the fools and pedants and reformers of the world that our only obligation is to condemn them, to draw apart into rapture—the reader is asked to wash his hands of them, and to become part of the sanctimonious anarchic ecstasy of the poem. The poet has made a separate peace; sitting among the lakes and flowers of a Swiss summer, he complacently dismisses the fools killing each other below, people who have never even realized that love is enough. I have heard only once his recording of his poem about the soldier from New York City who is killed by steel from the Sixth Avenue Elevated; but I shall never forget the firm superiority, the confident rejection of the voice as it said that you and I told him, Christ told him, Socrates told him, and he wouldn't listen; but part of the old Sixth Avenue

Elevated, in a Japanese shell—*that* made him listen. . . . Yes, Christ and Socrates did tell him (though it is odd to see that old soldier Socrates in this particular connection), and he didn't listen; but they told you and me and Mr. Cummings this and many other things, and we listened to few and lived by fewer. In the triumph of his poems there is one thing lacking, that slave who whispers: You too are mortal. But usually Mr. Cummings is moral about not being conventionally moral: he resembles a student of ethics who, after reading that some tribes feed the old and others eat them, decides that it is all right to do anything anywhere, that the self-expression of the knowing superior is the one true key to ethics—and from then on he looks with pharisaical impatience at those not elect, weak spirits caught in the bloody toils of morality.

The poems' relation to "Nature" is impressive in its purity and delight, but depressing in its affinity to that of picture-postcards; and Love, in the poems, is so disastrously neo-primitive, has been swept so fantastically clean of complication or pain or moral significance, that it seems a kind of ecstatic chocolate soda which is at once a sin—to the world—and a final good—to us happy few. For such poems Stendhal and Proust (and anyone who was ever in love, one is tempted to say) have lived and died in vain. One is bewildered by the complacency with which the poet accepts himself and his, and rejects or doesn't even notice the existence of the rest of the world. One of his poems lives along the line like Pope's spider, but hides at the heart of its sensitivity a satisfied inaccessibility to experience—for experience is, after all, what is different from oneself. He has hidden his talent under a flower, and there it has gone on reproducing, by parthenogenesis, poem after poem after poem. Because of this his poems are, year after year, the same poems; the only true changes are technical changes, ingenious discoveries exhaustively exploited. He is like a painter who has on every canvas charming and characteristic patches, colors that are a pleasure in themselves, but who has never once managed to paint a good picture. For I can't think of a single poem of his that can be called, in the most serious meaning of the phrase, a good poem. When one asks people to name one they seem oddly at a loss, and finally mention poems like *My father moved through dooms of shall* [sic] or *Anyone lived in a pretty how town*—attractive poems which are spoiled both by filling-in, the automatic repetition of technical novelties (as if you wrote a poem by discovering a novel formula and repeating it a dozen times), and by the willing shallowness of the attitude which produces them, that Renascence of Wonder of our own day. (And something as wonderfully promising as *The Enormous Room* is the most distressing disappointment of all—as though one could read *The House of the Dead* only in an adaptation by Paul Goodman and Kenneth Patchen.) Even Mr. Cummings's delectable freshness and innocence have come to seem professionally surprising in the way that, say, Mistinguette's legs are: how much care and avoidance, what cloistral resolution, have been necesssary to preserve intact this stock in trade!

Yet how wonderfully individual, characteristic, original, all his poems are. (Thinking how extraordinarily true to himself he has been, how false to every other man, one is forced to remember how far from "self-expression" great poems are—what a strange compromise between the demands of the self, the world, and Poetry they actually represent.) And Mr. Cummings's poems are full of perceptions pure as those in dreams, effects of wonderful delicacy and exactness; many a flower of rank sentiment twinkles at one such dewy petals that one gobbles it up like a cow. In fact, as soon as the reader lowers the demands he makes on art—pretends that it is, at best, no more than a delightful or ecstatic or in-genious diversion—the best poems become a thorough pleasure. For Mr. Cummings is a fine poet in the sense in which Swinburne is one; but in the sense in which we call Hardy and Yeats and Proust and Chekhov poets, great poets, he is hardly a poet at all. Marshal Zhdanov said, delighting me: *There is a great big hole in the foundations of Soviet music*; well, there is a great big moral vacuum at the heart of E. E. Cummings's poetry. As Louise Bogan has written, with summary truth: "It is this dele-tion of the tragic that makes Cummings's joy childish and his anger petulant." What delights and amuses and disgusts us he has represented; but all that is heart-breaking in the world, the pity and helplessness and love that were called, once, the tears of things, the heart of heartless-ness—these hardly exist for him.

E.E. Cummings:
The World of "Un"

Carl Bode*

When a poet as widely known as Cummings has both published his autobiography and issued his collected poems, it is a good time to look back over his work and reconsider it. The more so in this case because of a lurking suspicion about its quality. The suspicion is based on a curious cir-cumstance, one that should strike anybody who leafs through the essays about Cummings' verse. The fact is that the essays break down, almost without exception, into two kinds. The first, and far more frequent, are brief but generous appreciations written by his admirers. The sec-ond—there are only a handful of these—are longer studies; and the closer the scrutiny, the less favorable the appraisals prove to be.

*Reprinted from *Poetry*, 86 (1955), 358–63. Copyright 1955 by The Modern Poetry Association. Reprinted by permission of Carl Bode and the editor of *Poetry*.

If we reread Cummings from the beginning, a disappointingly low view of the poetry can all too easily emerge. If the criticism turns out to be caustic, moreover, the fault may be the poet's own. It may be generated by his persistent combination of cocksureness with technical inadequacy.

It is not strictly true that his career as a poet both began and ended with his first book, *Tulips and Chimneys*, which he published in 1923. Some of the poems quietly buried there were never to be exhumed. No later collection of his work, and no anthology either, would ever include such a piece of derivation as *Epithalamion*, with its perfectly banal rhetoric about "Thou aged unreluctant earth who dost / with quivering continual thighs invite / the thrilling rain." Nor would we be apt to read in reprint the commonplace couplets of *Puella Mea* ("Lovely as those ladies were / mine is a little love-lier") or the lines *Of Nicolette* ("right wildly beat / her heart"). All that these poems reflect is the enthusiasm of the college student who has earned an A in his English literature course.

But once we read past the tributes to Nicolette and other ladies likewise of incomparable beauty, several of the pieces which were later anthologized begin to appear. Their advent is marked by the first, tentative use of the little "i" and of the fragmented typography. *Always before your voice my soul, Thy fingers make early flowers*, and the poem beginning "the Cambridge ladies who live in furnished souls" are examples.

Here in fact is some of the best as well as some of the earliest Cummings in print. The kind of poem he managed in the course of time to make widely known is well represented. We see the sonnet, the conventional form of which is superficially concealed by blowing the words and phrases apart and by abandoning punctuation and the use of capital letters—although it should be added that Cummings was afterwards to go much further in those directions than he did in *Tulips and Chimneys*. Then there are the free-verse lyrics which represent an extension of this technique, a reduction, often, almost to absurdity. But not always. The lyric *in Just-spring*, for instance, turning as it does on the epithet "goat-footed" for the balloon man, suddenly extends far beyond childhood and the present.

The tricks of technique, or, if you will, the stylistic devices, appear in both crude and complex forms. One that Cummings particularly likes is paradox. Ultimately paradox was to become one of the main barriers between Cummings and the reader because of the way it defeated even the most assiduous attempts to make out the poet's meaning. Perhaps the most interesting thing, in terms of understanding his long career as a composer of verse, is to see the first simple use of the device. There is a poem in *Tulips and Chimneys* which begins "my love is building a building" and here this technique is to be found at its baldest. The building in question is "strong fragile," "skilful uncouth," "precise clumsy," and "laborious, casual." Normally, the advantage of paradox for a poet is that it increases the tension of his poetry. In Cummings it is too often merely a case of opposites which cancel out, leaving neither meaning nor emotion behind them.

Cummings' discontent with traditional rhyming anyone can doubtless sympathize with, and *Tulips and Chimneys* marks both his departure from it and his characteristic deviation thereafter. He takes masculine rhyme, feminine rhyme, internal rhyme, and assonance, and mixes them all loosely together. His rhyme effects are sometimes vivid and sometimes not, but they are never restrained. The same thing holds true for the sound patterns of his verses in general. Two of the most praised instances of his bold use of sound also serve to show his lack of subtlety. They are the "angry candy" in the sonnet about the Cambridge ladies and "the bigness of cannon / is skilful," which opens one of his free-verse poems about World War I.

His pungent humor is of a piece with his metrical effects. It is devoid of complications. At its best it is mingled with anger, and that combination has produced several poems which we should not willingly lose. The sonnet about the prostitute Kitty is certainly the most memorable among those in *Tulips and Chimneys*. Later this humor was, with an added measure of contempt, to result in *Poem, or Beauty Hurts Mr. Vinal*, which is probably his most acrid criticism of the boom-time America of the 1920's. And, infused with a deep though superficially jocular bitterness, it was to result in the poem on Olaf, the conscientious objector.

But more important perhaps than any of these things is Cummings' casual treatment of words. In the closest study of him made so far, *Notes on E. E. Cummings' Language*, R. P. Blackmur shows beyond any doubt that Cummings' chief fault is that he uses words without a particular meaning. He is especially apt to take a general term—his favorite is "flower"—and then try to conceal its emptiness from the reader by attaching a paradoxical adjective to it. Just how, for instance, is the bigness of cannon skilful? It can be doubted if there is any depth of meaning here beyond the mechanical one. It is always wise to start by suspecting that we the readers are at fault in not gauging the fullness of the poem; yet if Cummings has ever shown the sort of subtlety that rewards close reading, few critics have noticed it. From *Tulips and Chimneys* to his latest collection of verse, there seems to be little to discover.

It is possible, nevertheless, that we are wrong. Perhaps the pages of *i: six nonlectures* will yield different evidence. The value of a poet's autobiography lies in the light it can cast on his poetry, and so we can turn back to the "nonlectures" to see what they have to say.

They say nothing new. They report simply on a man whose verse is, at heart, the sentimental celebration of the individual. Beneath the cynicism and the physicality, beneath those broken lines and small letters, there is to be found a surprisingly old-fashioned lover who—without neglecting to sing about his own self-discovery—hymns the praises of his mistress. The later chapters of *i: six nonlectures* have many references to Cummings' belief in the importance and uniqueness of the individual—and notably, in this case, of the artist—that is to say, of Cummings himself. "Even success . . . cannot concern him otherwise than as a stimulus to further . . . selfdiscovering." "Selfhood" and "Self-transcendence" are the key words. And as to love between man and woman, "I am someone who proudly and humbly affirms that love is the mystery-of-mysteries."

Though his poems show more of weakness than of strength and though the poet's own comments about his writing offer us little new insight, the fact is that Cummings nonetheless has some significance in contemporary American poetry. Perhaps the problem in evaluating his work lies in the fact that we have not approached it properly. We may not have asked the right questions about it.

Blackmur's essay furnishes, despite its acumen, a classic example of that failing. He studies Cummings with all the delicate probing that characterizes his critical method. The essay on Cummings came out in 1930; a year later Blackmur's appraisal of Wallace Stevens appeared. Blackmur's careful reasoning and his close searching of Stevens' language afforded rich results; his poetry was correctly approached. But the similar analysis of Cummings produced nothing but the critic's conclusion that here was a trivial versifier. Blackmur, from his point of view, was right. I suggest, though, that we approach Cummings on a simpler level.

To do this, we must begin by granting that he is not a poet who has thought about every word in his verse. His work is not intense, it is not concentrated. He is not an intellectual poet; it is even permissible to guess that he has seldom revised his writing very much. Consequently, the virtues fashionable today are not his. The most important thing Cummings has to offer in their place is a naive delight in the sound of words.

For the sake of sound he seems willing to sacrifice both clarity and complexity. That is the reason for "angry candy" and other well known exhibition pieces. Sometimes there will be an approximation to meaning, of course—at rare intervals there will be more than that—but ordinarily sound rather than any real sense is the basic consideration. In a way there is a resemblance between Gertrude Stein and Cummings. According to Leon Howard's theory Gertrude Stein thought of words as things. In terms of medieval philosophy she was a realist rather than a nominalist. Cummings similarly may think of the very sounds of words as things and in this way can let himself be captivated by them.

and this day it was Spring is perhaps the median Cummings poem, representing the average almost exactly. It reads:

> and this day it was Spring. . . . us
> drew lewdly the murmurous minute clumsy
> smelloftheworld. We intricately
> alive, cleaving the luminous stammer of bodies

(eagerly just not each other touch) seeking, some
street which easily trickles a brittle fuss
of fragile huge humanity. . . .
                    Numb

thoughts, kicking in the rivers of our blood, miss
by how terrible inches speech—it
made you a little dizzy did the world's smell
(but i was thinking why the girl-and-bird
of you move. . . . moves . . . . and also i'll admit—)

till, at the corner of Nothing and Something, we
        heard
a handorgan in twilight playing like hell

There seems to be almost a childish delight in such sounds as "drew
lewdly," and "murmurous minute." And then there is the senseless attraction in the assonance of "trickles a brittle" as well as the more meaningful
(if trite) juxtaposition of "bird" with "girl." At times the chiming is faint
enough to be accidental, though usually, one guesses, it is not. The sound
complex, "intricately alive, cleaving" with its mingled "l's," "y's," and
"c's," is a case in point; so is "fragile huge humanity." Often alliteration
alone is to be heard but generally Cummings wants a little more than
that.

If we take this love of sound and add one other thing to it, we have
the technical basis for Cummings' poetry. The other element, already
mentioned, is his love of paradox. The paradox, like the assonance, is apt
to be simple. It is often merely a reverse. Lectures become nonlectures;
Cummings himself is an unthing; he is a poet who chatters unpoetically.
Or, at the extreme, in the lyric *this mind made war*, we read such a stanza
as:

                unfools unfree
                undeaths who live
                nor shall they be
                and must they have.

This is the world of the simple switch; this is the world of "un."

Are briskly vibrating sound and verbal paradox enough? Cummings
himself suggests that only twenty of his poems best show his work as an artist, and it may be hazarded that perhaps half that number will continue
to be reprinted. In his own defense he says that poetry must be read with
love. And yet the question for all but a few of his poems is whether they
are worth the loving. The critical consensus remains against him, and
with reason. He is still a poet who is considerably more talked about than
he deserves to be, a man who has made his vogue out of a large amount
of—at best—casually semi-private writing.

Six of One and Six
Hundred of the Other

John Logan*

There are two kinds of purity in the work of E. E. Cummings, one of art and one of the heart. The first is signified by his heroic unconcern for tyrants (such as money, "Mostpeople," various isms, and the laws of inertia as they apply to literature); the second, by the constant compassion in what he makes. The two together have always distinguished him. Thus in his first book *The Enormous Room* we find the language he invented, "The Zulu . . . shoulderless, unhurried body, velocity of a grass-hopper, soul up under his arm-pits, mysteriously falling over the own-ness of two feet, floating fish of his slimness half a bird. . . ." There is also an immense compassion: such a book is in fact best understood as an incantation, I should like to say prayer, offered for persons he loved in the war—both in hope of their wellbeing and as a reparation in human art for those times of inhumanity when, as another of his "criminal" and confined friends wrote, "the hoar frost grip[s] thy tent."

And now we have a book from Cummings which is not only marked by art and by love but which is about them. It is about them because it is about self-transcendence, which is why it is called *i*: we note that it could also have been called *i* if it had been about selfishness, but this would be less accurate and Cummings is, well, careful with words.

He writes in the fifth of his *six nonlectures*:

> Let us make no mistake: Him of the play so named is himself and nobody else—not even Me. But supposing Him to exemplify that mythical entity "the artist," we should go hugely astray in assuming that art was the only self-transcendence. Art is a mystery: all mysteries have their source in a mystery-or-mysteries who is love . . . nor could all poetry . . . begin to indicate the varieties of selfhood; and consequently of selftranscendence.

To close this "fifth lesson" Cummings quotes the great serpent-scene from *Anthony and Cleopatra* together with the hymn to the Blessed Virgin composed by Dante to open the final canto of the *Comedy*. I translate the first two verses to show Cummings' point:

> Virgin mother child of your son
> More low more high than any creature
> Fixed end toward which all plans run
>
> Your self transcended human nature
> So well its maker did not shun
> To take His self its shape and feature

*Reprinted from *Poetry*, 86 (1955), 353–58. Copyright 1955 by The Modern Poetry Association. Reprinted by permission of John Logan and the editor of *Poetry*.

One may add little on the possibilities of selfhood in the high sense. However, we may note the connection between the notion of transcending ("climbing over") oneself and the notion of ecstasy ("standing outside"); the one follows the other: and without both there is neither love nor art. Thus Cummings gives us a "sixth lesson," and final one, whose subjects are "ecstasy and anguish, being and becoming; the immortality of the creative imagination and the indomitability of the human spirit."

Allied to his celebration of the individual human spirit are Cummings' apparent anti-patriotism and his apparent anti-intellectualism, which are large themes of *i*. Both are signs of fundamental affirmations. The apparent anti-patriotism is a goad to a higher notion of self than is usual, hence a goad, as well, to a higher sense of the ends of freedom. The apparent anti-intellectualism is basically an affirmation of the *mystery* of things, which Cummings believes to be more compatible with "feeling" than with knowing, supposing the latter activity to be a kind of "measuring" that excludes love. At heart the quarrels of Cummings are a resistance to the small minds of every kind, political, scientific, philosophical, the literary, who insist on limiting the real and the true to what they think they know or can respond to. As a preventive to this kind of limitation, Cummings is directly opposed to letting us rest in what we believe we know; and this is the key to the rhetorical function of his famous language.

Certainly one comes from *i: six nonlectures* with a heightened respect both for the Cummings rhetoric and the poetry. One will not forget in reading the book that it is the work of one of the greatest lyric poets who write in our language; it is a master's examination of himself and his work. Who is now over sixty years old. And this is the most exciting possible kind of book.

i begins with a wonderful yarn about a child of remarkably loving, remarkably intelligent, and remarkably heroic parents. It tells of his education in "cerebral Cambridge" and "orchidaceous Somerville" (Mass.), in the "little barbarous Greenwich perfumed fake," where he says he first breathed, and in Paris ("love rose in my heart like a sun and beauty blossomed in my life like a star"). It is the story of his first friends, such as Harvard's Professor Royce, his first books, and his first singing.

In the last group of three lectures, since for the adult Cummings "The question 'Who am I' is answered by what I write," we are given his own selection of his poems and prose (largely from *XAIPE, IXI, EIMI, Him*, and *Santa Claus*) with his comments on them. The whole is supplemented, as were the last fifteen minutes of each of the "nonlectures" when they were given at Harvard on the Charles Eliot Norton Professorship in 1953, by his own selection of the poetry which has formed him.

It is a joy that this book, the best existing introduction to Cummings' poetry, is so closely followed now by the monumental *Poems 1923-1954*. This volume restores the more than one hundred pieces omitted from the

1938 *Collected Poems* (such as the amazing long, opening Keatsian poem "Epithalamion" from Cummings' first book of verse *Tulips and Chimneys* [1923]) and adds the contents of *50 Poems* (1940), *IXI* (1944), and *XAIPE* (1950). Together the six hundred poems represent a prodigious accomplishment in American verse.

One often reads that Cummings has been saying the same thing in the same way since he started to write. This is quite false. For example, he abandons quite early the Poundian archaisms which give a poem like *Puella Mea* its remarkable and exquisite flavor. Again there are poems in *No Thanks* (1935) which employ a greater range of invention than those of any previous volume (for example the stunning nos. 2, 9, 13, 48). And the last three volumes contain pieces more profound than anything he wrote earlier; among them *hate blows a bubble of despair into, one's not half two . . . , nothing false and possible is love, my father moved through dooms of love, no man if men are gods . . . , love is more true than reason will deceive,* and *i thank God for most this amazing.*

Reading these latter poems one smiles at the term "charming" so often applied to his work—frequently as a technique of damning. Such a term does not touch the depth of these poems, or the conjugal mystique of *it is at moments after I have dreamed* or *o by the by* (which looks like it is about kites). And even less does such a term meet the violence, the anger, the bawdiness, the bitterness of some of his most memorable work.

Though *Poems 1923-1954* contains an astonishing number of astonishingly varied sonnet forms, still it raises more acutely than any other modern book, except possibly the later work of Joyce or Pound, the problem of the relation of the poem to its appearance on the page. I dare say we assume on the whole that the typography of a poem is unimportant to the poem—partly because poetry existed for ages before print, partly because of the blind alleys (for poetry)—ending in visible allegory or even illustration—which some have explored with typography, and partly because of the authority of certain modern critics, notably R. P. Blackmur. The question is crucial to Cummings, for if it be true that typography is on principle always irrelevant to essential poetic then a large body of his work dearest to him and most interesting to us must fall. And this book will be the occasion for re-opening and -examining the whole problem.

Cummings does not for the most part employ shapes literally related to the sense of his poems (as did George Herbert in a number of fine poems) or symbolically related ones; rather he employs shapes we would be apt to call abstract, i.e., non-representational. Cummings has a noteworthy alternate profession as a painter; and he is a modern painter: he would no more paint a Christmas tree with its commonly acknowledged shape than he would write a poem about a Christmas tree (he has such a poem) in that shape. Now the choice of shape, among poets interested in them for their poems, is relevant to the general ideas of shape in the visual art of the time. I don't know enough to say which art movements influenced Cummings most, dadaism, say, or surrealism, or cubism, or . . . ? Though from what I have seen of his painting I would suppose cubism had—in any case I am concerned here with the aesthetic of his poems, not his painting, and that could well be different. What I wish to note is equally true of the three modern movements I named: they share with the baroque (which so influenced Herbert) an interest in dissolving surfaces. Applied to poems, this means that they must not look as we *expect* poems to look. The aim of course is different in each case; the baroque wanted to transfigure, to analyze toward mathematical and theological infinity; it had a positive interest in the dissolution of surface. The dadaist had a negative interest, not to transfigure but to disenchant, to debunk; and the cubist to disorganize (though in the best only to reorganize more perfectly).

The relevance of dadaism and cubism to Cummings' poetics goes far beyond the surface of his poems—one thinks of the disenchantment of the language of the American-English lyric accomplished by his many poems reproducing the speech of prostitutes and the various dialects of working men, or one thinks of the positive perfections of verse he achieves out of fractured forms.

But I wish to emphasize here that even so far as the *appearance* of the poem is directly concerned, it is not itself the end of the interest in shape for Cummings (as it was not for Herbert): rather the language of the poem is the end of this interest, as it must be for a poet—whether or not he is also a painter. We have still a great deal to learn about just how Cummings uses appearances to serve the ends of language art (there exist initial studies by Theodore Spencer and others); my own spotty investigation has led me to three conclusions. First, the typographical inventions are instruments for controlling the evocation of the poem in the mind of the reader; they are organic and essential where they are successful and are only ornamental and precious where either the poem or the reader fails. Techniques of punctuation, word-breaking and -placing are means of exorcizing the temporal necessities of language with its falsification of the different temporal rhythms of experience; the latter rhythms are often quicker than those of language and may be doubled, occurring simultaneously or else in some kind of conflict on the one hand or reinforcing phase on the other. This is a traditional problem and it is especially great in lyric poetry, which cannot put to use the time lag of language in the way that epic poetry can. Rhyme, counterpoint techniques like alliteration, stanza periods, and other smaller or larger units of rhythmic control are all aids for solving the problem of the disparate times between language and experience; each of them was invented by somebody.

Second, the orthographical inventions—altered spellings, irregular use of lower case, etc., are expansions of the ancient poetic method of connotation, where a single word is pressed for richness latent in it but unrealized in the common spelling and appearance of it.

Third, the grammatical inventions (or re-introductions such as the use of Latin word orders) are designed some of them to break up the usual patterns of response so that the reading *can be* brought under the control of the poet, allowing him to do his work (this is a rhetorical function shared to a certain extent by typographical and orthographical inventions as well); others of them are designed to bring that possibility into act. A prime problem in accomplishing the latter is (following Pound and Fenollosa) to secure the maximum number of active verbs and to place them most effectively within the period. One of Cummings' achievements has been to gain the *effect* of the active verb, with its closeness to elemental dynamic reality, in other parts of speech (thus: "disintegrat i o n" and "stic-ky" and "onetwothreefourfive"); and again, to make verbs themselves apparently more active (thus: "SpRiN,k,LiNg" and "kIss" and ".press" and "ex:ten:ded" and swallow) s" and "stiffenS"). Many of the examples seem exceedingly simple; that is a characteristic of discovery.

I have mentioned the rhetorical function of Cummings' language: let me add here that each of the above methods acts rhetorically to prevent the reader from resting in what he thinks he knows and what he expects; without this, poetry would be impossible, and as humans become more and more self-consciously and self-satisfiedly "knowing," as more and more they "smash . . . why . . . into because," the means for bringing this about will have to be more and more radical. I should say that is a central meaning of Cummings' work.

Although *Poems 1923–1954* will for a good long time be the main object of Cummings studies, it is good to report that E. E. is by no means through. The new book represents the contents of all his *books* of verse published up until 1954 (the last was in 1950); but it does not contain the recent verse. A good many pieces scattered through the magazines during the past four years have come to my attention (e.g., in *Poetry, Quarterly Review of Literature, Times Literary Supplement, Accent*—"do lovers love? why then to heaven with hell. / Whatever sages say and fools, all's well."), and no doubt there are others. Cummings must be well on his way to the next book. Meanwhile, shout Viva! Shout XAIPE! For of this newest book he can be proud throughout his immortality—and that is a heaven of a long untime.

[Review of 95 *Poems*]

John Berryman*

Cummings, like Dr. Williams, is a westerner, of course, versing briskly away in his mid-sixties to everyone's delight, loaded with merited honors, impenitent, irregular, mannered. Mannerism, curiously, is a greater danger in western style than it is in eastern; it sticks out. What Cummings would do without parentheses is not easy to see. He makes use of them in all but seven of his ninety-five new poems, needs them in most, and some poems could not have been conceived without them: see *19, 20, 23*. They are the more obtrusive because he uses little other pointing—exception made for

s.ti:rst;hiso,nce;ma:n

which says "stirs this once man." What can the obsession with parentheses mean to Cummings? Simultaneity, no doubt, and inextricable relation, and offhandedness, informality. But I wonder whether they do not constitute also a sort of instinctive defense invoked by his talent against one of its worst faults, a hollow rhetoric of which *77* is the most embarrassing example in his new book. Along with his jerky, maze-like little poems has always gone an organ-like, Keatsian propensity, which has given him (and us) some of his stunning successes, but which he is quite right to distrust, for when the little poems fail they are only trivial, but when the others fail they are false.

Cummings is extremely sentimental, a fact long partly disguised by his satirical and tough-guy attitudes and still partly disguised by some of his language, but more patent throughout this book than ever before. I am not objecting, just reporting. The eternizing of which he has always been very fond—it is not done in Shakespeare's manner but it is eternizing all the same—is more frequently in evidence too. Otherwise the new book is as usual: love poems galore, moons, flowers, dreams, thrushes, miracles, vignettes on drunks and floozies, harridans, nice old ladies, businessmen, disquisitions on "why" and time. It is littered with the trademarks of his fine poems of the past, "little" and its allies, "un-," "almost," *x* "by" *y*. It should not be read in large chunks. The most effective poems, I think, are *13, 16, 76* and *95*, but there are amusing and touching passages in many others. Nothing, unless I am wrong, is up to the standard of his finest work, and the very loud poems are mostly bad. What is truly amazing is the scarcity of allusion to old age: *57, 61*, a few others. It is a pity that one very dark poem, *30*, is not better. Cummings' high spirits are partly an act, naturally, one in which he has been engaged for so long that he must in some degree be taken in by it himself, and so some of his deepest feelings scarcely emerge.

*Reprinted from the *American Scholar*, 28 (1959), 388, 390. Copyright Kathleen Donahue Berryman. Reprinted by permission of Kathleen Donahue Berryman.

[Review of 95 *Poems*]

Edward M. Hood*

The first poem in this latest collection by E. E. Cummings is typical of the volume as a whole.

l(a

le
af
fa

ll

s)
one
l

iness

An unqualified emotion, with no context, is asserted and compared to falling leaf: *asserted*, not embodied. The typography creates an almost impenetrable visual complexity of surface—the poem strikes the eye, not the ear—to disguise the vapidity of the language and give a "modern" appearance to a poem of romantic sentimentality. The leaf image is conventional and random, not established in any context except Cummings' private feelings about it. Any emotional and intellectual vitality is not objectified, but is prior to the poem. The world "loneliness" is indeed a "vehicle": an empty conveyance into which Cummings tries to unburden himself of a feeling (the "tenor); then he shoves it, like a wheelbarrow, towards the reader, hoping it may contain what he thought he put in it. Whether it does or not will depend on the reader's willingness to feel a charitable sympathy towards a stranger's cry of distress—not his *distress*, but his declaration of it. The poem is not an experience arrested, qualified, and publicized in language (like, for instance, Emily Dickinson's "Renunciation is a piercing virtue"); it is an abstraction, a mere idea of experience, an assertion of it. The erratic typography may elicit our closer attention; but it gives us no assurance of the reality, of the concrete truth of the distress. We end by having to "take Cummings' word for it"; it is not, as Pound would say, *there on the page*. Because the word, despite its pretensions, is not really there either. There is only the dry husk of a word, floating as aimlessly as the falling leaf.

The nervous glitter of the poem's surface—it *looks* so like the fragmentation and recalcitrance of real experience—blinds the infatuated reader to its emptiness, its drab conventionality, very much as the bland

*Reprinted from *Shenandoah*, 10 (1959), 49–53. Copyright © 1959 by Washington and Lee University, reprinted from *Shenandoah: The Washington and Lee University Review* with the permission of the editor.

paradoxes, snappy rhymes, and chic allusions of a Cole Porter lyric delude one into supposing that something actually is being said. Such tough-mindedness is only a glossy patina, and what the mesmerized reader sees in it is not a stable core of intelligible, objective experience, but merely the reflection of his own fatuity.

Cummings is so determined to freshen language (and, thereby, perception) by flouting its conventions that he ends by destroying convention, language, and perception itself. Linguistically, public contexts and traditions of usage form conventions, and it is from these that Cummings tries to escape. Language and perception are made possible only by society, by convention, just as only they make society possible: "the complete consort, dancing together." But Cummings cannot play upon and extend convention; he must smash it, escape society and the public tradition, and be individual to the point of anarchy. Thus his language tends to isolation and privacy. Its only vital context is his own mind, which remains, for us, permanently unknowable. *Non serviam!*

> crazy jay blue)
> demon laughshriek
> ing at me
> your scorn of easily
>
> hatred of timid
> & loathing for (dull all
> regular righteous
> comfortable) unworlds
>
> thief crook cynic
> (swimfloatdrifting
> fragment of heaven)
> trickstervillain
>
> raucous rogue &
> vivid voltaire
> you beautiful anarchist
> (i salute thee
>   (Poem 5)

This is one of the few successful poems in the volume* because Cummings has here become sufficiently detached partially to see his posture of Romantic envy of "free" nature as childish, as diabolism or anarchism. There is a kind of facile ingenuity in the paradoxes. But Cummings falls short of the crucial insight here: that anarchy is the blindest compulsion, that the proper use of convention, the discipline of technique ("regular" and "righteous"), promise our only liberation. Chaos is not freedom; isolation is not escape. And destroying the syntax and conventions of

---

*Other poems which seem to me successful, or interesting for various reasons, are Nos. 10, 35, 42 (the sestet), 49, 52, 72, 91, and 94.

language does not free it: "Be bold, be bold, be not too bold." Distortion *may* be creative, but it is not equivalent to creation. Whatever else this "crazy jay blue" can do, he cannot write this poem. He can only "laughshriek." It took an adult mind to write this poem—Cummings the poet, not Cummings the "raucous rogue" and "beautiful anarchist," which he so frequently, so sadly, pretends to be, with such unfortunate results:

> dim
> i
> nu
> tiv
>
> e this spark is e
> mpty (everyb
> ody's elsewher
> e except me 6 e
>
> nglish sparrow
> s) a
> utumn & t
> he rai
>
> n
> th
> e
> raintherain
>   (Poem 24)

Dr. Williams has written that Cummings "avoids the cliché first by avoiding the whole accepted modus of english." This poem is obviously an avoidance of conventions of metrics and syntax. Whether it avoids platitude is another question. After we excogitate, transpose, and reassemble the elements of the poem, it is to be seriously doubted whether our experience is enlarged or our perception freshened. The note of autumnal loneliness (struck repeatedly in this new volume) is a familiar one, a mood of adolescent romanticism in which everyone can participate vicariously simply by letting down the guard of a critical intelligence and extending a little sympathetic indulgence. Everyone, after all, likes roses and birds and love, and most everyone equates loneliness with deep seriousness.

Moreover, the deliberate unconventionality of surface assures the reader of the difficulty, the tough-witted modernity, the complexity, which he has been taught to look for, so that when he has unscrambled and "mastered" the poem's surface, and seized the vague cliché and worn-out mood which the surface conceals, by indulging that very conventionality and sentiment at the center of the poem, he can congratulate himself on having made a difficult, rare and enhanced discovery. This is the strategem which a Cummings most usually employs: not to avoid the cliché, but to conceal it. Perception is not renewed; it is counterfeited. The carefully calculated anarchism of style and attitude, where not simply flat, becomes frequently a little ridiculous, like an urchin sticking out his tongue to razz his adults—as in these stanzas from Cummings' embarrassing little poem on the Hungarian revolt, "Thanksgiving (1956)":

> uncle sam shrugs his pretty
> pink shoulders you know how
> and he twitches a liberal titty
> and lisps "i'm busy right now"
>
> so rah-rah-rah democracy
> let's all be thankful as hell
> and bury the statue of liberty
> (because it begins to smell)
> (Poem 39)

It is just this sort of raucous roguery—Cummings in knee-britches, playing the little monster—that leads to the gratuitous shocks of syntax, the exploration of "thrill" effects, which finally deaden so much of the language thus brutalized . . . as the useless inversion of "living" dulls rather than sharpening the impact of these two lines:

> a total stranger one black day
> knocked living the hell out of me—
> (Poem 58)

We leave this volume, which begins with poems of loneliness and ends in celebrations of love, with the disquieting sense that neither experience has been made real. The brittle glitter of the surface betrays, by its very nervousness and strain, the vacuum of thought and feeling within. If this image is perhaps reminiscent of Cole Porter or the Great Gatsby, then it should reveal Cummings in a very characteristic posture: the aging but incorrigible Child of the Twenties.

E.E. Cummings

Horace Gregory*

The years immediately following a writer's death are usually a severe test of his fame. After a few tributes to his memory there is usually silence, or if not silence, a small groundswell of counter-statement expressing fears that he has been over-praised. Such was the immediate fate of D. H. Lawrence's reputation, and a touch of the same blight for a brief time

*Reprinted from *Commonweal*, 79 (1964), 725–26. Reprinted by permission of Commonweal Publishing Co., Inc.

stained F. Scott Fitzgerald's—and today Robinson Jeffers and Hemingway are undergoing a similar trial.

Cummings' reputation since his death a year ago is the rare exception to this rule. For the past ten years it has been steadily growing, and the publication of his posthumous book, *73 Poems*, reaffirms a living spirit. This is to say that his readers will feel no sense of decline or of weariness in his last poems. If anything, his lyric phrasing is lighter, more adroit than ever. But why do the poems of Cummings' later years seem more "alive" than those which pleased so many during the 1920's? The first reason is cumulative and may seem very small and strange, yet its reiteration works its way into subconscious memory.

The great majority of Cummings' poems lack periods at the close of their last lines. The absence of a full stop suggests silence between poems and books, rather than a period signifying "the end." This is a way (and by means of deliberate lack of punctuation) of allowing a poem to breathe, to give it air as well as space for sound. Another reason is that his poems held to beliefs in miracles, to the mysteries of rebirth, of man being "continually reborn." This is very like a Bergsonian philosophy of continual "Evolution" or "Becoming."

In the introduction to his *Collected Poems* Cummings wrote (and with conscious wit used the word "becoming" in its two-fold meaning): "We are human beings; for whom birth is a supremely welcome mystery, the mystery of growing: the mystery which happens only and whenever we are faithful to ourselves. You and I wear the dangerous looseness of doom and find it becoming."

Number 5 in his 73 Poems shows how a deliberate economy in punctuation keeps the poem moving in space as well as stressing its images of growth ("blossoming") and the transcendental realities of "dream:"

> the first of all my dreams was of
> a lover and his only love,
> strolling slowly (mind in mind)
> through some green mysterious land
>
> until my second dream begins—
> the sky is wild with leaves; which dance
> and dancing swoop (and swooping whirl
> over a frightened boy and girl)
>
> but that mere fury soon became
> silence: in huger always whom
> two tiny selves sleep (doll by doll)
> motionless under magical
>
> foreverfully falling snow.
> And then this dreamer wept: and so
> she quickly dreamed a dream of spring
> —how you and i are blossoming

The succession of dreams, a dream within a dream, and "this dreamer wept" makes one think of Blake, but to say Cummings resembles Blake in any other way is quite untrue: so far as English sources are concerned, his lyrical heritage is the line of the sixteenth and seventeenth century Courtly Makers. One of his miracles was to make their music youthful and pure again, a recreation in a new language. In the American tradition, his position is no less singular, for if one does not press the resemblance too far, one finds in his later poems a New England affinity to the poems of Emily Dickinson. This is not a matter of influence or subconscious derivation—and his gift was as masculine as hers was feminine: it is in the sharpened metaphors both draw from nature, in the mastery of a highly selective, yet flawlessly keyed vocabulary, in the dramatic use of aphorisms, in the creation of strict conventions in which their style is so memorably defined, in the transcendental quality of their visions.

> for any ruffian of the sky
> your kingbird doesn't give a damn—
> his royal warcry is I AM
> and he's the soul of chivalry
>
> true to his mate his chicks his friends
> he loves because he cannot fear
> (you see it in the way he stands
> and looks and leaps upon the air)

Surely no American poet since Emily Dickinson has written a brief fable with greater clarity, wit, and vividness: and this is still another reason why Cummings' poetry continues to be read and enjoyed by so many. Instinctive as that response may be, and however strange some few of his typographical arrangements may have seemed forty years ago, the sense that his poetry *is* poetry in its ancient meaning is strongly felt. Cummings' songs and sonnets treating of love and death, of immortality, and of spring are among the classics of modern poetry. And his achievement is unique in our time: a lyrical integration of satire, religious feeling and art.

[Review of *Selected Letters of E.E. Cummings*]

Robert B. Shaw*

In a section of light verse, [Babette] Deutsch has reprinted a parody of E. E. Cummings which appeared in 1941 as a review of his *50 Poems*; it begins

> : dearmrcummings it is
> late
> r than you th
> ink

The same criticism has been leveled at Cummings many times since: that he repeated himself unmercifully, behaving as if the 'twenties had never ended. This was in my mind as I turned to Cummings's *Selected Letters*, which have been edited well and unobtrusively by F. W. Dupee and George Stade. I have felt censorious in just this way about Cummings's poetry: it never develops, I told myself. After reading the letters I saw why: Cummings himself never developed. His character, his basic tone was formed at a remarkably early age and remained essentially unchanged throughout his life; he began and ended as a bohemian aristocrat, an avant garde reactionary, effortlessly embodying his contradictions.

All his time was spent in being himself or in projecting himself in terms of his riotous art. After the prison camp experience (which produced some of his more memorable letters, as well as *The Enormous Room*) Cummings settled down to an almost unvaried routine, wintering in Greenwich Village, summering at the family farm in New Hampshire, now and then (but less and less frequently) travelling in Europe. In all this he pursued his painting and writing with intensity as great as any writer of his time was to show. He worked in ferocious privacy, shunning the "Life Goes To A Garret type of hullaballoo via MesserLuce's murmurdons". Except for a brief menial stint with P. F. Collier & Son between Harvard and World War I, he never had a job to distract him. Few of his close friends, except for Pound and Dos Passos, were eminent writers. His friendships in any case were few, were formed early, and were longlasting.

Cummings's loyalty to his friends is one of the most admirable of his traits to come to light in his letters. When Ezra Pound (whom Cummings now and then addressed as "Nuncle") was being pointedly avoided by nearly everybody on account of his treasonous, or deranged, activities,

*Reprinted from *Poetry*, 115 (1970), 278–80. Copyright © 1970 by The Modern Poetry Association. Reprinted by permission of Robert B. Shaw and the editor of *Poetry*.

Cummings did not join in the desertion. He wrote angrily to a group that urged Pound's "rehabilitation":

> In this UNworld of "ours", lots of UNpoets and plenty of UNcountries (UNamerica, for example) need rehabilitating the very worst way. But whoever or whatever he may be, Ezra Pound most emphatically isn't UNanyone or UNanything

And yet to Pound he wrote, no doubt in response to a tirade:

> talents differ: if heroical thine be cursing swine & ringing nex, our tolerant unhero may only re-remark (vide 6 nonlectures page 70)that "hatred bounces"

The letters to Pound are the trickiest of those included here—full of zany syntax, trilingual puns, and cheerfully foul-mouthed gossip about mutual friends and foes. Cummings's humor was his salvation as a writer, and probably—who knows?—as a person. It softened a crankiness which was at times vented at "procommunist-&-how-activities throughout the USA, sponsored by Mrs FD Roosevelt & her messianically-minded partner". He can never keep this tone up; soon he is back to limericks:

> 3 cheers for Aloysius Fitzgerald
> who, being nine-eights unapperald,
> went strolling the Strand
> with his pr-ck in his h-nd;
> proclaiming The End Of The Werald

Why *should* Cummings have had to develop? He was being what he was, a weird mixture of wisdom and naiveté, warmheartedness and crankiness; generosity and egotism; a Blake of lesser dimensions, half satirist, half sonneteer. Intricately hilarious, often deeply moving, these letters should send many readers, as they did me, back to the poems. Like the poems, the letters should be read a few at a time. Cummings comes on strong. It is a little shocking to think he has been gone seven years; in this book he seems very alive and well.

[Review of *Complete Poems 1913–1962*]

Helen Vendler*

The mystery of e. e. cummings' great aborted talent is not solved, only deepened, by his *Complete Poems*. His brave quixotry, still proclaiming itself in his 1968 volume as it had forty-five years earlier in

*First published in the *Yale Review*, 62 (1973), 412–19. Reprinted from *Part of Nature, Part of Us* by Helen Vendler. Reprinted by permission of Helen Vendler.

Tulips and Chimneys, has made him one of the poster gurus of a new generation: "one's not half two. It's two are halves of one," says the motto shining poignantly on a brilliant yellow-orange background, with a single flower as shy adornment of this revealed truth. In fact, cummings' first and last lines are nearly always, as in this case, his memorable ones, and most of his poems sag in the middle. While we all go round remembering "nobody, not even the rain, has such small hands," or "the single secret will still be man," or "there's a hell of a good universe next door, let's go," we rarely recall what led up to these declarations. Something is wrong with the relation of parts to wholes in cummings: we do not receive, as Coleridge thought we should, "such delight from the *whole*, as is compatible with a distinct gratification from each component *part*." Cummings was capable of stunning parts, and these parts glitter on the page like sparklers, float up like scraps of hurdy-gurdy music—but the sparks don't organize into constellations, the music falls apart into notes and remains unorchestrated. "Our genuine admiration of a great poet," Coleridge says, "is a continuous *under-current* of feeling; it is everywhere present, but seldom anywhere as a separate excitment." Whether this is true or not, it is certain that for the most part cummings provides only separate excitments, and is for that reason beloved of the young, who vibrate to his local effects and ask no more.

The disintegrative impulse was specially strong in cummings, and it is a wonder that he could put wholes together at all, he so much liked tinkering with words to take them apart, the dismemberment interesting him more, in some conspicuous examples, than the reintegration:

                                        r-p-o-p-h-e-s-s-a-g-r
                        who

    a)s w(e loo)k
    upnowgath
                    PPEGORHRASS
                                    eringint(o-
    eThe):l
            eA
              !p:
    S   a
                                (r
    rIvInG   .gRrEaPsPhOs)
                                                    to
    rea(be)rran(com)gi(e)ngly
    ,grasshopper;

Infinite amusement: scatter the alphabet across a page and watch the letters scramble to get back together again into words. But the energy to reintegrate lies in the preexistent word: the energy to disintegrate arises from the mischievously scissored poet, who is willing to allow a resurrection if he is permitted to dissect. His unreadable-aloud poems are cum-

mings' most original and charming contribution to English verse. Though
he may have learned the technique from the French, still he immortalized
it in English, proving once and for all that rhythm and meter, and even
sound, are not indispensable in poetry. Cummings' iconoclastic mind
must have reveled in his avant-garde visual arrangements, while his
painter's eye sensed their satisfying punning contours:

```
l(a

le
af
fa

ll

s)
one
l

iness
```

I wish there were more of these exquisite and fragile triumphs. But,
as Frost says, the truth keeps breaking in, or ought to, and cummings'
mind was abysmally short on ideas, however long on gently frivolous
games with letters. For some reason, one a biographer may eventually
reveal, cummings violently mistrusted mixed feeling, or mixed ideas. Ambivalence was not a possibility to him, and everything had to be all or
nothing. Where Keats could hear in the nightingale both ecstasy and req-
uiem, where Frost could hear the hard "diminished thing" in the oven
bird, cummings was unwilling to have any birdsong that was not unequivocally joyful:

```
"o purple finch
              please tell me why
this summer world(and you and i
who love so much to live)
                         must die"
"if i
     should tell you anything"
(that eagerly sweet carolling
self answers me)
                "i could not sing"
```

So there it is. Song can't tell, and certainly can't tell of death, but must go
on imperturbably carolling a babble of sweet sound. And the bird has the
last word: cummings does not want or will not permit Hardy's turning
from "the blessed Hope" of the aged darkling thrush to his own somber
and unconvinced mind. It could be said that cummings has the right to be
born an optimist, as Hardy to be a pessimist, and that such preferences
are radically a matter of temperament. But cummings' optimism excludes
too much; pain is scanted, and the perpetual analogy of man's life to the

seasonal cycle awakes in the reader angry logical resistance instead of the faith-filled acquiescence cummings must have hoped for. "Given much mercy," says cummings, "more than even the / mercy of perfect sunlight after days / of dark," he

> will climb;will blossom:will sing(like
> april's own april and awake's awake)

"Oh you will, will you?" we rudely reply, and this response is fatal to anything cummings wished for from us. We know that, but try as hard as we can no willing suspension of disbelief arises, and so we appear ungenerous Scrooges, hissing "bah, humbug" to the spirit of mercy, blossoming, life, love, and april which has dared to disturb our cynical universe. This myth of the sensitive poet immured in a greedy and unreceptive world was, not surprisingly, adopted by cummings himself, as he established himself in a saved little enclave with his appreciative reader where they together could look out and repudiate all the damned everyone else, the Scrooges, the "mostpeople":

> The poems to come are for you and for me and are not for mostpeople—it's no use trying to pretend that mostpeople and ourselves are alike. Mostpeople have less in common with ourselves than the squarerootofminusone. You and I are human beings; mostpeople are snobs (*New Poems*, 1938).

It is not hard to see who is the snob here. Such a position is certainly constricting to a poet, and it provoked in cummings that affectation of superior wisdom which is one of the most irritating things in his verse:

> seeker of truth
>
> follow no path
> all paths lead where
>
> truth is here

It is true that Emerson wrote things nearly as bad, but he had more intellect (or genius) to use on the exotic Indianisms and Orientalisms from which such poetry springs. Good poems often acknowledge, as interior appeals, the regions they eventually dismiss, but cummings gives no temptations houseroom. Others are in error, and *he* points the way to truth, allying himself, in a disarming want of modesty, with those humble supporters the sun, the moon, the stars, and the earth: these primal things say Why and Who and Be and Now and May, but "the greedy the people" (in the poem so named) ally themselves, chary and wary and busy and cunning and craven as they are, with Because and Which and Seem and Until and Must. The world is so clearly divided into the Good and the Bad, and cummings is so sure which is which and whose side he is on, that we are left gasping. Of course we too are against the greedy, and so on, and that is why it is so hard to object to cummings. We cannot exactly deny his "values," and we are all, I suppose, in favor of the sun, the moon, and the stars. We may, however, doubt that these sublime objects do exactly utter the imperatives cummings attributes to them. How much truer and more painful, even if we do not agree with its espousal, is Wordsworth's stoic farewell to Why, Who, Be, Now, and May:

> I, loving freedom, and untried,
> No sport of every random gust,
> Yet being to myself a guide,
> Too blindly have reposed my trust . . .
> Me this unchartered freedom tires;
> I feel the weight of chance-desires.

In the same poem, Wordsworth gave full acknowledgment to the wish for an ethos like cummings':

> Serene will be our days and bright,
> And happy will our nature be,
> When love is an unerring light
> And joy its own security.

Cummings seems never to have felt any misgivings about his creed—or, if he felt them, he only raised his voice more defiantly in his utopian affirmations. The affirmations become, in the *Complete Poems*, ever more stereotyped, until one could write a cummings poem oneself simply by juggling the cummings syntax and the cummings counters: young, new, yes, frail, love, bright, dream, doom, flower, moon, small, deep, touch, least, sweet, brief, guess, kiss, lost, and on and on and on.

The murderous devaluation of intellect in cummings has yet to be explained. Perhaps it comes from seeing all those Cambridge ladies living in furnished souls; perhaps intellect stood in cummings' mind for his parents. In any case, a guerrilla war against intellect is being conducted almost perversely all through the *Complete Poems*:

> —the best gesture of my brain is less than
> your eyelids' flutter which says
>
> we are for each other
>   . . . not
> all matterings of mind
>
> equal one violet

Cummings protests so much (far more than Wordsworth ever did) that nature is better than mind that the brain and the mind in his poetry take on sinister potential. His willed atrophy of both is matter for regret, especially since his satiric talent was the product of a sharp malicious intellect enjoying its own precision. If cummings had not been so afraid of what are now called "negative feelings," we might have had less slush about love and april and more wit; if he had kept in mind more often the

ironic circumstances under which "love" is conducted, we might have had
more poems like the immortal one about the necking couple:

may i feel said he
(i'll squeal said she
just once said he)
it's fun said she

(may i touch said he
how much said she
a lot said he)
why not said she

(let's go said he
not too far said she
what's too far said he
where you are said she)

may i stay said he
(which way said she
like this said he
if you kiss said she

may I move said he
is it love said she)
if you're willing said he
(but you're killing said she

but it's life said he
but your wife said she
now said he)
ow said she

(tiptop said he
don't stop said she
oh no said he)
go slow said she

(cccome?said he
ummm said she)
you're divine!said he
(you are Mine said she)

Aggression and pathos arise together here as they cannot in cummings' sentimental verse. Early in the *Complete Poems* two cummings-
selves elbow each other for room: the cummings who sketches, with brilliant economy, low-life Paris—madams, whores, sailors, bars, sidewalks;
and then there is the cummings, inheritor of the troubadours, who sings
ballades of love. In many of the poems of *Tulips and Chimneys* (1923)
cummings allows both selves a say, but somehow, in later years, a disjunction took place, and the pretty and the miserable ceased to communicate
with each other in his verse. His delighted humor (visible in poems like

"my sweet old etcetera" and "nobody loses all the time") thinned mysteriously; his dancing rhythms ("anyone lived in a pretty how town") were given less and less play; his caprices of letter-jokes became less joyous and more contrived; his satire (especially on women) became uglier; and only the dogged sentimentality remained, spreading like a proliferating growth until it crowded out the rest, pretending its name was love and joy when its name really was fear of all that the earlier self had justly tried to include. The final dwarf of cummings is a disappointment to American letters. He remains a poet who is best represented by his anthologized self—by olaf glad and big, by the little lame balloon-man, by uncle sol, by the little couple on the wedding-cake, by ignorance tobogganing into know and trudging up to ignorance again. Cummings was happiest in ignorance, even though he was shy of saying so in his own voice and, for all his sonnets on sensitive love, he had a hankering after the know-nothing, the gross, and the violent. In every future selection from his verse (if only to give his young admirers some perspective) after the obligatory printing of "nobody, not even the rain, has such small hands," there should be printed the Archie-Bunker rant of the newly republished "the boys i mean are not refined," a poem praising the "boys" who "do not give a shit for wit" and "do not give a fart for art":

> the boys i mean are not refined
> they cannot chat of that and this
> they do not give a fart for art
> they kill like you would take a piss
>
> they speak whatever's on their mind
> they do whatever's in their pants
> the boys i mean are not refined
> they shake the mountains when they dance

The admiration for boys who can "shake the mountains when they dance" (and who can hump their girls thirteen times a night) *because* they hate art and wit is a measure of cummings' self-hatred, and the measure of self-hatred is the measure of sentimentality.

Nevertheless, cummings' early volumes done in the twenties—roughly, the first half of this collection—remain a heady experience-in-retrospect, a joke on all New England proper "poyetry," and a preserved exhilaration scampering through Cambridge halls and raising indignant dust.

ESSAYS

Notes on E.E. Cummings' Language

R.P. Blackmur*

In his four books of verse, his play, and the autobiographical *Enormous Room*,[1] Mr. Cummings has amassed a special vocabulary and has developed from it a special use of language which these notes are intended to analyze and make explicit. Critics have commonly said, when they understood Mr. Cummings' vocabulary at all, that he has enriched the language with a new idiom; had they been further interested in the uses of language, they would no doubt have said that he had added to the general sensibility of his time. Certainly his work has had many imitators. Young poets have found it easy to adopt the attitudes from which Mr. Cummings has written, just as they often adopt the superficial attitudes of Swinburne and Keats. The curious thing about Mr. Cummings' influence is that his imitators have been able to emulate as well as ape him; which is not so frequently the case with the influence of Swinburne and Keats. Mr. Cummings is a school of writing in himself; so that it is necessary to state the underlying assumptions of his mind, and of the school which he teaches, before dealing with the specific results in poetry of those assumptions.

It is possible to say that Mr. Cummings belongs to the anti-culture group; what has been called at various times vorticism, futurism, dadaism, surrealism, and so on.[2] Part of the general dogma of this group is a sentimental denial of the intelligence and the deliberate assertion that the unintelligible is the only object of significant experience. These dogmas have been defended with considerable dialectical skill, on the very practical premise that only by presenting the unintelligible as viable and actual *per se* can the culture of the *dead intelligence* (Brattle Street, the Colleges, and the Reviews) be shocked into sentience. It is argued that only by denying to the intelligence its function of discerning quality and order, can the failures of the intelligence be overcome; that if we take things as they come without remembering what has gone before or guessing what may come next, and if we accept these things at their face value,

*First published in the *Hound & Horn*, 4 (1931), 163–92. Reprinted from *Language as Gesture* by R.P. Blackmur, copyright 1952 by Richard P. Blackmur, renewed © 1980 by Elizabeth Blackmur. Reprinted by permission of Harcourt Brace Jovanovich, Inc.

we shall know life, at least in the arts, as it really is. Nothing could be more arrogant, and more deceptively persuasive to the childish spirit, than such an attitude when held as fundamental. It appeals to the intellect which wishes to work swiftly and is in love with immediate certainty. A mind based on it accepts every fragment of experience as final and every notion as definite, yet never suffers from the delusion that it has learned anything. By an astonishing accident, enough unanimity exists among these people to permit them to agree among themselves; to permit them, even, to seem spiritually indistinguishable as they appear in public.

The central attitude of this group has developed, in its sectaries, a logical and thoroughgoing set of principles and habits. In America, for example, the cause of the lively arts has been advanced against the ancient seven; because the lively arts are necessarily immediate in appeal and utterly transitory. Thus we find in Mr. Cummings' recent verse and in his play *Him* the side show and the cabaret set up as "inevitable" frames for experience. Jazz effects, tough dialects, tough guys, slim hot queens, barkers, fairies, and so on, are made into the media and symbols of poetry. Which is proper enough in Shakespeare where such effects are used ornamentally or for pure play. But in Cummings such effects are employed as substance, as the very mainstay of the poetry. There is a continuous effort to escape the realism of the intelligence in favor of the realism of the obvious. What might be stodgy or dull because not properly worked up into poetry is replaced by the tawdry and by the fiction of the immediate.

It is no great advantage to get rid of one set of flabby generalities if the result is merely the immersion of the sensibility in another set only superficially less flabby. The hardness of the tough guy is mostly in the novelty of the language. There is no hardness in the emotion. The poet is as far from the concrete as before. By denying the dead intelligence and putting on the heresy of unintelligence, the poet only succeeds in substituting one set of unnourished conventions for another. What survives, with a deceptive air of reality, is a surface. That the deception is often intentional hardly excuses it. The surface is meant to clothe and illuminate a real substance, but in fact it is impenetrable. We are left, after experiencing this sort of art, with the certainty that there was nothing to penetrate. The surface was perfect; the deceit was childish; and the conception was incorrigibly sentimental: all because of the dogma which made them possible.

If Mr. Cummings' tough-guy poems are excellent examples of this sentimentality, it is only natural that his other poems—those clothed in the more familiar language of the lyric—should betray even more obviously, even more perfectly, the same fault. There, in the lyric, there is no pretense at hardness of surface. We are admitted at once to the bare emotion. What is most striking, in every instance, about this emotion is the fact that, in so far as it exists at all, it is Mr. Cummings' emotion, so that our best knowledge of it must be, finally, our best guess. It is not an emotion resulting from the poem; it existed before the poem began and is a result of the poet's private life. Besides its inspiration, every element in the poem, and its final meaning as well, must be taken at face value or not at all. This is the extreme form, in poetry, of romantic egoism: whatever I experience is real and final, and whatever I say represents what I experience. Such a dogma is the natural counterpart of the denial of the intelligence.

Our interest is not in the abstract principle, but in the results of its application in poetry. Assuming that a poem should in some sense be understood, should have a meaning apart from the poet's private life, either one of two things will be true about any poem written from such an attitude as we have ascribed to Mr. Cummings. Either the poem will appear in terms so conventional that everybody will understand it—when it will be flat and no poem at all; or it will appear in language so far distorted from convention as to be inapprehensible except by lucky guess. In neither instance will the poem be genuinely complete. It will be the notes for a poem, from which might flow an infinite number of possible poems, but from which no particular poem can be certainly deduced. It is the purpose of this paper to examine a few of the more obvious types of distortion which Mr. Cummings has practiced upon language.

The question central to such a discussion will be what kind of meaning does Mr. Cummings' poetry have; what is the kind of equivalence between the language and its object. The pursuit of such a question involves us immediately in the relations between words and feelings, and the relations between the intelligence and its field in experience—all relations which are precise only in terms themselves essentially poetic—in the feeling for an image, the sense of an idiom. Such relations may only be asserted, may be judged only tentatively, only instinctively, by what seems to be the disciplined experience, but what amounts, perhaps, only to the formed taste. Here criticism is appreciation. But appreciation, even, can take measures to be certain of its grounds, and to be full should betray the contant apprehension of an end which is the necessary consequence, the proper rounding off, of just those grounds. In the examinations of Mr. Cummings' writings the grounds will be the facts about the words he uses, and the end will be apprehended in the quality of the meaning his use of these words permits.

There is one attitude toward Mr. Cummings' language which has deceived those who hold it. The typographical peculiarities of his verse have caught and irritated public attention. Excessive hyphenation of single words, the use of lower case "i," the breaking of lines, the insertion of punctuation between the letters of a word, and so on, will have a possible critical importance to the textual scholarship of the future; but extensive consideration of these peculiarities today has very little importance, carries almost no reference to the *meaning* of the poems. Mr. Cummings' experiments in typography merely extend the theory of notation by adding to the number, *not* to the *kind*, of conventions the reader must bear in mind, and are dangerous only because since their uses cannot readily be defined, they often obscure rather than clarify the exact meaning. No doubt the continued practice of such notation would produce a set of well-ordered conventions susceptible of general use. At present the practice can only be "allowed for," recognized in the particular instance, felt, and forgotten: as the diacritical marks in the dictionary are forgotten once the sound of the word has been learned. The poem, after all, only takes wing on the page, it persists in the ear.[3]

Considering typographical peculiarities for our present purposes as either irrelevant or unaccountable, there remain the much more important peculiarities of Mr. Cummings' vocabulary itself; of the poem *after* it has been read, as it is in the mind's ear, as it is on the page only for reassurance and correction.

If a reader, sufficiently familiar with these poems not to be caught on the snag of novelty, inspects carefully any score of them, no matter how widely scattered, he will especially be struck by a sameness among them. This sameness will be in two sorts—a vagueness of image and a constant recurrence of words. Since the one depends considerably upon the other, a short list of some of Mr. Cummings' favorite words will be a good preliminary to the examination of his images. In *Tulips and Chimneys* words such as these occur frequently—thrilling, flowers, serious, absolute, sweet, unspeaking, utter, gradual, ultimate, final, serene, frail, grave, tremendous, slender, fragile, skillful, carefully, intent, young, gay, untimid, incorrigible, groping, dim, slow, certain, deliberate, strong, chiseled, subtle, tremulous, perpetual, crisp, perfect, sudden, faint, strenuous, minute, superlative, keen, ecstatic, actual, fleet, delicious, stars, enthusiastic, capable, dull, bright. In listing these as favorite words, it is meant that these words do the greater part of the work in the poems where they occur; these are the words which qualify the subject matter of the poems, and are sometimes even the subjects themselves. Observe that none of them, taken alone, are very *concrete* words; and observe that many of them are the rather *abstract*, which is to say typical, *names* for precise qualities, but are not, and cannot be, as *originally important* words in a poem, very precise or very concrete or very abstract: they are middling words, not in themselves very much one thing or the other, and should be useful only with respect to something concrete in itself.

If we take Mr. Cummings' most favored word "flower" and inspect the uses to which he puts it, we should have some sort of key to the kind of poetry he writes. In *Tulips and Chimneys* the word "flower" turns up, to a casual count, forty-eight times, and in ♂, a much smaller volume, twenty-one times. We have among others the following: smile like a flower; riverly as a flower; steeped in burning flowers; last flower; lipping flowers; more silently than a flower; snow flower; world flower; softer than flowers; forehead a flight of flowers; feet are flowers in vases; air is deep with flowers; slow supple flower of beauty; flower-terrible; flower of thy mouth; stars and flowers; mouth a new flower; flower of silence; god's flowers; flowers of reminding; dissonant flowers; flower-stricken air; Sunday flower; tremendous flower; speaking flower; flowers of kiss; futile flowers, etc., etc. Besides the general term there is a quantity of lilies and roses, and a good assortment of daisies, pansies, buttercups, violets, and chrysanthemums. There are also many examples of such associated words as "petals" and "blooms" and "blossoms," which, since they are similarly used, may be taken as alternative to flowers.

Now it is evident that this word must attract Mr. Cummings' mind very much; it must contain for him an almost unlimited variety and extent of meaning; as the mystic says god, or at least as the incomplete mystic repeats the name of god to every occasion of his soul, Mr. Cummings in some of his poems says flower. The question is, whether or not the reader can possibly have shared the experience which Mr. Cummings has had of the word; whether or not it is possible to discern, after any amount of effort, the precise impact which Mr. Cummings undoubtedly feels upon his whole experience when he uses the word. "Flower," like every other word not specifically the expression of a logical relation, began life as a metaphor, as a leap from feeling to feeling, as a bridge in the imagination to give meaning to both those feelings. Presumably, the amount of meaning possible to the word is increased with each use, but only the meaning *possible*. Actually, in practice, a very different process goes on. Since people are occupied mostly with communication and argument and conversation, with the erection of discursive relationships, words are commonly spoken and written with the *least* possible meaning preserved, instead of the most. History is taken for granted, ignored, or denied. Only the outsides of words, so to speak, are used; and doubtless the outsides of words are all that the discursive intellect needs. But when a word is used in a poem it should be the sum of all its appropriate history made concrete and particular in the individual context; and in poetry all words act *as if* they were so used, because the only kind of meaning poetry can have requires that all its words resume their full life: the full life being modified and made unique by the *qualifications* the words perform one upon the other in the poem. Thus even a very bad poem may seem good to its author, when the author is not an acute critic and believes that there is life in his words merely because there was life (and a very different sort of life, truly) in the feelings which they represent. An author should remember, with the Indians, that the reality of a word is anterior to, and greater than, his use of it can ever be; that there is a perfection to the feelings in words to which his mind cannot hope to attain, but that his chief labor will be toward the approximation of that perfection.

We sometimes speak of a poet as a master of his words, and we sometimes say that a man's poetry has been run away with by words—meaning that he has not mastered his words but has been overpowered by his peculiar experience of certain among them. Both these notions are commonly improper, because they represent misconceptions of the nature of poetry in so far as they lay any stress upon originality, or the lack of it, in the poet's use of words. The only mastery possible to the poet consists in that entire submission to his words which is perfect knowledge. The only originality of which the poet is properly capable will be in the choice of order, and even this choice is larely a process of discovery rather than of origination. As for words running away with a poet or a poem, it would be more accurate to say that the poet's *ideas* had run away with him than his words.

This is precisely what has occurred with Mr. Cummings in his use of the word "flower" as a maid of all work. The word has become an idea, and in the process has been deprived of its history, its qualities, and its meaning. An idea, the intellectual pin upon which a thought is hung, is not transmissible in poetry as an important element in the poem and ought only to be employed to pass over, with the greatest possible velocity, the area of the uninteresting (what the poet was not interested in). That is, in a poem whose chief intent was the notation of character and yet required a descriptive setting, the poet might well use for the description such vague words as space and time, but could not use such words as goodness or nobleness without the risk of flatness. In Mr. Cummings' poetry we find the contrary; the word "flower," because of the originality with which he conceives it, becomes an idea and is used to represent the most interesting and most important aspect of his poem. Hence the center of the poem is permanently abstract and unknowable for the reader, and remains altogether without qualifications and concreteness. It is not the mere frequency of use that deadens the word flower into an idea; it is the kind of thought which each use illustrates in common. By seldom saying *what* flower, by seldom relating immitigably the abstract word to a specific experience, the content of the word vanishes; it has no inner mystery, only an impenetrable surface.

This is the defect, the essential deceit, we were trying to define. Without questioning Mr. Cummings, or any poet, as to sincerity (which is a personal attitude, irrelevant to the poetry considered) it is possible to say that when in any poem the important words are forced by their use to remain impenetrable, when they can be made to surrender nothing actually to the senses—then the poem is defective and the poet's words have so far deceived him as to become ideas merely.[4] Mr. Cummings is not so much writing poetry, as he is dreaming, idly ringing the changes of his reveries.

Perhaps a small divagation may make clearer the relation of these remarks to Mr. Cummings' poems. Any poetry which does not consider itself as much of an art and having the same responsibilities to the consumer as the arts of silversmithing or cobbling shoes—any such poetry is likely to do little more than rehearse a waking dream. Dreams are everywhere ominous and full of meaning; and why should they not be? They hold the images of the secret self, and to the initiate dreamer betray the nerve of life at every turn, not through any effort to do so, or because of any inherited regimen, but simply because they cannot help it. Dreams are like that—to the dreamer the maximal limit of experience. As it happens, dreams employ words and pictorial images to fill out their flux with a veil of substance. Pictures are natural to everyone, and words, because they are prevalent, seem common and inherently sensible. Hence, both picture and word, and then with a little stretching of the fancy the substance of the dream itself, seem expressible just as they occur—as things created, as the very flux of life. Mr. Cummings' poems are often nothing more than the report of just such dreams. He believes he knows what he knows, and no doubt he does. But he also believes, apparently, that the words which he encourages most vividly to mind are those most precisely fitted to put his poem on paper. He transfers the indubitable magic of his private musings from the cell of his mind, where it is honest incantation, to the realm of poetry. Here he forgets that poetry, so far as it takes a permanent form, is written and is meant to be read, and that it cannot be a mere private musing. Merely because his private fancy furnishes his liveliest images, is the worst reason for assuming that this private fancy will be approximately experienced by the reader or even indicated on the printed page.

But it is unfair to limit this description to Mr. Cummings; indeed, so limited, it is not even a description of Mr. Cummings. Take the Oxford Book of English Verse, or any anthology of poems equally well known, and turn from the poems printed therein of such widely separated poets as Surrey, Crashaw, Marvell, Burns, Wordsworth, Shelley, and Swinburne, to the collected works of these poets respectively. Does not the description of Mr. Cummings' mind at work given above apply nearly as well to the bulk of this poetry as to that of Mr. Cummings, at least on the senses' first immersion? The anthology poems being well known are conceived to be understood, to be definitely intelligible, and to have, without inspection, a precise meaning. The descent upon the collected poems of all or of any one of these authors is by and large a descent into tenuity. Most of their work, most of any poet's work, with half a dozen exceptions, is tenuous and vague, private exercises or public playthings of a soul in verse. So far as he is able, the reader struggles to reach the concrete, the solid, the definite; he must have these qualities, or their counterparts among the realm of the spirit, before he can understand what he reads. To translate such qualities from the realm of his private experience to the conventional forms of poetry is the problem of the poet; and the problem of the reader, likewise, is to come well equipped with the talent and the taste for discerning the meaning of those conventions as they particularly occur. Neither the poet's casual language nor the reader's casual interlocution is likely to be much help. There must be a ground common but exterior to each: that is the poem. The best poems take the best but not always the hardest reading; and no doubt it is so with the writing. Certainly, in neither case are dreams or simple reveries enough. Dreams are natural and are minatory or portentous; but except when by accident they fall into forms that fit the intelligence, they never negotiate the miracle of meaning between the poet and the poem, the poem and the reader.

Most poetry fails of this negotiation, and it is sometimes assumed that the negotiation was never meant, by the poet, to be made. For the poet, private expression is said to be enough; for the reader, the agitation of the senses, the perception of verbal beauty, the mere sense of stirring life in the words, are supposed sufficient. If this defense had a true premise—if the poet did express himself to his private satisfaction—it would be unanswerable; and to many it is so. But I think the case is different, and this is the real charge against Mr. Cummings: the poet does not ever express himself privately. The mind cannot understand, cannot properly know its own musings until those musings take some sort of conventional form. Properly speaking a poet, or any man, cannot be adequate to himself in terms of himself. True consciousness and true expression of consciousness must be external to the blind seat of consciousness—man as a sensorium. Even a simple image must be fitted among other images, and conned with them, before it is understood. That is, it must take a form in language which is highly traditional and conventional. The genius of the poet is to make the convention apparently disappear into the use to which he puts it.

Mr. Cummings and the group with which he is here roughly associated, the anti-culture or anti-intelligence group, persists to the contrary. Because experience is fragmentary as it strikes the consciousness it is thought to be essentially discontinuous and therefore essentially unintelligible except in the fragmentary form in which it occurred. They credit the words they use with immaculate conception and there hold them unquestionable. A poem, because it happens, must mean something and mean it without relation to anything but the private experience which inspired it. Certainly it means something, but not a poem; it means that something exciting happened to the writer and that a mystery is happening to the reader. The fallacy is double: they believe in the inexorable significance of the unique experience; and they have discarded the only method of making the unique experience into a poem—the conventions of the intelligence. As a matter of fact they do not write without conventions, but being ignorant of what they use, they resort most commonly to their own inefficient or superficial conventions—such as Mr. Cummings' flower and doll. The effect is convention without substance; the unique experience becomes a rhetorical assurance.

If we examine next, for the sake of the greatest possible contrast, one of the "tough" poems in *Is 5*, we will find a similar breach with the concrete. The use of vague words like "flower" in the lyrical poems as unexpanded similes, is no more an example of sentimental egoism than the use of vague conventions about villains. The distortion differs in terms but is essentially identical.

Sometimes the surface of the poem is so well constructed that the distortion is hard to discover. Intensity of process occasionally triumphs over the subject. Less frequently the subject itself is conceived directly and takes naturally the terms which the language supplies. The poem numbered One-XI in *Is 5* is an example in so far as the sentimental frame does not obscure the process.

> now dis "daughter" uv eve (who aint precisely slim) sim
>
> ply don't know duh meanin uv duh woid sin in
> not disagreeable contras tuh dat not exacly fat
>
> "father" (adjustin his robe) who now puts on his flat hat.

It is to be noted in this epigram, that there is no inexorable reason for either the dialect or the lapses from it into straight English. No one in particular is speaking, unless it be Mr. Cummings slumming in morals along with he-men and lady social workers, and taking it for granted that the dialect and the really refined language which the dialect exercises together give a setting. There are many other poems in *Is 5*, more sentimental and less successful, where the realism is of a more obvious sort; not having reference to an ideal so much as to a kind of scientific reality. That is, there is an effort to ground an emotion, or the facts which make the emotion, in the style of the character to whom the emotion happens. It is the reporter, the man with the good ear for spoken rhythms, who writes out of memory. The war poems and the poem about Bill and his chip (One-XVI) are examples. Style in this sense (something laid on) is only an attribute; is not the man; is not the character. And when it is substituted for character, it is likely to be sentimental and melodramatic. That is, the emotion which is named in the poem (by one of its attributes) is in excess of its established source (that same attribute). There is a certain immediate protection afforded to this insufficiency by the surface toughness, by the convention of burlesque; as if by mocking oneself one made sure there was something to mock. It is a kind of trickery resulting from eager but lazy senses; where the sensation itself is an excess, and appears to have done all the work of intuition and intelligence; where sensation seems expert without incorporation into experience. As if sensation could be anything more than the idea of sensation, so far as poetry goes, without being attached to some central body of experience, genuinely understood and *formed* in the mind.

The intrusion of science into art always results in a sentimental realism and always obfuscates form when that science is not kept subordinate to the qualitative experience of the senses—as witness the run of sociological novels. The analogues of science, where conventions are made to do the work of feeling instead of crowning it, are even more dangerous. Mr. Cummings' tough guy and his hard-boiled dialects are such analogues.

Mr. Cummings has a fine talent for using familiar, even almost dead words, in such a context as to make them suddenly impervious to every ordinary sense; they become unable to speak, but with a great air of being bursting with something very important and precise to say. "The bigness of cannon is *skillful* . . . enormous rhythm of *absurdity* . . . *slimness* of *evenslicing* eyes are chisels . . . electric Distinct face haughtily vital *clinched* in a swoon of *synopsis* . . . my friend's being continually whittles *keen* careful futile *flowers*," etc. With the possible exception of the compound *evenslicing* the italicized words are all ordinary words; all in normal contexts have a variety of meanings both connotative and denotative; the particular context being such as to indicate a particular meaning, to establish precisely a feeling, a sensation or a relation.

Mr. Cummings' contexts are employed to an opposite purpose in so far as they wipe out altogether the history of the word, its past associations and general character. To seize Mr. Cummings' meaning there is only the free and *uninstructed* intuition. Something precise is no doubt intended; the warrant for the belief is in the almost violent isolation into which the words are thrown; but that precision can seldom, by this method, become any more than just that "something precise." The reality, the event, the feeling, which we will allow Mr. Cummings has in mind, is not sensibly in the word. It is one thing for meaning to be difficult, or abstruse—hidden in its heart, that is. "Absent thee from *felicity* a while," Blake's "Time is the *mercy* of eternity" are reasonable examples; there the mystery is inside the words. In Mr. Cummings' words the mystery flies in the face, is on the surface; because there is no inside, no realm of possibility, of essence.

The general movement of Mr. Cummings' language is away from communicable precision. If it be argued that the particular use of one of the italicized words above merely makes that word unique, the retort is that such uniqueness is too perfect, is sterile. If by removing the general sense of a word the special sense is apotheosized, it is only so at the expense of the general sense itself. The destruction of the general sense of a word results in the loss of that word's individuality; for in practice the character of a word (which is its sense) is manifest only in good society, and meaning is distinguished only by conventional association. Mr. Cummings' use of words results in a large number of conventions, but these conventions do not permeate the words themselves, do not modify their souls or change their fates; they cannot be adopted by the reader because they cannot be essentially understood. They should rather be called inventions.

If we take a paragraph from the poem beginning on page thirty in *Is 5*, we will discover another terminus of the emotional habit of mind which produced the emphasis on the word "flower" in *Tulips and Chimneys*.

> the Bar. tinking luscious jugs dint of ripe silver with warmlyish wetflat splurging smells waltz the glush of squirting taps plus slush of foam knocked off and a faint piddle-of-drops she says I ploc spittle what the lands thaz me kid in no sir hopping sawdust you kiddo he's a palping wreaths of badly Yep cigars who jim him why gluey grins topple together eyes pout gestures stickily point made glints squinting who's a wink bum- nothing and money fuzzily mouths take big wobbly footsteps every goggle cent of it get out ears dribbles soft right old feller belch the chap hic sum- more eh chuckles skulch. . . .

Now the point is that the effect of this whole paragraph has much in common with the effect of the word "flower." It is a flower disintegrated, and the parts are not component; so that by presenting an analysis of his image Mr. Cummings has not let us into its secret: the analysis is not a true analysis, because it exhibits, finally, what are still only the results, not the grounds, of his private conventions, his personal emotions. It is indubitable that the words are alive; they jostle, even overturn, the reader in the assurance of their vitality; but the notion of what their true vitality is remains Mr. Cummings' very own. The words remain emotive. They have a gusty air of being something, but they defeat themselves in the effort to say what, and come at last to a bad end, all fallen in a heap.

The easiest *explanation* of the passage would be to say that each separate little collection of words in it is a note for an image; an abstraction, very keen and lively in Mr. Cummings' mind, of something very precise and concrete. Some of the words seem like a painter's notes, some a philologist's. But they are all, as they are presented, notes, abstractions, ideas—with their concrete objects unknown—except to the most arbitrary guess. The guess must be arbitrary because of the quantity, not the quality, of the words employed. Mr. Cummings is not here overworking the individual words, but by heaping so many of them together he destroys their individuality. Meaning really residual in the word is not exhausted, is not even touched; it must remain abstract and only an emotional substitute for it can be caught. The interesting fact about emotional substitutes in poetry, as elsewhere, is their thinness, and the inadequacy resulting from the thinness. The thinness is compulsory because they can, so far as the poem is concerned, exist only as a surface; they cannot possess tentacular roots reaching into, and feeding on, feelings, because the feelings do not exist, are only present by legerdemain. Genuine emotion in poetry perhaps does not *exist* at all; though it is none the less real for that, because a genuine emotion does not need the warrant of existence: it is the necessary result, in the mind, of a convention of feelings: like the notion of divine grace.

In *Tulips and Chimneys* (p. 109) there is a poem whose first and last lines supply an excellent opposition of proper and improper distortion of language.

> the Cambridge ladies who live in furnished souls . . .
>   the
> moon rattles like a fragment of angry candy.

In the context the word "soul" has the element of surprise which is surprise at *justness*; at *aptness*; it fits in and finishes off the notion of the line. "Furnished souls" is a good, if slight, conceit; and there is no trouble for the reader who wishes to know what the line means: he has merely to *extend* his knowledge slightly, just as Mr. Cummings merely extended the sense of his language slightly by releasing his particular words in this particular order. The whole work that the poet here demands of his reader is pretty well defined. The reader does not have to *guess*; he is enabled to *know*. The reader is not collecting data, he is aware of a meaning.

It would be unfair not to quote the context of the second line.

> . . . the Cambridge ladies do not care, above
> Cambridge if sometimes in its box of
> sky lavender and cornerless, the
> moon rattles like a fragment of angry candy.

We can say that Mr. Cummings is putting beauty next to the tawdry; juxtaposing the dead with the live; or that he is being sentimentally philosophical in verse—that is, releasing from inadequate sources something intended to be an emotion.[5]

We can go on illustrating Mr. Cummings' probable intentions almost infinitely. What Mr. Cummings likes or admires, what he holds dear in life, he very commonly calls flowers, or dolls, or candy—terms with which he is astonishingly generous; as if he thought by making his terms general enough their vagueness could not matter, and never noticed that the words so used enervate themselves in a kind of hardened instinct. We can understand what Mr. Cummings intended by "moon" and "candy" but in the process of understanding, the meaning of the words themselves disappears. The thrill of the association of "rattles" with "moon" and "angry" with "candy" becomes useless as a guide. "Rattle" and "angry" can only be continued in the meaning of the line if the reader supplies them with a force, a definiteness of suggestion, with which Mr. Cummings has not endowed them.

The distortion is here not a release of observation so keen that commonplace language would not hold it; it is not the presentation of a vision so complete that words must lose their normal meanings in order to suggest it. It is, on the contrary, the distortion of the commonplace itself; and the difficulty about a commonplace is that it cannot be known, it has no character, no fate, and no essence. It is a substitute for these.

True meaning (which is here to say knowledge) can only exist where some contact, however remote, is preserved between the language, forms, or symbols in which it is given and something concrete, individual, or sensual which inspired it; and the degree in which the meaning is seized will depend on the degree in which the particular concreteness is realized. Thus the technique of "meaning" will employ distortion only in so far as the sense of this concreteness is promoted by it. When contrast and contradiction disturb the ultimate precision of the senses the distortion involved is inappropriate and destructive. Mr. Cummings' line about the moon and candy does not weld a contradiction, does not identify a substance by a thrill of novel association. It leaves the reader at a loss; where it is impossible to *know*, after any amount of effort and good will, what the words mean. If it be argued that Mr. Cummings was not interested in meaning then Mr. Cummings is not a serious poet, is a mere collector of sensations, and can be of very little value to us. And to defend Mr. Cummings on the ground that he is in the pretty good company of Swinburne, Crashaw, and Victor Hugo, is partly to ignore the fact that by the same argument all four also enjoy the companionship of Mr. Guest. Such defense would show a very poor knowledge of the verses of Mr. Cummings, who is nothing if not serious in the attempt to exhibit precise knowledge. His interest in words and in their real meaning is probably greater than that of most poets of similar dimensions. He has consciously stretched syntax, word order, and meaning in just the effort to expand knowledge in poetry; and his failure is because he has gone too far, has lost sight of meaning altogether—and because, perhaps, the experience which he attempts to translate into poetry remained always personal to him and was never known objectively as itself. By his eagerness Mr. Cummings' relation to language has become confused; he has put down what has meant much to him and can mean little to us, because for us it is not put down—is only indicated, only possibly there. The freshness and depth of his private experience is not denied; but it is certain that, so far as its meaning goes, in the poetry into which he translated it, sentimentality, empty convention, and commonplace rule. In short, Mr. Cummings' poetry ends in ideas *about* things.

When Mr. Cummings resorts to language for the *thrill* that words may be made to give, when he allows his thrill to appear as an equivalent for concrete meaning, he is often more successful than when he is engaged more ambitiously. This is true of poets like Swinburne and Poe, Shelley and the early Marlowe: where the first pair depended almost as much upon *thrill* as Mr. Cummings in those poems where they made use of it at all, and where the second pair, particularly Marlowe, used their thrills more appropriately as ornament: where all four were most successful in their less ambitious works, though perhaps not as interesting. Likewise, today, there is the example of Archibald MacLeish, whose best lines are those that thrill and do nothing more. So that at least in general opinion Mr. Cummings is in this respect not in bad company. But if an examination of thrill be made, whether in Mr. Cummings' verse or in that of others, it will be shown that the use of thrill has at heart the same sentimental impenetrability that defeats the possibility of meaning elsewhere. Only here, in the realm of thrill, the practice is comparatively less illegitimate. Thrill, by itself, or in its proper place, is an exceedingly important element in any poem: it is the circulation of its blood, the *quickness* of life, by which we know it, when there is anything in it to know, most intimately. To use a word for its thrill, is to resurrect it from the dead; it is the incarnation of life in consciousness; it is movement.[6]

But what Mr. Cummings does, when he is using language as thrill, is not to resurrect a word from the dead: he more often produces an apparition, in itself startling and even ominous, but still only a ghost: it is all a thrill, and what it is that thrilled us cannot be determined. For example in *XLI Poems*, the following phrases depend considerably for their effect upon the thrill that is in them: "Prisms of sharp *mind*; where strange birds *purr*; into the *smiling* sky *tense* with *blending*; ways cloaked with *renewal*; sinuous riot; *steeped* with burning flowers; little kittens who are called *spring*; electric Distinct face haughtily vital clinched in a *swoon* of synopsis; unreal *precise* intrinsic fragment of actuality; an orchid whose *velocity* is *sculptural*; scythe takes *crisply* the *whim* of thy *smoothness*; perpendicular *taste*; wet stars, etc., etc. (The italics are mine.)

Take especially the phrase, "scythe takes *crisply* the *whim* of thy *smoothness*." We know in the poem that it is the scythe of death and that it is youth and beauty (in connection with love) that is to be cut off. So much is familiar, is very conventional; and so the conventional or dead emotion is placed before us; the educated reader receives it and reacts to it without a whimper. But Mr. Cummings must not have been content with presenting the conventional emotion in its conventional form; he felt bound to enliven it with metaphor, with overtones of the senses and the spirit: so that he substituted for the direct statement a rather indirect image combining three unusually sensed words for the sake of the *thrill* the special combination might afford. As the phrase stands there is no precision in it. There is a great suggestion of precision about it—like men going off to war; but precisely *what* is left for the reader to guess, to supply from his own heart. By themselves *whim* and *smoothness* are abstract quality words; and in order for them to escape the tensity, the dislocated strain, of abstractness and gain the intensity, the firm disposition, of concrete meaning, they should demand a particular reference.

Smoothness is probably the smoothness of the body and is used here as a kind of metonymy; but it may be pure metaphor and represent what is really to die—the spirit—taken in its physical terms; or it may be that all that is to be understood is a pure tautology. And so on. Even with this possible variety of reference, *smoothness* would not be very objectionable, were it the only word in the phrase used in this way, or were the other words used to clarify the *smoothness*. But we have also the noun *whim* bearing directly on *smoothness* and the adverb *crisply* which while it directly modifies *takes*, really controls the entire phrase. Taken seriously *whim*, with reference to the smoothness of either the body or the spirit or the love it inspires, is to say the least a light word; one might almost say a "metrical" word, introduced to stretch the measure, or because the author liked the sound of it, or enjoyed whimsy. It diminishes without limiting the possibilities of *smoothness*. Because it is here, in the phrase, it is inseparable from the phrase's notion of smoothness; yet instead of assisting, tends to prevent what that notion of smoothness is from being divulged.

Crisply is even more difficult to account for; associated with a scythe it perhaps brings to mind the sound of a scythe in a hayfield, which is surely not the reference here intended; it would be very difficult for such a crispness to associate itself with death, which the scythe represents, or *whim*, or *smoothness* in either the spiritual or fleshly sense. If it implies merely a cleanness, a swiftness of motion in the apparition of death, some other word would have seemed better chosen. If this analysis be correct, the three words are unalterably combined by the force of *crisply* in such a way as to defeat the only possible sense their *thrilling* use would have had. They are, so to speak, only the notions of themselves and those selves must remain forever unknown. All we are left with in such a phrase as this is the strangeness which struck us on our first encounter; and the only difference is that the strangeness is the more intensified the more we prolong the examination. This is another test of poetry: whether we understand the *strangeness* of a poem or not.[7]

As it happens there is an exquisite example of the proper use of this strangeness, this thrill, in another poem of Mr. Cummings: where he speaks of a cathedral before whose face "the streets turn *young* with rain." While there might be some question as to whether the use of *young* presents the only adequate image, there is certainly no question at all that the phrase is entirely successful: that is, the suggestive feeling in *young* makes the juncture, the emotional conjugation, of streets and rain transparent and perfect. This may be so because there is no element of essential contradiction, in the terms of feeling, between the emotional word *young* and the factual word *streets* and *rain*; or because, positively, what happens to the context by the insertion of *young* is, by a necessary leap of the imagination, something qualified. *Young* may be as abstract a word by itself, as purely relative and notional a word, as any other; but here it is brought into the concrete, is fixed there in a proper habitation. Just because reference is not commonly made either to young streets or young rain, the combination here effected is the more appropriate. The surprise, the contrast, which lend force to the phrase, do not exist in the poem; but exist, if at all, rather in the mind of the reader who did not foresee the slight stretch of his sensibility that the phrase requires—which the phrase not only requires, but necessitates. This, then, is a *strangeness* understood by its own viableness. No preliminary agreement of taste, or contract of symbols, was necessary.

The point is that Mr. Cummings did not here attempt the impossible, he merely stretched the probable. The business of the poet who deals largely with tactual and visual images, as Mr. Cummings does, for the meat of his work, is to escape the prison of his private mind; to use in his poem as little as possible of the experience that happened to him personally, and on the other hand to employ as much as possible of that experience as it is data.

It is idle for a critic to make the familiar statement that the mind of the writer is his work, or that "the style is the man," when by mind and man is meant the private experience of the author. So far as, in this sense, the mind *is* the work, or the style *is* the man, we can understand the work or the style only through an accidental unanimity; and what we understand is likely to be very thin—perhaps only the terms of understanding. For the author himself, in such circumstances, can have understood very little more. He has been pursuing the impossible, when the probable was right at hand; he has been transcending his experience instead of submitting to it. And this is just what Mr. Cummings does in the phrases quoted above.

It would be ungracious to suppose that as a poet "a swoon of synopsis" did not represent to Mr. Cummings a very definite and very suggestive image. But to assent to that image would be a kind of *tour de force*; the application of such assent would imply that because the words appear, and being words contain notions, they must in this particular instance exhibit the undeniable sign of interior feeling. The proper process of poetry designs exactly what the reader will perceive; that is what is meant when a word is said to be inevitable or *juste*. But this exactness of perception can only come about when there is an extreme fidelity on the part of the poet to his words as living things; which he can discover and control—which he must learn, and nourish, and stretch; but which he cannot invent. This unanimity in our possible experience of words implies that the only unanimity which the reader can feel in what the poet represents must be likewise exterior to the poet; must be somehow both anterior and posterior to the poet's own experience. The poet's mind, perhaps, is what he is outside himself with; is what he has learned; is what he knows: it is also what the reader knows. So long as he is content to remain in his private mind, he is unknowable, impenetrable, and sentimental. All his words perhaps must thrill us, because we cannot know them in the very degree that we sympathize with them. But the best thrills are those we have without knowing it.

This essay has proceeded so far on the explicit assumption that the poems of Mr. Cummings are unintelligible, and that no amount of effort on the part of the reader can make them less so. We began by connecting Mr. Cummings to two schools, or groups, which are much the same essentially—the anti-culture group which denies the intelligence, and the group, not limited to writers, of which the essential attitude is most easily defined as sentimental egoism or romantic idealism. Where these schools are most obviously identical is in the poetry they nourish: the avowed interest is the relentless pursuit of the actual in terms of the immediate as the immediate is given, without overt criticism, to the ego. Unintelligibility is a necessary consequence of such a pursuit, if by the intelligible we mean something concrete, qualified, permanent, and public. Poetry, if we understand it, is not in immediacy at all. It is not given to the senses or to the free intuition. Thus, when poetry is written as if its substance were immediate and given, we have as a result a distorted sensibility and a violent inner confusion. We have, if the poet follows his principles, something abstract, vague, impermanent, and essentially private. When every sensation and every word is taken as final and perfect, the substance which sensations report and for which words must stand remains inexplicable. We can understand only by accident.

Of course there is another side to the matter. In a sense anyone can understand Mr. Cummings and his kind by the mere assertion that he does understand. Nothing else is needed but a little natural sympathy and a certain aptness for the resumption of a childish sensibility. In much the same way we understand a stranger's grief—by setting up a private and less painful simulacrum. If we take the most sentimental and romantic writers as they come, there will be always about their works an excited freshness, the rush of sensation and intuition, all the ominous glow of immediacy. They will be eagerly at home in the mystery of life. Adroitness, expertness, readiness for any experience, will enlighten their activities even where they most miserably fail. They are all actors, ready to take any part, for they put themselves, and nothing else, into every part they play. Commonly their real success will depend on the familiarity of the moments into which they sink themselves; they will depend on convention more than others, because they have nothing else to depend on.

So with the poetry of Mr. Cummings we might be altogether contented and pleased, were he himself content with the measure of his actual performance. But no poetry is so pretentious. No poetry ever claimed to mean more; and in making this claim it cannot avoid submitting itself, disastrously, to the criticism of the intelligence. So soon as we take it seriously, trying to discover what it really says about human destiny and the terms of love and death, we see how little material there is in this poetry except the assurance, made with continuous gusto, that the material exists. We look at the poetry. Sometimes one word, in itself vague and cloudy, is made to take on the work of an entire philosophy—like flower. Sometimes words pile themselves up blindly, each defeating the purport of the others. No feeling is ever defined. No emotion betrays a structure. Experience is its own phantoms, and flows willy-nilly. With the reality of experience the reality of language is lost. No metaphor crosses the bridge of tautology, and every simile is unexpanded. All the "thought" is metonymy, yet the substance is never assigned; so in the end we have only the thrill of substance.

Such an art when it pretends to measure life is essentially vicarious; it is a substitute for something that never was—like a tin soldier, or Peter Pan. It has all the flourish of life and every sentimental sincerity. Taken for what it is, it is charming and even instructive. Taken solemnly, as it is meant to be, the distortion by which it exists is too much for it, and it seems a kind of baby-talk.

NOTES

1. As of 1930. There would seem little modification of these notes necessary because of *Eimi* or the subsequent volumes of verse.

2. The reader is referred to the late numbers of *transition* for a serial and collaborative expression of the latest form which this group has assumed: the Battle of the Word. [As of 1930.]

3. It is not meant to disparage Mr. Cummings' inventions, which are often excellent, but to minimize an exaggerated contemporary interest. A full discussion of the values of notation may be found in *A Survey of Modernist Poetry* by Laura Riding and Robert Graves (London: Heinemann, 1927), especially in Chapter III which is labeled: "William Shakespeare and E.E. Cummings: A study in original punctuation and spelling." Their point is made by printing sonnet 129 in its original notation beside a modern version; the point being that Shakespeare knew what he was doing and that his editors did not.

4. It should be confessed that for all those persons who regard poetry only as a medium of communication, these remarks are quite vitiated. What is communicated had best remain as abstract as possible, dealing with the concrete as typical only; then "meaning" will be found to reside most clearly in the realm of ideas, and everything will be given as of equal import. But here poetry is regarded not at all as communication but as expression, as statement, as presentation of experience, and the emphasis will be on what is made known concretely. The question is not what one shares with the poet, but what one knows in the poem.

5. That is, as the most common form of sentimentality is the use of emotion in *excess* of

its impetus in the feelings, here we have an example of emotion which fails by a great deal to *come up* to its impetus. It is a very different thing from understatement, where the implications are always definite and where successful disarming.

6. Cf. Owen Barfield's *Poetic Diction* (London: Faber and Gwyer, 1928), p. 202. "For what is absolutely necessary to the present existence of poetry? Movement. The wisdom which she has imparted may remain for a time at rest, but she herself will always be found to have gone forward to where there is life, and therefore movement, *now*. And we have seen that the experience of esthetic pleasure betrays the real presence of movement. . . . But without the continued existence of poetry, without a steady influx of new meaning into language, even the knowledge and wisdom which poetry herself has given in the past must wither away into a species of mechanical calculation. Great poetry is the progressive incarnation of life in consciousness." That is, we must know what thrills us; else being merely thrilled we are left gasping and aghast, like the little girl on the roller coaster.

7. Barfield, *Poetic Diction*, pp. 197–98: "It (strangeness) is not synonymous with wonder; for wonder is our reaction to things which we are conscious of not quite understanding, or at any rate of understanding less than we had thought. The element of strangeness in beauty has the contrary effect. It arises from contact with a different kind of *consciousness* from our own, different, yet not so remote that we cannot partly share it, as indeed, in such a connexion, the mere word 'contact' implies. Strangeness, in fact, arouses wonder when we do not understand; esthetic imagination when we do."

The Poems and Prose of E.E. Cummings

John Peale Bishop*

It is impossible for me as I reread the poems of E. E. Cummings not to recall the emotion with which I first read *Tulips and Chimneys*. Their freshness and grace have not been lost, but to these qualities there was then added a rare excitement of discovery. This was early in the summer of 1922; John Dos Passos had loaned me a copy of the manuscript which Cummings on going abroad had left in his hands that he might arrange, if he could, for its publication. The following year, Thomas Seltzer was persuaded to bring out *Tulips and Chimneys*, but only in a much shortened form. About half the poems I had read in manuscript did not appear in print until much later and then scattered through volumes which wore other titles.

The *Collected Poems* contains whatever from earlier books the poet "wishes to preserve." A number of the most youthful poems have been dropped; some twenty recent compositions have been added.

No one can quarrel with a poet's selection from his own work. Still, I cannot but regret that since the manuscript of which I have just spoken was scattered, it has not been possible for anyone to trace the develop-

*Reprinted from the *Southern Review*, 4 (1938), 173–86. Reprinted by permission of the *Southern Review*.

ment of Cummings from poem to poem. The order in which the poems have now been arranged still represents little more than the accidents of publication. In the pages that follow I shall not hesitate to take into consideration some of the poems which have disappeared from *Tulips and Chimneys*. And though it is too early to take a historical view of Cummings, it may aid in "placing" him if I return to my first encounter with his poetry. I cannot do otherwise.

He appeared as a young and romantic poet. But he was one unmistakably of his time. That he derived from Keats and had been instructed by the poets of the last century was obvious; but even in the earliest poems, where their trace is most strong, the movement of Cummings' verse is already his own. His charm, at once, is his rapidity. The influence of the romantic tradition was soon left behind; but not the romantic attitude. That was authentic and not taught—at least, not by the English poets. It stood no more in critical favor than it does now, however the cry against it in some quarters has changed. This poetry was aware, as only poetry can be, of what was going on. The sensibility of the poet was singularly uncontaminated. He defied, indeed, every principle which Ezra Pound had taught us was right for poetry; and there was none of us then who had not listened with attention to Pound. Here was no effort for the one precise word; instead adjectives, which were Pound's abhorrence, were piled one on another in a sort of luminous accumulation. If Cummings, in writing, had kept his eye on the object, it was of no avail, for the objects had their outlines distorted, or else they dissolved, leaving behind only an impression of their qualities. Here was a poetry as shining and as elusive as quicksilver. If there was anything precise about it, it was, as Cummings was to note later, that precision which aims at creating movement. Yet none but a poet could have been so preoccupied with words; nor could anyone not a poet have so enlivened them with his presence.

Here was no Prince Hamlet, nor was meant to be; here was quite another figure, fine, impertinent, full of shocks and capers, in the midst of some absurd mockery suddenly turning surpassingly lyrical. Here was Mercutio.

The impulse which the romantics of the early nineteenth century had given poetry had long been exhausted. By the turn of the century, it had so definitely expired that when Francis Thompson came along, it was scarcely possible for him, a belated romantic, to create poetry. He could only make elaborate garlands for its corpse.

When romanticism reappeared, it was not at once recognized. It had changed its aspect. It appeared as the reverse of itself. But a coin has the same value, whether it falls heads or tails. And though we may prefer to call the poetry that was written in the years close to the War, and for some time after it, antiromantic, its ultimate value is romantic. And this was so, even though almost every critical opinion, including that of the poets themselves, was against anything of the sort. For no other poetry was possible.

Classical poetry is necessarily moral. It can come into existence only when there is a moral order which both society and the poet can accept. The *grand siècle* produced such a poetry in France. When T. S. Eliot espoused the cause of classicism in literature, it is to be noted that he came out for Catholicism. He had to have some sort of authority in morals, even though the only one available should be his collection of English Bishops, some living and some dead, those who are most alive spiritually being those who are actually dead. Mr. Eliot is not so much a classicist as a poet who at times is like Flaubert in trying to strip romanticism from his soul and at times is like the saints who would rid themselves while still in the flesh of every accident of birth and change.

A romantic immorality must return whenever civilization is found no longer an aid but a hindrance to the accomplishment of desires. The alternative is asceticism. A protest was bound to be made by a generation in which the individual had suffered so much from society and suffered, as he felt, under the most false pretenses. The armies and the governments of this world had ignored the lonely man; but death had not ignored him. It was only to the individual that death paid any attention. It was this contrast between this death of a man—I have seen them dug up out of the earth of France at Montfaucon—this death known in the flesh that lives and loves and rots, and the impersonal casualty lists put out by the governments that gave everyone who went through the War a permanent distrust and horror of abstract forms of information. The gap was too great. Death was not forgotten. For death was an enemy of the individual even more redoutable than society, for he was inescapable. Nevertheless, awareness of his imminence had its compensations. He was a silence increasing the intensity of every sound. Romantic emotions reappear in every generation and always at that moment when the young first conceive their own annihilation. At that moment, regardless of the state of society in which they find themselves, there follows an assertion of whatever they conceive themselves to be in their own right. This consciousness is enhanced for the young to whom death is continuously present, as in war. In Cummings there is an untiring protest against everything that stands in the way of a man's knowing himself alive and a praise and exaltation, which otherwise would be excessive, for whatever comes to the aid of that awareness.

> Among
>
>   these
>   red pieces of
> day(against which and
> quite silently hills
> made of blueandgreen paper
>
> scorchbend ingthem

-selves-U
pcurvE, into:
                    anguish(clim
b)ing
s-p-i-r-a-
l
and, disappear)
                    Satanic and blasé
a black goat lookingly wanders

There is nothing left of the world but
into this noth
ing il treno per
Roma si-gnori ?
jerk.
ilyr, ushes

    This is an example, and by no means an extreme one, of Cummings'
method. A momentary relationship is established between the poet and a
black goat wandering at twilight among the Italian hills. Then the train
departs and this particular landscape is gone. Presumably the goat continues to wander, to browse, or whatever it is a goat must do to pursue its
life. The sky has darkened and into a dimness in which nothing can be
seen, the train, after a pause, proceeds. The goat is not a symbol of
anything. He is what Cummings would call an actual miracle. He is a
creature of the outer world who is capable of becoming a creation of the
mind. It now becomes the poet's task to set down, without falsification,
this fragment of time, which is not so insignificant as it seems, since it is
like no other since the beginning of the world. And in that instant
something has happened to the poet to assure him that he is alive. And
Cummings belongs to a generation which for years after the War, and not
only because of the War, needed constantly to be assured that it was
among the living.
    The world can be known only in its momentary aspects; for once the
moment has passed, whatever has been known must change. The importance of the moment increases, once we have admitted the discontinuity
of the mind. The mind in Cummings has become its own material. The
center no longer holds and he ends by becoming fascinated by the speed of
its fragments. By sticking strictly as may be to what he knows, by staying
within the record of sensations, Cummings has been able to do what a
generation of poets in Europe, with considerably less success, attempted
to do. Whether they were called Futurists in Italy, or Dadaists in France,
or by other names in other countries, their aims have been more completely accomplished by Cummings than by any poet on the continent. He
has the advantage of being an American, with whatever that implies in
the way of a natural appetite for disorder. He had, too, in a degree that
none of the others had, the sensibilities and the wit of a poet.

II

At the time when Cummings' manner was formed, it seemed not only possible, but imperative, that every element of technique should be recreated. He was aware of Joyce's experiments in prose in *Ulysses*; some of them he has repeated, concentrating them, as he might well do in the smaller space of a poem; in his own prose he has carried them still further, especially in *Eimi*, by accelerating their performance. He had before him the example of Picasso, who had already passed through three or four periods, each representing a progress in emotion and a prodigious renewal of technique. What could be more natural than that Cummings, who is painter as well as poet, should attempt to emulate in literature the innovations of his contemporaries in painting? In Picasso, as in some others who were renewing the painter's art, he saw what intensity might follow distortion of line and immensity of form. And Cummings has taught himself to see somewhat as they see, but without losing his personal vision. He juxtaposes words as they do pigments. The effect is not altogether a happy one, for what is gained in intensity may be lost in meaning. When a painter distorts a line, he may increase its functional value; but a sentence can easily be so dislocated that it will no longer work. The impressionist method, so apt to seize the aspect of a momentary world, permits Cummings to rely on the vaguest associations. It has led him as a poet, not to weight, but merely to touch his words with meaning. In fact, the significance of his words is often in their position. Then, too, it is probably the example of the Post-Impressionists and the Picasso of the *papier collé* period that has persuaded him to admit to his poetry much that was tawdry, trivial, and lewd—material whose advantage to him is certainly in part that it has hitherto been considered inadmissible.

Cummings has his own punctuation, his own typography, and not only his own speech and prosody, but his own grammar. What he has aimed to do is to set down all that his mind, prompted by the sensations of the body, inevitably and spontaneously knows. His art is personal. It could not well be anything else; for it reposes upon a conviction that each man's world is his own and that no other can be known. "Regarded as an existence which appears in a soul, the whole world for each is peculiar and private to that soul."[1] Other poets have professed some such philosophy, but, so far as I know, Cummings is the first actually to carry it into his writing. He does not write as a common sense dualist. He was born and brought up in Cambridge, Massachusetts; and though he has constantly cried his repudiation of his birthplace and all its academic works, including the late Josiah Royce, it is only as a child of Cambridge that he can be so passionately private and peculiar. In Russia, he met a compatriot, a young woman reporter, who told him he was not part of the world. Their conversation is related in *Eimi*. Cummings' reply is unhesitating: "Quite so. Actually the world is a part of me. And—I'll egocentrically tell the world—a very small part."

Ever since T. S. Eliot published his essay on *Tradition and the Individual Talent* the personal in poetry has been suspect. Mr. Eliot in that essay quotes Remy de Gourmont on Flaubert, and it is, of course, very largely from admiration of the incomparable display of impersonal art in *Madame Bovary* that this opposition to the personal in literature has risen. Now one can share that admiration without being sure that what was not impossible for a practitioner in the art of prose narration is also practicable for the poet, particularly the lyric poet. Mr. Eliot has held up to us "The Phoenix and the Turtle," and he was, at the time he did it, right to do so, for it was then a neglected poem. But there is in all Shakespeare only one "Phoenix and the Turtle," and against it may be placed one hundred and fifty-odd sonnets. They, to be sure, represent a disciplined art. And all must in the end come back to a question of discipline and not of personality. The objections which may properly be brought against Cummings are not that his art is personal and that therefore it is unintelligible, because on such grounds we should also have to declare there is no knowing Proust or any number of other writers whose worlds are not less private than that of Cummings. Rather it may be said of him that he is constantly trying to affect us by other than purely literary means. He attempts to seduce us without departing from his solitude. Cummings' faults are those of the sensitive writer, and the interest of his poetry is that it is a product of his sensibility. No one poem is unintelligible. On the contrary, it is much more likely that if we try to take it as complete, its meaning will be too soon exhausted. For its concern is with the immediate and with the moment. It may charm or amuse; but it is only by Cummings' poetry as a whole that we are profoundly impressed. It is not unattached to his personality; but the interest of that personality is in its singular capacity to report the age.

The problem is not one of escaping personality (for that way impotence lies) but of transcending it. And that a poet may do in one of two ways: he may dramatize his personal desires directly, or he may find in the outer world some drama, into whose actors he can fuse his own desires and in whose catastrophe he can, though only on an imaginative plane, resolve his personal conflict. The one method is that of *La Vita Nuova*, the other is that of *The Divine Comedy*. It is the more mature work, which, in Dante's case, is the more profoundly personal. But Cummings has almost no imagination. He is said to be confined in his own world; but it is a world which has too much in common with ours to make communication impossible. He is subject there to a conflict of contrary desires: he would be like others, and yet utterly unlike; he would be like the man who suffers, but not like the man who dies. He has taken the only known way to immortality. Out of this conflict he has made his poems, both lyrical and satirical. But nothing has made him a dramatic poet.

III

Cummings' prose has never had anything like the attention it deserves. *The Enormous Room* came out in 1921, when a reaction had set in against almost all that had then been written about the War. It did not exploit that reaction and failed, as so many later books did not, to profit from it. *Eimi*, which is an account of a journey made through the U.S.S.R. in 1931, appeared the following year, in the midst of the depression communism. It was derided or ignored. And yet, *The Enormous Room* has the effect of making all but a very few comparable books that came out of the War look shoddy and worn. It has been possible to read it, as I have done, at intervals over the seventeen years since its publication, and always to find it undiminished. So it has slowly found readers. But those who were attracted to *The Enormous Room*, because of the compassion Cummings showed there for the lowly and despised, were repulsed by *Eimi*, which makes it clear that he will have nothing to do with the communist effort to improve the condition of mankind. The one book is, nevertheless, the complement of the other, and the only change in Cummings to be marked between them is the change from youth to maturity. And in *Eimi*, he makes every other writer on Russia appear dishonest or credulous.

These books have behind them what must be regarded as the two most important events of our time. And the backgrounds, in so far as they affect his narratives, are set before us with great vividness. The incidental characters are presented with an admirable skill and they remain convincing, even though in the parts they play there is almost always some exaggeration, comic or pathetic. For again and again, as Cummings produces a character, we are reminded of Dickens. But the center of *The Enormous Room* is not the War, nor that of *Eimi* the Russian Revolution. At the core of each is a spiritual crisis.

In 1917, Cummings was confined for some months, at the behest of the French government, in a detention camp, along with a number of others, whom, for reasons of their own, the French officials suspected of being spies. Cummings, who until his arrest had been an ambulance driver in an American unit, encountered in that huge barracks at La Ferté-Macé, which he calls the Enormous Room, a sad assortment of men. They from being his companions in misery become, whether they speak or not—and the most eloquent are those who have the smallest command of words—his counselors in compassion. He was here in the backwash of the War. Some of these men were its wrecks; more of them, war or no war, the common scum of humanity. Among them the narrator met a problem much older than the War. In his own soul he met it: the significance of human suffering. He met it with the intensity of youth and knowing that upon some solution of it depended his sanity. It is a problem much greater than that of injustice, for it includes it. And it is worth noting that it is not with its injustice that Cummings reproaches the French government, but with its stupidity, in confining to the Enormous Room specimens of humanity as small as these.

The mind provides no answer to the problem of suffering. The answer must come from elsewhere. There are good men and bad in the Enormous Room, there are brave men and cowards. There is that truculent, bullying pimp called the Fighting Sheeney, there is that grave and handsome Gypsy known as the Wanderer. Men come and go in this imprisonment, which they are not allowed to call a prison. They are made very real to us in their great variety; they reveal themselves and none is like another. They have, nevertheless, something in common. Their pain is real and they share their misery. They are, in a way, like those mountebanks painted by the young Picasso, those starved and wandering Spaniards, whose long drawn skulls seem not made for any thought, but only to contain the burden of suffering humanity. There are eyes which meet Cummings in prison which are very like those in the Picasso paintings; they have been beyond the blue of the horizon and they know there is nothing there that is not also here.

The answer, even for a poet, is not in words. The climax of *The Enormous Room* is reached in the episode of Supplice. Supplice is a Pole and what he speaks of anybody else's language is very little; there is one of his compatriots in prison, but even he says he cannot understand Supplice's Polish. He is the most abject of men; below him is nothing conceivable, and he is tortured by those who, but for him, would know themselves on the bottom. He is attracted to excrement; it is he who every morning, without being ordered, bears away from the Enormous Room the refuse from so many human bodies. What Supplice has to say is only pathetically little more than nothing. What he has to impart is as tremendous as humility.

When Cummings has done with Supplice, he has only one portrait to follow, drawn on a comparable scale: Jean le Nègre. Jean is black, swaggering, immense. He has been arrested in Paris for impersonating an English officer. In prison he is far from silent; but what is remarkable about his speech is not its amazing mixture of childish French and pidgin English, nor even his capacity for lying. It is that Jean does not know himself when he is lying and when he is not. His is the mind of a child, an utterly timeless mind, without memory; what is true today may be false tomorrow. He is at one time the child of a sixteen year old father and a mother who died before he was born; at another he is the son of the Lord Mayor of London and the Queen. Only laughter could resolve these contradictions. But wherever he came from, Jean is the only person in his gallery who could follow Supplice and make a proper contrast. For what can oppose the poverty of the spirit, but the pride of the body? Jean is all laughter, sinew, and sensuality.

Here, at the very start, we have in Cummings what has been called his cult of unintelligence. He was one who could not but seek a wholesome being. He emerged from imprisonment profoundly shaken. Where else is he to look for what he sought in a world dead at the top if not below? And in Cummings there is from now on, in all he writes, an exaltation of the lowly and the lively. He is himself, and he accepts his common lot. With the others, he suffers; he exults alone, and in a world of his own. But something happens to alter this attitude shortly after he crosses the Polish border into the Soviet Union and in the customs house encounters upon the wall, framed in bunting, the colored photograph of Nicolai Lenin.

IV

The style which Cummings began in poetry reaches its most complete development in the prose of *Eimi*. Indeed, one might almost say that, without knowing it, Cummings had been acquiring a certain skill over years, in order that, when occasion arose, he might set down in words the full horror of Lenin's tomb. It is brought to us through every sense: the acid stench of numberless multitudes endlessly waiting, endlessly treading downward into the darkness to look on the maker of their world, the corpse of the man with the small, not intense, face and the reddish beard, secret, being dead, as when alive, intransigent even in mortality. For in Russia, Cummings was not only in a new country; he was in a new world. Impressions pressed, one on another, in such confusing rapidity that no one with less than his skill could possibly have caught and recorded them. Sensations are transformed into words at the moment they arrive in the consciousness; there they confront other words, and are confused with recollections from the world beyond Russia and the instantaneous reactions of Cummings' spirit. All these are given as they occurred, or at least we have the illusion that they are, so that they must be read as rapidly as they are recorded. *Eimi* demands much the sort of attention, prompt and yet easily scattered, with which we discover from a few pages of the morning newspaper what went on in the world the day before. Not the least of its interest is what it has to show of the workings of a contemporary mind. It is more or less incidental that the mind happens to be Cummings'.

Russia no doubt has changed since 1931, but mostly in such a way as to make apparent to every one of good will what Cummings was almost alone in seeing when he went there seven years ago. He had been warned, before going, that because of his lack of political and economic training he was not at all prepared to understand Russia. He was peculiarly prepared to see the Russians.

It was precisely because he did not approach them through theories that he saw through their pretenses with such astonishing honesty of vision. He was the child who saw, not the King, but the Kremlin, naked.

He was certainly not interested in discovering for himself how far

Comrade Stalin had been able to carry out the predictions of *The Communist Manifesto*. He did not care how many motors had been turned out under the Five Year Plan. He had come from the land of Detroit. He had never, I am almost sure, read *The Communist Manifesto*. If there were words from any political document in his head they were from a much older one, which had been drawn up and signed by none but Americans. And if the Declaration of Independence had not existed, Cummings in Russia, I dare say, would have invented it. His sole interest in government was the effect on the governed. What he wanted to know was not what material progress had been made by the workers since the Revolution. What he wanted to know about the socialist experiment was whether it was better prepared than the democracy he had left to assure to those under it the rights to life, liberty, and the pursuit of happiness. The rights of man were not inalienable in the America of 1931. Least of all, in the cities where were most machines.

He found in Russia not liberty, but a joyless experiment in force and fear. He found not life, but in men and women a willingness not to live if only they were allowed not to die. Apathy made possible the Stalin régime. Apathy supported it and it was this same apathy which accounted as no native lack of ability could do for the drabness, the ineffectiveness, the filth of all the Russians were supposed to do. A lack of comfort might mean many things and not be serious; it might even be admirable; only if it meant a dearth of spirit was it appalling. The country was in a state of civil war, which had, perhaps, been deliberately protracted. But it had been much worse. Anything was better, as one Russian woman explained to Cummings, than the time when "they made us lie down at the point of the bayonet." The Russians had long been unhappy; they were now, it might be, somewhat less so; but their suffering, whatever it was, was suffering in silence. Cummings understands that the despair of the individual may become the enthusiasm of the masses. For what else is propaganda for? But as for the efforts of the Soviet Government to increase the happiness of the Russians, he sums them up in one succinct phrase—"Pippa passes the buck!"

The Red Dawn has faded into the most depressing of days. But Cummings does not, as so many of the later commentators do, attribute the failure of the Russian Revolution to Stalin. No revolution can do more for a people than restore it to itself, and not much more could be done for the Russians than to massacre their former masters. For every one of them looks over his shoulder before he speaks—and that not only on account of the political police; every man is suspect where no man trusts himself. But in so far as any one man is responsible for this world in which the Russians do not live it is Lenin. Stalin is an idea become action. It was Lenin who first converted the idea into an act.

Lenin inherited a doctrine, which he attempted to impose upon the Russians. And this, to Cummings, is among all others the unforgivable crime. A poet may be as violent as he wants with words and make them obey his will. But for a man to do likewise with living men and women, he must be more than a man. And that Lenin was not. He was not a source of power, however much power he acquired. He was a secondary figure like Cromwell, like Saint Paul. The poet works with form as his end. The reformer starts with a formula. The distance between them is as great as the distance between life and nonexistence, between the life of the spirit and the suicide of the soul known as dialectical materialism. Lenin probably believed that he had come into the world that men might have life and have it more abundantly. But the almost immediate effect on whoever accepted his doctrines was an acceptance of lifelessness. He took away from his followers the little life they had.

Cummings seems to have gone to Russia very much as he went to imprisonment, not altogether unwillingly, knowing that an important experience awaited him there, without in the least knowing what the experience would be. In Russia he was not granted his experience; he was prepared for it. In prison he had accepted suffering as inseparable from the life of man. But in Russia he was repulsed by the spectacle of untold multitudes suffering and willing to suffer in silence. He was appalled. In the Enormous Room he had been taught to know himself a man among others. But in the Soviet Union, he saw that something more than patience, something more than compassion, was needed to make a man.

Throughout *Eimi*, Cummings maintains an analogy, never too hard pressed, between his own progress from circle to circle of soviet society and Dante's passage through Hell. The moment at which he emerges to see the stars is when he returns to Europe, where it is once more possible for him to assume the full responsibility of being a man. In prison he had learned a passive acceptance of his lot. It was on his return to freedom (his ticket was sold him in Constantinople by a pleasant young Englishman to travel towards Paris by International Express) that he experiences that sense of the wholeness of life—that complete vision which includes both divinity and depravity—that allows him, as he approaches the borders of Italy, without permission, to call upon the name of Dante. For now he knows there is but one freedom, a freedom active and acquiescent in the vision, the freedom of the will, responsive and responsible, and that from it all other freedoms take their course.

"He that knoweth the eternal is comprehensive; comprehensive, therefore just; just, therefore a king; a king, therefore celestial; celestial, therefore in Tao; in Tao, therefore enduring."

And with that quotation he knows he is forever beyond the U.S.S.R.

NOTES

1. It is not Cummings, but T. S. Eliot, who, in his notes to *The Waste Land*, quotes this remark from F. H. Bradley.

Latter-Day Notes on
E.E. Cummings' Language

Robert E. Maurer*

The language that E. E. Cummings uses in his poems, no less than his more widely noticed experiments with typography and his sometimes startling choice of themes, is an expression of the fundamental basis of his life: he is aggressively an individualist, and, more than that, a protestant, as he makes clear in the autobiographical portions of his recent book, *i: six nonlectures*. The nonlectures themselves are an expression of his protestantism; when he was offered the Charles Eliot Norton Professorship of Poetry at Harvard for the academic year 1952–1953, he accepted only on the condition that he would not have to teach; and, though he was "extremely glad," as he said, to be giving the six "socalled lectures," he protested against the very idea of lecturing ("lecturing is presumably a form of teaching"[1]) by calling his talks "nonlectures," and by choosing to be autobiographical rather than professorial.

In the nonlectures he reveals that as a boy he reacted against the teacup society of his home in Cambridge, where his father was a professor at Harvard and later a clergyman, by making excursions into "sinful Somerville." His pattern of protest continued as he reacted against the well-scrubbed nice boys of Harvard by frequenting, in his college days, Boston's Old Howard burlesque house; against the authoritarianism of the Norton-Harjes Ambulance Corps, which he joined in 1917, by choosing to remain with a friend even though his steadfastness resulted in his going to a French prison; and, after he began to publish his writings, against polite society in general by glorifying the most abject of men and using prostitutes, stripteasers, and gangsters as the subjects of poems. An inveterate protestant almost automatically comes to sense in himself an aura of separateness, of aloneness; and because he wills himself a significant and very personal insight into all experience, it is understandable that, if he is a writer, he should want to fashion a language in keeping with the uniqueness of his viewpoint. Thus Cummings protested against "gentlemen poeds" and "Longfellow . . . dead" by throwing away their linguistic principles and working out new ones of his own.

In this activity he was not alone. Cummings grew to artistic maturity in a period, the time just after the First World War, in which experimentation was not only common but almost expected of all serious young artists. Men who rejected all the ideological traditions and values of pre-war bourgeois society used artistic experimentation in a negative way as a means of destroying as many shibboleths as they could; positively, it enabled them to express their new-found individualistic relation to the

*Reprinted from the *Bucknell Review*, 5 (1955), 1–23. Reprinted by permission of the *Bucknell Review* (Associated University Presses).

world about them. The young writers of poetry were trying, as F. J. Hoffman and Charles Allen have expressed it in their book, *The Little Magazine*, to get rid of the poetic clichés that made meaning deceptively easy and to substitute for them an "awareness of complexity." Modern poetic language, they said, "violates . . . conventional recognition, and aims essentially to make the reader discard it altogether, to reform his attention and to reconsider his standards of acceptance."[2] Cummings, in working toward this aim, has used language with no concession to conventional recognition; he has always wanted his reader to drop all the accoutrements of the grammarian and the rhetorician that he may be wearing as protective clothing and to approach his poems, as it were, naked and unafraid. The reader should be free of preconceptions about English poetry, unafraid to "reconsider his standards of acceptance."

This is not to say, however, that Cummings does not know rules and tradition. He is instead a prime example of the old adage that an artist must know all the rules before he can break them. Cummings is no primitive, though he sometimes uses words as a child does; he is no Walt Whitman with a barbaric yawp, no untutored child of the prairie working in what is essentially an alien medium. He was writing poetry, according to his non-lectures, at the age of six—indeed, he was by then in his second poetic phase, in which he thought that a good poem is one that does good; his third phase opened when an uncle presented him with "The Rhymester" and he discovered verse forms—rondels, ballades, villanelles, rondeaus. Shortly thereafter Professor Josiah Royce, a neighbor, introduced him to the sonnets of Rossetti, and, as he says, "I've been writing sonnets ever since."[3] He learned Greek in public school. At Harvard he received "a glimpse of Homer, a more than glimpse of Aeschylus Sophocles Euripides and Aristophanes, and a deep glance at Dante and Shakespeare"[4]; through his friends there he grew to love Sappho, Catullus, Horace, Blake, and Keats. His first book of poems, *Tulips and Chimneys* (1923), revealed the fact that he had had a classical education, although the poems in it that looked forward to his later writing were much more noteworthy than those which were traditionalist. And although he continues to work in the sonnet—perhaps his most memorable poetry is in this form—he long ago abandoned the language of Rossetti and Keats for one which fits his highly personal insight into experience. At its most highly developed state, in his later books, Cummings' language becomes almost a foreign one, usually possible to figure out for a reader who knows English, it is true; but he will get its full meaning only if he has read a great deal of Cummings and if he "knows the language."

It is unfortunate that most of the critical appraisals of Cummings' poetry were made early, shortly after his first books were published. Since those days—the twenties—were full of literary and artistic ferment, and a new poetic talent was to many people at least as exciting as a new baseball player, it is natural that he should have received a great deal of attention then; it is perhaps also natural that as the first shock caused by his poetry died down into acceptance of what seemed a fixed technique of an established poet, the critics should have turned their eyes elsewhere. Cummings, too, was somewhat out of the mainstream in the thirties. He was not popular with the New Critics because he was too personal and unintellectual; he did not think or write in their groove. Nor was he popular with the critics of the left who demanded their own variety of social consciousness in a writer. His "immorality" was too blunt for the Humanists, and his verse was too uncommunicative for the attackers of the cult of unintelligibility. When his last three volumes of verse came out, no one took the trouble to give Cummings the reappraisal that his poetry needed and deserved; very few people noticed the fundamental change of attitude which manifested itself in his growing reverence and dedication to lasting love; even fewer noted the development in his use of language.[5] Thus in 1955 an essay, "Notes on E. E. Cummings' Language," by Richard P. Blackmur,[6] written in 1930, remains the only extensive treatment of the subject; and too many people think of his language, as they think of the subject matter of his poetry, as if it were all of a piece, which it most emphatically is not.

The man who in 1923 could publish such an echo of poets immemorial as:

> i like
> to think that on
> the flower you gave me when we
> loved
>   the far-
> departed mouth sweetly-saluted
> lingers.
>
>   (from *Tulips and Chimneys*, "Amores," VI:36)[7]

in 1944 was writing:

> what if a dawn of a doom of a dream
> bites this universe in two,
> peels forever out of his grave
> and sprinkles nowhere with me and you?
> Blow soon to never and never to twice
> (blow life to isn't:blow death to was)
> —all nothing's only our hugest home;
> the most who die, the more we live
>
>   (from *I x I*, XX: 401)

The progression is tremendous, not only of language but of thought, of rhythmic patterns, of density, of originality, These examples are not taken out of context merely to make a point; almost any poem from *Tulips and Chimneys* could be set alongside almost any poem from *I x I* (1944), in which the latter verse appears, and the contrast would be just as great.

In 1952 Mr. Blackmur appended a note to his republished essay saying, "There would seem little modification of these notes necessary because of *Eimi* or the subsequent volumes of verse,"[8] but this statement is an oversimplification. Many of the things that Mr. Blackmur said are still accurate descriptions of some of the phenomena of Cummings' language; the trouble is that his remarks are incomplete. They do not consider Cummings' later practices of using one part of speech as another, of leaving out words so that the resulting condensation is so dense as to be almost impenetrable, of thoroughly scrambling English word order with the same effect. Mr. Blackmur was instead occupied with such things as Cummings' tough-guy attitude and his romantic egoism, with his overuse of certain favorite words to which he seemed to assign private meanings, and with the question of whether such diction did not make his poetry impenetrable. Mr. Blackmur concluded unequivocally that it did; and, if in 1952 he saw no need for modification of his notes, one assumes that he still thinks so. He does not mean to say that Cummings is isolated in his fault, however; he puts him in the company of Surrey, Crashaw, Marvell, Burns, Wordsworth, Shelley, and Swinburne, and he asserts: "Most of their work, most of any poet's work, with a half a dozen exceptions, is tenuous and vague, private exercises or public playthings of a soul in verse."[9] Since the work of these poets, tenuous and vague though it may be, has been studied with profit, it may not be amiss to give some attention to what is a great obstacle to complete perception of Cummings' poetry, his use of language.

Cummings, a man who admires the paradox enough to utilize it constantly in his work, has a knack for unconsciously exemplifying it himself. Although his language, especially in the later books, is intricate and difficult, what he asks of his reader is, as always, the frank approach of a child; and it is this attitude which he himself takes to his mother tongue and to its tenets and rules. Of course, such an approach is consistent with that most salient feature of his viewpoint, his glorification of the child (or the "maturely childish" adult) ; he is, when he fashions language as a child would, merely practicing what he preaches. It is doubtful whether he ever said to himself, "I shall form and use words as if I have not completely mastered the idiom of the English language, although I know its rules"; but this is precisely what, in his first ventures into unusual language, he began to do. He divested himself of the literate adult's prejudices against such things as double negatives, redundant superlatives and comparatives, and non-dictionary words.

A child will construct his language by means of analogy, forming the past tense of irregular verbs by adding the *-ed* suffix (*runned, swimmed,* and so forth), and forming all comparatives or superlatives by adding the normal *-er* or *-est* (*beautifuler, chiefest*), or stepping up the power of a word such as *last*, which is already superlative, and saying *lastest*. Intent on making his point clear and only half certain of the niceties of grammar, a child will repeat negatives or superlatives in triple measure, and so will Cummings. A line from one of his poems, "somebody might hardly never not have been unsorry,perhaps" (from *ViVa*, XXVII:242) rivals if it does not outclass in bristling negatives such famous lines as Chaucer's "He never yit no vileineye ne sayde" and Shakespeare's "Nor what he said, though it lacked for a little,/ Was not like madness." That Cummings has not outgrown his childish technique of word forming is shown by his comparisons in the following fragment, from *I x I*, which match those of any child who is determined to make his admiration amply known:

> which is the very
> (in sad this havingest
> world)most merry
> most fair most rare
> —the livingest givingest
> girl on this whirlingest
> earth?
> why you're
> by far the darlingest

(from *I x I*, L: 420)

His creation of *havingest, livingest, givingest,* and *whirlingest* carries the child's habit of adding *-est* to all adjectives one step further: he has added the suffix to words which are rarely if ever used as adjectives at all—*having* and *giving*—thus not only creating a non-dictionary superlative but changing the part of speech of his base word. *Living* and *whirling*, of course, are often used as adjectives; but they are not normally compared.

He uses a similar technique in the following passage, in which he is pointing out the spiritual quality of the moon:

> whO perfectly whO
> flOat
> newly alOne is
> dreamest

(from *no thanks*, 1 : 277)

By making an adjective out of a word that is normally a noun or a verb, *dream*, he exercises his habit of assuming that the cubbyholes into which words are put are flexible; by doing so he is enabled to express concisely an idea which in English has no one-word equivalent: that a natural phenomenon can contain the quality of dreams to a great degree. The same kind of part-of-speech derangement may be seen in his use of *wonderful* in this passage:

> And if somebody hears
> what i say—let him be pitiful:

> because i've travelled all alone
> through the forest of wonderful,
>
> (from *Xli Poems*, "Sonnets," XII : 158)

Here he is giving unusual weight to a normally overused and colorless word by changing its grammatical classification. The "forest of wonderful" he speaks of is the beauty of his loved one; the line might have read "through the forest of her wonderful beauty," in which case the figure would have been the same but the surprise of language would have escaped. Similarly, he combines the "childish" technique of using redundant comparatives with the highly sophisticated element of paradox in the following lines:

> love is more thicker than forget
> more thinner than recall
>
> (from *50 Poems*, 42: 381)

Sometimes, in the simplest of his word coinages, he merely creates a new word by analogy as a child would without adding any shade of meaning other than that inherent in the prefix or suffix he utilizes, as in the words *unstrength* and *untimid*, which appeared in his first book. The meaning of *unstrength* is not precisely different from that of *weakness*, although the latter has certain derogatory connotations which the former may lack (possibly this is the reason why Cummings coined it for the particular passage in which it is used); but certainly *untimid* is no different from *not timid*, although it is less complimentary than *brave*. The chief advantage of the coined words in such cases is that they add a bit of freshness to a poem. In a later book, however, Cummings took the same prefix, *un*, and added it to a word in such a way as to form a pun: in *manunkind*. Here attention is focused on what is not present, as it was in *unstrength*; but by placing *un* in the middle of the word he in effect changed the suffix *kind* to the adjective *kind* and ended with the quite normal adjective *unkind* modifying *man*. The result is not merely a coined word; it is a new idea, which happens to be an apt and concise expression of one of Cummings' convictions.

Less startling, perhaps, than his extensions on a child's way of forming language is his habit of combining two or more words to form a single new one. Quite often these combinations are little more than normally hyphenated words without the hyphen, or a mere printing together of two or more words to give an effect of wholeness, of one quality, as when he describes a color as *yellowgreen* or *yellowand bluish*, or when he describes a movie actress as *muchmouthed*. Sometimes, however, the printing of several words together adds a commentary on the words: by saying "*poorbuthonest* workingman," for instance, Cummings is scornfully implying that the words have become a cliché. Or he may print words together in order to regulate the speed of reading and come closer to the nature of the action being described, as when he writes "and break onetwothreefourfive pigeonsjustlikethat" in imitation of Buffalo Bill's phenomenally rapid shooting.

Such word coinages as have been mentioned so far are only slight digressions from the conventions of good English, but they do help to give Cummings' writing the distinctive stylistic character it had had practically from the beginning. Thus in *Tulips and Chimneys*, although the greater part of his language is conventional and sometimes even banally "poetic," one finds such unusual usages as *unstrength, purpled, Justspring, eddieandbill, puddle-wonderful, almostness, greentwittering, quiveringgold, flowerterrible, starlessness, fearruining, timeshaped, sayingly.* Except for *sayingly* and *almostness*, which are among the first examples of his changing one part of speech into another, and *unstrength*, there is nothing very startling about most of these words. The mere printing of two words together, as in *greentwittering*, might be considered more a typographical technique than a linguistic one, although it is apparent that when Cummings combines two words to form one adjective he usually creates a new concept by the juxtaposition of two unlike descriptives: *flowerterrible, timeshaped.* (It is such language as this that Mr. Blackmur objects to; he would say that it is impossible to determine the exact meaning of such words as *flowerterrible* and *timeshaped*, and undoubtedly he is right.) *Tulips and Chimneys* abounds with such words and with phrases that are made up of conventional words in unconventional juxtapositions, such as "the convulsed orange inch of moon," "little accurate saints thickly which tread," "a skilful uncouth prison," "a polite uproar of knuckling silent planes," "brittle towns," "chattering sunset," "the square virtues and the oblong sins."

These phrases that (one must agree with Mr. Blackmur) convey a thrill but not a precise impression swarm through the book but are not able to occupy it exclusively. In contrast to them are many images which depend for their power upon the unexpected but which manage to convey an accurate reproduction of the poet's thought, which show, indeed, that the poet *had* a thought and not merely a rush of words. Such a poem as "La Guerre," II (39), shows Cummings in control of his images and his words:

O sweet spontaneous
earth how often have
the
doting
        fingers of
prurient philosophers pinched
and
poked

thee
, has the naughty thumb
of science prodded

thy

    beauty   .how
often have religions taken
thee upon their scraggy knees
squeezing and

buffeting thee that thou mightest conceive
gods
    (but
true

to the incomparable
couch of death thy
rhythmic
lover

    thou answerest

them only with

    spring)[10]

Cummings is in control, too, in the three "Chansons Innocentes" (pp. 21–23), and in the sonnet whose first line Mr. Blackmur quotes in rare approval: "the Cambridge ladies who live in furnished souls" (p. 58); although, as Mr. Blackmur points out, the last four lines of this sonnet go off into one of his thrilling but not precise metaphors:

. . . . the Cambridge ladies do not care, above
Cambridge if sometimes in its box of
sky lavender and cornerless, the
moon rattles like a fragment of angry candy

The volume *Tulips and Chimneys* has been unavailable for a long time. One is surprised, therefore, upon going back to its full text as reprinted in the new *Poems: 1923–1954*, to find that Cummings' first volume of poems, though it has long been a famous book, is not a uniformly good one. It contains the tired romanticism of "Epithalamion" and "Of Nicolette," the embarrassing lushness of "Puella Mea" and "Orientale," the unoriginal love thoughts of "Amores"; it is packed with original but probably imprecise images of the kind quoted above; it displays such juvenile sentiments as "your little voice / Over the wires came leaping / and i felt suddenly / dizzy" (p. 38), and "her heart breaks in a smile—and she is Lust . . . . / mine also, little painted poem of god" (p. 60). In short, the volume is the work of a young man whose taste is not yet impeccable nor his mastery of his medium secure. The poems are not, of course, dated; but some of them were written when he was in college, and almost ten years later he did not exclude them from his first collection. Many *were* excluded from his miscalled *Collected Poems*, which appeared in 1938, and today it comes as a shock to find that Cummings used to write lines like "Lover, lead forth thy love unto that bed" (p. 6), or "Eater of all things lovely—Time!" (p. 20), or ". . . right wildly beat / her heart at every kiss of daisy-cup" (p. 8). It is typical of the unevenness of *Tulips and Chimneys* that on the same page with the sophomoric "her heart breaks in a smile—and she is Lust. . . ." appears the fresh and well-stated image, "whose least amazing smile is the most great / common divisor of unequal souls" (p. 60).

The language of *Tulips and Chimneys*, then, like the imagery, the verse forms, the subject matter, and the thought, is sometimes good, sometimes bad. But the book is so obviously the work of a talented young man who is striking off in new directions, groping for original and yet precise expression, experimenting in public, that it seems uncharitable to dwell too long on its shortcomings. Edmund Wilson, who, although a year younger than Cummings, seemingly never was immature as a critic, wrote, shortly after *Tulips and Chimneys* came out, ". . . a master is precisely, as yet, what Mr. Cummings is not. . . . A poet with a real gift for language . . . he strikes often on ethereal measures of a singular purity and charm . . . but he never seems to know when he is writing badly and when he is writing well. . . . his emotions are familiar and simple. They occasionally even verge on the banal." But Mr. Wilson concluded: "for the fact that, though not yet fully grown, he is a genuine lyric poet at a time when there is a great deal of writing of verse and very little poetic feeling—Mr. Cummings deserves well of the public."[11]

Mr. Wilson was not speaking of Cummings' language as distinct from the other elements of his poetry, but what he had to say applies to Cummings' linguistic usages in *Tulips and Chimneys* and in the two books which soon followed it, *AND* and *Xli Poems*. These books were published within three years and are fairly much alike (although the typographical distortions that reach extremes in *AND* were barely hinted at in the first book); in style and in subject matter the three books are the work of the same youthful poet. Although his control over his material is firmer in *Xli Poems* than in *Tulips and Chimneys*, and although his mature style begins to be suggested, *Xli Poems* still contains such lines as "i will wade out / till my thighs are steeped in burning flowers" (p. 139) and such conventionally "poetic" thoughts as "my soul slowly which on thy beauty dreamest" (p. 152) and "Time shall surely reap, / and on Death's blade lie many a flower curled" (p. 154).[12]

All three books, however, are indelibly the work of Cummings; in one of the first poems in *Tulips and Chimneys*, for instance, appears this double-barreled hint of his later style and of one of the first principles which are to underlie all his work:

> each is a verb, miraculous
> inflected oral devious,
> beneath the body's breathing noun
>
> (from "Puella Mea": 19)

When Cummings refers to something as a "verb," he means that it is alive, vital; this is the highest compliment he can pay, just as he indicates the quintessence of individuality in a person by calling that person an "is."

Although, as Mr. Blackmur points out, the early books are punctuated with favorite words (*thrilling, flowers, utter, skillful, groping, crisp, keen, actual, stars,* etc.)[13] almost as copiously as another author would use commas, an awareness of these words is not unrewarding if one wishes to understand Cummings. The words *flower* and *stars*, are, as he uses them, not mere substantives representing a thing in nature but are metaphorical shorthand for concepts which Cummings finds admirable: the flowers, for example, representing growth, being, aliveness; the stars standing for the steadfastness of beauty in nature.

Such adjectives as he continually uses (Mr. Blackmur lists a great many), though they are admittedly overworked in the early books to the point of tiresomeness, are nevertheless indicative of his viewpoint: he admires phenomena that can be described as crisp, keen, actual, gay, young, strong, or strenuous, and dislikes the groping, the dim, the slow, the dull. In reading the early poetry, it is often necessary to know which of Cummings' words are, in Hayakawa's terms, "purr words" and which are "snarl words" in order to get any meaning from the poem. As Cummings progressed, he outgrew his penchant for such expressions as "thy whitest feet crisply are straying" (p. 11) and grew into his mature style, which is something infinitely more precise, often more concrete, and which relies more on such straightforward words as nouns and verbs than on piled-up adjectives for its effects.

To refer, however, to Cummings' words as nouns and verbs is to make things sound much simpler than they are, for the one outstanding characteristic of his mature style is his disrespect for the parts of speech. It would be more accurate instead to say that he *uses* words as nouns, for instance, which are not normally so; it would be hard to find any one of his later poems which does not utilize a word in a sense other than its usual one. *Yes* is used as a noun to represent all that is positive and therefore admirable, *if* to stand for all that is hesitating, uncertain, incomplete. The style thus becomes spare; the later books contain many poems written in extremely short lines, lines which, utilizing the simplest words, say a great deal. For instance, these two fragments from *I x I*:

> yes is a pleasant country:
> if's wintry
> (my lovely)
> let's open the year
>
> (from XXXVIII: 412)
>
> *   *   *   *   *
>
> who younger than
> begin

> are,the worlds move
> in your
> (and rest,my love)
> honour

(from XXXV: 410)

It is possible, of course, to argue that in the above stanzas *yes*, *if*, and *begin* do not convey precise meanings, that, since they are not used within their historical framework, no one but the poet can possibly know exactly what he meant to convey. This is an objection that, if it is accepted, is unanswerable; and the person who reads with such an assumption by his side will never make any sense out of Cummings's poems. But again, by accepting the fact that the poet may be saying something worthwhile and may be seriously trying to convey both truth and beauty as he sees it, one will try to look through the poet's eyes. To understand Cummings fully, more so than in understanding most other poets, it is necessary for one to have read much of Cummings. To a reader familiar with his techniques such a statement as "yes is a pleasant country" is as penetrable as a deep, clear pool; it might, however, seem more opaque to one reading him for the first time. Such words as *yes* and *if* take on a historical meaning within the body of his poetry, a meaning not divorced from their traditional ones but infinitely larger: *yes*, for instance, conventionally is used in a particular situation; as Cummings uses it, *yes* represents the sum of all the situations in which it might be used. And such a technique as "who younger than / begin / are" is not too complicated to be used by some practitioners of the art of writing for mass consumption, as witness the first line of a very popular song from *South Pacific*: "Younger than springtime, you are."

One of Cummings' most universally liked poems, "my father moved through dooms of love" (*50 Poems*, 34: 373), is extremely dense linguistically as a result of its suffusion with such words as *sames*, *am*, *haves*, *give*, *where*, *here*, *which*, *who*, *why*, *begin*, *pure*, *now*, *beyond*, *must*, and *shall* used as nouns. Again, it is helpful, if not necessary, to know the basic assumptions of Cummings, to know what he likes and what he dislikes, in order to interpret these reincarnated words. The following couplet will serve as an example:

> and should some why completely weep
> my father's fingers brought her sleep:

(p. 374)

A word such as *why* in an otherwise simple, straightforward passage such as this calls attention to itself at once; it causes a linguistic shock. Its startling effect is not due merely to the fact that it is used as a noun, since *why* does sometimes function in this fashion, in such expressions as "get to the *why* (bottom) of the situation," or "there is a terrible *why* (enigma) involved in this." However, it is immediately obvious that such normal substantive meanings of the word are not called into play in Cummings' couplet, and the reader must use his own resourcefulness in exploring the possibilities of new meaning.

In these two particular lines *why* actually presents no difficulty, for it is placed in the context of a concrete dramatic situation that is perfectly understandable: the *her* in the second line indicates that *why* is the substantive antecedent of the pronoun and that it can therefore be assumed to represent some feminine noun of a general character, such as *girl* or woman. If, however, *girl* or *woman* should be substituted for *why*, the startling quality of the first line would surely be lost, as would much of Cummings' meaning, which is ascertainable as much from the nature of the word *why* itself as from its use in context. In normal interrogative usage *why* presupposes an unanswered question and a mind searching for answers. If these conditions are fitted into the dramatic situation that is portrayed in the couplet—a girl weeping and given peace through sleep—the elements fit together: she is mentally puzzled, unable to answer the questions in her mind, miserable because she is mixed up. So that without further extensions the passage conveys an exact meaning, if not all that Cummings intended.

Just as do *yes, if,* and *begin* in the passages quoted above, *why* takes on an aura of meaning within the body of his poetry, a meaning that it is impossible to illustrate from this single example. Babette Deutsch has described Cummings' use of these words as follows:

> His later poems make words as abstract as "am," "if," "because," do duty for seemingly more solid nouns. By this very process, however, he restores life to dying concepts. "Am" implies being at its most responsive, "if" generally means the creeping timidity that kills responsiveness, and "because" the logic of the categorizing mind that destroys what it dissects. Here is a new vocabulary, a kind of imageless metaphor.[14]

Why, Miss Deutsch might further have explained, generally means to Cummings a state of uncertainty, a searching for direction from sources outside oneself, an unspontaneous demanding of reasons and causes in the face of life. A person who is a *why* is generally a subject for ridicule, being, like an *if*, a timid creature who thinks, fears, denies, follows, unlike an all-alive *is*. However, in the couplet above the measure of Cummings' father's compassion and stature is that he sees this particular *why* as a pitiful creature, to whom he brings solace through love.

Right though she is in assigning meanings to Cummings' am's, if's, and *because's*, Miss Deutsch does not get to the root of the technique used in these words when she describes them as examples of "imageless metaphor." Metaphor has as its base the use of comparison and analogy, of the verisimilitude within dissimilitude that exists between two images, actions, or concepts. Actually, a closer insight into the real nature of these words is found in Mr. Blackmur's study, though, in contrast to Miss

Deutsch's commitment to the technique, his definition of the process comes within a general attack on Cummings' language. He says at the end of his essay that all of Cummings' "thought" (the quotes are Mr. Blackmur's) is metonymy, and that the substance of the metonymy is never assigned to anything. "In the end," he concludes, "we have only the thrill of substance."[15] Metonymy is based on reduction rather than comparison: an object associated with a thing is substituted for the thing itself (as *crown* for *king*), or a corporeal object is used to represent an abstract concept or idea (as *heavy thumb* for *dishonesty*). When Mr. Blackmur says that Cummings' metonymy contains only the "thrill of substance," he means that in the case of such a word as *flower*, one of Cummings' favorite metonymical vehicles, the substance—flower—is there but the idea of which it is a reduction is neither present nor ascertainable. If the reader receives a "thrill" from such a word as *flower*, well and good; but Mr. Blackmur asserts that a thrill is all he will receive.

It must be remembered that Mr. Blackmur's essay was written after only the earliest of Cummings' books had appeared; none of them exemplify his mature style—in those days *flower* and *star* were about as far as he had gone in the direction of metonymy. In his use of *why*, however, he has extended not only the uses to which a particular word can be put but also the accepted limits of metonymy: he has taken an abstract word and made it stand for a host of ideas, the negative characteristics mentioned above. Mr. Blackmur's "thrill of substance" is therefore not applicable to Cummings' present use of metonymy, for such words as *why* do not represent a substance and certainly, if they are isolated, convey no thrill. That it is possible for *why* to induce a thrill is seen in the lines quoted above, but the thrill comes not from the "substance" of *why* but from the uniqueness of its use; perhaps also there is a thrill of comprehension which comes when the implication of the metonymy strikes the reader.

Again, if one accepts Mr. Blackmur's argument it is unanswerable; he would say that to derive an implication from a metonymical concept is not enough, that the idea or object which the "substance" represents must be precisely known. However, there must perhaps have been a day when *heavy thumb* was not a universally accepted reduction for dishonesty; the person who created this particular metonymy must have been doing a rather original thing, and his created expression must have had to go through a process of recognition into acceptance before it came to be unquestioned. That Cummings' metonymical usages are unlikely to go through this particular process is immaterial; such metonymies as *why* and *yes* are a little too subtle, too closely based on a poet's private convictions, to find a place in ordinary language. It should not be concluded, however, that their meaning cannot be understood—that their substance cannot be assigned—just as readily as was the meaning of *heavy thumb* by a person who was willing to apply to the metonymy the knowledge that he possessed about butchers, green-grocers, and bakers.

To understand a Cummings metonymy, one can bring his plain common sense to bear first, and, in the case of such expressions as "who younger than / begin / are" or "and should some why completely weep," common sense is often enough to establish a correct meaning. But the reader who can apply to the metonymy not only his judgment but his experience with Cummings will have an advantage in that he will have in his mind an accumulation of meanings for such a word as *why* and will therefore be able to identify a complete, rounded concept whenever he comes upon the "substance." *Why*, as the couplet above illustrates, is a reduction for the puzzled, questioning state of mind. In another context, one much more indefinite than that of the couplet, another meaning is suggested:

> doubting can turn men's see to stare
> their faith to how their joy to why
>
> (from *I x I*, XL: 413)

Without knowing the complete metonymical function of *why*, the reader of this passage can come to a common-sense understanding of its meaning—here *why* refers to the joylessness that comes from lack of faith—even though the lines contain three other reductions: *see*, *stare*, and *how*. And when the reader has penetrated the following use of *why*, which is much the most difficult of the three examples, he is well on his way to recreating the larger body of meaning of which *why* is a reductive part:

> proudly depths above why's first because
> (faith's last doubt and humbly heights below)
> kneeling,we—true lovers—pray that us
> will ourselves continue to outgrow
>
> all whose mosts if you have known and i've
> only we our least begin to guess
>
> (from *I x I*, XXXIV: 409)

Here in a passage saturated with metonymical words and paradoxical combinations Cummings' meaning is clear enough: proudly true lovers will continue to grow to a far greater extent than all those who are limited by their timidity and unresponsiveness, who do not continuously transcend themselves as lovers mysteriously do; lovers are beyond the restrictions of niggling reason, which is represented in these lines by the words *why* and *because*. Hence, from the three fragments which have been studied, *why* takes on its full metonymical meaning: in the first quotation it is associated with the troubled mind, in the second with the mind that lacks faith, in the third with the reasoning, unintuitive mind.

In short, his technique in creating new uses for such words as *if, why, because, which, how, must, same, have,* and *they* on the one hand and *now, am, yes, is, we, give,* and *here* on the other is to accumulate meanings for each of them that total up to the same kind of positive and negative oppositions that are set against each other throughout his work: tulips and chimneys, as he put it in the title of his first book of poems; beauty and ugliness; love and hate; the one and the many. As in the three examples cited for *why,* he makes each of these words self-subsistent in terms of the context in which they appear, and, by varying the meanings in each usage, makes the words metonymical reductions for a whole set of concepts. In a way he is creating an easy cipher of meaning, penetrable but not completely so at first sight. And is this not also the case of any author who utilizes a few dominant symbols in order to express his special insight into experience, who must make each use of a symbol function in its context and yet adds to its meaning with each repeated use? (Hawthorne's repeated use of light and shadow in his works might be cited as an example of this method.) The success of a metonymous or symbolic system of this sort depends partly upon the degree to which the poet objectifies and clarifies his conception of the world, partly upon the effects of freshness and vitality his language produces; when one comes across such lines as the following there can be no doubt that Cummings is successful in both respects:

> she laughed his joy she cried his grief
> bird by snow and stir by still
> anyone's any was all to her
>
> (from *50 Poems,* 29: 370)

Using a traditional rhetorical pattern in the second line (*little by little* serves as a model for it), he superimposes a metonymous structure: *bird* and *snow* are reductions of summer and winter; *stir* and *still,* of all manner of activities. The net result of such a line is a new and delightful sense of linguistic invention, precise and vigorous.

To say that Cummings is successful in objectifying his conception of the world and in achieving a freshness and vitality of language is not to diminish the difficulty of many of his poems. Nor is it meant to say that his metonymical usages are not over-worked, just as were his favorite adjectives in *Tulips and Chimneys.* What was originally a fresh idea, and what still has great power if used with discrimination—his utilizing abstract words to be the "substance" of a metonymy—can become boring, tiresome, and even meaningless if called upon constantly to carry the whole weight of a poem. Just as the word *flower,* which obviously was a symbol for something, when used in every poem became a mere word, to be accepted and passed over, so a constant succession of *which's* and *who's* and *why's* and *they's* begins to roll off the tongue too quickly for the mind to make the transference from the "substance" to the idea for which it stands; and the force of the metonymy is lost. A poem written almost exclusively in these words loses, too, its beauty and grace; one-syllable abstract words are not particularly melodious, and a poem in which they are not frequently interspersed with words which are more interesting in themselves, or more concrete, is likely to plod along (like Pope's "And ten low words oft creep in one dull line"), one metonymy after another, never skipping or dancing or singing.

However, at the same time that Cummings developed the metonymy to its ultimate use he was growing in another direction: many of his poems became much more, not less, musical than his earlier ones. In the earlier books he had placed his dependence upon the sonnet form, often upon a grand manner, and sometimes upon free verse; but he very seldom wrote a poem which cried out to be sung, which could be read only with a joyous, pronounced rhythm. Such poems as these occur frequently in the last three books. Cummings has given up being grand and derivative and become simple and himself. If he utilizes old verse forms, they are more likely to be of the nursery rhyme than of the Spenserian stanza. His lines, as has been mentioned, are often short; his meter is usually iambic; his words—when they are not metonymies—are colloquial. As a result, one can read these poems with a sense of the child's pure delight in poetry; Cummings himself has become more maturely childish as he has grown.

The rhythmical poems do utilize the typical abstract word metonymies—it is a rare poem in his later books which does not; even his satires make use of them to some extent—but the metonymies are likely to be placed in the context of concrete words and lively happenings. Such a poem as the following, from *I x I*, in which the metonymies are made to stand alone with only a little help from such semi-abstract words as *hell*, *paradise*, *eternal*, and *distinct*, becomes the exception rather than the rule:

> as any(men's hells having wrestled with)
> man drops into his own paradise
> thankfully
>   whole and the green whereless truth
> of an eternal now welcomes each was
> of whom among not numerable ams
>
> (leaving a perfectly distinct unhe;
> a ticking phantom by prodigious time's
> mere brain contrived:a spook of stop and go)
> may i achieve another steepest thing—
>
> how more than sleep illimitably my
> —being so very born no bird can sing
> as easily creation up all sky

(really unreal world,will you perhaps do
the breathing for me while i am away?)

(XVIII: 399)[16]

In contrast to such an unfocused plethora of metonymies (it is interesting to note that this poem falls back on some of the old favorite modifiers: *eternal, perfectly, distinct, steepest, illimitably*, and loses force because of them) is the next poem but one in the same volume. Here is the new joyous rhythmical manner in a poem in which metonymies are contrasted to such concrete *things* as wind, leaves, sun, hills, sleet, snow, and to such forceful verbs as *bloodies, yanks, blow, hanged, drowned, flays, strangles*, and *stifles*. The final stanza of this poem has already been quoted in the introduction to this article; for purposes of specific illustration of the techniques that have just been studied, it is well to note the first two stanzas also:

what if a much of a which of a wind
gives the truth to summer's lie;
bloodies with dizzying leaves the sun
and yanks immortal stars awry?
Blow king to beggar and queen to seem
(blow friend to fiend:blow space to time)
—when skies are hanged and oceans drowned,
the single secret will still be man

what if a keen of a lean wind flays
screaming hills with sleet and snow:
strangles valleys by ropes of thing
and stifles forests in white ago?
Blow hope to terror;blow seeing to blind
(blow pity to envy and soul to mind)
—whose hearts are mountains,roots are trees,
it's they shall cry hello to the spring

(XX: 401)[17]

In the third stanza of this poem Cummings becomes personal; he speaks of "me and you," and the last couplet is triumphantly affirmative of the power of two people—two lovers—to live despite whatever may happen to "this universe":

—all nothing's only our hugest home;
the most who die,the more we live

This progression from the external to the personal, from the outer world of "mostpeople" to the inner world of "us," finds its expression, sometimes quietly, sometimes with childish innocence, sometimes with a dauntless courage, in poem after poem in the volume *I x I*. Cummings concludes the book with

we're anything brighter than even the sun
(we're everything greater

than books
might mean)
we're everyanything more than believe
(with a spin
leap
alive we're alive)
we're wonderful one times one

(from LIV: 423)

And, as he begins one of the most beautiful of his sonnets: "one's not half two. It's two are halves of one:" (XVI: 398). This whole conception of i-you-we (or my-your-our) becomes one of Cummings' most frequently used metonymies. Its impact, to anyone who knows that "two are halves of one," is immediate. When Cummings starts out a poem:

o by the by
has anybody seen
little you-i
who stood on a green
hill and threw
his wish at blue

(from LIII :422)

and then continues:

blue took it my
far beyond far
and high beyond high
bluer took it your
but bluest took it our
away beyond where

the reader does not have to be told why "our" should be "bluest." In the i-you-we metonymy the whole is greater than the sum of its parts, and the metonymy itself becomes a prime example of Cummings' ability to use the simplest words as a shorthand for concepts which represent his own convictions. It is fitting that his most musical poems should be the ones, like those from which the last three quotations were taken, in celebration of i-you-we; for to Cummings love is still the most joyous of all things. Mature love to him becomes not more sober and settled but more intensely lyrical, less tortured, more a thing for singing and dancing and child-like delight. *We* takes its place along with *yes* and *now* and *is* as the metonymies for all that is best in this "really unreal world."

NOTES

1. *i: six nonlectures* (Cambridge: Harvard Univ. Press, 1953), p. 3.

2. F. J. Hoffman et al., *The Little Magazine* (Princeton: Princeton Univ. Press, 1946), p. 116.

3. *i: six nonlectures*, p. 30.

4. *i: six nonlectures*, p. 47.

5. One writer, James G. Southworth, in 1950 included a chapter on Cummings in his *Some Modern American Poets* (Oxford: Oxford Univ. Press, 1950), and despite the fact that he then had before him (or should have had) all of Cummings' books of poetry except the most recent, *Xaîpe*, he persisted in describing what he did in *Tulips and Chimneys*. He paid some lip service to the later books, but justified his peculiar emphasis on a poet's first efforts by saying that ". . . as is now generally recognized by most of his readers, no important changes have occurred in his methods since his early work" (p. 141).

6. Reprinted in *Language as Gesture* (New York: Harcourt Brace Jovanovich, 1952), pp. 317–340.

7. References to Cummings' poems will give the original volume in which they appeared and their number in that volume, then, following the colon, the page on which the poem is to be found in the new collection of Cummings' *Poems 1923–1954* (New York: Harcourt, Brace, 1954).

8. "Notes on E.E. Cummings' Language," in *Language as Gesture*, p. 317.

9. "Notes on E.E. Cummings' Language," p. 326.

10. From *Poems 1923–1954* (New York: Harcourt, Brace, 1954), p. 39. Copyright, 1923, 1951, by E.E. Cummings.

11. "Wallace Stevens and E.E. Cummings," in *The Shores of Light* (New York: Farrar, Straus and Young, 1952), pp. 50–53.

12. It is interesting to note that there is almost no satire in the original *Tulips and Chimneys*, and what there is seems strangely mild. In *&* appears the first of his sharply barbed poems, "here is little Effie's head / whose brains are made of gingerbread" (p. 95), and in *XLI Poems*, "Humanity i love you" (p. 151).

13. "Notes on E.E. Cummings' Language," p. 321.

14. *Poetry in Our Time* (New York: Henry Holt, 1952), p. 113.

15. "Notes on E.E. Cummings' Language," p. 340.

16. From *Poems 1923–1954* (New York: Harcourt, Brace, 1954), p. 399. Copyright, 1944, by E.E. Cummings.

17. From *Poems 1923–1954* (New York: Harcourt, Brace, 1954), p. 401. Copyright 1944, by E.E. Cummings. The final stanza of this poem is quoted earlier in the essay.

Timeless Prose

Kingsley Widmer*

There would appear to be a minor but significant prose literary tradition which is, apparently, peculiarly American. A brief examination of one twentieth century example of this type, E. E. Cummings' *The*

*Reprinted from *Twentieth Century Literature*, 4 (1958), 3–8. Reprinted by permission of *Twentieth Century Literature*.

Enormous Room, may suggest a crucial problem of modern prose form. The type, if a rather amorphous body of work of considerable dissimilarity can be so identified, might be defined by several predominant characteristics: a conscious violation and avoidance of traditional prose forms; the attempt to turn narrative prose into lyric poetry without the traditional formal order of poetry; the mixture of aesthetic functions—documentary, autobiographical, fictional and poetic; and the experimentation with logical, causal and temporal relationships in the effort to achieve different kinds of aesthetic experience. The last and, as I shall try to indicate, the most crucial point, may be put more simply: prose which attempts to get outside the limits of time.

Parts, at least, of James Agee's *Let Us Now Praise Famous Men*, of the "stories" of Anais Nin, of the "biographies" and "essays" of Henry Miller, of the fantasies of Kenneth Patchen, of the "novels" of Thomas Wolfe, and, in general, of long works usually identified as "poetic-prose," such as Djuna Barnes' *Nightwood*, belong to a tradition of imaginative prose which probably needs to be distinguished from the more usual forms of the novel.[1] It is possible that these works partly replace, in function at least, various more explicit Continental traditions of meditation, journal and prose-poem—forms which are mostly absent in serious American literature. There are, of course, pre-twentieth century American prototypes, not only Whitman—the most evident influence on many of these writers—but also Thoreau and Melville in their formal eccentricities. And, not least, works of the type discussed here show in more extreme form, and at a greater remove from most academic "great traditions," the insistent and pervasive principles of style, order and meaning.

We must, then, at least momentarily put aside some of our usual expectations for prose narrative when examining these works. But to do this requires some other principle of expectation—not simply a responsive sensibility. Much of expectation depends on temporal order. When we read a work like E. E. Cummings' *The Enormous Room*, a highly stylized and subjectivized account of a few months in a French prison in World War I, the temporal order is hard to find. Like Cummings' later record of a few weeks in the prison-atmosphere of Soviet Russia in the 1930s, *Eimi* (I am I; individualist Cummings' manner of emphasizing his total lack of illusion about collectivism's denial of the self), *The Enormous Room* may first appear to have no other aim than the poeticization of a sensitive and idiosyncratic individual's miscellaneous experiences and ruminations.

However, the technique of *The Enormous Room*, with its elaborately personal metaphoric style, is actually far removed from the poetic order of the lyric poem because of the book's endless flow and elaboration, in contrast to the lyric's economy and condensation. Cummings calls *The Enormous Room* a novel.[2] The occasional critical comments on the book usually identify it as a "poetic form." But the modern poetic organization of experience, as we know it in the lyric poem (and the lyric is the basis of most of Cummings' techniques here), takes temporal limitation as the means for extending in depth the meaning of discrete and relatively isolated moments—units of knowledge without a relevant before and after, so that the poem is a self-sufficient experience. This is also characteristic of the twentieth century long poem, such as "The Wasteland," "The Bridge" and *The Cantos.* Cummings, the experimentalist, attempts to turn an individualized and non-mythic narrative into what is essentially a lyric poem. To do so, he has had to remove the before-and-after and cause-and-effect of time from a series of connected episodes in order to make them all "timelessly" equal.

We might briefly examine the difficulty by asking what Cummings does to three conventional aspects of time: chronological time (usually indicated by the clock, calendar and historical progression of public events), rhetorical time (verbal order, which is usually the grammar of before-and-after and the logic of cause-and-effect) and novelistic time (plot and pattern).[3]

Chronological time. The Enormous Room is an account of what happened to the author "between the later part of August, 1917, and the first day of January 1918."[4] Such is the *hidden* narrative framework, and a few additional details are given (as in a comic interview with an official), but most of the remaining account is outside the calendar and the clock in the subjective flow of response and its hyperbole. True, winter comes ("early") and Christmas is celebrated in the enormous room of the prison, but the dominant units of time become impressions of objects and actions—usually in surrealistic disjunction—such as emptying the urinals, trips to the courtyard or the frigid *douché*, unexpected visual arrangements and the recurrence of sounds and smells. The lack of an external frame of time is appropriate to the prison experience where outside events were not known, and could not anyway have much meaning to the prison's capricious order and the gratuitous entrapment of its inmates. But the lack of chronological time is not compensated for by a remembered past or a planned future, and the events tend to be an arbitrary flow without source, center point or purpose (to rephrase Aristotle). Perspective is absent. And while this may sometimes be true of actual experience, it may not be adequate to give experience coherence in art.

The "timeless" substitute for chronology is the unit of heightened sensation. As in most of Cummings' work, the style is dominated by visual fragments. Pom-Pom's throwing away a cigarette butt, the Zulu's slowly spreading smile, the Wanderer's gestures—the characters and their names are themselves the creation of subjective response to visual fragments and their exotic associations—form the chronology in most of the narrative, and provide its irregular recurrences and periodicities. The time, thus, is whimsically dependent on whether or not the narrator is awake, aware and responding, and not on the object. In this solipsistic scheme, how often the Zulu smiles (and thereby whether he is really happy or not) or how much Pom-Pom smokes (and thereby is satisfied or not), is totally unknowable. Thus all objects tend to lose their own independent reality. Because these things only exist as responses, and only in the whimsical terms of one peculiar point of view, the knowledge of the place and its people—the declared purpose of the book—paradoxically disappears.

Rhetorical time. The only experience, then, which exists with any certainty is the language and its evocations. Without an outer order of reality, time is a purely verbal scheme. Thus the style is characterized by verbal approximations of time ("splutter-fizz-pop");[5] verbal substitutions for unknown and unknowable time (a missing day exists as "a glass of *pinard* (plus or rather times the astonishing exhaustion bequeathed me by my journey)";[6] or; and most often, paradoxical descriptions in which all logical time is annihilated ("a train *rushed lazily* across the earth").[7] Also, the isolation of a detail—focusing one moment on a nose, another moment on a shoe, then on a sneeze, then on a urinal—from its context, and hence from any continuity, makes any progression arbitrary or fortuitous.

That this stylistic destruction of time is basic to the view of the author and is a self-conscious part of the book's principle, is revealed about one-third of the way through the narrative. The prison is summarized as "a vast grey box in which are laid helter-skelter a great many toys, *each of which is itself completely significant apart from the always unchanging temporal dimension.*"[8] To turn the dreary actualities of the prison into things of pure joy, they must be put in the time dimension of eternity and separated from all normal continuities and values—"individualities distinct from time itself."[9] Each event therefore becomes uniquely significant, but loses causality ("events no longer succeed each other"[10]), loses potentiality for change (which comes from "the minutes, months and the other treasures of freedom"[11]), and, indeed, loses actuality (each becomes "an amputation of the world.") Thus the only context for anything is its aesthetic presentation. This artifice-of-eternity, which also appears in Proust, Joyce, and even in Faulkner, is the glorification of the aesthetic experience and the denial of all temporally bounded meanings. Indisputably, such artifice creates style, but something else is lost along with the coherence of mortal time.

The aesthetic egoism of this procedure, of course, is an unabashed theme throughout Cummings' poetry on the assumption that eternity is purely immanent and is contained in the heightened personal "now." And it becomes the one criterion for all values. When, in one of Cummings' most serious poems, a thief-of-life is caught, "someone called they / made him pay with his now."[12] The reverse point is made in the satiric poems: "progress is a comfortable disease."[13] While the style is perhaps most effective in the satiric work, the obverse exaltation of timelessness is most important to Cummings. Time is the enemy of those who live in the eternal realms of "dooms of love."[14] The cure for all is the destruction of time—most simply represented by rhetorical and syntactical violence—so to "blow soon to never, and never to twice."[15] Thus one achieves the faith of "the centuries of original soon,"[16] and arrives in the paradisical "Ever-Ever land."[17] Creating one's own rhetorical, and ultimately mythic, time,[18] after having destroyed chronological and logical time, is the apotheosis of the word-manipulator, the artist.

Novelistic time. The fragmentation of chronological time and the subjective eternalizing of rhetorical time, however, cannot give coherence to a prose narrative. The middle sags and the ending flattens out since the account is neither going anywhere nor has any point to arrive at. At best the pyrotechnics of style can only partly obscure the disorder. But we should also note that Cummings, perhaps a more effective writer than his egoistic time aesthetic would logically allow, actually does impose, intermittently, a time-pattern on the material. Not only do the metaphors repeat themselves (contrary to his doctrine of uniqueness) but they are also partly arranged in one of the most traditional of patterns: a secularized Christian narrative symbolism. Thus the chapter titles: "I Begin a Pilgrimage," "A Pilgrim's Progress," "Apollyon," "An Approach to the Delectable Mountains" and "Three Wise Men" (among others). While the use of Bunyan and the pilgrimage is only partial, and probably would not justify the ingenuity of systematic exposition, it does give elements of order at several levels to the poetic narrative. The pilgrimage is a temporal scheme for the progression *towards* viewing all *sub specie aeternitas*. It also suggests an emphatic scheme of values linking together the otherwise wilful subjective responses: charity, pacifism, defiance of secular authority, brotherly love and personal revelation. The pilgrimage rhythm is a *temporal* order for the attainment of these values and a deepening of felt awareness. In good part because of this pattern, *The Enormous Room* is not simply an aesthetic exercise in whimsical subjectivism, though severely marred by a manipulative exuberance.

This, or any other partial temporal order, however, does not appear in Cummings' later "timeless" narrative, *Eimi*. There the assertion of the ego ("I-I-I-I") and its being ("isness") in timelessness ("the eternal now") becomes a treadmill to tedium. By a wilful use of "poetic" devices, narrative prose can lose both its claim to immediacy and to the coherent fullness of experience. For there is a separate yet never wholly independent world in time which gives art its significance and purpose. The effort of Cummings' art to deny time is most simply evident in the frequent collapse of the tone into sentimentality and arbitrary whimsicality.[19] The awareness of an external order of time in art provides the corresponding senses of anguish, tragedy, purpose and mortal limit which deepen the significance of the human artifice.

It might be suggested, then, that the experimental prose forms—and the contemporary use of the more traditional novelistic forms, as well, since many of them have been moving in the direction of artistic wilfulness and the stasis of elaborate poetic language—have a drastic limitation despite their internal richness and sensitivity. The aesthetic is not sufficient; there must be a temporal pattern from outside the artwork (and the artist). Obviously, it does not have to be the mechanical clock-time of scientific rationalization nor the allegorical progress towards eternity of Christian symbolism. But in the extended artwork, as in the extension of human life, there is the inextricable significance of the unfolding of mortal time.

NOTES

1. The only one of these works whose time method appears to have been analyzed at length is *Nightwood*. See Joseph Frank, "Spatial Form in the Modern Novel," *Critiques and Essays on Modern Fiction*, ed. John W. Aldridge (New York: Ronald Press, 1951), pp. 43–66. Why "breaking up temporal sequence," a main principle in these works, should be a "spatial" concept is not quite clear in Frank's treatment. The metaphor, probably taken from modern physical theory, is not particularly relevant to literature, and so is ignored here.

2. "Introduction," *The Enormous Room* (New York: Modern Library, 1934), p. vii. However, the introduction was written in 1932 (the same year as *Eimi*), ten years after the first book was originally published, and so is not necessarily a statement of original intention.

3. The categories are my own since the more technical philosophical terms are not generally familiar. See, for the latter, Hans Meyerhoff, *Time in Literature* (Berkeley: University of California Press, 1955), p. 85, where the "six aspects of time characteristic of literature" are summarized. Meyerhoff is primarily concerned with philosophical properties rather than literary forms. While his work has a number of valuable points about time in modern literature, particularly pp. 11–84, the discussion in this essay is pointedly directed against one of his main contentions. He holds that the creation of various autonomous temporal orders in literature is coherent because "referred to or seen within the perspective of the *same self*," p. 37. My contention, developed below, is that the identity of the "self" (whether author, narrator or the persona of a character) is adequate to create style but not what Meyerhoff calls "significance." Coherent meaning requires a time scheme from outside the art work.

4. *The Enormous Room*, p. 313. The crucial chronological information has been withheld until the end of the book.

5. *The Enormous Room*, p. 29.

6. *The Enormous Room*, p. 97 (Sic.).

7. *The Enormous Room*, p. 49 (My italics.).

8. *The Enormous Room*, p. 113 (My italics.).

9. *The Enormous Room*, pp. 113.

10. *The Enormous Room*, p. 114.

11. *The Enormous Room*, p. 115.

12. *1 x 1* (New York: Henry Holt, 1944), p. III.

13. *1 x 1*, p. XIV.

14. *Collected Poems* (New York: Harcourt, Brace, 1938), poem 298.

15. *1 x 1*, p. XX.

16. *Collected Poems*, poem 167.

17. *Collected Poems*, poem 297.

18. Or as Cummings would have it, "*The actual or kinetic aspect of our otherwise merely real non-existence.*" *The Enormous Room*, p. 176 (his italics). One could find a pos-

sible philosophic source for this, and similar poetic-metaphysical statements of time in Cummings: see Henri Bergson, *Time and Free Will* (London: Allen and Unwin, 1910), pp. 222–31. But, more importantly, there is an indebtedness in both attitude and technique to the poetry of Guillaume Apollinaire and some of his contemporaries. The revolt against the personal meaninglessness of both mechanical and traditional modes of time, and the effort to create the autonomous aesthetic time of simultaneity and association, has been pervasive in twentieth century literature. Most of these temporal schemes are willed subjectivity rather than scientific time or the timeless idealism traditionally expressed in Zeno's paradox.

19. The formalist criticism of why Cummings' language is meant to be taken seriously, but frequently cannot be, was stated, and perhaps over-stated, by R. P. Blackmur. "Notes on E. E. Cummings' Language," *The Double Agent* (New York: Arrow Editions, 1935), pp. 1–29.

E.E. Cummings and the Modernist Movement

Norman Friedman*

E.E. Cummings occupies an anomalous position in modern poetry. On the one hand, he is often thought of, usually by those hostile to the modernist tradition, as an avant-gardist, an impossibly obscure poet, a leading figure in what Max Eastman once called the Cult of Unintelligibility. On the other hand, he is frequently regarded, usually by those committed to the modernist aesthetic, as a romantic, a perpetual adolescent, and a sentimentalist. Now, for a poet whose stance is that of a nonconformist, one whose policy it is to disregard fads, fashions, and reviewers, such an anomaly might not be particularly bad news. As he himself put it, in the author's dialogue with the reader which forms the Introduction to *The Enormous Room*:

> Ah-but (now that you mention it) [says his interlocutor] isn't love just a trifle oldfashioned?
> I dare say [replies the poet].
> And aren't you supposed to be ultramodernistic?
> I dare say.

But for those of us whose interest lies in trying to understand the varieties of contemporary poetry, it might be of some value to look into the causes of this anomaly and thereby to evaluate more justly Cummings' true place in our literature.

I think, to begin with, that there *are* adequate grounds in Cummings' poetry for such apparently contradictory opinions, because his work does contain both modernist and more romantic elements. He is not

*Reprinted from *Forum*, 3 (1962), 39–46. Reprinted by permission of *Forum*. The "Post Script" was written specifically for this volume and appears here by permission of the author.

modern, for example, in his lack of sophistication and ambivalence, in the simplicity and naturalness of his symbolism, in his directness of affirmative statement, and so on. On the other hand, he shares with poets like Yeats, Pound, Stevens, Eliot, and Auden, an opposition to scientific rationalism and the commercialistic vulgarity of modern middleclass life, an insistence upon the value of the irrational and intuitive, an interest in technical and stylistic experimentation, a single-minded devotion to the role of the artist and the function of poetry, and so on. But rather than fixing upon one element or the other as characteristic, and then evaluating his work on such a partial basis, I would prefer to attempt an explanation of what is characteristic in terms of the ways in which these two elements are related—and inter-related—in his poetry.

I

But first, let us consider in more detail the ways in which he diverges from the modernist tradition, and the reasons for this divergence. His subjects, for example, differ in content or in treatment, or both, from those of the moderns. Where he is likely to sing of the joys of spring, they are prone to discuss its sorrows; where he praises the insights of childhood, they analyze its conflicts; where he treats of landscapes and seasons in terms of an affirmative vision, they see them as symbols of man's alienation. They both share an interest in the waste land of modern life, but where he sees it as an object of satire, they treat it as a tragic dilemma. They both are concerned with twentieth-century man's loss of sexuality and creativity, but where he simply asserts the value of these things, they are caught in the coils of disgust and guilt. Cummings is one of the few poets today, for example, who writes straight-forward but serious love poetry. If he exalts the individual, they wonder how the Individual is to be reconciled with Society. Where they trace adult conflicts back to their parents, he writes poems of unashamed filial piety.

If we are realizing more and more that the poor Victorians were as much the poets of doubt as of faith, we have always known that the moderns have tried to make faith out of doubt—as Robert Penn Warren's Willie Stark tried to make good out of evil—because there isn't anything else to make it out of. There is no doubt in Cummings; his love hasn't a why or because or although: it exists for no reason, and for that reason it cannot be doubted. It is self-contained, self-sufficient, self-creating, and altogether apart from cause and effect. As he explains in his Introduction to George Herriman's *Krazy Kat*:

> This hero [Offissa Pup] and this villain [Ignatz Mouse] no more understand Krazy Kat than the mythical denizens of a twodimensional realm understand some threedimensional intruder. The world of Offissa Pup and Ignatz Mouse is a knowledgeable power-world, in terms of which our

unknowledgeable heroine is powerlessness personified. The sensical law of this world is *might makes right*; the nonsensical law of our heroine is *love conquers all*. To put the oak in the acorn: Ignatz Mouse and Offissa Pup (each completely convinced that his own particular brand of might makes right) are simple-minded—Krazy isn't—therefore, to Offissa Pup and Ignatz Mouse, Krazy is. But if both our hero and our villain don't and can't understand our heroine, each of them can and each of them does misunderstand her differently. To our softheaded altruist, she is the adorably helpless incarnation of saintliness. To our hardhearted egoist, she is the puzzlingly indestructible embodiment of idiocy. The benevolent overdog sees her as an inspired weakling. The malevolent undermouse views her as a born target. Meanwhile Krazy Kat, through this double misunderstanding, fulfills her joyous destiny.

Let's make no mistake about Krazy. A lot of people "love" because, and a lot of people "love" although, and a few individuals love. Love is something illimitable; and a lot of people spend their limited lives trying to prevent anything illimitable from happening to them. Krazy, however, is not a lot of people. Krazy is herself. Krazy is illimitable—she loves. She loves in the only way anyone can love: illimitably. She isn't morbid and she isn't longsuffering; she doesn't "love" someone because he hurts her and she doesn't "love" someone although he hurts her. She doesn't, moreover, "love" someone who hurts her. Quite the contrary: she loves someone who gives her unmitigated joy. How? By always trying his limited worst to make her unlove him, and always failing—not that our heroine is insensitive (for a more sensitive heroine never existed), but that our villain's every effort to limit her love with his unlove ends by a transforming of his limitation into her illimitability. If you're going to pity anyone, the last anyone to pity is our loving heroine, Krazy Kat. You might better pity that doggedly idolatrous imbecile, our hero; who policemanfully strives to protect his idol from catastrophic desecration at the paws of our iconoclastic villain—never suspecting that this very desecration becomes, through our transcending heroine, a consecration; and that this consecration reveals the ultimate meaning of existence. But the person to really pity (if really pity you must) is Ignatz. Poor villain! All his malevolence turns to beneficence at contact with Krazy's head. By profaning the temple of altruism, alias law and order, he worships (entirely against his will) at the shrine of love.

What are the reasons for these differences? The modernist views his complex techniques as attempts to capture in aesthetic form that which is otherwise inexpressible. Cummings' experiments may also be viewed as means to a similar end; only the end is conceived in a somewhat different way in each case, and hence is approached along a rather different route. The modernist's view of the world—and an obsession with the knowledgeable power-world occupies a large portion of that view—is complicated and his notion of ultimate truth is complex. For him, reality is a many-sided affair and it is poetry's job to capture that reality. As Eliot explained long ago in his essay on "The Metaphysical Poets":

We can only say that it appears likely that poets in our civilization, as it exists at present, must be *difficult*. Our civilization comprehends great variety and complexity, and this variety and complexity, playing upon a refined sensibility, must produce various and complex results. The poet must become more and more comprehensive, more allusive, more indirect, in order to force, to dislocate if necessary, language into his meaning.

And this is a job that no other mode of human apprehension and discourse—least of all, science—is fitted for. The modernist's view of poetry, therefore, is correspondingly subtle. He wants, on the one hand, to disengage poetry from the necessity of rational verification as well as from the pressures of personal and practical utility, and on the other hand, to endow it with a truth-value and a usefulness of its own. This he does by developing his notion of "another kind of truth" and reformulating the concept of utility. Truth, for the modernist, is not limited to mere matters of fact, but includes as well the ways in which values arise from and modify in turn these matters. This is the way Whitehead puts it:

> What is wanted is an appreciation of the infinite variety of vivid values achieved by an organism in its proper environment. When you understand all about the sun and all about the atmosphere and all about the rotation of the earth, you may still miss the radiance of the sunset. There is no substitute for the direct perception of the concrete achievement of a thing in its actuality. We want concrete fact with a high light thrown on what is relevant to its preciousness (*Science and the Modern World*, Ch. XIII).

Reality, then, is in this view no single thing, and no single approach will therefore ever grasp the whole of it. As Yeats wrote at the end of his life: "It seems to me that I have found what I wanted. When I try to put all into a phrase I say, 'Man can embody truth but he cannot know it.' " If it is the job of the poem to embody insights into this reality, then it cannot be confined to any single attitude. And a whole host of devices have been developed to capture this complexity. There is, to begin with, the modernist's obsession with the expressive powers of language and the ways in which these powers may be increased. Connotation, suggestion, irony, ambiguity—these are some of the terms used to examine and discuss such powers. There is, secondly, his similar concern with diction and rhythm, with tone and texture. There is, thirdly, his interest in figures of speech and symbols as ways of multiplying meanings and tapping more primitive levels of awareness. There is, fourthly, his suppression of connectives and transitions in order to preserve uncontaminated the essential poetry of a poem and to avoid the rational and the logical.

And there is, finally and most characteristically, his development of a new concept of the poetic speaker known as the Mask, in which every protagonist is conceived of as containing his opposite, even as having his own built-in-self-mocker. In this way is the poem disengaged from the private personality of the poet and objectified. The speaker in Yeats's "Sailing to Byzantium," for example, while turning his mind to immortal things, can at the same time see himself from the opposite perspective as "but a paltry thing, / A tattered coat upon a stick." Or Pound's Mauberley, while dedicating himself to art, can simultaneously say of himself:

> "I was
> And I no more exist;
> Here drifted
> An hedonist."

Or Eliot's Prufrock can lament, even as he toys with the idea of doing something heroic:

> And I have seen the eternal Footman hold my coat,
>   and snicker,
> And in short, I was afraid.

Or Auden's speaker, as he concludes a noble reflection about love as the cure for the evils coming to a head in "September 1, 1939," can say:

> May I, composed like them
> Of Eros and of dust,
> Beleaguered by the same
> Negation and despair,
> Show an affirming flame.

Or Roethke's speaker can say, as he mourns the death of a student he loved:

> Over this damp grave I speak the words of my love:
> I, with no rights in this matter,
> Neither father nor lover.

In each case there is this characteristic double-view, this undercutting, this deliberate acknowledgement of one's more foolish side, this insistence upon the un- or anti-heroic.

Complex reality: complex poem. Tension, conflict, reconciliation of opposites, ambivalence, metaphor, drama, paradox—these are the basic terms of modernist criticism. The poem is an image of reality and a heuristic device—for it has utility in that it teaches us how to see—as well as an organic and "useless" aesthetic object, reflexive, severed from the poet, self-generating, and indivisible. Thus has the modernist attempted to resolve the ancient form-content dilemma: What is said in the poem is not what it "means," for what it means is inseparable from the *way* it is said. John Ciardi's recent poetry textbook is called, with calculated intent, *How Does a Poem Mean?*—not, you may notice, *what* does a poem mean. When all is indirect, the reader has to infer the meaning for himself, and since he must make such inferences on the basis of the total context, then it may be said that the meaning is inseparable from that context. Thus a prose paraphrase can never equal the poem, for it is precisely the way in which a poem's meanings are embodied that gets left behind in the abstraction which is paraphrase. So it is said that poetry is what is lost in translation.

But Cummings' picture of the world is somewhat different, and so his techniques vary accordingly in their nature and function. Or perhaps I ought to say "worlds," for in the Introduction to *The Enormous Room* he remarks: "I live in so many: which one do you mean?" His interlocutor replies: "I mean the everyday humdrum world, which includes me and you and millions upon millions of men and women." Is not this a distinction resembling that mentioned earlier between the sensical and knowledgeable power-world of Offissa Pup and Ignatz Mouse, and the nonsensical world of love inhabited by Krazy Kat? The point in Cummings is that to lose the two-dimensional everyday world is to gain the threedimensional world of understanding. This is a world without conflict, where hope has no opposite in fear; a world without contingency, without compromise, without contradiction, without limits, and without fixity. It is the world of what's possible, and hence is the source of all our values. It is the world which Cummings refers to as "dream," "magic," "mystery," and "miracle." It is the world, in short, which gives meaning and significance to our everyday humdrum world. Evil—and he sees plenty of it around him, for he is no naive optimist—exists in this latter world, but for him it is the result of a corrupt will rather than an inherent part of the universe. Fear is what corrupts that will and love is what cures it—this it does by a paradoxical surrender, for a loss of self is a loss of fear. It's not so much, therefore, that he sees reality as a single thing, as that he doesn't see the good and the bad as necessarily intertwined. His world is complicated, but his vision of it is not complex.

And his view of poetry is correspondingly simple. The persuasion of the lover who urges his lady to accept the threedimensional freedom of surrender and the castigation of the critic who deplores twodimensional man's voluntary slavery to his fears—these are the stuff of his poetry, the lyric and the satire:

> you shall above all things be glad and young.
> For if you're young,whatever life you wear
>
> it will become you;and if you are glad
> whatever's living will yourself become.
> Girlboys may nothing more than boygirls need:
> i can entirely her only love
>
> whose any mystery makes every man's
> flesh put space on;and his mind take off time
>
> that you should ever think,may god forbid
> and(in his mercy)your true lover spare:

for that way knowledge lies,the foetal grave
called progress,and negation's dead undoom.

I'd rather learn from one bird how to sing
than teach ten thousand stars how not to dance

(New Poems, #22)

when god decided to invent
everything he took one
breath bigger than a circustent
and everything began

when man determined to destroy
himself he picked the was
of shall and finding only why
smashed it into because

(IXI, #XXVI)

These, plus descriptions of and reflections on landscapes and seasons, which open, as we shall see, gateways to the infinite. For Cummings, as much as the modernist, conceives also of "another kind of truth."

Nor is his conception of poetic form any less "organic." For it is no necessary part of a theory which holds that form and content are inseparable to require ambivalence, irony, and the rest. A poem may aim at a single affirmative expression and still depend upon the way it does so for its proper significance to be grasped. That which is inexpressible may be inexpressible not so much because it is complex as because it is ineffable. If Cummings has shown no interest in the modernist Mask, in the techniques of discontinuity, in mythic symbols, he has explored—even more deeply than the modernist—certain possibilities of language. These are, specifically, the grammatical shift, syntactic disarrangement, experiments in the free verse stanza, and the mingling of different levels of diction. To these devices he has added certain others of his own: the controversial typographic displacements, and the unconventional handling of punctuation and capitalization. Aside from causing what is said to be inseparable from the way it is said, these devices, rather than serving as subtle nets to snare the elusive variety and complexity of the everyday world, function instead to make the reader see and feel and understand directly and immediately the nonsensical world of love. To change the word order radically, for example, or to break words typographically, prevents the reader from following a sentence rationally and consecutively, so that when he does see the pattern he grasps it all at once rather than abstractly from point to point. "I am abnormally fond of that precision which creates movement," he says in the Foreword to is 5. Such techniques do not communicate meanings; they provoke insights. As the Introduction to Krazy Kat puts it: "We understand that, just as there is something—love—infinitely more significant than brute force, there is something—wisdom—infinitely more significant than mental prowess. A remarkably developed intelligence impresses us about as much as a sixteen-inch biceps. If we know anything, we know that a lot of people can learn knowledge (which is the same thing as unlearning ignorance) but that no one can learn wisdom. Wisdom, like love, is a spiritual gift."

In one sense, then, Cummings' problem is the reverse of the modernist's: rather than framing a complex mirror to reflect a complex reality, he is treating simple subjects and attitudes in a complicated way. And the complication is an attempt to freshen what might otherwise be taken as an ordinary idea and to wake it up for us. There are many themes that we have taken so much for granted that they have become clichés, and it is these clichés which the modernist avoids like the plague. The work of Cummings represents an alternative course, for he has undertaken to drain the swamps themselves: a cliché is not necessarily false because people no longer think or feel while uttering it. To love one's lady wholeheartedly, to revere one's parents, to look back with gratification upon one's childhood, to say joyous things at the arrival of spring, to praise the individual—to do these things places one in imminent danger indeed of falling into the heart of cliché-land itself. But to say that Cummings' well-known poem on his father reminds one, as a certain reviewer has done, of a *Reader's Digest* Most Unforgettable Character I've Ever Met sketch is simply to ignore the way the poem is written in favor of its message:

> though dull were all we taste as bright,
> bitter all utterly things sweet,
> maggoty minus and dumb death
> all we inherit,all bequeath
>
> and nothing quite so least as truth
> —i say though hate were why men breathe—
> because my father lived his soul
> love is the whole and more than all
>
> (*50 Poems*, #34)

But isn't it a central modernist doctrine that poetic excellence derives not intrinsically from the poem's subject but rather from its *treatment* of the subject? In this way the modernist supports and confirms his notion of organic form, for if certain subjects are more "poetical" than others, then form and content *are* separable. Thus has the modernist argued for the extension of poetic subject matters to include the non-poetic and the antipoetic, the ugly, the sordid, and the shocking. Thus has he managed his separation of poetry from the comparatively crude pressures of conventional morality. For he believes in the power of the artistic imagination to transform and give significance to any subject, however unpromising or unconventional. And he is right. Why, therefore, should he deny this power to the poet's vision when it comes to the cliché?

For Cummings' problem is to say what has been said to death. Those, however, who confuse his love lyrics with the verses on Valentine cards are committing the "heresy of paraphrase," they are victims of the stock response:

> never could anyone
> who simply lives to die
> dream that your valentine
> makes happier me than i
>
> but always everything
> which only dies to grow
> can guess and as for spring
> she'll be the first to know

(*95 Poems*, #46)

He is saying things which sound familiar but are no longer familiar when he gets through with them. It is the difference between hypocrisy and the real thing, the meretricious and the genuine, the commercial and the creative: on the surface both might look alike and a description of each might even sound alike, but each is held together on entirely different principles. When Cummings talks about love he may sound to the inattentive reader like Cole Porter, but he is not only actually feeling what he is talking about, he is also talking about it in an entirely fresh way:

> i carry your heart with me(i carry it in
> my heart)i am never without it(anywhere
> i go you go,my dear;and whatever is done
> by only me is your doing,my darling)
>   i fear
> no fate(for you are my fate,my sweet)i want
> no world(for beautiful you are my world,my true)
> and it's you are whatever a moon has always meant
> and whatever a sun will always sing is you
>
> here is the deepest secret nobody knows
> (here is the root of the root and the bud of the bud
> and the sky of the sky of a tree called life;which grows
> higher than soul can hope or mind can hide)
> and this is the wonder that's keeping the stars apart
>
> i carry your heart(i carry it in my heart)

(*95 Poems*, #92)

What redeems this poem from ordinariness is the distinction of its language—to be found in its delicacy and balance of phrasing, in its purity of tone, and in its careful management of the sonnet form—and the depth of its source in a profoundly mystical view of life—implied in the concept of "fate" and "world," as well as in the tree-root-bud imagery toward the end.

So, when you come right down to it, what we thought was only too familiar turns out to be actually ineffable. The manner of expression *is* inseparable from what is being expressed: if he talks in a way no one ever thought of before, then what he is saying represents what no one has ever thought of before either. His poetry is not merely what oft was thought but ne'er so well expressed, after all. Draining the swamps of cliché-land takes us into the heart of the mystery. For what *is* love, anyway? Or innocence, for that matter? Or an individual? Are we really weary of these themes because they are so boringly obvious? Or because we don't understand them, and never have?

II

Thus, in another sense, the complexity of Cummings' techniques represents an attempt to express the inexpressible. And here he joins the modernists in a common enterprise. For the ultimate aim of poets like Yeats, Pound, Stevens, Eliot, and Auden, is to achieve a "unification of sensibility," a vision of the timeless moment. The net result of attempting to express the variety and complexity of a various and complex world, of aiming at a sense of the concrete thing in its vivid and varied actuality, is—unity. The unity of a vision which transcends, without excluding, variety. This is truly another kind of truth, a kind which science not only does not, but also can not, duplicate. For science, although it may aspire to a unified field theory, can only do so in terms of its own proper limits: in being necessarily bound to the measurable and the verifiable, it can never approach the immeasurable and the intuitive. And the transcendent vision of the poet is of the immeasurable and the intuitive. The modernist movement—often castigated as being negative and dehumanizing—may be properly understood only in terms of its culminating affirmation. Here, for example, is the conclusion of Yeats's "A Dialogue of Self and Soul":

> When such as I cast out remorse
> So great a sweetness flows into the breast
> We must laugh and we must sing,
> We are blest by everything,
> Everything we look upon is blest.

Or the conclusion of Eliot's *Four Quartets*:

> Quick now, here, now, always—
> A condition of complete simplicity
> (Costing not less than everything)
> And all shall be well and
> All manner of thing shall be well
> When the tongues of flame are in-folded
> Into the crowned knot of fire
> And the fire and the rose are one.

Or the still point at the center of Pound's *Cantos*, in Canto XLIX:

> Sun up; work
> sundown; to rest
> dig well and drink of the water
> dig field; eat of the grain
> Imperial power is? and to us what is it?
>
> The fourth; the dimension of stillness.
> And the power over wild beasts

Or the lovely conclusion of Stevens' "Sunday Morning":

> Deer walk upon our mountains, and the quail
> Whistle about us their spontaneous cries;
> Sweet berries ripen in the wilderness;
> And, in the isolation of the sky,
> At evening, casual flocks of pigeons make
> Ambiguous undulations as they sink,
> Downward to darkness, on extended wings.

Both the modernist and Cummings are, at the last, striving for the transcendental vision. For Cummings, too, it is the result of a direct perception of the concrete thing. Here is #48 of *95 Poems*:

> someone i am wandering a town(if its
> houses turning into themselves grow
>
> silent upon new perfectly blue)
>
> i am any(while around him streets
> taking moment off by moment day
> thankfully become each other(one who
> feels a world crylaughingly float away
>
> leaving just this strolling ghostly doll
> of an almost vanished me(for whom
> the departure of everything real is the
> arrival of everything true)and i'm
>
> no(if deeply less conceivable than
> birth or death or even than breathing shall
>
> blossom a first star)one

The basic, the real difference between them is that, while the modernist feels he must reach this vision only after long struggle and much difficulty, Cummings goes right to it directly. For the modernist, direct perception refers to the twodimensional world we live in every day, while for Cummings it refers to the immortal natural world in terms of which we may grasp the threedimensional world of understanding. For the one a transcendent insight is the result of deliberate discipline; for the other it is a felt experience. The modernist achieves it by a painful dialectic process of balancing tensions and for him it is difficult to surrender; Cummings achieves it by immediate intuition, and for him to surrender is joyful. What the one is seeking, the other already has.

This means that the modernist wants to achieve unity without giving up anything—without surrendering, for example, his maturity of outlook with its sad knowledge of how good and evil are rarely a matter of black and white. As we have seen, he hedges his bets. He wants a vision of infinite possibility without surrendering his tragic sense of the inevitability of failure and of his self-involvement in the will of fate. He wants the Just City on earth to pave the way to the Heavenly City above; he wants to remain in History while living outside of Time. He wants to rediscover and awaken the primitive levels of his being without discarding Civilization and Culture. He wants to achieve the threedimensional world without surrendering the twodimensional world.

Now this results indeed in a "dramatic" sort of poetry, in an especially *human* sort of poetry, and I would be the last to wish it away. It is, in effect, the poetry of the modern intellectual and it has a wide appeal among modern intellectuals, and it would have an even wider appeal if it were not so difficult to read. Certainly Eliot, for one, has yearned all along for a large audience, and he has even taken lately to decrying (the final irony!) the isolation of modern poetry among academic coteries and recommending that it be removed from the curriculum and be read simply for fun. Modern poetry is certainly, from my experience, popular among undergraduates. It speaks frankly to us about what we must be feeling, and even teaches us what we ought to be feeling. It proposes to face the difficult world we live in without flinching, and the solution to our problems it offers is not an easy one—to be achieved, if at all, only after much effort. It is, in short, about *us*. For we find it hard to give up the knowledgeable power-world, too.

Indeed, the modernist objection to Cummings is based upon the modernist assumption that the affirmative vision has to be "earned." Cummings, it is said, is naive and sentimental because his affirmation came early and stayed late. His career is not marked by that climax of spiritual conversion found in the careers of poets like Yeats, Eliot, and Auden (although no such pattern is found in the careers of Frost, Stevens, and Pound, for example). He did not struggle through the darkness toward the light. He was apparently born knowing what he knows. And thus he is called a perpetual adolescent.

Cummings does not hedge his bets. He is not obsessed with the "mature sensibility," because he knows that is just what sells us out in a pinch. He is not weighed down by the Tragic Vision because he knows we *do* create our fate. Failure doesn't bother him because he has accepted it from the start as a condition of freedom. He is not concerned with History and the City because he knows that when men act in groups they are motivated by abstractions. He is not in pursuit of the Primitive because he *is* a primitive, and he knows that if Culture doesn't come naturally it had better not come at all.

His is not a poetry about us and our Situation. And isn't there something more difficult after all in such a poetry, a poetry which comes telling us we can be different? Isn't it easier, more faddish even, to write of Exile and Alienation and the Symbol? More condescending to show us images of our own ambivalent and anxious selves? More flattering to assure us that affirmations *are* difficult, and that they are to be achieved, if at all, only—later? Isn't there something finally sentimental, irredeemably melodramatic even, in insisting upon the darkness which must precede and accompany our vision of the light? Doesn't this attitude justify us to ourselves, telling us what we are instead of what we might become? Isn't the divided self in manifest danger of becoming in turn a stock response, the modern cliché?

III

So if the two common opinions are both right in saying that Cummings is a romanticist and a modernist, we have seen that these elements are not so simply defined as we had thought. Neither really understands him, but each misunderstands him differently. It is in the way modernism and romanticism are intertwined that the essence of his work is to be found. His "romantic" vision turns out to be ultimately modern, while his "modern" techniques turn out after all not to be the ones favored by the modernists. Having to express what is equally inexpressible, he is equally experimental. But his techniques vary from theirs in that, while his vision has the same goal as theirs, his begins where theirs leaves off.

Neither the modernist nor Cummings, however, has sold us short about one thing: neither has committed the old Victorian error of seeing the transcendent in terms of absolutes, in terms of abstractions. No systems, no dogmas of the supernatural have been erected to take the place of our vanished certitudes. Both have realized that what killed religion was not its dogmas but rather the fact that it formulated them as dogmas. Although both deplore what middle-class vulgarity has made of the world, neither tells us the old lie that the natural world is unreal. As the modernist tells us that no formulation of the transcendent is or can be final—

> Shall she not find in comforts of the sun,
> In pungent fruit and bright, green wings, or else
> In any balm or beauty of the earth,
> Things to be cherished like the thought of heaven?
> (Stevens, "Sunday Morning")

so Cummings shows us that the never-changing infinite can only be found in the ever-changing finite:

luminous tendril of celestial wish

(whying diminutive bright deathlessness
to these my not themselves believing eyes
adventuring,enormous nowhere from)

querying affirmation;virginal

immediacy of precision:more
and perfectly more most ethereal
silence through twilight's mystery made flesh—

dreamslender exquisite white firstful flame

—new moon!as(by the miracle of your
sweet innocence refuted)clumsy some
dull cowardice called a world vanishes,

teach disappearing also me the keen
illimitable secret of begin

(Xaipe, #71)

If the modernist does not often delight in the physical world as Cummings
does, being torn by its transiency and its mortality, he nevertheless will
not forsake it, and in the end he blesses it too. As the modernist constantly
shifts his ground, so Cummings says:

> never to rest and never to have:only to grow.
> Always the beautiful answer who asks a more beautiful
>   question

(Introduction to Collected Poems)

If life can be said to have a secret, and if that secret can be expressed
in words, then this is it. Even a faith such as Cummings' is never fixed,
never final. Each poem for him is a new beginning, but neither evil nor
old age nor death are ever far from his sight as he sings afresh of the
familiar but inscrutable glory of love:

> being to timelessness as it's to time,
> love did no more begin than love will end;
> where nothing is to breathe to stroll to swim
> love is the air the ocean and the land
>
> (do lovers suffer?all divinities
> proudly descending put on deathful flesh:
> are lovers glad?only their smallest joy's
> a universe emerging from a wish)
>
> love is the voice under all silences,
> the hope which has no opposite in fear;
> the strength so strong mere force is feebleness:
> the truth more first than sun more last than star

—do lovers love?why then to heaven with hell
Whatever sages say and fools,all's well

(*95 Poems*, #94)

POST SCRIPT

It is not to register my disagreement with an essay I wrote over twenty years ago that I requested the editor of the present volume to permit me to add a note to it here. Upon reading it over for the purpose, I do feel I would alter some of the emphases—"simple subjects and attitudes" strikes me now as altogether too much of a concession to the opposition, however rhetorical—and correct a point here and there—"no interest in . . . the techniques of discontinuity" is certainly wrong and is contradicted by the remainder of the paragraph. My basic point remains, however, and I still believe that Cummings differs from certain of the other modernists in that his transcendental vision is achieved without that balancing and reconciling of opposites which is characteristic of theirs.

But I do want now to reemphasize their similarities, for I see that I was identifying modernism rather too closely with the doctrines of what was then called the New Criticism. I was of course raised on those doctrines, and a good part of my intellectual life has been spent in trying to extend them and to adapt them to my greater commitment to Cummings. Over the years I have come to realize that the New Criticism was only a local variation of the larger movement of modernism, which is indeed characterized, as my essay suggests, by its attempts to achieve a holistic vision by means of the devices of fragmentation and recombination. The particular interpretation put upon those devices by the New Criticism happened to have stressed the clash of opposites, the "earning" of affirmation, the use of mythic substructures, the sophisticated and self-critical speaker, and "maturity" of vision, but this interpretation is far from an adequate account of the whole of modernism.

What I have come to appreciate more fully of late, and what I want to explore more deeply, is the profound and pervasive influence of orientalism—Buddhism and Taoism, Noh drama, the Upanishads, Confucius, Haiku, the ideogram, and so on—on modernism, and indeed upon the whole evolving process of romanticism from the nineteenth century to the present day. One has only to mention Emerson, Thoreau, and Whitman in the previous century, and Yeats, Pound, and Eliot in our own time, to realize how profound and pervasive it is.

The point is that modernism when seen from this perspective takes on a somewhat different cast than when seen too exclusively from the perspective of the New Criticism, even though it too bears certain significant affinities with that other perspective. What strikes me as central in this oriental influence is that it offers a needed alternative to either the alienation of modern culture or the New Critical struggle to *incorporate* that alienation in its effort to transcend it. Orientalism, or that aspect of it which I see as operative here, finds wholeness by accepting what is, and transcendence by immersion in the here and now. Rather than balancing and reconciling opposites, it surrenders that whole mental and societal system whereby opposites are engendered in the first place, and substitutes an awareness of and a oneness with the organismic unfolding of process.

This is not the entire story, of course, for such a vision is not simply as passive and quietistic as it may at first seem, and much remains to be said about the kinds of energy and action it can foster and contain. Enough has been said, however, to indicate that, if this involves a larger view of modernism, it most surely entitles Cummings to a larger and clearer place within that movement. I have brought out certain elements—and problems—in Cummings' orientalism in my essay, "Cummings Posthumous," also reprinted here, and I hope to explore the issue further at some future time.

E.E. Cummings: The Now Man

L.S. Dembo*

"Here is a thing," wrote E. E. Cummings in a little piece called "Fair Warning"; "To one somebody, this 'thing' is a totally flourishing universal joyous particular happening deep amazing miraculous indivisible being." To other "somebodies," the tree, here described, is something mechanical or functional:

> Somebody number one is a poet. Actually he is alive. His address is: Now. All the other somebodies are unpoets. They all aren't alive. They all merely are not unexisting—in a kind of an unkind of unreality or When. Here is another thing: whatever happens, everybody cannot turn the Nowman's Now into When; whatever doesn't, nobody can turn the Whenman's When into Now.[1]

This theme recurs in the introduction to the *Collected Poems*:

> We can never be born enough. We are human beings; for whom birth is a supremely welcome mystery, the mystery of growing: the mystery which happens only and whenever we are faithful to ourselves. You and I wear the dangerous looseness of doom and find it becoming. Life, for eternal us, is now; and now is much too busy being a little more than everything to seem anything, catastrophic included.[2]

*Reprinted from *Conceptions of Reality in Modern American Poetry* by L.S. Dembo, copyright © 1966 by the Regents of the University of Calfornia. Reprinted by permission of L.S. Dembo and the University of California Press.

This Bergsonian conception of spontaneous existence, for both subject and object, the idea of physical and mental life as perpetual birth and growth, as constant *becoming*, is, of course, reminiscent of the ultimate values of Williams, Stevens, and Hart Crane. And, again, as in these poets, the problem of perception and response is crucial.

Although in so frankly a primitivistic ethos as Cummings', ideal perception and response are not really a matter of exotic vision, Cummings is inclined to make the same kind of distinctions that one would find in objectivist theory. There are the deluded rationalists (bourgeois society) and the enlightened irrationalists (poets):

> A poet is somebody who feels, and who expresses his feeling through words. . . .
> A lot of people think or believe or know they feel—but that's thinking or believing or knowing; not feeling. And poetry is feeling—not knowing or believing or thinking. . . .[3]

As with the objectivist, the poet's experience with language is experience with logos and ultimate truth:

> Ineluctable preoccupation with The Verb gives a poet one priceless advantage: whereas nonmakers must content themselves with the merely undeniable fact that two times two is four, he rejoices in an irresistible truth (to be found on the title page of the present volume) [*Is* 5].[4]

Similarly, Cummings' ideas concerning the "self" and its relation to the external world, nature, follow a logic not remote from the objectivist's. To begin with, identity with "Life" means "self-transcendence" and what would be called by "mostpeople" nonidentity, since to be "most truly alive" means to transcend the social self and to acquire the natural one (selflessness) that comes with response to the universe.[5] The Now Man is "on the one hand a complete fanatic, dedicated to values beyond life and death," and on the other he is "a profoundly alive and supremely human being."[6] He dives "out of tinying time / (into supreme Now)," seeking "new / textures of actual cool stupendous is" (p. 267).[7] As "Being," stupendous Is represents both physical nature and supernature, just as "Now" is both a moment and eternity. Existence is, in a sense, the final "para-thing" (Stevens) and it is not surprising to find that in Cummings, as in Fletcher, Aldington, Crane, Williams, and Stevens, death itself is regarded as a form of being, or at least intimately associated with the process of *becoming*. The "sweet spontaneous earth" defies the "fingers of prurient philosophers," and responds only to a more elemental suitor:

> true
> to the incomparable
> couch of death thy
> rhythmic
> lover

                    thou answerest
              them only with
                        spring)

                                        (p. 39)

  To "live suddenly without thinking / under honest trees" (p. 121), to
live with "feeling," then, implies a sympathetic union (in the sense of
Hazlitt) of mind and object, a union in which the "organic" object, in a
state of continual growth, defines consciousness. The reply of the wind to
the speaker in "the wind is a Lady" (p. 79) suggests the indistinguish-
ability of mind and object in the ideal experience. To the question, "why
do you touch the flowers as if they were ideas)," the green Lady replies,

            "because, sir
      things which in my mind blossom will
      stumble beneath a clumsiest disguise, appear
      capable of fragility and indecision

      —do not suppose these
      without any reason and otherwise . . .
      different from the i am who wanders

      imminently across the renewed world"

That is, despite appearances, the mind does not treat the object as an
"idea" in abstraction; rather the object, "blossoming" in the mind, constitutes its very nature. In short, what seems "capable of fragility and in-
decision" is what actually makes up the force of life. Looked at from
another point of view, the poet himself, ideally a nonidentity and
therefore an Individual, must be "slender and fragile," borrowing "contact from that you and from / this you sensations, imitating a few fatally /
exquisite . . . things" (p. 237). "When my sensational moments are no
more / unjoyously bullied by vilest mind" (active reason rather than
passive feeling), only then is the Now of eternal spring possible. Exquisite
things, "fragile splendors," "luminous" objects—para-things and unpar-
ticularities—are fatal to the reason and social self; they are similarly part
of the "doom" that is the rhythmic lover of "life," the eternity that
characterizes Now. To die in time and be reborn in timelessness is the
poetic aim of life.
  It is in these terms that one can understand Cummings' appreciation
of Hart Crane, whom he saw as being able "to invent growth's likeness"—
that is, to carry out the true function of poetry: "Drunk and becauseless
(talking about a cyclone, telling how at last with the disappearance even
of impossibility himself found actually himself and suddenly becoming
the cyclone; not perishing and not surviving; Being). . . ."[8] The
equivalent experience in Cummings is suggested in a poem in which a
tree, addressing the wind, says

> i
> wait the sweet
> annihilation of swift
> flesh. . . .
>
> . . . .
>
> O haste
>   annihilator
> drawing into you my enchanting
> leaves.   (p. 135)

The absorption of the tree into the wind, of the poet into eternity, is the death that is in reality growth.

The preoccupation with being-as-being has, as we saw in both Williams and Stevens, its negative side: explicitly, confrontation with the contingent may involve terror no less than joy. I am thinking specifically of Williams' "Portrait of an Author," discussed earlier, in which the apprehension of an existence that resisted all human conceptions of it left the poet "with shrinking heart / and startled empty eyes—peering out / into a cold world." A dialogue between lover and lady walking alone at night appears to reflect this problem in Cummings' poem, "touching you i say" (p. 218). "Everything / turns into something else, and slips away," says the frightened girl; "These leaves are Thingish with moondrool." The poet tries to comfort her by providing a humanized conception, even though he is himself partially overcome with the changing reality of the spring night:

> "along this particular road the moon if you'll
> notice follows us like a big yellow dog. You
>
> don't believe? look back. (Along the sand
> behind us, a big yellow dog that's. . . . now it's red
> a big red dog that may be owned by who
> knows)
>   only turn a little your. so. And
>
> there's the moon, there's something faithful and mad"

That if one turns one's head the moon will become a dog might be comforting, but even so, in a thingish world, the dog will prove as mad as faithful—as changing as constant.

Yet whatever the interpretation of such poems as this, the "invention of growth's likeness," the imitation of being and becoming, remains the central poetic in Cummings' work. The dissolution of syntax ("Who pays attention to the syntax of things will never wholly kiss you"), involving the dissolution of conventional conceptualization, has been, of course, a distinguishing feature of Cummings' poetry. Insofar as Cummings is usually attempting to achieve an effect of "Nowness," to remove all sense of temporal or causal (as opposed to "organic") progression, we can profitably recall Pound's definition of the "Image" as an instantaneous presentation that gives that "sense of freedom from time and space limits; that sense of sudden growth." "Sudden growth" (if I may use Pound's expression out of context) seems to be precisely the paradoxical quality that Cummings is seeking to effect in poems describing natural phenomena—sunsets, moonrises, and thunderstorms, for example. "Growth" is development in time, and the conception of "instantaneous growth" is a logical contradiction that is the metalogical verity of any vitalistic outlook.

A thunderstorm appears to Cummings as three moments, coming in so rapid a succession as to constitute a single moment:

```
n (o) w
        the
how
      dis(appeared cleverly)world
iS Slapped:with;liGhtninG
!
   at
which (shal)lpounceupcrackw(ill)jumps
of
   THuNdeRB
            loSSo!M . . .
```

The next moment is similarly introduced with "n,o;w:":

```
            theraIncomIng
      o all the roofs roar
                  drownInsound. . . .
```

And finally,

```
            But l!ook—
                  s
   U
      n:starT birDs(lEAp)Openi ng
   t hing ; s(
   —sing
      )all are aLl(cry alL See)o(ver All) Th(e grEEn
   ?eartH)N,ew                                          (p.250)
```

The graphic imitation, which is relatively straightforward in this poem, contributes to the effect of spontaneous growth, just as the whole experience is essentially an "imagistic" one.

The attempt to capture motion (that is, paradoxically, to give the illusion of motion in a "moment") is equally apparent in this poem about a striptease dancer (p. 320):

```
            sh estiffl
            ystrut sal
            lif san
            dbut sth
```

```
epoutin(gWh.ono:w
s li psh ergo
wnd ow n,
                    r
Eve
aling 2 a
-sprout (eyelands). . . .
```

(Stiffly struts, all ifs and buts: the pouting Who [proper name?] now slips her gown down, revealing two asprout islands.) And, again, in the poem about a grasshopper (p. 286):

```
            r-p-o-p-h-e-s-s-a-g-r
        who
    a)s w(e loo)k
    upnowgath
            PPEGORHRASS
                        eringint(o-
    aThe):l
            eA
                lp:
    S. . . .
```

The word "now" appears in each of the three poems cited, and, indeed, it is the quality of "nowness," immediacy, that is common to all of them. But in each of the poems there also appears a reference to vision ("But l!ook," "See," "Eyelands," "Eyes," "a)s w(e loo)k / up"); to say nothing of the whole matter of the graphic technique itself. The truth is that the act of perception, as distinct from the object as such, is the central element in these pieces. If the last poem cited attempts to imitate a leaping grasshopper, it also tries to create a verbal equivalent that has an effect on the eye similar to that of the actuality; just as the grasshopper is out of focus in the process, and comes into focus only after he has come to rest, so the word that signifies him, suddenly regarded ("as we look up"), is jumbled throughout the poem, finally to "become rearrangingly, 'grasshopper.' " The striptease dancer is similarly a chaos of broken movements transformed into broken words, and if her breasts are "islands," they are also a place where the eye lands. She represents an "object" with the power to "absorb" the beholder, psychologically and aesthetically as well as sexually:

```
seethe firm swirl hips whirling climb to
GIVE
(yoursmine mineyours yoursmine
!
i()t)
```

As a beholder, the poet in Cummings' world is, like the objectivist, the man who apprehends and recreates the true nature of the object, the true nature here being "growth," "vitality," "rhythm." Thus the poet can say,

> myself is sculptor of
> your body's idiom:
> the musician of your wrists;
> the poet who is afraid
> only to mistranslate
>
> a rhythm in your hair. . . .
>
> (p. 209)

But in emphathizing with his subject as objectivist, the poet also involves himself with it as mystic; in the lines just cited, the speaker is lover as well as poet. "Art is a mystery," says Cummings; "all mysteries have their source in a mystery-of-mysteries who is love: and if lovers may reach eternity directly through love herself, their mystery remains essentially that of the loving artist whose way must lie through his art, and of the loving worshipper whose aim is oneness with his god."[9] And in another poem, we find,

> "to be, being, that i am alive
> this absurd fraction in its lowest terms
> with everything cancelled
> but shadows
> —what does it all come down to? love? Love." . . .
>
> (p. 212)

If poetry is a form of love, what characterizes love characterizes poetry, and as the "mystery-of-mysteries" love is the quintessential awareness of being "alive," or, again, the ultimate form of "self-transcendence." The poet as aestheticist responds to the Lady's beauty:

> nothing which we are to perceive in this world equals
> the power of your intense fragility. . . .

As lover, he is transfigured:

> whose texture
> compels me with the colour of its countries,
> rendering death and forever with each breathing
>
> (p. 263)

The kind of death the Lady renders (the "dooms of love") is the death from time into eternity, both sexually and spiritually:

> And then all her beauty is a vise
>
> whose stilling lips murder suddenly me,
>
> but of my corpse the tool her smile makes something
> suddenly luminous and precise

>—and then we are I and She. . . .
>
>what is that the hurdy-gurdy's playing   (p. 116)

The hurdy-gurdy, if not a distraction after the act, is possibly an appropriate accompaniment, like the hand organ, in another poem, "at the corner of Nothing and Something . . . / playing like hell."

In Cummings' realism, the passivity of the lover before the beauty of the Lady (or if not the beauty, the charisma of her person) is analogous to the receptivity of the Now Man before the power of existence. Just as the object determines consciousness, so the Lady determines the lover's being:

>   create
>me gradually (or as these emerging now
>hills invent the air)
>   breathe simply my each how
>my trembling where my still invisible when.   (p. 267)

The poet's role in this mystical experience is solely to express his feeling without conception and without evaluation ("nor has a syllable of the heart's eager dim / enormous language loss or gain from blame or praise.") for it is only the thought "born of dream"—the feeling that survives "wish and world" that matters.

The primitivistic conception of experience that underlies Cummings' poetry, for all its foundation in realism, can, in one sense, be seen as resolving itself in the direction of idealism. Since we have been talking about natural objects as existents and phenomena as process, we might recall Sartre's exposition of the problem in *What Is Literature?*: "Each of our perceptions is accompanied by the consciousness that human reality is a 'revealer,' that is, it is through human reality that 'there is' being, or, to put it differently, that man is the means by which things are manifested. It is our presence in the world which multiplies relations."[10] This formulation, which finds its prototype in Renaissance humanism and idealism, implies that human consciousness, being the means by which reality is expressed, "encompasses" reality. Or, to recall Stevens again, the idea of reality is a human "fiction." Bergson's statement on the aim of art is in complete harmony with Cummings' poetic: "Could reality come into direct contact with sense and consciousness, could we enter into immediate communion with things and with ourselves, probably art would be useless, or rather we should all be artists, for then our soul would vibrate in perfect accord with nature."[11] The idealistic converse of this realistic proposition is that nature requires the artist to make itself known, just as a Now Man is necessary to the spontaneity (the *idea* of spontaneity) that governs Cummings' world. The poet might often feel that he has failed to invent growth's likeness or to "fabricate the unknown," but he never fails to appreciate the nature of "growth" and the extent of his failure, and it is precisely upon such appreciation that Cummings' world depends. Those poems in which the speaker laments his inability to translate his experience are, needless to say, part of the rhetoric of translating the experience of defining reality. Beyond the translation is the subjective apprehension; beyond the subjective apprehension there is nothing. I would be foolish to insist that Cummings is actually an idealist; he is indeed a realist—just so long as one appreciates the truism that in poetic realism the aesthetic response of the poet is a crucial element.

NOTES

1. *E.E. Cummings: A Miscellany*, ed. by George Firmage (New York: Argophile, 1958), p. 12.

2. *Collected Poems* (New York: Harcourt, Brace, 1938), n.p.

3. *E.E. Cummings: A Miscellany*, p. 13.

4. Foreword to *is 5* (New York: Liveright, 1926). Reprinted as part of *i: six nonlectures* (New York: Atheneum, 1962), p. 64.

5. I might acknowledge at this point two useful studies: Norman Friedman's *E.E. Cummings: The Art of His Poetry* (Baltimore: Johns Hopkins Press, 1960) and Barry Marks' *E.E. Cummings* (New York: Twayne, 1964).

6. *i: six nonlectures*, p. 81.

7. All quotations are from *E.E. Cummings, Poems, 1923–1954* (New York: Harcourt, Brace, 1954), which supersedes *Collected Poems*.

8. *i: six nonlectures*, p. 65.

9. *i: six nonlectures*, p. 82.

10. Jean-Paul Sartre, *Literature and Existentialism* (New York: Citadel, 1949), p. 38.

11. *Le Rire*, translated as "Laughter" in *Comedy*, ed. by Wylie Sypher (New York: Random House, 1956), pp. 157–58.

Language as a Reality in E.E. Cummings

James P. Dougherty*

Though for forty years all influential critics have been dismissing E. E. Cummings, we are still talking about him. Recently there have been signs that he may survive a more important judgment, that of younger poets hungry for new post-Eliotian, post-mythological resources. The little magazines are printing poems more or less indebted to Cummings' experiments with typography or with grammar and syntax. Charles Olson in the "Projective Verse" manifesto established Cummings with Pound and Williams as pioneers and patrons of Field Composition, which has become the orthodoxy of the Sixties.[1] And, together with Pound and

*Reprinted from the *Bucknell Review*, 16 (1968), 112–22. Reprinted by permission of the *Bucknell Review* (Associated University Presses).

Apollinaire, he is honored as a prophet by the Concrete Poetry movement in Europe and South America—a movement just now coming to this country.

Cummings poses the question of how we are to discuss a major minor poet in such a way that we can acknowledge both his achievements and his limitations. Close reading, which assumes that intricacy is value, fails us here for two reasons: as Graves and Riding pointed out, grammatical or typographical contortion are not in Cummings the outward sign of complex thought that they are in Donne, Hopkins and Eliot;[2] and the poems most desperately needing explication are as a rule the least successful—the ones in which Cummings was more concerned with pleasing himself than with speaking to an audience, and which justify Blackmur's accusation of a private language, inaccessible to the reader.[3] A man opinionated beyond the point of shrillness, he is seldom ironic, self-contradictory, or ambiguous, in the style of Stevens or Yeats. And liberal and conservative critics will beg forever the question whether he "matured," that is, came to agree with them. I wish to return to the topic that has occasioned much of the hostile criticism: Cummings' use of language.

Cummings shares with many post-Romantic writers a distrust of what they call abstraction, meaning by the word "an absolute not of my own devising." Abstractions lack the rich potential of significance which they find in concrete reality; or they lack the emotional and psychological power of sensory things; or they cannot coerce readers in a skeptical, empiric age. Frost in "For Once, Then, Something," cannot decide whether the gleam beyond the surface of the well is Truth—or just a pebble of quartz. Stevens mocks at "fops of fancy" producing "memorabilia of the mystic spouts" ("Le Monocle de Mon Oncle"). Yeats in "The Tower" declines "to choose Plato and Plotinus for a friend / Until imagination, ear and eye, / Can be content with argument and deal / In abstract things." Pound, to avoid the reductions of abstraction, undertakes an enormous periphrasis of the good state, which is the *Cantos*. Yet none of these writers really escapes from "abstraction," since language of necessity generalizes, and since "loneliness," "imagination," "art" and "Usura" are abstractions which these writers have charged with poetic significance.

In Cummings' prose we find the familiar romantic contempt for "abstraction"—in *Eimi* for example, his journal of a trip to Russia, in which he writes:

> Machinemade "civilization" isolates every human being from experience(that is , from himself)by teaching mankind to mistake a mere gadgety interpretation(e.g.the weatherman's prediction)of experience for experience itself(e.g.weather).[4]

His objections to "abstraction" however refer not to the generalizing process itself, but rather—as he says in his introduction to the Modern

Library edition of *The Enormous Room*—to the reciprocal process of imposing abstractions on particular individuals as categories that deny the
freedom and uniqueness of their identities.[5] Cummings of course, like the
other moderns, has never hesitated to impose his own absolutes ("mostpeople," "unanimals," etc.) upon others when the poetic occasion suits.

This dualism of concrete individual and universal category is the
basis of an obvious division in Cummings' poetry. Many of his poems,
especially those constructed through idiosyncratic compositions of type,
seek just to present weather without interpretation: a particular moment
of the poet's sensory experience, the typographic arrangement imitating
the disorder and simultaneity of several perceptions, or else the action or
quality of the things perceived. In these poems, Cummings aims for an
immediacy beyond the uneditorialized report of the Imagist. His well-
known "grasshopper" poem is an instance.

The perennial problem for the Imagist, however, is the transition
from experience to significance—the need, as Williams said at the beginning of *Paterson*, "to make a start / out of particulars / and make them
general." Symbolic realism, in which an object is cumulatively charged
with meaning through the terms and limits of its description and through
direct commentary—in which two farmers mending a wall become types
of two complex attitudes toward definition and limitation—was evidently
not congenial to Cummings, for he seldom attempts this transition. Either
his poems imitate the disorder of pure phenomena, or else take form from
the development of a general observation proceeding from his neo-
romantic philosophy of primitivist, anti-intellectual vitalism. This division corresponds generally with the division of his work into poems for the
eye, which because of their typographic irregularity can be compre-
hended only visually, and poems for the ear, which can be both read and
spoken. Among the latter are "pity this busy monster,manunkind," "my
father moved through dooms of love," and "anyone lived in a pretty how
town"—some of his best-known poems.[6] What constitutes "the concrete"
in them is interesting.

Commenting on his play *Him*, Cummings once wrote that its
dialogue "renders vivid a whole bevy of abstractions," "thus creating [per-
sonal] values."[7] These three poems also vivify abstractions, or, more accurately, general truths. One is an exhortation concerning our whole race
("pity . . . manunkind, / not") and two are parables expounding Cummings' vision of the heroic life as lived by idealized and generalized heroes,
"my father" and "anyone." These subjects, so universal as to be almost
amorphous, are tied to the concrete and the definite—and so rendered
vivid—in two ways, one conventional and one peculiarly Cummings'. The
first is the conceit yoking a concrete term with an abstraction—as
Marvell's "deserts of vast eternity" or Dickinson's "the carriage held but
just ourselves / And Immortality." Cummings does this repeatedly in the
series of aphorisms that make up "pity this busy monster,manunkind":

"progress is a comfortable disease"; "electrons deify one razorblade / into a mountainrange"; "lenses extend / unwish through curving wherewhen"; "there's a hell / of a good universe next door ;let's go." These conceits are particularly effective because each presents in miniature the structure of the whole poem, a tension between the affective world of sense and the neutralized world of intellectual construct. Similar conceits can be found in the other poems. In the elegy for his father he condemns a world in which "freedom [is] a drug that's bought and sold," and "conform the pinnacle of am." In the other poem, the townspeople "sowed their isn't they reaped their same."

But all three poems, especially the last two, depend for their immediacy on Cummings' unusually developed sense of the reality of a third poetic world, neither that of material objects nor that of immaterial significances but that of language itself—words, their orthography and grammar—a world so obvious that most theories of the particular and the general in poetry ignore it altogether.[8] Cummings is in this sense an anti-nominalist, an extreme realist, for whom words themselves have important concrete reality both in sound and in physical extension. His typographic poems develop out of this sense that a written word is a set of printed characters that can be pried apart to reveal new words, or distributed on the page so as to coerce the eye and the mind into special rhythms of comprehension. His sense of sound is responsible for such arrangements as "death and life safely beyond" in the "manunkind" poem, or, in the elegy to his father, "keen as midsummer's keen beyond / conceiving mind of sun," in which a compound adjective, "keen beyond mind's conceiving" is reorganized for the sake of sound and rhythm. Of course, in disturbing syntax to create euphonies, rhymes or rhythms, Cummings is balancing near the edge of the technical self-indulgence that has reduced the coherence—and hence the stature—of many of his poems. But he risks this because of his confident orientation in the universe of English structure and his confidence that the same familiarity with their language has given his readers better sea legs than they know. Elsewhere he preserves syntactical pattern and normal inflections as a guide to the reader, while substituting his own neologisms: "he sang his didn't he danced his did"; "my father moved through theys of we." The technique is familiar from Lewis Carroll.

But the result is not like Carroll's, for the neologisms are not private nonce words like "snark" and "toves," whose meanings we guess from the context of the one poem, but familiar public words like "they" and "did," whose meaning we establish by considering the situations in which they are normally used in the total context of our language. An easy example, from the elegy to his father, is

> newly as from unburied which
> floats the first who,his april touch
> drove sleeping selves to swarm their fates

We comprehend "which" as a metaphor for "some inanimate thing" and "who" as "a human person," because we are familiar with the assignments of these terms in our normal speech. Yet the unusual thing about these metaphors is that the vehicle in each case, instead of being a definite, concrete, and sensory thing, is just a function-word, without any corresponding object in reality. Each is a metonymy, founded on syntactics rather than semantics, representing an object not by another *object* associated with it (as "pen" for "poetry"), but by a *word* associated with it. Here too, writer and reader depend upon an intense realization of the system of language, distinct from the world of entities to which language refers. The reader experiences the pleasure of wit, of negotiating the transfer from vehicle to tenor, of seeing what was not stated, but the metaphor does not illuminate for him a hitherto unapprehended connection between actual things, as Shelley thought it must, but rather between a word in itself and a general class of things.

The same practice can be found throughout "my father moved through dooms of love" and the metaphors are not always so obvious as "which" and "who." In the opening lines—"my father moved through dooms of love / through sames of am through haves of give," the pattern "through x of y" is three times repeated, but only gradually the relationship of its two terms becomes clear, that x is what must be risked if y is to be attained. We can establish this by a general familiarity with how "same" is related (for Cummings) to "am"; and "have" to "give" and "they" to "we."

What emerges from the elegy is a parable, presenting his father as a creative, dynamic man dedicated to increasing the joy and vitality of his neighbors. It is a parable without episodes, without particular details; it is not about Edward Cummings, Harvard '83, who lived at 104 Irving Street in Cambridge and died in 1926, fourteen years before this poem was published; like the other poem, it is about "anyone": anyone who meets the poet's definition of true humanity. Yet we acknowledge that "my father moved through theys of we / singing each new leaf out of each tree" has an immediacy, a precision, that would not exist in a paraphrase such as "any man, seeking to express his love for other men and his sense of physical participation in the natural world, exposes himself to grave risks of rejection, alienation and failure, risks which must be embraced to be overcome." It is not that the paraphrase lacks accuracy or completeness of statement, but that it wants intensity and organization of sound.

Such sentiments could have been concretized in more conventional ways, as Robinson does in "Flammonde"—itself a parable, but a highly detailed one—or as Eliot does negatively in *The Waste Land*, or as Lawrence in his novels, certainly more important works than Cummings'; and one measure of this superiority must be their delineation of theme in the world of concrete things, persons and situations. But this is not Cummings' method. In these poems many of his conceits negotiate abstract with abstract: instead of deserts of vast eternity, or a hell of a good universe next door, we have "theys of we," "haves of give," and "pure so now and now so yes." Without one foot firmly in the definite, can the mind leap as it does with Marvell's metaphor? How does Cummings render vivid the generalizations of these poems?

Partly by traditional techniques like "singing each new leaf out of each tree." Partly by the wit of syntactic metaphors like "which" and "am." But also by attending closely to the sound and rhythm of the words themselves, and by the creation of repetitive rhythms in the patterns of English syntax.

Cummings' obvious conviction is that "am" is a more vital word than "being"; or, in another couplet, "and should some why completely weep / my father's fingers brought her sleep," that "why" has a verbal precision and economy not to be attained by any list of comfortless feminine questioners, nor any individual questioner chosen to be a type. This precision and economy are achieved not in the world of objects to which words refer—as Stevens in "The Emperor of Ice-Cream" finds ice cream the exact vehicle for all transient sensory experience—but rather in what Edith Sitwell would call the "texture" of the poem, the orchestration of sounds.

The poem's base is an octosyllabic couplet, from which Cummings deviates only by two expanded lines (3 and 51), and by four lines unrhymed (15–18) and four linked *abab* (63–66). On this base he develops a great variety of rhythmic effects, by reversing feet—

néwly as fróm unbúrĭed which

. . . .

nó líar loóked hím in the héad

laying spondees over an iambic base—

that if(so timid aír is fírm)

("that" being a demonstrative, correlative to "this" in line 5), or shifting a line into falling rhythms—

singing each morning out of each night

When he lets the iambs march unhampered he mutes them with a slanted rhyme:

and pure so now and now so yes
the wrists of twilight would rejoice

Though the opening stanzas establish a medial caesura, Cummings in about half the poem's lines shifts its position:

woke dreamers / / to their ghostly roots

. . . .

my father's fingers / / brought her sleep

or eliminates it altogether:

> Lifting the valleys of the sea

or uses two:

> that if / / (so timid / / air is firm)

The "anyone" poem has a less rigorous structure. Its base is a four-stress line and a four-line stanza. The lines vary in length from four syllables (8, 21, 36) to twelve (23); the first two lines of each stanza rhyme and the last two are free, except in the second and the last stanzas where they are joined by assonance. The few regular lines are iambic, but trochees and dactyls dominate in the polysyllabic words and in the poem as a whole. By his inversions in the first two lines—whatever insoluble semantic difficulties he thus creates—Cummings declares the poem's rhythmic alternatives:

> anyone lived in a pretty how town
> with up so flóating mány bells down)

Though the "manunkind" sonnet begins and ends with quatrains, *abab . . . efef*, the central six lines are linked irregularly and borrow rhymes from the first quatrain: *c(a)dcdb*. Within the decasyllabic base, stresses vary from three (1.4) to six (1.5), feet are reversed at every position in the line, and the caesura thrashes back and forth from following the first syllable (1.2) to preceding the penultimate (1.14).

In spite of Cummings' demonstrable concern for the musicality of these poems, his equal interest in conveying an idea prevents them from becoming "pure poetry" or verbal tone poems. Yet the relationship between grammar and meaning is not always obvious. The phrase I have already labored over will serve again: "my father moved through dooms of love." "Through x of y" is not a conventional way of linking risks and possibilities, as one sees by substituting some such set as "through tackles of touchdown." Yet Cummings' intent emerges, as I remarked above, from the massing of "sames of am," "haves of give," "depths of height," "griefs of joy," and "theys of we." Further, the construction suggests a close linking of the two acts, the necessity of embracing the first as the way to the second. In the "anyone" poem, there is a similar but even looser use of patterns. "He sang his didn't he danced his did" commences one of several sequences in that poem; in the next stanza, the townspeople "sowed their isn't they reaped their same." In between, we have been told that these people "cared for anyone not at all," and so we know to look for an opposition between the pattern as applied to "anyone" and the same pattern applied to "women and men." Given this opposition, we can inquire why to sow one's isn't is an act inferior to singing one's didn't; without this opposition, on which the whole poem is based, it would be impossible to establish that singing is better than sowing (being play instead of work) and that "didn't" is healthier than "isn't" (being a refusal to act rather than a denial of being). Subsequently the pattern is used several times to contrast the behavior of the hero with that of the town. But at poem's end it is used in a somewhat different way:

> Women and men(both dong and ding)
> summer autumn winter spring
> reaped their sowing and went their came
> sun moon stars rain

This last stanza is wholly a matter of rhythms: denoted rhythms of celestial motion, seasonal change, and human generation, but also textural rhythms, for every line is a pattern used earlier in the poem, its content or order slightly different but its rhythm recapitulating a theme developed throughout the poem. "Reaped their sowing and went their came" does tell us something about the cosmic forces before which "anyone" capered; but it is also employed musically, without regard to denotation.

Both poems, and many others by Cummings, make this absolute use of syntactical patterns, as rhythmic settings into which the poet introduces words that convey his idea with little help from the pattern's normal function. "Anyone lived in a pretty how town" has six such patterns, four of them contained in the stanza just quoted; a fifth illustrates this practice even more clearly. In the poem's twelfth line Cummings writes "noone loved him more by more," and in the stanzas that follow, the phrase "x by y" is used as an incantatory refrain, making grammatical sense only occasionally but conveying nevertheless the world of "anyone" and "noone":

> when by now and tree by leaf
> she laughed his joy she cried his grief
> bird by snow and stir by still
> anyone's any was all to her

and eventually it is used to offer, without explicit predication, the hope of rebirth:

> busy folk buried them side by side
> little by little and was by was
>
> . . . . "... . . .
>
> all by all and deep by deep
> and more by more they dream their sleep
> noone and anyone earth by april
> wish by spirit and if by yes.

The definite imagination finds nothing to seize upon in such a stanza, yet it is impossible to imagine Cummings' delicate parable built of more tangible stuff. Philosophically he is close to the psychic-regeneration themes of Shelley and Whitman; yet their assertions, whether made flatly or in metaphor, seem crude and so dogmatic as to try our credulity. In Cummings' poem most of the work of affirmation is done in phrases like "earth by april" which contain no apparent predications and are but tenuously connected with the sentences they surround. The words of consolation, "earth," "april," "wish," "spirit," "if," and "yes," are introduced into a pattern the poet has developed earlier, and it is this rhythmic pattern in itself, rather than any predicative sentence, that carries conviction. Throughout the poem, idea is inseparable from sound and rhythm, and the role of concrete detail and symbolic events is deliberately diminished.

Thus, in the three idea-poems we have considered, there is a progressively greater departure from the phenomenological world of definite persons, things, and actions. This is the world in which most modern poets have rooted themselves, in order to escape the intangible, unaffective and imprecise language of abstraction. Cummings is capable of depicting this physical world with hypersensitive accuracy in his "immediate" poems, and sometimes capable of using it for such conceits as "electrons deify one razorblade . . ." or for the seasonal references ("sun moon stars rain") which tie so many of his poems to the definite. But he is seldom able to move, within one poem, from the phenomenal world to developed general discourse, and herein lies one of his limitations as a poet. In some of his best-known and most ambitious poems, he is writing a tissue of abstractions or generalizations, vivified not so much by tangible symbols as by an appeal to the tangibility of language itself. First, by a peculiar conviction of the reality of a universe of language, in which one can depict the unwishes of unpeople, in which "magical omnipotence" can be wound up one more turn to "hypermagical ultraomnipotence," and in which great liberties with customary grammar are taken in the knowledge that his reader's resources of comprehension have been developed but never fully exploited by his normal reading. Second, his generalizing poems are made vivid by his unusual awareness of the concrete reality of words themselves, occupying physical space on the printed page and, when artistically distributed, directing the eye in mimetic rhythms; or creating certain patterns of sound and syntax which often are repeated until their grammatical function is submerged in their audial reality. In Cummings' poems of statement, we can sometimes praise the wit, or even the vision, of his sentences. But we must always look to the cunning, vivid texture of verbal arrangements and of the words taken as realities in themselves.

NOTES

1. This essay, first published in *Poetry New York*, No. 3 (1950), pp. 19–20, is more accessible in *The New American Poetry*, ed. Donald M. Allen (New York: Grove Press, 1960), pp. 386–97.

2. Robert Graves and Laura Riding, *A Survey of Modernist Poetry* (London: Heinemann, 1927), p. 75.

3. "Notes on E.E. Cummings' Language," in *The Double Agent* (New York: Arrow Editions, 1935), pp. 1–29.

4. *Eimi* (New York: Grove Press, 1958), p. 142. See also his defense of Ezra Pound, which describes national states as a "geographical abstraction," quoted in *i: six nonlectures* (Cambridge: Harvard Univ. Press, 1953), p. 69.

5. *The Enormous Room* (New York: Modern Library, 1934), p. viii.

6. *Poems 1923–1954* (New York: Harcourt, Brace, 1954), pp. 397, 373–75, 370–71.

7. Quoted in *i: six nonlectures*, pp. 79–80.

8. Connotation and denotation, tenor and vehicle, intension and extension, concrete and universal, etc. René Wellek, in "The Mode of Existence of a Literary Work of Art," in *Theory of Literature* (New York: Harcourt, Brace, & World, 1965), does acknowledge a "sound-stratum" and a "syntactic structure" before proceeding to higher things.

Him and the Modern Theatre

Manuel L. Grossman*

When it was first produced by the Provincetown Players in the spring of 1928, E. E. Cummings' play *Him* became the subject of a lively critical debate. Reviewers from the New York papers, with the exception of John Anderson of the *Evening Journal* who recognized certain merits in the play, could hardly have been less favorable in their comments. The consensus was expressed by Alexander Woollcott who labeled *Him* "fatiguing, pretentious, and empty."[1] George Jean Nathan added that it was "incoherent, illiterate, preposterous balderdash."[2] The battle was joined. These judgments were balanced by the more cautious views of Gilbert Seldes, Stark Young, and Edmund Wilson, each of whom concluded that although *Him* had its "flaws," it was, nevertheless, a significant dramatic achievement.

Forty years later, a retrospective analysis of the critical reception afforded *Him* reveals that what were most vehemently criticized then—a confusing dramatic structure and a lack of unity and development—are the very qualities that justify renewed interest in the play today. We can perhaps now see that in its disunified structure and ambiguous development *Him* was anticipating many of the important innovations of the modern theatre that have moved theatre away from the realm of discursive logic and the conventional unities and into the "Theatre of the Absurd." This study will examine *Him* within the context of the "Theatre of the Absurd" in an effort to determine in what ways the play was a forerunner of the modern theatre.

Him is a two-part exploration of the role of the artist in the modern

*Reprinted from the *Quarterly Journal of Speech*, 54 (1968), 212–19. Reprinted by permission of Manuel L. Grossman and the *Quarterly Journal of Speech*.

world. One aspect of the play examines his inner life; the other, his relationship to society.

The first theme concerns the ambivalent struggles of the artist to achieve self-transcendence.[3] Cummings presents the struggle in five scenes which depict the relationship of the poet Him—"an artist, a man, and a failure"—and his beloved Me. Him is torn between his art of writing plays and his love for Me. Confronted with the problem of conflicting desires and fearful that the two are mutually exclusive, he is forced into the dilemma of choosing between them.

The second theme expresses the conflict between individuality and conformity, life versus death. According to Cummings, the artist must choose life over death. He must choose integrity, sincerity, and feeling, rejecting sterile logic, overintellectualism and sameness.[4]

This concept of life versus death, expressed by the playwright as the struggle of the artist to remain an individual despite the seductions of conformity, is embodied in the play through various symbolic figures. Act One, scene one, introduces the two major death symbols—the "Three Weirds" and the Doctor. The "Three Weirds" appear to be a debased modern variation on the Fates of mythology and the Weird Sisters of *Macbeth*. Unlike these figures, who, at least, evoked an aura of mystery, the "Three Weirds" are simply provincial non-entities who let loose a constant stream of mixed clichés, advertising slogans, and other inanities. As if to stress their sterility and particularly Americanized brand of cliché, they are addressed either as "One, Two, and Three" or as "Stop, Look and Listen."

The Doctor, a symbol of the forces of science, represents empty intellect and abstraction. As a symbol of science, he is made responsible for the conformists that society has spawned.[5] This idea is expressed by the play within a play which comprises Act Two. Each scene of this act reveals the Doctor in a new disguise: in turn a businessman, a soap-box orator, a detective, an American tourist, a circus barker, and a self-appointed enforcer of the moral code.

This play within a play is also a multi-leveled burlesque, poking fun at the most popular forms of drama of the period while at the same time ridiculing the follies of modern man. In one of the most interesting of these scenes, Cummings burlesques modern dress historical drama by presenting a bawdy version of Mussolini's rise to power as it might have been staged at the Old Howard Burlesque House in Boston. Other scenes heap ridicule on the superficiality of the American male (three middle-aged drunks playing croquet and tennis *sans* implements in the early hours of the morning), modern man's gullibility about science (the Doctor in the guise of a soap-box orator peddling an elixir for civilization's ills), Freudian psychology (an Englishman who totes around his unconscious in a trunk), and American tourists.

On the opposite pole, the Freaks, "the unhappy residue of noncon-

formists society has left behind," who appear in the last act, are the symbols of courageous individualism in a world pervaded by conformity.[6]
They are the Nine Foot Giant, the Queen of Serpents, the Human Needle,
the Tattooed Man, the Missing Link, Six Hundred Pounds of Passionate
Pulchritude, the Eighteen Inch Lady, and the King of Borneo. This
courage to be different is predictably disturbing to the "Three Weirds" in
their roles as respectable members of society. Thus "Miss Look Weird,"
after hearing of the exploits of the Eighteen Inch Lady in Russia, asks
slyly, "What was she doing among the Bolsheviki?" And in a Freudian
touch, one of the other "Weirds" gasps, upon hearing the Barker's introduction of the Queen of Serpents, "I hate snakes, ugh!" Finally, "Miss
Listen Weird," noting the unabashed confidence and pride of Six Hundred Pounds of Passionate Pulchritude, is led to snort, "You'd think
people would have a little shame, wouldn't you?"[7]

Although this brief description provides an idea of some of the basic
action of the play, it leaves certain questions unanswered. What, for example, is the source of *Him*'s complexity, and why did the play cause such
a furor among the critics? A partial answer must be sought in Cummings'
intention in writing the play. Cummings appears to have written *Him* as
a protest against what he termed the "conventional theatre." Throughout
his lifetime, he displayed a great disdain toward the "legitimate" theatre.
Once asked by *Vanity Fair* to write about his impressions of the then current American drama, he agreed only on the condition that he not be required to see any of the seven plays they asked him to write about since
"he had never attended the theatre in his life and could not find any particular reason for doing so now."[8]

Cummings preferred burlesque and the circus to conventional
theatre. He left no doubt about this when he wrote that the National
Winter Garden (a famed New York Burlesque House) was "a singularly
fundamental institution, whose Scratch is a noble clown, whose first wink
is worth the struttings of a hundred thousand Barrymores, who are the
unmitigated bunk: since the direction of all spectacle lives in Aristophanes
and the 'theatre' has a great future behind it, said 'future' being the Circus."[9] In the same essay he offered a rationale for this view: ". . . the
creations of the National Winter Garden possess, in common with the
sculpture of Gaston Lachaise, the painting of John Marin and the music of
Igor Stravinsky, the virtue of being intensely alive; whereas the productions of the conventional theatre, like academic sculpture and painting
and music, are thoroughly dead—since 'art,' if it means anything, means
to be intensely alive, the former constitute art and the latter are balderdash."[10]

Although Cummings was disdainful of what had passed for theatre,
he saw hope for the future. By developing new audience-performance
relationships and new kinds of involvement, he felt that this form could
be transformed from "a box of negligible tricks" and "a pennyintheslot

Manuel L. Grossman   195

peep show parlour" into something "intensely alive." He even offered some suggestions for doing the job. Cummings felt, first of all, that the "picture-frame stage," a concept that was in his view "inorganic, mechanical and sterile," had to be replaced by a more dynamic approach to staging plays. Moreover, he discussed various alternatives.

One of these was the "space stage," a concept with which he had become acquainted when as a guest critic for *The Dial* he had reviewed Friedrich Kiesler's International Theatre Exposition. Another was the circus which Cummings described as "a gigantic spectacle, *which is surrounded* by an audience,—in contrast to our modern theatres, where an audience and a spectacle merely confront each other."[11] (Elsewhere, he suggested that the latter confrontation was "rotten" to the core.)[12]

But curiously enough, it was Coney Island, that teeming New York Amusement Center, to which Cummings turned as the most promising model for a new theatre. At Coney Island, that "extravagant fusion of the circus and the theatre," he miraculously discovered—"THE AUDIENCE IS THE PERFORMANCE."[13]

> It [Coney Island] resembles the theatre, in that it fosters every known species of illusion. It suggests the circus, in that it puts us in touch with whatever is hair-raising, breath-taking and pore-opening. But Coney Island has a distinct drop on both theatre and circus. Whereas at the theatre we are merely deceived, at Coney Island we deceive ourselves. Whereas at the circus we are merely spectators of the impossible, at Coney we ourselves perform impossible feats—we turn all the heavenly somersaults imaginable and dare all the delirious dangers conceivable.[14]

Variations on these proposals were incorporated into the stage plan for *Him*. By using a rotating room with a window and a mirror as his basic set, Cummings was able to create an interesting variation on the proscenium stage. Norman Friedman in his book, *E. E. Cummings: the Growth of a Writer*, explained how this was accomplished: Cummings "uses a room with a window and a mirror for the Him-Me scenes, but he rotates it four times during the course of the play, so that it ends where it began, with actors and audience confronting one another through the invisible mirror. One of the things which is accomplished by this device . . . is that the audience is encouraged to regard the room as having four walls, and not as having three walls plus an illusory fourth."[15]

Another convention which was perhaps somewhat more baffling to critics was the manner by which Cummings indicated that *Him* was a dream play. The following stage direction, introduced during Act One, scene one, and appearing intermittently throughout the play, was the only concrete indication that the action took place in the subconscious of Me about to be anesthetized for an operation: "A flat surface on which is painted a DOCTOR anesthetizing a WOMAN. In this picture there are two holes corresponding to the heads of the physician and of the patient, and through these holes protrude the living heads of a man and a woman."[16]

Other scenes took place on a completely bare stage with a curtain and few props. A scene that undoubtedly enraged the critics was one in which the curtain rose, stayed up for about one minute, and then fell with no other action taking place. This, as one astute critic has noted, was "pure Dada."

In his attempt to create new kinds of involvement for his audience Cummings went to even greater lengths in *Him*. He presented a play which boldly juxtaposed serious and comic incidents. Thus the tender love scenes between Him and Me were invariably followed, with hardly a transition, by bawdy comedy or riotous "who's-on-first" type mistaken identity slapstick. None of this apparently bothered Cummings, a devotee of the circus and the burlesque show, two forms of popular theatre which rarely make a hard and fast distinction between what is serious and what is comic.

Moreover, the way in which the various scenes in *Him* were presented, with all of the action being given more or less equal dramatic value, made it very difficult for one to decide which was more important to the playwright, the love affair or the horseplay. Or as Robert Maurer put it, . . . "the twenty lions were always on stage . . . but where were they orchestrated."[17]

Cummings provided a kind of rationale for both the unusual juxtapositions and the seemingly unorchestrated quality of the play in an article that he wrote about the glories of the *Folies Bergère*: "By the laws of its own structure, which are the irrevocable laws of juxtaposition and contrast, the revue is a use of everything trivial or plural to intensify what is singular and fundamental. In the case of the *Folies Bergère*, the revue is the use of ideas, smells, colours, Irving Berlin, nudes, tactility, collapsible stairs, three dimensions and fireworks to intensify Mlle. Josephine Baker."[18] Thus Cummings may have offered *Him* in the same spirit as he took the *Folies Bergère*.

The confusion that this kind of approach might produce could hardly have disturbed the playwright; for, according to Cummings, it was just this kind of confusion which, like "the down-rush of a first-rate roller coaster, infused the three-ring circus with thrilling experiences of a life-or-death order."[19]

The play's oblique dialogue and indirect manner of presenting conflict must have complicated matters even more. In his play *Him* Cummings replaced conventional dramatic dialogue with something closer to the way that people actually speak to each other. The dialogue between Him and Me, for example, was more effective in revealing their immediate psychological states than in advancing the dramatic situation. Moreover, the basic conflict between the two lovers, the fact that Me's pregnancy is bringing about their separation, is hinted at indirectly through certain birth references, but is never stated explicitly.

The anti-realistic attitudes of the playwright, the unusual stage directions, the juxtaposition of serious and comic elements, and the indirect way of introducing essential information—all of these—contributed to the complexity of *Him* and added to the perplexity of the critics. For the daily reviewers this perplexity usually turned to anger. Alexander Woollcott, George Jean Nathan and Brooks Atkinson agreed that the play neither made sense, nor said anything new. As for Cummings, Woollcott proposed that he was "one of those playwrights . . . cousins to the surgeon who needs no knowledge of anatomy and to the architect who really couldn't be bothered with anything so Victorian as specific gravity."[20] Nathan chimed in that "for utter guff, this Cummings' exhibition has never been surpassed within the memory of the oldest play-reviewer operating in Manhattan."[21]

John Anderson of the *Evening Journal*, however, took exception to the cavalier treatment that Cummings' play received from the New York daily critics. Anderson tried to give *Him* its due when he noted that "it doesn't quite come off . . . but none of its flaws quite destroy the sharp perception behind it, and the quivering intensity of its writing."[22]

The monthly reviewers for the literary magazines were more evenly divided about the play. John Hyde Preston, the critic for the *Saturday Review of Literature*, allowed Cummings no quarter. "This new play (which is not a play at all, but a mess of formless talk with a not very clear idea behind it)," Preston proposed, "is the *reductio ad absurdum* of his talents and his highly modernistic Symbolism."[23] Echoing these sentiments, John Mason Brown in *Theatre Arts Monthly* curtly stated that "it is not a play, it can not be enjoyed, and it can not be understood."[24]

But there were others—Gilbert Seldes, Edmund Wilson, and Stark Young, in particular—who defended the play. Although these critics, without exception, admitted that *Him* needed cutting and tended to lack unity, they were impressed with its bawdy comedy, poetic intensity, and lyric beauty. They were unanimous in their praise of the love scenes between Him and Me, love scenes in which, as Wilson aptly put it, Cummings "has succeeded with an original and marvelous eloquence, not merely in letting us hear what the lovers say, but also in making us feel what they feel, experience what they experience."[25]

In the forty years that have passed since the first controversial performances of *Him*, a new approach to the theatre with a whole series of new stage conventions has begun to develop. According to Eugène Ionesco, one of its principal exponents, this form of theatre rests upon the philosophical assumption that "cut off from his religious, metaphysical and transcendental roots, man is lost; all his actions become senseless, absurd, useless."[26] With this statement as the basis for his thinking, Martin Esslin has defined the new form as the "Theatre of the Absurd."

In this "Theatre of the Absurd," a more or less direct reaction against realistic theatre, psychologically motivated characters and conventional plots are abandoned and emphasis is placed, in Esslin's words, upon creating "a language based on concrete images rather than argument and discursive speech."[27] Thus, as Esslin has proposed, one of the most significant aspects of the "Theatre of the Absurd" is that it "strives to express its sense of the senselessness of the human condition by the open abandonment of rational devices and discursive thought."[28]

This non-discursive element that relates the "Theatre of the Absurd" to the modern artist's attempts to transcend the realm of discursive meaning is especially important. In his book *The Banquet Years*, a study of avant-garde art from 1885 to the First World War, Roger Shattuck has pointed out that these attempts stemmed from the modern artist's desire to explore the subconscious world, to capture what Sergei Eisenstein termed "inner speech."[29]

The basic intention behind this approach was, according to Shattuck, to express the idea of simultaneity or "to grasp the moment in its total significance, or, more ambitiously, to manufacture a moment which surpasses our usual perception of time and space."[30] It is particularly revealing that Shattuck finds the clearest statement of this intention in the dialogue with an imaginary author which Cummings wrote and had published on the book jacket of *Him*:

> Author: Well?
> Public: What is *Him* about?
> Author: Why ask me? Did I or didn't I make the play?
> Public: But you surely know what you're making . . .
> Author: Beg pardon, Mr. Public, I surely make what I'm knowing.
> Public: So far as I'm concerned, my very dear sir, nonsense isn't everything in life.
> Author: And so far as you're concerned, 'life' is a verb of two voices—active, to do, and passive, to dream. Others believe doing to be only a kind of dreaming. Still others have discovered (in a mirror surrounded with mirrors) something harder than silence but softer than falling; the third voice of 'life,' which believes itself and which cannot mean because it is.[31]

It is important to note that Esslin has recognized this passage as a "perfect statement of the philosophy of the 'Theatre of the Absurd,' in which the world is seen as a hall of reflecting mirrors, and reality merges imperceptibly into fantasy."[32]

It should not be surprising that the author of *Him* and the playwrights of the Absurd hold a similar attitude toward communication. The attitude of the absurdists is pointed up by Esslin when he says that "the form, structure and mood of an artistic statement can not be separated from its meaning, its conceptual content; simply because the art as a whole is its meaning, *what* is said in it is indissolubly linked with the *manner* in which it is said, and cannot be said in any other way."[33] Thus, when Samuel Beckett answered Alan Schneider's query about the meaning of *Waiting for Godot* with "If I knew, I would have said so in the play,"[34] he neatly summed up the attitude of the absurdists toward communication.

Cummings not only shared the absurdists' position "against interpretation," but perhaps went further in proposing that the question of communication was irrelevant to the true artist. This idea was most succinctly expressed in the second scene of *Him*, in which the poet describes his art as a perilous acrobatic act, balancing three chairs in the sky. When asked what will happen to the chairs (the completed work) by Me, Him answers, "the chairs will all fall by themselves down from the wire and be caught by anybody, by nobody; by somebody whom I don't see and who doesn't see me; perhaps by everybody."[35] And so Cummings cleverly offers a denial that the artist is responsible to anyone but his muse.

Stemming perhaps from a common intention, the attempt to express "the third voice of 'life,' " and a shared attitude toward communication, E. E. Cummings' *Him* and the plays of the "Theatre of the Absurd," particularly those of Beckett and Ionesco, reveal interesting similarities. There are, first of all, structural similarities. The absence of a clearly articulated plot and a linear dramatic development, which was so roundly attacked by the critics of Cummings' play, has become an integral part of absurdist plays. In *Waiting for Godot*, for example, these qualities are pushed to an extreme: the characters are types, and the idea of the story gives way to the exploration of a static situation ('nothing happens, nobody comes, nobody goes, it's awful').

Still another area of similarity concerns the use of the conventions and techniques of the popular theatre. In trying to go beyond the confines of the conventional theatre, playwrights such as Beckett and Ionesco have followed a path similar to that taken by Cummings in *Him*. They have incorporated various techniques from popular theatre into their work. In the case of Beckett these techniques—cross talk comic dialogue, slapstick gestures, and pratfalls—have been derived from vaudeville and farce. In this way, as Ruby Cohn has stated in her book *Samuel Beckett: The Comic Gamut*, theatre has become his "immediate metaphor of the world."[36]

For Ionesco, the metaphor is derived from the Punch and Judy show. By resorting to the basic convention of this form, the revealing of the strings, Ionesco has attempted to express a new form of theatre. "To push the theatre beyond that intermediary zone that is neither theatre nor literature was to put it back into its proper framework, to its natural limits. What was needed was not to disguise the strings that moved the puppet, but to make them even more visible, deliberately apparent, to go right down to the very basis of the grotesque, the realm of caricature, to transcend the pale irony of witty drawing-room comedies. . . ."[37]

Because of their interest in popular theatre, where comic and serious elements often merge, these playwrights have also adopted the technique of juxtaposition that plays such a prominent role in *Him*. As a matter of fact, they have gone even further in this direction. They have developed a form of drama, based on the idea of expressing theatrical concerns in comic terms, which might be labeled the "comedy of the absurd." By using "comic means" for "serious ends" Beckett's theatre can express life as "no more than the comedy of life,"[38] and Ionesco can strive to convey what he himself refers to as the "tragedy of comedy."[39]

Despite the fact that it has been possible to note similarities in the approaches of Cummings, Beckett, and Ionesco, it is important to prevent these from blinding us to at least one essential difference: Cummings does not share the all-encompassing pessimism of the exponents of the "Theatre of the Absurd." In particular, he does not share the view that man is cut off from all transcendental values. One of the basic themes of *Him*, for example, is that the artist must strive for self-transcendence.

Nevertheless, enough parallels have been noted to justify the view that both in terms of intentions and approach, E. E. Cummings anticipated many of the innovations of the "Theatre of the Absurd." Moreover, the ambiguities and non-linear development which so confused and enraged the critics of *Him* have become a more or less acceptable component of the modern theatre.

Examining *Him* today, it is impossible to deny that parts of the play are badly overwritten and much that was extraneous has been needlessly included; but it is difficult to deny that the passage of time has made this play more, rather than less, important. As Martin Esslin has expressed it, ". . . the theatre Jarry and Cummings created has found its public."[40]

NOTES

1. Charles Norman, *The Magic Maker* (New York: Macmillan, 1958), p. 242.

2. Gilbert Seldes, "The Theatre," *The Dial*, 85 (1928), p. 75.

3. In one of his rare attempts at explanation, Cummings described this struggle as follows: ". . . I recognize immediately . . . three mysteries: love, art, and self-transcendence or growing . . . we should go hugely astray in assuming that art was the only self-transcendence. Art is a mystery: all mysteries have their source in a mystery-of-mysteries who is love: and if lovers may reach eternity directly through love herself, their mystery remains essentially that of the loving artist, whose way must lie through his art, and of the loving worshipper whose aim is oneness with his god." E.E. Cummings, *i: six nonlectures* (Cambridge: Harvard Univ. Press, 1953), p. 82.

4. *i: six nonlectures*, p. 111.

5. *i: six nonlectures*, p. 68.

6. This same idea was used by Alfred Jarry in a little known *Guignol* play entitled *Par la Taille*. In this play the Giant and the Hunchback contest for the love of a girl with the "Average Man."

7. E.E. Cummings, *Him* (New York: Liveright, 1927), pp. 135, 136, and 140.

8. *E.E. Cummings: A Miscellany Revised*, ed. George J. Firmage (New York: October House, 1965), p. 86.

9. *E.E. Cummings: A Miscellany Revised*, p. 144.

10. *E.E. Cummings: A Miscellany Revised*, pp. 129–30.

11. *E.E. Cummings: A Miscellany Revised*, p. 112.

12. *E.E. Cummings: A Miscellany Revised*, p. 151.

13. Here Cummings seems to have anticipated the kind of "environmental theatre" that Antonin Artaud proposed in *The Theatre and Its Double* and the exponents of Happenings and Action Theatre have been experimenting with lately.

14. *E.E. Cummings: A Miscellany Revised*, p. 150.

15. Norman Friedman, *E.E. Cummings: The Growth of a Writer* (Carbondale: Southern Illinois Univ. Press, 1964), p. 54.

16. Cummings seemed to have borrowed this idea from Coney Island, where painted surfaces depicting comic scenes contain holes corresponding to the heads of the caricatured figures, through which one can protrude one's own head, thereby becoming part of the comedy.

17. Robert E. Maurer, "E.E. Cummings' *Him*," *Bucknell Review*, 6 (1956), 10.

18. *E.E. Cummings: A Miscellany Revised*, p. 163.

19. *E.E. Cummings: A Miscellany Revised*, p. 113.

20. Norman, p. 241.

21. Seldes, p. 75.

22. Norman, p. 247.

23. Norman, p. 227.

24. John Mason Brown, "Valedictory to a Season," *Theatre Arts Monthly* (June 1928), p. 392.

25. Edmund Wilson, *The Shores of Light* (New York: Farrar, Straus and Young, 1952), pp. 284–85.

26. Martin Esslin, *The Theatre of the Absurd* (Garden City, New York: Doubleday, 1961), p. xix.

27. Esslin, p. 294.

28. Esslin, p. xix.

29. Roger Shattuck, *The Banquet Years* (Garden City, New York: Doubleday, 1961), p. 341.

30. Shattuck, p. 345.

31. Shattuck, p. 341.

32. Esslin, p. 289. Esslin also proposes, pp. 296–97, that the "Theatre of the Absurd" carried the search for a non-discursive form of expression into "the concrete imagery of the stage," a medium which, in his opinion, is "particularly suited to the communication of complex images. . . ."

33. Esslin, p. 12.

34. Esslin, p. 12.

35. *Him*, p. 13.

36. Ruby Cohn, *Samuel Beckett: The Comic Gamut* (New Brunswick, New Jersey: Rutgers Univ. Press, 1962), p. 297.

37. Esslin, p. 91.

38. Jacques Guicharnaud, *Modern French Theater* (New Haven: Yale Univ. Press, 1961), p. 215.

39. Roger Shattuck, "Superliminal Note," *Evergreen Review*, 13 (May–June 1960), 31.

40. Esslin, p. 289.

E.E. Cummings and
Popular Culture

Patrick B. Mullen*

It is generally overlooked that E.E. Cummings had an avid interest in various forms of American popular culture, especially burlesque, circuses, amusement parks, comic strips, animated cartoons, and movies. During the 1920's and 1930's, Cummings wrote many essays on mass culture which appeared in popular magazines such as *Vanity Fair* and journals of the arts such as *Stage* and *Cinema*. In these articles and in some of his other prose, Cummings reveals a great deal about his own concepts of art and poetry, and also provides some penetrating insights into American culture as manifested in popular entertainment. To Cummings, burlesque and the other popular arts were alive with a spontaneous, unrehearsed quality. He wanted to capture the same quality of spontaneity in his poetry, both in content and technique. In a limited way, Cummings wrote about popular culture of the 1920's–1930's much the same as Tom Wolfe was writing about it in the 1960's. Cummings was one of the few writers of his day to deal with mass entertainment, and his fondness for it shows through in his poetry.

Burlesque had a more direct influence on Cummings' poetry than the other popular forms. He was a devoted fan of burlesque and went many times to the Old Howard in Boston, and the National Winter Garden and Irving Place Theatre in New York. An article by Cummings about burlesque entitled "You Aren't Mad, Am I?" appeared in the December, 1925, issue of *Vanity Fair*. In it he discussed burlesque as a true art form because it was "intensely alive; whereas the productions of the conventional theatre, like academic sculpture and painting and music, are thoroughly dead."[1] This antagonistic attitude toward high art is typical of Cummings and can be considered a part of his general anti-intellectualism. He claims that since burlesque is modern and abstract and loved by the masses, the critics who say that modern art is not for the masses are completely wrong.

In analyzing the art of burlesque Cummings emphasizes its incongruous and paradoxical qualities: " 'opposites' occur *together*. For that reason, burlesk enables us to (so to speak) *know around* a thing, character, or situation."[2] In ordinary painting, on the other hand, we can only know one side of a thing. As an example of "knowing around" Cummings cites his favorite burlesque comic Jack Shargel, whom he called one of the "two very great actors in America."[3] Cummings was almost reverential when he wrote that around Shargel "there hung very loosely some authentic *commedia dell'arte*."[4] Opposites occur together when

*Reprinted from *Journal of Popular Culture*, 5 (1971), 503–20. Reprinted by permission of the *Journal of Popular Culture*.

Shargel delicately and lightly tosses a red rose to the floor. It floats downward and when it lands, a terrific ear-splitting crash is heard.

> Nothing in 'the arts' . . . has moved me more, or has proved to be a more completely inextinguishable source of 'aesthetic emotion,' than this *knowing around* the Shargel rose; this releasing of all the unroselike and non-flowerish elements which—where 'rose' and 'flower' are ordinarily concerned—*secretly or unconsciously* modify and enhance those rose—and flower—qualities to which (in terms of consciousness only) they are 'opposed.'[5]

Another example of opposites occurring together in slapstick comedy is the trick pistol which instead of giving a loud smoky discharge drops an innocuous sign with "bang" written on it.

Cummings has transferred the juxtaposition of opposites in burlesque into one of his favorite poetic techniques. One of the poems which employs this uses a description of a burlesque strip-teaser to contrast the picture of a famous university professor.

> curtains part)
> the peacockappareled
> prodigy of Flo's midnight
> Frolic dolores
>
> small in the head keen chassised like a Rolls
> Royce
> swoops smoothly
>   outward(amid
> tinkling-cheering-hammering
>
> tables)
>
> while softly along Kirkland Street
> the infantile ghost of Professor
> Royce rolls
>
> remembering that it
>
> has for
> -gotten some-
> thing ah
>
> (my
>
> necktie[6]

The intellectual professor Josiah Royce of Harvard is contrasted to the physical image of the stripper Dolores. The non-intellectual qualities of Dolores are illuminated by the spiritual Professor Royce and *vice versa*. For the absentminded professor to forget his necktie is humorous, but there is a state of pathos here which arises from his absentmindedness. Dolores is "keen chassised like a Rolls Royce," but Cummings uses the inversion of this to create a pun and point up the opposite nature of Royce.

The pun itself illustrates opposites occurring together in word play which enables the reader to "know around" both the stripper and the professor. This poem also captures the spontaneity and eye appeal of burlesque with the sound image of "tinkling-cheering-hammering tables."

The verbal comedy of the burlesque comic also appealed to Cummings' sense of the ridiculous. In the foreword to *Is 5*, Cummings uses burlesque in explaining his theory of technique.

> I can express it in fifteen words, by quoting The Eternal Question And Immortal Answer of burlesk, viz. 'Would you hit a woman with a child?—No, I'd hit her with a brick.' Like the burlesk comedian, I am abnormally fond of that precision which creates movement.[7]

The joke expresses some of Cummings' favorite poetic techniques: movement, incongruity, and surprise. These same elements are inherent in his juxtaposition of opposites, but surprise can arise from other incongruities. For instance, in one of his poems on the effect of science on mankind, Cummings juxtaposes incongruous elements for humorous and satiric purposes. In "pity this busy monster, manunkind"[8] the line occurs, "Progress is a comfortable disease." A new understanding of progress is gained by modifying "disease" with a word which is associated with an opposite feeling. Cummings views scientific progress as a morally destructive process. Later in the same poem he says, "electrons deify one razorblade / into a mountainrange." Again there is the juxtaposition of incongruous elements—electrons, razorblades, and mountainranges—to point up the absurdity of man's self image as the tamer of the universe. The incongruity between man's scientific illusions and the reality of his insignificance leads to Cummings' famous advice in the last two lines, "listen: there's a hell / of a good universe next door; let's go." Part of the surprise humor in the ending arises out of the contrast between the colloquial tone of these words and the pseudo-technical tone of the rest of the poem, "hypermagical ultraomnipotence."

Science and technology represent the dead world of nonfeeling and nonloving, and Cummings satirizes them mercilessly. But burlesque was a part of the alive world which he celebrated in many of his poems and articles. In one article, "Burlesque, I Love It," which appeared in *Stage* in March of 1936, Cummings analyzed the history of burlesque and how the advent of strippers such as Dolores was brought about. In the early days of burlesque, which Cummings observed at the Old Howard in Boston, there were no strippers, and the women were just trimmings. In the next phase, after the First World War, the comedian became king, and burlesque achieved the status of a true art form. This period was observed by Cummings at the National Winter Garden in New York. After the Winter Garden folded and the Irving Place Theatre took its place, the focus of burlesque changed from the comedian's humor to feminine pulchritude. John Dos Passos took Cummings to Irving Place one day, and

Cummings witnessed the strip tease for the first time. The comedian was no longer the center of attention.

> Humor, filth, slapstick, and satire were all present, but they functioned primarily to enhance the Eternal Feminine. And when you saw that Feminine you understood why. It was no static concept, that pulchritude. It moved, and in moving it revealed itself, and in revealing itself it performed such prodigies of innuendo as made the best belly dancer of the *Folies Bergere* entr'acte look like a statute of liberty.[9]

Here again is Cummings' fascination with movement; the stripper who best exemplified movement was June St. Clare.

> To see June St. Clare walk the length of the Irving Place stage, or the Apollo stage, or any other stage, is to rejoice that a lost art has been revived. There have been epidemics of women who swam when they walked and of women who floated when they walked. When Miss St. Clare walks, she walks.[10]

Cummings transfers his love of movement to the printed page in his poetry. Cummings' poems never sit still; they move across the page in unusual typography, and the words themselves often suggest movement. Marshall McLuhan noticed this element in Cummings' poetry. "The poet at the typewriter can do Njinsky leaps or Chaplin-like shuffles and wiggles."[11] In one poem Cummings attempts to emulate the bumps and grinds of a stripper performing her act. He demonstrated his belief that woman could be the most beautiful expression of movement and aliveness.

```
sh estiffl
ystrut sal
lif san
dbut sth

epoutin(gWh.ono:w
s li psh ergo
wnd ow n,
                  r
Eve


aling 2 a
-sprout eyelands)sin
uously&them&twi
tching,begins

unununun?
butbutbut??
tonton???
ing????

—Out-&
        steps;which
```

flipchucking
.grins
gRiNdS

d is app ea r in gly
eyes grip live loop croon mime
nakedly hurl asquirm the
dip&giveswoop&swoon&ingly

seethe firm swirl hips whirling climb to
GIVE
(yoursmine mineyours yoursmine
!
i( )t)[12]

The letters and words are so arranged as to suggest the mystery and "peek-a-boo," tantalizing, teasing quality of the stripper. We never see it all, but we see enough to keep us interested. When she slips her gown down she reveals two sprouting islands ("eyelands"), a very sensual image for breasts. The halting and provocative unbuttoning of her gown is suggested by the repetition of parts of the word until they all fall together, and by the question marks at the end of each line. When the stripper grinds, the words grinds ("gRiNdS"). The vicarious participation of the men in the audience almost becomes an orgasm at the end of the poem. Besides the type swooping all over the page, the words also imply movement, "struts," "slips," "twitching," "steps," "flipchucking," "grinds," "loop," "mine," "hurl," "swoop," "swirl, "whirling," and "climb." The words and typography suggest the spontaneity of the burlesque art which the poem describes.

Another popular form of entertainment which delighted Cummings was the circus, and like burlesque it too was noted for movement. In an article in *Vanity Fair* of October, 1925, he noticed the movement which made it come alive. "Movement is the very stuff out of which this dream is made. Or we may say that movement is the content, the subject matter, of the circus-show, while bigness is its form."[13] The circus as an art form has something which even burlesque lacks, a sense of reality. "Within 'the big top,' as nowhere else on earth, is to be found Actuality."[14] There is nothing phoney when the lion tamer faces the lion and when the trapeze artist defies death. Again, there are opposites occurring together as the terror of death is juxtaposed with the antics of the clowns. "At positively every performance Death Himself lurks, glides, struts, breathes, is. Lest any agony be missing, a mob of clowns tumbles loudly in and out of that inconceivably sheer fabric of doom, whose beauty seems endangered by the spectator's least heartbeat or whisper."[15] The circus appealed to Cummings because it captured the spontaneity of life just as burlesque did. In comparison, the theatre was stilted, confined, and formal.

In discussing the circus, Cummings defines what art means to him:

. . . . let us never be fooled into taking seriously that perfectly superficial distinction which is vulgarly drawn between the circus-show and 'art' or 'the arts.' Let us not forget that every authentic 'work of art' is in and of itself alive and that, however 'the arts' may differ among themselves, their common function is the expression of that supreme alive-ness which is known as 'beauty.'[16]

"Aliveness" and "beauty" seem to be the qualities which Cummings seeks in art, and if painting, fiction and drama ever lack them, then they are not art in those instances; but if mass forms of entertainment, the burlesque and circus, have them, then they are appreciated as true art. One of Cummings' poems celebrates the appreciation of live beauty as opposed to intellectual pseudo-artistic concepts of beauty.

> mr youse needn't be so spry
> concernin questions arty
>
> each has his tastes but as for i
> i likes a certain party
>
> gimme the he-man's solid bliss
> for youse ideas i'll match youse
>
> a pretty girl who naked is
> is worth a million statues[17]

Cummings is saying that beauty should appeal to the emotion, not the intellect. His belief in living beauty is couched in the vulgar language of the common man for the purpose of humor in this poem, but this does not lessen the strength of his conviction. He puts these words in the mouth of an uneducated man to make them more convincing; they would not ring true if an intellectual said them. The reader laughs at the last two lines, yet he cannot help but realize that there is some truth here. The living breathing beauty of a woman is what many artists have tried to capture in paintings and sculpture, but the original model is still the most inspiring of all.

Cummings also saw beauty and aliveness in amusement parks, especially his favorite, Coney Island. "The incredible temple of pity and terror, mirth and amazement, which is popularly known as Coney Island, really constitutes a perfectly unprecedented fusion of the circus and the theatre."[18] Besides displaying beauty and aliveness, Coney Island performs a unique function of fusing humanity; ". . . nowhere else in all of the round world is humanity quite so much itself."[19] The swimmer at Coney Island swims in the populace, not the water, adding to the "spontaneous itselfness." The performance at this "circus-theatre" is joined with the audience, a fact which is significant for art. The audience participates by doing circus tricks themselves, by riding the death-defying roller coasters and loop-the-loops. To Cummings, ". . . the essence of Coney Island's 'circus-theatre' consists in *homogeneity*. THE AU-

DIENCE IS THE PERFORMANCE, and vice versa."[20] Cummings seems to have anticipated the current interest in participatory arts, widely expressed in the "living theatre" and in art which requires the viewer to enter its structure or manipulate it in some way. Having actors embrace members of the audience and using electronic media are not the only ways to involve the audience; the printed page has long been used to make the reader participate in an experience. This is what Cummings attempts to do in his poetry, to fuse the reader with the poem, to make the poem become the reader. He wants the poem to be an emotional experience for the reader. Most of Cummings' poems could be offered as examples of this, especially his love poems and nature poems.

One example of a nature poem will suffice for illustration. Cummings attempts to draw the reader into a scene in nature by making it a transcendental emotional experience.

                    & sun &

                    sil
                    e
                    nce
                    e

                    very

                    w
                    here
                    noon
                    e

                    is exc

                    ep
                    t
                    on
                    t

                    his

                    b
                    oul
                    der
                    a

          drea(chipmunk)ming[21]

Part of the involvement of the reader is achieved by waiting until the last line to reveal that the poem is about a chipmunk. This surprise is intensified by spreading the words down the page so that the reader has to put them together before he can understand them. The intellectual process involves the reader on one level and leads him to emotional involvement on another level. The reader must put together the key phrase of the poem, "everywhere no one is except on this boulder." At this moment nothing else exists except the chipmunk. The simple observation of the sleeping chipmunk becomes a transcendental experience for Cummings and the reader. Cummings has transcended the corporeal world of reality and reached a truer world of the imagination through the chipmunk. The reader is supposed to feel the same emotional transference by reading and comprehending the poem.

Another form of mass entertainment which Cummings analyzed was the comic strip. He wrote an article entitled "A Foreword to Krazy" which appeared in the 1946 spring number of *Sewanee Review*. Before him, Gilbert Seldes had written of George Herriman's comic strip character Krazy Kat in *The Seven Lively Arts*. The situation between Krazy Kat, Offissa Pupp, and Ignatz Mouse is summed up by Cummings: "Dog hates mouse and worships 'cat,' mouse despises 'cat' and hates dog, 'cat' hates no one and loves mouse."[22] But each of the characters is symbolic, with Krazy as the central symbol. "Krazy is herself. Krazy is illimitable—she loves. She loves in the only way anyone can love: illimitably."[23] Her love is combined with wisdom; she recognizes their situation and loves anyway. Krazy transcends reality because of her love and wisdom. "Always (no matter what's real) Krazy is no mere reality. She is a living ideal. She is a spiritual force, inhabiting a merely real world—"[24] Marshall McLuhan has said of the comic strip as art, "Popular art is the clown reminding us of all the life and faculty that we have omitted from our daily routines."[25] Krazy Kat's love reminds us of the "spiritual force" which is missing from our lives. Cummings' poetry was not directly affected by his appreciation of comic strips, but there is a parallel between his interest in Krazy and one of the main themes of his poetry, love. Like George Herriman, Cummings uses the symbolism of a comic situation to awaken our dead sensibilities to a spiritual awareness of love.

Cummings often used the comic exuberance of youth to evoke an awareness of love in his readers.

> Jimmie's got a goil
> goil
> goil,
> Jimmie
> 's got a goil and
> she coitnly can shimmie
>
> when you see her shake
> shake
> shake
> when
> you see her shake a
> shimmie how you wish that you was Jimmie.
>
> Of for such a gurl
> gurl
> gurl,

                                            oh
        for such a gurl to
        be a fellow's twistandtwirl

        talk about your Sal-
                        Sal-
                            Sal-,
                                    talk
        about your Salo
        -mes but gimmie Jimmie's gal[26]

The earthly love described here can be a spiritual force to transcend the
merely real world, just as a comic strip character can symbolize transcendent love. Some of the fast-paced, visual humor of the comic strip is captured by Cummings' use of rhythm, language, and typography. The
rhythm of the poem and the repetition of "goil goil goil" suggests a child's
chant of derision. Phonetic spelling, "goil," "coitnly," and "gurl," enables
Cummings to approximate actual chants of the streets of New York. The
visual effect of spreading the repetitious words across the page is to make
the reader say them as a chant. The word fusion of "twistandtwirl"
creates the illusion of quickness and agility with which Jimmie's "goil"
dances. The comic comparison between the Biblical, mythical Salome
and the sexy teenager of the streets not only creates bathetic humor but
also stresses Cummings' preference for real earthly sexuality over abstract
concepts of beauty. Cummings celebrates the sparkling aliveness, the
earthy desires, and the electric energy of youth. These qualities of youth
are a part of Cummings' ideal, and he tried to retain some of them all his
life. He was often accused of being an "adolescent songster," and this
remark probably gave him great delight because he tried to maintain the
aliveness of youth in his adult life. This may partially explain his fondness
for entertainments associated with childhood and adolescence: circuses,
amusement parks, comic strips, and animated cartoons.

    Cummings' love for comic strips was intensified when they took on
the motion of animated cartoons. In an article entitled "Miracles and
Dreams" in the June, 1930, issue of *Cinema*, Cummings discussed the
benefits of movie cartoons. His fascination with film animation lies in the
fact that this is a world where nothing is impossible: animals talk, rabbits
save other rabbits from being tied to railroad tracks, trains split in half,
people walk on air. Miracles take place when we are in this dream world.

> Given this purely miraculous condition, such trifles as impossibility don't
> trouble us at all; everything (even a banana) being "really" something
> else. Let contradictions contradict—to the pure all things are impure, but
> we, by heaven, understand our dream symbols. . . .[27]

Here again are the opposites occurring together, and a new awareness and
understanding arising from it. The awareness comes about through
laughter at the contradictions. At the end of the article Cummings, in ad-

dressing the reader, emphasizes the importance of laughter. "And if you—this means you—are an abnormal individual so healthy, so fearless, so rhythmic, so human, as to be capable of the miracle called 'laughter,' patronize your neighborhood wake-up-and-dreamery!"[28]

Cummings often created a dream world, a world where the impossible is possible, in his poems, and laughter was often the vehicle for entering this realm. One of these creations is the world of candy figurines atop a wedding cake.

> this little bride & groom are
> standing) in a kind
> of crown he dressed
> in black candy she
>
> veiled with candy white
> carrying a bouquet of
> pretend flowers this
> candy crown with this candy
>
> little bride & little
> groom in it kind of stands on
> a thin ring which stands on a much
> less thin very much more
>
> big & kinder of ring & which
> kinder of stands on a
> much more than very much
> biggest & thickest & kindest
>
> of ring & all one two three rings
> are cake & everything is protected by
> cellophane against anything(because
> nothing really exists[29]

Lloyd Frankenberg says of the poem, "This is a little world to itself. The poem is of a size with the cake; constructed, like it, in tiers of progressive excitement; and all frosting."[30] The whimsical humor comes from the building intensity throughout the poem. The reader is swept along by rhythms and sounds, much as a viewer is moved by the rapid action in an animated cartoon, until he is almost breathless and limp by the time the climax occurs in the last line. Cummings builds the reader up tier by tier through the unreality of the cake and then hits him with a startling metaphysical statement. Our world is separated from reality just as the cake is cut off from the outside by cellophane. We are no more real than figurines on top of a cake. The poem is a statement of Cummings' transcendent vision: the physical world is not the ultimate reality, and we can only reach reality through the imagination and emotions. The laughter evoked by the surprise statement at the end is a vehicle for seeing beyond the physical and into the spiritual.

Laughter is also the central element in another of Cummings' movie favorites, Charlie Chaplin. Cummings was a life-long fan of Chaplin's cinematic creations. Chaplin and Jack Shargel were the two comedians whom Cummings called the "two very great actors in America." Cummings captures the "Chaplin-like shuffles and wiggles" in the way he places the type on the page. Chaplin's creation "The Tramp" is closely akin to many of the personages in Cummings' poetry, the hoboes, balloonmen, organ grinders, and other social misfits who bring joy into the lives of others. Cummings' technique of combining pathos with humor is parallel to the feeling evoked by "The Tramp." He is probably the only modern American poet who can achieve to the same degree this fusion of pity and joy. Cummings' Uncle Sol is a victim of circumstances in the tradition of Chaplin's "Tramp."

nobody loses all the time

i had an uncle named
Sol who was a born failure and
nearly everybody said he should have gone
into vaudeville perhaps because my Uncle Sol could
sing McCann He Was A Diver on Xmas Eve like Hell Itself which
may or may not account for the fact that my Uncle

Sol indulged in that possibly most inexcusable
of all to use a highfalootin phrase
luxuries that is or to
wit farming and be
it needlessly
added

my Uncle Sol's farm
failed because the chickens
ate the vegetables so
my Uncle Sol had a
chicken farm till the
skunks ate the chickens when

my Uncle Sol
had a skunk farm but
the skunks caught cold and
died and so
my Uncle Sol imitated the
skunks in a subtle manner

or by drowning himself in the watertank
but somebody who'd given my Uncle Sol a Victor
Victrola and records while he lived presented to
him upon the auspicious occasion of his decease a
scrumptious not to mention splendiferous funeral with
tall boys in black gloves and flowers and everything and

> i remember we all cried like the Missouri
> when my Uncle Sol's coffin lurched because
> somebody pressed a button
> (and down went
> my Uncle
> Sol
>
> and started a worm farm)[31]

Uncle Sol's pathetic ventures become a comic series of pratfalls in a Chaplinesque vein. The reader laughs at Sol's misadventures, but he also sympathizes with him as an underdog. The quick, unpunctuated flow of colloquial words in the poem suggests the intensity and spontaneity of "The Tramp's" comic movements. The ironic humor of the first line which is not revealed until the last line parallels the surprise effect of Chaplin's satiric situations. Sol is even the type of man who should have been in vaudeville, probably as a comic. The juxtaposition of opposites for humorous effect is also seen in this poem: Sol's "splendiferous funeral" is juxtaposed to his worm farm. The incongruity, futility, and absurdity of every man's life is mirrored and exaggerated in the story of Uncle Sol. There is a deeper meaning, then, just as there is always something serious beneath the antics of Charlie Chaplin in his best films. Other Cummings' poems which reflect Chaplinesque technique and subject matter are "in Just-spring," "my uncle Daniel," and all of the poems about Joe Gould, the Greenwich Village beggar.

Cummings' poetry was only indirectly influenced by popular culture, but he definitely absorbed the rhythms and styles of America from 1920 through 1960 as they were expressed in mass entertainment. He considered burlesque, circuses, amusement parks, comic strips, animated cartoons, and movies as true art forms, because, at their best, they demonstrate qualities of aliveness, spontaneity, and beauty. Cummings' interest in mass culture shows his own anti-intellectualism. He wanted no part of an art that was just for a small elite; functioning art had to appeal to the masses. Several of these popular arts exhibit techniques found in Cummings' poetry: the juxtaposition of opposites, incongruity, movement, and surprise. The themes of many of Cummings' poems have similarities with mass entertainment: love, women, youth, and comedy. Cummings saw the popular arts as a means of transcending reality, and his poetry often functions in the same way. Thus, Jack Shargel's rose, June St. Clare's walk, circus clowns, Krazy Kat, and Charlie Chaplin in the realm of entertainment and the stripper Dolores, the chipmunk, Jimmie's "goil," the candy figurines, and Uncle Sol in the realm of poetry are symbolic forces of the imagination which permit the mind to escape the mundane world. Laughter is often a means to this end. Humor runs through all the forms of popular culture which appealed to Cummings, and his own work is made up of many humorous poems. No matter how great or how small the actual influence of popular arts was on Cummings' poetry, there is no doubt that he was in harmony with American mass culture. Thus, Cummings' prose essays on entertainment can be studied by literary critics to better understand his poetry, but they can also be investigated by scholars of American culture in order to gain new perspectives on the artist and his relationship to popular art forms of the 20th century.

NOTES

1. *E.E. Cummings: A Miscellany Revised*, ed. George J. Firmage (New York: October House, 1965), p. 129.

2. *E.E. Cummings: A Miscellany Revised*, p. 127.

3. *E.E. Cummings: A Miscellany Revised*, p. 127.

4. *E.E. Cummings: A Miscellany Revised*, p. 293.

5. *E.E. Cummings: A Miscellany Revised*, p. 128.

6. *Poems, 1923-1954* (New York: Harcourt, Brace, 1954), p. 169.

7. *Poems*, p. 163.

8. *Poems*, p. 397.

9. *E.E. Cummings: A Miscellany Revised*, pp. 294–295.

10. *E.E. Cummings: A Miscellany Revised*, p. 295.

11. *Understanding Media: The Extensions of Man* (New York: McGraw-Hill, 1964), p. 230.

12. *Poems*, p. 320.

13. *E.E. Cummings: A Miscellany Revised*, p. 113.

14. *E.E. Cummings: A Miscellany Revised*, p. 113.

15. *E.E. Cummings: A Miscellany Revised*, p. 113.

16. *E.E. Cummings: A Miscellany Revised*, p. 114.

17. *Poems*, p. 177.

18. *E.E. Cummings: A Miscellany Revised*, p. 150.

19. *E.E. Cummings: A Miscellany Revised*, p. 150.

20. *E.E. Cummings: A Miscellany Revised*, p. 151.

21. *73 Poems* (New York: Harcourt Brace Jovanovich, 1963), No. 58.

22. *E.E. Cummings: A Miscellany Revised*, p. 323.

23. *E.E. Cummings: A Miscellany Revised*, pp. 324–25.

24. *E.E. Cummings: A Miscellany Revised*, p. 327.

25. *Understanding Media*, p. 153.

26. *Poems*, pp. 170–71.

27. *E.E. Cummings: A Miscellany Revised*, p. 213.

28. *E.E. Cummings: A Miscellany Revised*, p. 214.

29. *Poems*, p. 337.

30. *Pleasure Dome: On Reading Modern Poetry* (Boston: Houghton Mifflin, 1949), p. 175.

31. *Poems*, pp. 173–74.

Cummings: One Man Alone

Malcolm Cowley*

"Gertrude Stein who had been much impressed by *The Enormous Room* said that Cummings did not copy, he was the natural heir of the New England tradition with its aridity and its sterility, but also with its individuality."
—*The Autobiography of Alice B. Toklas*, p. 208.

I

It was a curious background for a rebel poet. Edward Estlin Cummings was born (1894) and brought up on a quiet street north of the Harvard Yard, one where distinguished professors lived. William James and Josiah Royce were neighbors, and Charles Eliot Norton had a wooded estate nearby that bordered on Somerville and its Irish tenements. Cambridge in the early 1900s . . . good manners, tea parties, Browning, young women with their minds adequately dressed in English tweeds. I think it was T.S. Eliot who said that life there was so intensely cultured it had ceased to be civilized. The younger poet's family was part of that life. Edward Cummings, the father (Harvard '83), had been an instructor in sociology, but then had become a clergyman, preaching in Boston as the assistant, the colleague, and finally the successor of Edward Everett Hale at the South Congregational Society, Unitarian. Sometimes on Sundays little Estlin, as the family called him, passed the plate. The father, famous for rectitude, was also president of the Massachusetts Civic League and was later executive head of the World Peace Foundation.

The son attended a public high school, Cambridge Latin, where he tells us that the admired principal was a Negro.[1] Sending Estlin there was apparently one of his father's democratic ideas, and another—when the son went on to Harvard, class of '15—was to have him live at home for the first three years. That encouraged his bookish habits and also cut him off from college life, including the club system and its societies, waiting clubs, and final clubs—always something ahead to make students act with propriety for fear of being blackballed. Cummings joined nothing but the Musical Society and the board of a literary magazine that had published some of his early poems. There were two such magazines at Harvard in those days, *The Monthly* and *The Advocate*, and they looked down on each other—or, to be accurate, they nodded to each other coldly from the facing doors of their respective sanctums on the dusty third floor of the Harvard Union. The Monthlies thought that the board of *The Advocate*, which then appeared fortnightly, was composed of journalists,

*First published in the *Yale Review*, 62 (1973), 332–54. Reprinted from *A Second Flowering* by Malcolm Cowley. Copyright © 1956, 1967, 1968, 1970, 1972, 1973 by Malcolm Cowley. Reprinted by permission of Viking Penguin Inc.

clubmen, athletes, and disciples of Teddy Roosevelt, a former editor, with not a man of letters among them. The Advocates suspected that the Monthlies were aesthetes (as indeed most of them came to be called), scruffy poets, socialists, pacifists, or worse. It was for *The Monthly* that Cummings chose to write.

In his last undergraduate year he took a room at college and became a gossiped-about figure in the group that surrounded *The Monthly*. It was the only time in his life that he formed part of a group, but even then he stood apart from most of the others and preferred to keep his relations one to one. He was intensely shy and private in the Cambridge fashion. Still, among the ones he saw often were Dos Passos, Robert Hillyer the conservative poet (though with some distrust on both sides), S. Foster Damon ("who opened my eyes and ears," Cummings was to write, ". . . to all ultra, at that moment, modern music and poetry and painting"), and two very rich young men, James Sibley Watson and Scofield Thayer, who greatly admired his poems and drawings. Cummings decided to stay at Harvard for a year of postgraduate work. At commencement he was awarded a degree *magna cum laude*, with honors in Literature, Greek and English. He was also chosen to give the Disquisition and shocked his classmates and their parents—those who listened—by speaking on "The New Art," with examples from Amy Lowell and Gertrude Stein.

At the time he was in full revolt against almost everything—except personal integrity—that Cambridge and his father stood for. Cleanliness, godliness, decorum, public spirit, then chastity went by the board. Cummings developed a taste for low life, something that teemed in Boston. One night the Boston police were embarrassed to find his father's car, with its clergyman's license plates, parked outside a joint near Scollay Square. Cummings and Dos Passos, both virgins at the time, were not "upstairs"; they were drinking in the parlor while holding a polite conversation with the madam.

> When you rang at Dick Mid's Place
> the madam was a bulb stuck in the door.

In the autumn after his postgraduate year, Cummings went to New York, where he spent three months at the only office job he was ever to hold. The experiment having failed by reason of pure boredom, he went to work seriously on his drawing and painting (the drawing was often inspired; the paintings were impressionistic and weak in color). He took no part in the debate over preparedness for war, one which shook the country in the winter of 1916–17 and which, as a minor effect, disrupted the board of *The Harvard Monthly*. Four of the editors were pacifists, the other four were superpatriots, all eight were impractical, and they couldn't agree on what to print. In April 1917, when Congress declared war, *The Monthly* disappeared from Harvard, but not from memory. An editorial that carefully didn't mention the war explained that publication was being suspended because of "existing circumstances." Cummings by that time was on his way to France as a volunteer in the Norton-Harjes Ambulance Corps.

On the old *Touraine* of the French Line, a tub that wallowed its way through the submarine zone, he met William Slater Brown, another New Englander. Brown, lately a student at Columbia, was a pacifist proud of knowing the anarchist Emma Goldman. Cummings was mildly patriotic, but he didn't allow opinions, at the time, to interfere with his friendships. Through a mistake at headquarters, the two young men were not immediately assigned to an ambulance unit and had a month to spend in Paris. They roamed the streets in all the glow of youth, went to the Russian Ballet, and learned to speak passable French, apparently with the help of Paris ladies ("little ladies more / than dead exactly dance / in my head"). Finally they went to the front in Section 21, whose commanding officer, Lieutenant Anderson, distrusted them because they wore dirty coveralls and were too friendly with the French mechanics. An artillery company quartered in their village had mutinied that spring, and Brown talked about war weariness in letters to friends (as well as in one to Emma Goldman). A French censor reported his remarks to Lieutenant Anderson, who said that Brown was a dangerous character and that Cummings should be arrested too. Cummings might have been cleared—of what charge? there was none—but a sense of personal honor kept him from assuring the military examiners that he detested all Germans. Together the friends were shipped off to La Ferté, to a detention barracks that Cummings was later to celebrate as "the Enormous Room."

The three months he spent there were another watershed, after the rebellion of his last two years at college. Confined with men of all nations, mostly illiterate, even inarticulate, all used to living outside the law, Cummings found that he liked some of them—especially those he called the Delectable Mountains—vastly more than he liked his college classmates. They gave him a new sense of human values: individuals could be admired for their generosity and courage, but social authority was always and everywhere stupid. By example they encouraged him to exalt feeling over knowledge, and they also gave him a new aesthetic. He was soon to say, on page 249 of *The Enormous Room*, "that there is and can be no such thing as authentic art until the *bons trucs* (whereby we are taught to see and imitate on canvas and in stone and by words this so-called world) are entirely and thoroughly and perfectly annihilated by that vast and painful process of Unthinking which may result in a minute bit of purely personal feeling. Which minute bit is Art."

The honors student in Literature, Greek and English was busy unthinking his five years at Harvard and was getting ready to write poems that would each, he hoped, embody a moment of intensely alive and personal feeling. Meanwhile Dr. Edward Cummings, having learned of his son's disappearance, made vigorous efforts first to find where he was, a difficult task in itself, and then to obtain his release. As pastor of the South Church, he was not without friends in Washington. When the French received official inquiries, they gave the son another farcical hearing and finally set him free. Brown, with his letters as evidence, was condemned to the military prison at Précigny, from which nobody had come out living since the first days of the war. There he fell victim to scurvy, but Dr. Cummings was busy with his problem, too, and he was released before the disease had crippled him.

After the Armistice, Brown and Cummings rented a Greenwich Village apartment that became a model of squalor. Cummings liked to roam through the Lower East Side and the Syrian quarter near the southern tip of Manhattan. He was painting "all the time," Brown says, but was also writing scores, even hundreds of poems in many new manners. Meanwhile the death of *The Harvard Monthly* had an unexpected sequel. Scofield Thayer and Sibley Watson had bought a moribund political fortnightly, *The Dial*, which they set about transforming into the most distiguished magazine of the arts that had appeared in this country. In some ways and in some contributors it carried on the tradition of *The Monthly*, this time with a national audience. The first issue, for January 1920, featured the poems and drawings of E.E. Cummings. I remember how they provoked indignant remarks from more conservative poets and, in particular, how Bobby Hillyer fumed.

In the autumn of that year Cummings wrote *The Enormous Room* at his father's house near Silver Lake, New Hampshire. He wrote it at the father's suggestion and partly to keep Dr. Cummings from suing the French government for a million dollars; also he wrote it very fast, in a style close to the spoken idiom he had fashioned for himself over the years. Dr. Cummings had the manuscript copied by his secretary, then went over it with a blue pencil, crossing out the bad words and making other minor changes (for example, a character whom the son called Jesus Christ was renamed Judas). It was hard to find a publisher, but the new firm of Boni and Liveright was more venturesome than others, and Dr. Cummings persuaded them to accept the book. When it appeared in 1922, it was read with enthusiasm by younger writers, and the free-ranging, partly colloquial, partly involved style had a lasting effect on American prose. *The Enormous Room* was not a commercial success. Horace Liveright, who thought he had been fooled, came to dislike the book so much that he wouldn't allow the unsold copies of the first edition to be remaindered; he sold them for wastepaper.[2]

II

In the years from 1923 to 1926 Cummings published four books of poetry: *Tulips and Chimneys*, *&* (he wore his titles cut short), *XLI Poems*, and *Is 5*. Many or most of the poems in all four were written either at college or during the burst of activity and experiment that followed his release from the detention barracks at La Ferté, but the first and the last book stand somewhat apart from the other two. In *Tulips and Chimneys* there are some of his recent experiments, but there are also earlier long pieces full of oriental or medieval color, and these seem utterly traditional in their effort to be exotic. Only one of them has life in it, "All in green went my love riding," a lyrical ballad that is a gifted exercise in Preraphaelitism. The fourth book, *Is 5*, contains many satirical pieces written in what seems to have been a new manner for Cummings. "Poem, or Beauty Hurts Mr. Vinal," "she being Brand-new," "workingman with hand so hairy-sturdy," "my sweet old etcetera": these and others deal mostly with contemporary subjects, using catch phrases and advertising slogans that are strictly of the time (as note "pretty littleliverpillhearted-Nujolneeding-There's-A-Reason americans" in the diatribe against Harold Vinal, a harmless lyric poet from Maine); yet their wit and their headlong rhythms give them an inner life that makes them nearly indestructible. Among all the books of poetry that Cummings published, *Is 5* is still the liveliest.

None of the first four books was a popular success. The audience for poetry was even smaller at the time than in earlier and later periods, and most of it shared Mr. Vinal's tastes for conventional beauty. With Cummings the critics were severe: they condemned his fleshly realism, his experiments with typography, and his custom of using a small "i" for the first-personal pronoun. "e.e. cummings" they called him, with a visible curl of the lip. But the more his work was condemned by critics, the more it was admired by many of the younger writers and the more he was adopted as one of their spokesmen, along with Dos Passos and Hemingway. Fitzgerald had been the first spokesman, but rebels lost faith in him when he appeared too often in *The Saturday Evening Post*. Cummings too was making a keep-alive compromise, by writing prose pieces for *Vanity Fair*, but most of these were signed with a pseudonym. As for his private life, he kept it private, and that added to his prestige.

He wasn't often seen at parties in the middle 1920s, though hostesses tried to capture him and though he had overcome his shyness to the point of liking to have an audience. "I've watched him operating among strangers," another poet said rather envyingly. "He starts talking to one person in a low confidential voice and the person starts laughing. Then another person drifts up, glass in hand, and bends forward to hear what is being said. Cummings talks lower, faster, and funnier, without cracking a smile, and a third person appears. Pretty soon the whole room is grouped around Cummings, everybody laughing, everybody with eyes on him so as not to miss a word." "Jesus, he was a handsome man," as he had written of Buffalo Bill. He had large, well-shaped features, carved rather than molded, eyes set wide apart, often with a glint of mischief in them, and in those days a good deal of fine khaki-colored hair. "Doesn't he look like a faun!" I heard a young woman say. "Or like a bad boy," another said, also admiringly. In later years, when he had lost most of the hair and the rest was clipped off, he looked more like a bare-skulled Buddhist monk.

He was the most brilliant monologuist I have known. What he poured forth was a mixture of cynical remarks, puns, hyperboles, outrageous metaphors, inconsequence, and tough-guy talk spoken from the corner of his wide, expressive mouth: pure Cummings, as if he were rehearsing something that would afterward appear in print. Sometimes it did: "His Royal Highness said 'peek-a-boo' and thirty tame fleas left the prettily embroidered howdah. . . . Thumb-prints of an angel named Frederick found on a lightning-rod, Boston, Mass." Perhaps the style of those harangues is better suggested by his *i: six nonlectures* as these were delivered at Harvard in the early 1950s. The second nonlecture, for instance, starts by praising the world in which he grew to manhood: "a reckless world, filled with the curiosity of life herself; a vivid and violent world welcoming every challenge; a world worth hating and adoring and fighting and forgiving: in brief, a world which was a world." Then, after ridiculing the later ideal of "quote security unquote," he tells a story that has to be repeated in his own words.

> Back in the days of dog-eat-dog [he says] . . . there lived a playboy; whose father could easily have owned the original superskyscraper-deluxe; a self-styled Cathedral of Commerce, endowed with every impetus to relaxation; not excluding ultraelevators which (on the laudable assumption that even machinery occasionally makes mistakes) were regularly tested. Testing an ultraelevator means that its car was brought clean up, deprived of safety devices, and dropped. As the car hurtled downward, a column of air confined by the elevator shaft became more and more compressed; until (assuming that nothing untoward happened) it broke the car's fall completely—or so I was told by somebody who should know. At any rate, young Mr. X was in the habit not only of attending these salubrious ceremonies, but of entering each about-to-be-dropped car, and of dropping with it as far as the laws of a preEinsteinian universe permitted. Eventually, of course, somebody who shouldn't know telephoned a newspaper; which sent a reporter; who (after scarcely believing his senses) asked the transcender of Adam point-blank why he fell so often. Our playful protagonist shrugged his well-tailored shoulders—"for fun" he said simply; adding (in a strictly confidential undertone) "and it's wonderful for a hangover."
>
> Here, I feel, we have the male American stance of my adolescence; or (if you prefer) the adolescent American male stance of what some wit once nicknamed a "lost generation"; whereof—let me hastily append—the present speaker considers himself no worthy specimen. My point, however, isn't that many of us were even slightly heroic; and is that few of us declined a gamble. I don't think we enjoyed courting disaster. I do feel we liked being born.

In Cummings' published work, that passage is one of the very few in which he used the pronoun "we" as referring to any group larger than the one composed of the poet and his love. Usually other groups were "they," alien and hostile. But "we," meaning his generation, were reckless persons who liked to accept a challenge, and "we" sometimes gambled with death simply "for fun" and to reaffirm our joy in being alive. That is surely a theme or feeling that pervaded the 1920s; an adolescent feeling, if you will—Cummings makes that concession to critics—but one to which he looked back in the 1950s with a continuing sense of we-ness.

The 1920s had other favorite themes and one is amazed, in rereading his early work, to find out how often Cummings expressed them. Of course he was a lyric poet in the bad-boy tradition, broadly speaking, of Catullus and Villon and Verlaine. Of course he kept returning to the standard lyrical subjects of love, death, April, and the special quality of a moment. But traditional as he was on one side of his work, and determinedly unique on another, he was also a man of his generation. Much oftener than one might expect, he said what other young writers were saying at the time, or would soon be saying, and he usually said it with more ingenuity and morning freshness.

I won't revert to themes directly connected with his adventures in wartime: the feeling that death was omnipresent and life all the more to be enjoyed; the other feeling, for American ambulance drivers, that they were spectators of the greatest show on earth; and the notion that everyone in authority was stupid and that only common soldiers deserved sympathy. All this one finds in his early poems, together with other war-connected themes. More than other postwar writers, Cummings made fun of the big words, especially when spoken by politicians. Better and more amusingly than others he expressed his mistrust of almost everyone over thirty: "o the sweet & aged people who rule this world(and me and you if we're not very careful) . . . OH the bothering dear unnecessary hairless old." But Cummings also wrote poems on other themes that were popular with a whole generation of rebel writers, and here I might give a few examples.

There is first of all the revolt against Victorian standards, especially those prescribing chaste language and chaste behavior. Cummings made himself a leader in the revolt by describing, explicitly and often, the act of sex. Thus, in his second book of poems, &, there are nine rather labored sonnets recording visits to various prostitutes, including "Cecile . . . Alice . . . Loretta, cut the comedy, kid . . . Fran Mag Glad Dorothy."

There is the expatriate theme of praise for "superb and subtle" Paris, with its churches at twilight, its cafés, its streets that "turn young with rain," and its little ladies.

There is the tourist without Baedeker wandering beside his mistress among Roman ruins. "Ponder, darling, these busted statues," he tells her; but then he exhorts her to turn aside from the unimportant past and "instigate constructive horizontal business."

There is the spectator's report on New York as another such Greatest

Show as the war had been. Dos Passos embodied the report in a long novel, *Manhattan Transfer*, but Cummings was more succinct:

> by god i want above fourteenth
>
> fifth's deep purring biceps, the mystic screech
> of Broadway, the trivial stink of rich
>
> frail firm asinine life

There is the supercilious delight in advertising slogans and the habit of using them in poems. Cummings used them only for satire—"what's become of Maeterlinck / now that April's here / (ask the man who owns one / ask Dad, He knows)"—but later Hart Crane and others began to exploit them seriously.

There is the contempt for citizens who lead ordinary lives, "impersons" who accept the slogans at face value.

There is the utter scorn for conventional poets still feeding on the past:

> if we are to believe these gently O sweetly
> melancholy trillers amid the thrillers
> these crepuscular violinists among my and your
> skyscrapers—Helen & Cleopatra were Just Too Lovely,
> The Snail's On The Thorn enter Morn and God's
> In His andsoforth.

There is the respect for rebels of all sorts, even for Communists in those early days. Thus, in his report of a Paris demonstration broken up by the police, Cummings says that "the communists have fine Eyes . . . none look alike," whereas the police, "tidiyum, are very tidiyum reassuringly similar."

There is compassion for outcasts, not excluding the drunk lying in his pool of vomit as people carefully step around him, and there is the feeling that poets are outcasts too, for all their pride. "why are these pipples taking their hets off?" Cummings asks in an idiom borrowed from Krazy Kat of his favorite comic strip. He answers:

> the king & queen
> alighting from their limousine
> inhabit the Hôtel Meurice(whereas
> i live in a garret and eat aspirine)

There is finally the deep strain of anti-intellectualism that I have already mentioned. Among its manifestations is a prejudice against scientists and "pruient philosophers" who poke and prod the earth, combined with praise for a child's direct vision that sees the earth as "mud-luscious" and "puddle-wonderful."

There is, in fact, almost every theme that was to be widely treated by new writers in the 1920s, except for Hemingway's theme of giving and accepting death, and Fitzgerald's theme of the betrayed suitor for the very soul of money. Cummings spoke of money not often and then with the disdain of a barefoot friar. Besides the themes he treated, his poems embody various attitudes that lay behind them: the passion for reckless experiment in life and art, the feeling that a writer's duty was to be unique, and the simple determination to enjoy each moment and make the most of having been born. In spite of his aloofness, it is no wonder at all that the rebel writers had come to regard him as an indispensable spokesman for their cause.

The question in the middle 1920s was what Cummings would do next.

III

His next work, to their surprise, was for the theater and it was not so much a play as a brilliant vaudeville. *Him* (1927) was abused by the drama critics, but it was deliriously enjoyed by the younger people in the audience. Once again Cummings had spoken for them, and *Him* is in fact so much "of the twenties"—in the attitudes it reveals toward women, politics, Negroes (here admired for their sexual freedom), and the life of art—that it has seldom or never been revived. During the original production by the Provincetown Players, the very small auditorium was crowded every night, but the production was expensive, the Players were losing money they didn't have, and the piece had to be withdrawn after a few weeks. Cummings went back to painting and writing verse.

A new book of poems, *VV* (which he also called "*ViVa*"), appeared in 1931 and was a mild disappointment to his readers. Mostly the book deals with the same themes as his earlier work, but it is less exuberant than *Is 5*—much less of a hurrah than the title promises—and it speaks less directly for the poet's generation. There is a growing bitterness in the satires directed against politicians, generals, and run-of-the-mine people. The bitterest of all has proved to be the most enduring: it is the ballad of blond Olaf, the conscientious objector who is prodded with bayonets, then beaten to death while repeating "I will not kiss your f.ing flag." As a general thing, however, the development revealed in the book is a matter much less of tone than of technique.

Although Cummings' technique is a confusing subject, one argued back and forth since his poems first appeared in *The Dial*, much of it depends on the elaboration of a few devices that are fairly simple in themselves. Too much of it so depends, a reader may end by feeling. The two principal devices employed in *VV* had appeared at times in his earlier work, but here he carries them both to extremes. One is the calligram—or picture writing, to use a more general term—and the other is the word scramble, which might also be called the cryptogram. Cummings' use of the two devices has been discussed more than once, and I do not propose to resume the discussion here. It is enough to say that when he combines calligram with cryptogram, as he sometimes does in *VV*, the result in three or four cases is something beyond my ability to decipher. Even worse, a deciphered statement may be one that Cummings has made elsewhere, in plainer words, and thus it leaves a reader with the impression that his time and the poet's have both been wasted. *VV* is the most ingenious of Cummings' books, but—aside from the ballad of blond Olaf, a tribute to the poet's mother, and a few other moving poems—it is by far the least successful.

On the technical side, however, *VV* gives more than a hint of two additional devices that the poet was to cultivate more intensively in his later books. One of these is his use of negative terms—especially those formed by the prefixes "un-," "im-," and "not-" and the suffix "-less"—to imply special shades of meaning. In Poem XLII, for instance, he speaks of an "upward deep most invincible unthing," which I should take to be a spiritual essence. Poem LXVII tells of watching "unhands describe what mimicry," and here I don't know exactly what he means, although "unhands" would be a sinister word in Cummings' idiom. In later books one finds a host of such expressions: "an undream of anaesthetized impersons," "a notalive undead too-nearishness," "unfools unfree / undeaths who live," "till unwish returns on its unself," and the adjective "whereless," one that might pass into general usage. The poet says of politicians who want to save the world, "scream, all ye screamers, till your if is up / and vanish under prodigies of un." If such prodigies do not unexist, it is because Cummings has performed them.

The other device is the game he was beginning to play with parts of speech. It is a game with elastic rules or none at all: roughly, any part of speech can be transformed into any other. Verbs, adjectives, pronouns, even some adverbs and conjunctions, are used instead of nouns. Nouns become verbs ("but if a look should *april* me"), or they become adverbs by adding "-ly," or adjectives in the superlative by adding "-est" (thus, instead of writing "most like a girl," Cummings has "girlest"). Adjectives, adverbs, and conjunctions, too, become participles by adding "-ing" ("onlying," "softlying," "whying"); participles become adverbs by adding "-ly" ("kneelingly"). Some of those practices are foreshadowed in *VV*, where one finds, for instance, "footprints on the sands of was"—of time, obviously, though "was" in later books becomes "the past." Also in *VV* one finds "the smallening World" and "laughtering blocks"—the latter a hideous phrase—as well as "togethering" and "foreverfully," both more effective. In the later books—which include *50 Poems* (1940), *1 x 1* (1944), *XAIPE* ("Rejoice!" 1950), and *95 Poems* (1958)—such coined words and transposed parts of speech come close to being a new language. An example in *50 Poems* is Poem 29, of which the first stanza reads:

> anyone lived in a pretty how town
> (with up so floating many bells down)

> spring summer autumn winter
> he sang his didn't he danced his did.

A translation—omitting the second line, which means whatever it means—might be, "The poet lived year by year in an ordinary town, where he sang his negations and danced his affirmations." Need one say that Cummings' new language has a marvelous way of lending strangeness to sometimes rather commonplace statements? It also serves as a means of avoiding various words that he detested. Later in the same poem, when he says that "noone loved him more by more," it is obvious that "noone" is the poet's wife. After his second divorce, Cummings was happily married for nearly thirty years, a fact attested by some of his finest poems, but the word "wife" appears in none of them.

Any words involved in his game with parts of speech acquired a plus or a minus value. Thus, "was" as a noun is minus: "is" and "am" and "become" are plus. "Who" is plus, but "which" is minus, especially when it refers to impersons, and so is the adjective "whichful." "It," another neuter, seems to be the negative of "he" or "him" and leads to "itmaking," a term of utter condemnation. "Where" and "when" are both minus as nouns; "wherelings" and "whenlings" are pitiable people, "sons of unless and children of almost"—one might say the Jukes and Kallikaks of Cummings world. The honorifics are "here" and "now." "beautiful is now," he says, and elsewhere, in a fine tribute to his father,

> this motionless forgetful where
> turned at his glance to shining here.

All such words have become abstractions, and the meanings they imply are ethical and metaphysical. Usually ethics and ontology are fatal subjects for modern poets, but Cummings was feeling impelled to venture into them. The anti-intellectual was about to become, in limited ways, an ideologist. There had been changes in his life and they had led to a number of ideas that were partly new for him and were completely opposed at the time to those held by "mostpeople," as he called the American public. When one looks back at his career, it would seem that he had to invent his new language as the only fresh and serviceable means of expressing the ideas in poetry.

IV

Changes in his life. . . . His father had been killed in a motor accident (at a grade crossing in a blinding snowstorm), his second marriage had broken up, and in 1931 he had made a trip to Russia. This last was a shattering experience, much on the order of Dos Passos' visit to Loyalist Spain in 1937. Cummings wrote a prose book about the trip (*Eimi*, 1933), which is hard to read because of its pointillist style, but in which the con-

clusions are forthright. Russia, he reported, was a country racked by fear
and suspicion. Living under the shadow of Stalin, Communists were the
bigoted defenders of a system that destroys individuals. Soon the same
conclusions were being stated in his poems:

> every kumrad is a bit
> of quite unmitigated hate
> (travelling in a futile groove
> god knows why)
> and so do i
> (because they are afraid to love

Cummings was not afraid to love, but he hated, too, and his hatred
(or call it his feeling of revulsion) circled out from Stalin and his
"kumrads" to wider and wider social groups. First to be encompassed
were politicians who abetted communism by making appeals to the same
public yearning for a better life. Cummings had always detested politicians, but now he raged against them:

> a politician is an arse upon
> which everyone has sat except a man

Reformers and crusaders, especially those who supported the New Deal,
came next into the circle of aversion:

> then up rose pride and up rose pelf
> and ghibelline and guelph
> and ladios and laddios
> (on radios and raddios)
> did save man from himself

Growing still wider, the circle was drawn about salesmen of every type:
"a salesman is an it that stinks . . . whether it's in lonjewray or
shrouds"—a salesman in shrouds being anyone in favor of entering World
War II on Stalin's side. Labor unions were still another abomination:

> when serpents bargain for the right to squirm
> and the sun strikes to gain a living wage—
> when thorns regard their roses with alarm
> and rainbows are insured against old age

—then, Cummings says, "we'll believe in that incredible unanimal
mankind." At this point the circle of those rejected has become so wide
that it includes almost everyone living except "you and me," that is, the
poet, his love, and perhaps a handful of friends.

Not since the trip to Russia had Cummings been a spokesman for his
literary generation. Most of its other members—with almost all the
younger writers—had been moving in an opposite direction from his.
During the 1930s a dream that haunted many was that of joining forces
with all the dispossessed and of moving forward shoulder to shoulder into

a brighter future. Even Hemingway shared the dream for a time. *To Have and Have Not*, published during the Spanish Civil War, has a hero who lives by his own law, but his dying words are "No matter how a man alone ain't got no bloody fucking chance." "It had taken him a long time to get it out," Hemingway adds in his own voice, "and it had taken him all his life to learn it." Steinbeck, a younger man, was more affirmative in *The Grapes of Wrath* (1939): he tells how the mistreated Okies in California acquired a sense of collective purpose, until each of them—as Preacher Casy prophesies before his death—was on the point of becoming only a little piece of "one big soul." Cummings had no patience with this religion of humanity, or with humanity itself. He was to write during World War II:

> pity this busy monster,manunkind,
>
> not. . . .
>
> > listen:there's a hell
>
> of a good universe next door;let's go

Long before that other war, his statements of opinion had begun to seem inopportune and embarrassing. *Eimi*, for instance, appeared at a moment when much of the book-reading public was entranced by the Russian Five Year Plan, and it proved to be a commercial disaster. Its publisher rejected Cummings' next book of poems. After extensive travels in manuscript, and with a change in title, this was finally printed at his own expense as *No Thanks* (1935). It was dedicated, with no thanks, to fourteen publishers: Farrar and Rinehart, Simon and Schuster, Coward-McCann, Limited Editions, Harcourt Brace, Random House, Equinox Press, Smith and Haas, Viking, Knopf, Dutton, Harpers, Scribners, and Covici Friede. Cummings' first *Collected Poems* (1938) had less trouble in finding a home, and the books that followed had none at all, but I can't remember that they were widely discussed. In the left-wing press, hardly anyone excoriated Cummings or pleaded with him sorrowfully, as some did with Dos Passos; the books were mostly passed over in silence, as if they were social blunders. Perhaps it was the feeling of simply not being heard that made the poet's voice too shrill in some of the later diatribes.

Most of the poems, however, didn't suffer in themselves from his changed opinions, as the later novels of Dos Passos undoubtedly suffered. Dos Passos had different problems, having cast himself in the role of contemporary Gibbon. One of his self-imposed tasks was to report events in such a way as to reveal underlying forces. If he had been wrong about those forces during his early career, mightn't he be equally wrong after his loss of faith in the workers' revolution? That question must have nagged at him—though he didn't mention it to others—and it would help to explain the discouraged tone of his later fiction. Cummings took no interest in historical forces. He was essentially a lyric poet, and in the best of his later work he continued to deal with the traditional lyric themes of love and death, of spring-time and the ineffable quality of moments. There was less exuberance than in the early poems, less inventiveness in spite of the game he played with parts of speech, but there was at times more depth, combined with the effort I mentioned to express a coherent attitude, almost a metaphysic.

This last was something that Dr. Edward Cummings would have understood, and indeed it represented, in some measure, a return to the father. Such returns can be traced in the lives of many writers: Dos Passos is one of them, but there are scores of examples from which to choose. How often rebellion against the father—perhaps under the sign of the mother—is revealed in early works, and how often the father's image looms behind the later career! A younger poet, Wendell Berry, has written about such a change in his own life. Of his father he says:

> Now he speaks in me
> as when I knew him first,
> as his father spoke
> in him . . .
>   and I have grown
> to be brother to all
> my fathers, memory
> speaking to knowledge,
> finally, in my bones.[3]

If Cummings too admired his father more and more, it was obviously not for the social doctrine one assumes that the father preached to his congregation at the South Church, Unitarian. It was for personal qualities: love, kindness, utter independence, and faith based on an inner rightness of feeling:

> Scorning the pomp of must and shall
> my father moved through dooms of feel;
> his anger was as right as rain
> his pity was as green as grain

The New England tradition to which the poet returned was not that of the Unitarians or of the Calvinists, much less of the Come-outers, but that preached by Emerson in the years after he left the pulpit and before he became an Abolitionist. It was the tradition of the autonomous individual standing before God (or the Oversoul), living by universal laws in harmony with nature, obeying an inner voice, and letting society take care of itself. Emerson . . . there is no record that Cummings ever read his essays, yet his ideas had once pervaded the Cambridge air, and Cummings' later poems are Emersonian in more respects than one.

Thus, Emerson in the flush of his thought was an individualist to such an extent that he could not conceive of history as a process involving social systems and masses of people. "An institution," he wrote, "is the lengthened shadow of one man . . . and all history resolves itself into the biography of a few stout and honest persons." He regarded events of the past as mere decorations of the contemporary mind. "This life of ours," he said, "is stuck round with Egypt, Greece, Gaul, England, War, Colonization, Church, Court and Commerce, as with so many flowers and wild ornaments grave and gay. I will not make more account of them." For Cummings too, history was supremely unimportant:

> all history's a winter sport or three:
> but were it five,i'd still insist that all
> history is too small for even me;
> for me and you,exceedingly too small.

Here "me and you" are of course the poet and his love, the only group to which Cummings proclaimed his loyalty. He could do so because "me and you" were really not a group; they were "wonderful one times one." For him almost every group of more than two was either mythical or malevolent, or both. "swoop(shrill collective myth)into thy grave," he exclaimed in that same poem. In other poems we read that the state is an "enormous piece of nonsense" and that its citizens (or "sit-isn'ts") are a huge "collective pseudobeast / (sans either pain or joy)." Emerson wrote, and Cummings would have agreed, that "Society everywhere is in conspiracy against the manhood of every one of its members." As a rule, however, Emerson expressed less hostility to groups than Cummings did; he simply disregarded them in his scheme of things (while acknowledging the existence of "races," as he called the English and the French; of course what he meant was nations). He was interested in the moral character of each nation, but not at all in its politics. I am sure he would have assented when Cummings said:

> a state submicroscopic is—
> compared with pitying terrible
> some alive individual

Cummings also wrote that "there are possibly 2½ or improbably 3 individuals every several fat thousand years," and here the echo seems unmistakable. Emerson had said in "The American Scholar," "Men in history, men in the word of to-day, are bugs, are spawn, and are called 'the mass' and 'the herd.' In a century, in a millennium, one or two men; that is to say, one or two approximations to the right state of every man." I can imagine that Emerson would have nodded happily—as Whitman would have nodded too—when Cummings suggested that any man truly alive contains the universe within himself:

> (his briefest breathing lives some planet's year,
> his longest life's a heartbeat of some sun;
> his least unmotion roams the youngest star)

Emerson was more of a mystic, in the technical sense of the word, than most critics have realized, and some of his essays refer explicitly to an "ecstatical state" in which the soul is reunited with the Oversoul.[4] Such a state is to be understood in a famous passage near the beginning of *Nature*: "Standing on the bare ground—my head bathed in the blithe air and uplifted into infinite space—all mean egoism vanishes. I become a transparent eyeball; I am nothing; I see all; the currents of the Universal Being circulate through me; I am part and parcel of God." Time and space being abolished at such moments, the soul is bathed in a higher Reason to be distinguished from mere Understanding. The distinction in Cummings' later poems is between "know" or "because," both contemptuous nouns in his language, and "feel," which is something to be honored ("my father moved through dooms of feel"). As for the states of ecstasy, they are possibly foreshadowed in the early poems by Cummings' effort to render the special quality of moments. In later poems that sense of the moment, the now, is so intensified that it comes close to being a mystical vision. "ten centuries of original soon"—that is, of history—are "plunged in eternal now." "dimensionless new alls of joy" flood over the poet as he perceives the "illimitably spiralling candy of tiniest forever." "now the ears of my ears awake," another poem ends, "and now the eyes of my eyes are opened." In passages like these Cummings appears to be writing as the latest—though I suspect not the last—of the New England Transcendentalists.

The parallel can be carried too far. Where Emerson was essentially a Neoplatonist, Cummings was a scoffer in his youth, then more and more a Christian. He does not think of Christ as the most perfect man, in Emerson's way of speaking, but rather prays to him as a divine intercessor. In theological terms his God is less immanent than Emerson's and more transcendent. He says in a poem addressed to God—here I translate into prose—"How should any tasting, touching, hearing, seeing, breathing, merely human being—lifted from the no of all nothing—doubt unimaginable You?" As regards a future life, one of the subjects on which Emerson remained ambiguous, Cummings lets us infer that he believes in the resurrection of the flesh. "our now must come to then," he tells his love in a late sonnet—

> our then shall be some darkness during which
> fingers are without hands;and i have no
> you:and all trees are(any more than each
> leafless)its silent in forevering snow
>
> —but never fear(my own,my beautiful
> my blossoming)for also then's until

Other poems of the time make it clear that "until," for Cummings, was the moment when lovers shall rise from the grave.

V

Cummings lived into the late summer of 1962 and continued working to the last day. His career, if not his opinions, had been remarkably self-consistent. Except for his painting, carried on through the years, and except for a few lively incursions into prose—of which *The Enormous Room* is the most durable—he had never worked at any trade except that of writing verse. "*Peintre et poète*," he had told a French policeman who asked his profession before arresting him; I think that was in 1923. Poet and painter—and nothing else—he remained to the end.

He wrote twelve books of poetry, including one that appeared after his death (*73 poems*, 1963), but not including collected or selected works. The books contain 770 poems in all, an impressive output for a lyric poet and one recalling that of another New Englander, Emily Dickinson. Most of the poems are as short as hers, with perhaps one-fourth of them variations on the traditional fourteen-liner. After the early romantic pieces in *Tulips and Chimneys*, Cummings never ventured again into longer forms. Not all the poems are on the same level, and some of the more ingenious ones remind me that there is a drawer in our house full of kitchen gadgets made of stamped tin and wire, all vastly ingenious—U.S. patent applied for—but many of them unworkable and most of them seldom used. Cummings' inventions, too, are sometimes gimcrack and wasted, but the best of them have enriched the common language. The best of his lyrics, early and late, and not a few of the sonnets—more, it seems to me, on each rereading—have a sweep and music and underlying simplicity that make them hard to forget. And where does he stand among the poets of our time? He suffers from comparison with those who built on a larger scale—Eliot, Aiken, Crane, Auden among others—but still he is unsurpassed in his special field, one of the masters.

One may feel that in his later years, when he was groping his way back toward Emerson, Cummings wrote rather more new poems than he had new things to say. He might have been more severe with his work, and with his acolytes, but he had earned the privilege, after all, of being a little self-indulgent. He did not abuse the privilege. Except for those six nonlectures at Harvard, his only concession to the public, and to the need for earning money, was reading his poems aloud to mostly undergraduate audiences in all parts of the country. It required physical courage, for by that time he was partly crippled by arthritis, wore a brace on his back that jutted out two inches from his shoulderblades, and had to read while sitting in a straight-backed kitchen chair. After reading for half an hour, he had to rest for ten minutes; then he came back to finish the program. Nevertheless he held and charmed the audience, which was usually acquainted with his work and well prepared to listen.

He was speaking in the McCarthy years to what had come to be known as the silent generation. Sometimes he scolded the youngsters, as at Harvard, for being obsessed with security. "What is that?" he asked them. "Something negative, undead, suspicious and suspecting; an avarice and an avoidance; a self-surrendering meanness of withdrawal; a numerable complacency and an innumerable cowardice. . . . How monstrous and how feeble seems some unworld which would rather have its too than eat its cake!" The youngsters, cautious as they were at the time, liked to dream about the romantic freedom of the 1920s. They specially enjoyed his early poems, with their recklessness and brio, but they did not object to the conservative Christian anarchism of the later poems. Once again Cummings, the man stubbornly alone, found himself accepted by others as a spokesman.

NOTES

1. Cummings' biographer, Charles Norman, says that the black principal, a woman, was at a grade school the boy attended.

2. Later he must have regretted the gesture, when he found that there was a revived demand for the book. *The Enormous Room* was reprinted three or four times during the 1920s.

3. From "The Gathering," *The Nation*, 31 January 1972, p. 151.

4. He is most explicit in "The Method of Nature," an address delivered at Colby College in 1841. The address, not often read today, is almost a handbook of "the perennial philosophy."

In Consideration of Cummings

William Heyen*

E. E. Cummings' *100 Selected Poems* was published in 1959. This selection, which includes work from *Tulips and Chimneys* (1923) through *Xaipe* (1950), was made by Cummings himself. These were the poems, no doubt, that he considered his best and perhaps most representative. I'd like to talk about a few of the lyrics in this volume, and to move from them to critical considerations that they inevitably raise.

I am now three sentences deep into my talk and already almost forced to stop. For there is a sense in which, from Cummings' point of view, from the assumptions and visions of his life and life's work, poems *do not* inevitably raise critical considerations. Poems are poems, and they are to be taken for what they are or are to be left alone. And when mind starts tampering with them, Cummings would say, we'll have the same

*Reprinted from *Southern Humanities Review*, 7 (1973), 131–42. Reprinted by permission of the *Southern Humanities Review*. The paper was first presented as a lecture at the University of Frieburg on November 11, 1971.

situation as occurs in one of his poems when the "doting / fingers of / prurient philosophers" poke and prod the earth to no avail. In the first of his *i: six nonlectures* (1953) Cummings quotes Rainer Maria Rilke: "Works of art are of an infinite loneliness and with nothing to be so little reached as with criticism. Only love can grasp and hold and fairly judge them." This is said so well and it sounds so good that it may be true, but I don't know just what "love" is; or, at least, I think that part of the love I bring to any poem is the result of something more than pure feeling. But this is to quarrel, of course, more with Cummings than with Rilke.

John Logan, an American poet who has written what is to my mind the single finest essay on Cummings, will allow me to get at least my hands unstuck from this tar-baby of a dilemma. In "The Organ-Grinder and the Cockatoo: An Introduction to E. E. Cummings" (*Modern American Poetry: Essays in Criticism*, ed. Jerome Mazzaro, 1970), Logan says that when Yvor Winters charged that Cummings "understands little about poetry," Winters missed the whole point. "It is not Cummings' job," says Logan, "to understand poetry; it's his job to write it; and it is up to the critics to understand and to derive whatever new machinery they need to talk about the poems. . . ." So, Logan will at least allow me to talk about the poet he believes to be "the most provocative, the most humane, the most inventive, the funniest, and the least understood" of his generation. I don't know whether I'm ready or ever will be to erect "new machinery," but at least I am not slapped in the face as I am by so many of Cummings' poems which accuse me of being a "most-people" with a 2 + 2 = 4 mentality should I ever attempt anything sensible or logical. For Cummings, of course, this irascibility in the face of criticism may be more of a mask than a true self. Certainly, one of his ploys is hyperbole. Richard Wilbur, in fact, tells a very winning story about visiting Cummings in Greenwich Village, about Cummings' nonchalantly mentioning some sort of article on him by a fellow named Blackmur which he hadn't seen, and about seeing a whole stack of *Hound and Horn*, the magazine with Blackmur's essay, in a corner. Cummings probably was more aware of criticism than he cared to admit. Although he was a loner, and although he persisted in his stylistic and thematic leaps and glides like a single salmon making its way upstream, many of his poems, like the one beginning "mr youse needn't be so spry / concernin questions arty," may be masks and defenses. In any case, I trust that Cummings' ghost wouldn't be offended by something a professor of mine used to say: "The major purpose of criticism is that sooner or later someone should say something."

When I think of Cummings, the first poem I think about is No. 28 from the selected volume. First collected in *is 5* (1926), it argues the mathematics of that title:

> since feeling is first
> who pays any attention

> to the syntax of things
> will never wholly kiss you;
>
> wholly to be a fool
> while Spring is in the world
>
> my blood approves,
> and kisses are a better fate
> than wisdom
> lady i swear by all flowers. Don't cry
> —the best gesture of my brain is less than
> your eyelids' flutter which says
>
> we are for each other: then
> laugh, leaning back in my arms
> for life's not a paragraph
>
> And death i think is no parenthesis

I am more than fond of this poem. I think it is imaginative and compelling, convincing and even deep. But what I have realized, and this is to strike to the center of the matter on my mind, is that it sometimes seems as though I could not possibly appreciate this poem or much of Cummings if I did not read it as though Cummings were masking himself in hyperbole, as though he deliberately or not established a persona and an emotional and mental world for his persona to inhabit. I want to read this poem as though it speaks better than its speaker knows. I want to say that its essential thrust is its duplicity. I want to say that Cummings does not go as far as many of his critics have said he has gone in denying rationality, intelligence, logic; that these abstractions are indeed his whipping boys, but in a more complex way than Cummings has been given credit for.

Certainly, any poem is a fiction; it is a poem's burden to convince us of the truth of what I. A. Richards called its "pseudo-statements." When Robert Frost says "Something there is that doesn't love a wall," his poem, to be successful, has to convince me, through its images and sounds and languages, that there is indeed something in nature that wants walls down. Whether or not (and I suspect not) there *is* some natural force that detests walls is beside the point. The fiction has to be convincing, at least temporarily. Frost himself defined poetry as "a momentary stay against confusion." In "Directive" he tells us to follow him and to "Drink and be whole again beyond confusion." Poetry, to my mind, is a refuge from chaos; even when poems seek to embody chaos, they give shape to it. But while every poem is a fictional construct, the problem is that so many of Cummings' poems assume the same insistent hatred for rationality that they seem in the end to be speaking the poet's own narrow belief.

> "since feeling is first / who pays any attention /
> to the syntax of things / will never wholly kiss you. . . ."

It is not true that feeling is always first. It seems to me that emotions often arise after thought. But Cummings' first line is the given of his poem, his speaker's assumption. It is very important, of course, that he convince his listener that he is right. For this is a seduction poem. He is telling his lady to make good use of time, to act from feeling, to abandon her "syntax" in the matters of, perhaps, time and the steps of proper courtship. Our Romeo has only words—I think of Ogden Nash's famous seduction poem: "Candy is dandy, / but liquor is quicker"—and one of the delights for us in visualizing the dramatic situation of this poem is in anticipating whether or not our swain will be successful in petting or bedding his lady. This is a digression of sorts, but the poem can be read as a defense of spontaneous poetry, as a confrontation between poet and muse. What it should not be read as is a blanket condemnation of rationality. Mind was a villain for Cummings when it became dissociated from feeling, when it made bombs or political systems without regard to human consequences.

Cummings' speaker in this poem finds perfect words and a wonderful sort of reasoning to convince his lady. He tells her that she will never really be kissed until she is kissed without forethought, that kisses are better than wisdom, that his brain's best gesture is nothing next to the flutter of her eyelids. Then he tells her that he knows, probably better than she does, just how she feels, that her eyes give her away. Then come the clinchers, the old visions of worms trying the chastity of virgins in their graves: "life's not a paragraph"—i.e., it is not something formal and organized and part of a larger composition; it is all we have. "And death i think is no parenthesis"—he argues, at the same time, that death is not parenthetical, is not a bit of extra information. Death is the final arbiter of everything. As Cummings writes in another poem, Doom "will smooth entirely our minds." What lady could resist the Gatsby-like plaintiveness of that last parenthetical statement uttered so offhandedly and matter-of-factly? What lady, in fact, could resist the inexorable logic of this poem?

What we have here, then, is a carefully contrived and logical lyric that argues feeling and the abandonment of inhibition to larger forces. What we have, also, is a conventional lyric, one reminiscent of seventeenth-century love songs or even of the songs of the medieval troubadors. I hear this conventional quality often in Cummings, in a poem like "All in green went my love riding" (No. 2), for example, or in "if i have made, my lady, intricate" (No. 29).

But to return to what I see to be the central problem of any consideration of Cummings: "since feeling is first" is one of any number of Cummings' poems that seem to argue against any display of rationality, mentality, intelligence, thought; that is, against the processes of the upper mind. Cummings is often considered charming and primitive and shallow as a thinker. And worse: an anti-intellectual. Norman Friedman, Cummings' first book-length critic, has said that many important critics—Edmund Wilson, Randall Jarrell, Louis Untermeyer, John Crowe Ranson,

F. O. Matthiessen—have just not known what to make of Cummings. Roy Harvey Pearce in *The Continuity of American Poetry* (1961) calls Cummings "hyper-consciously lyrical" and is among those who have not been able to justify Cummings' typography. (James Dickey says he is not interested in this aspect of Cummings; Richard Wilbur sees Cummings' experiments as basically reductive, a sacrifice of the ear to the eye; Max Eastman forty years ago saw Cummings as a leading member of the "cult of unintelligibility," a poet who turned punctuation marks loose on a page like bacteria to eat the insides out of otherwise healthy words.) But the central problem in regard to Cummings is what seems to be his permanent adolescence in so stridently defending life against any intrusion by mind. Is it possible that Cummings really believes all of those escapist things he seems to be saying? Poem after poem tells us that we "shall above all things be glad and young" (No. 54), that "all ignorance toboggans into know / and trudges up to ignorance again" (No. 84), that "anything's righter / than books / could plan" (No. 88), that the supreme facts of existence are that scientists and thinkers are bad guys and that "girls with boys / to bed will go" (No. 47). Does he really believe, as he said in his introduction to new poems included in *Collected Poems* (1938), "Never the murdered finalities of wherewhen and yesno, impotent nongames of wrongright and rightwrong"? Is there as much pure and obstinate resolution in Cummings' universe as there seems to be? I don't think so. I think that just as Whitman declared himself to be a poet of body and soul but had to spend a greater amount of time on armpits and breasts because they had been neglected in poetry, Cummings has to emphasize feeling as opposed to thought. We had had enough thought in our poetry (indeed, in our whole society of passionless Cambridge ladies and politicians and scientists). Any hyperbole on behalf of unimpeded emotion would help to balance the scales. Cummings relies on the shock value of unconventional statement presented no-holds-barred. Cummings' speakers speak what they believe now, and in hard words, as Emerson said any real man must. If Cummings' persona in "since feeling is first" seems to argue that any sort of mentality is useless and stupid, the poet I hear behind the poem's pose means what Emerson meant when he said that "Thinking is a partial act" and that a "man thinking" instead of a "thinking man" knew and felt that he had to live each moment of life to its utmost or he would lose his soul. The Cummings I hear is a reformer nagging and pleading for and bragging about a radical resolution of sensibility so that, as Thoreau says in *Walden*, life would be "like a fairy tale and the Arabian Nights' Entertainments. If we respected only what is inevitable and has a right to be, music and poetry would resound along the streets." In his 1946 essay "Lower Case Cummings" William Carlos Williams said that Cummings is addressing his language "to the private conscience of each of us in turn." Should any great number of us understand Cummings, said Williams, "the effect would be in effect a veritable revolution, shall we say, of morals? Of, do we dare to say, love?"

I would like at this point to quote from R. P. Blackmur, whose criticism of Cummings is archetypal:

> [In Cummings] there is no pretense at hardness of surface. We are admitted at once to the bare emotion. What is most striking, in every instance, about this emotion is the fact that, in so far as it exists at all, it is Mr. Cummings' emotion, so that our best knowledge of it must be, finally, our best guess. It is not an emotion resulting from the poem; it existed before the poem began and is a result of the poet's private life. Besides its inspiration, every element in the poem, and its final meaning as well, must be taken at face value or not at all. This is the extreme form, in poetry, of romantic egoism: whatever I experience is real and final, and whatever I say represents what I experience. Such a dogma is the natural counterpart of the denial of the intelligence.

Blackmur's chief complaint against Cummings is the deadness and personalism, though we may feel just the opposite, of Cummings' language, and even John Logan, chief among Cummings' admirers, admits that the older poet's vocabulary is "the least imaginative aspect of his work (coinages and composites aside.)" At the same time, Logan senses a great depth in many poems and tells us, in fact, that "Freud's analysis of the punnings, splittings, and composings in the language of dreams and jokes provides an insight into some of Cummings' effects, which to my knowledge no student has yet followed out."

What strikes me as off the track of Cummings in Blackmur is his insistence that a Cummings poem "must be taken at face value or not at all," that the emotion of a poem "is Mr. Cummings' emotion." I think that this is far from true, that seldom, if ever, is Cummings' language so flat or private that I am left with only an emotion of resolution, so to speak, one that existed before the poem. The question is, with so many of Cummings' poems: What is the relation between the sensibility of the poet and his speaker's sensibility? I don't think there are any simple answers to this. Each poem may be a case in itself. I think that "since feeling is first" ought to be read as a sort of inquiry, though this is too philosophical a word, into the tenability of the poem's fictions, and not as a statement of Cummings' belief in the good sense that spontaneous sex makes in the face of death, or as just another Cummings poem celebrating the poet's own epicureanism. Cummings was a craftsman—he left behind, I read somewhere, 150 pages of drafts for a 50-line poem alone—and his poems are artifacts that often unfold several levels of irony. Given Cummings' aesthetic, his sense of the poem as an object, his labor to promote nuance and suggestion, we owe it to him to read the poems very carefully, masks and all, and not to throw them into one small basket labeled The Poet's Belief. Cummings was not, in general, a poet of the anticipated, stock emotion. Consider the depth of "if there are any heavens my mother will(all by herself)have / one" (No. 31), a poem that sounds the losses of the heaven of love. And consider "somewhere i have never travelled, gladly beyond / any experience" (No. 35). It seems to me that these two are among the finest and most profound poems on the theme of love ever written. At his best, Cummings is far from immature, and his mind is far from flimsy, whatever "since feeling is first" or similar poems initially suggest. Cleanth Brooks, in *Modern Poetry and the Tradition* (1939), can say that Robert Frost's voice issues from a character who may be described as "the sensitive New Englander, possessed of a natural wisdom; dry and laconic when serious; genial and whimsical when not; a character who is uneasy with hyperbole and prefers to use understatement to risking possible overstatement." Brooks can go on to say, and I think with justification, that "The range of Frost's poetry is pretty thoroughly delimited by the potentialities for experience possessed by such a character." I do not think, though attempts have been made, that Cummings will be caught in this way. The Cummings voice behind even what might be called the childhood poems, "in Just- / spring" (No. 4) and "who knows if the moon's" (No. 13), for example, is elusive.

I have mentioned the duplicity of many of Cummings' poems, the depth, or the level of irony inherent in them. I have also urged a close reading. To talk about one of the two love poems mentioned earlier, poems of obvious complexity, would load the argument and involve a long discussion. Blackmur also objects to Cummings' "tough guy" poems (poems of Jazz effects, tough dialects, barkers, prostitutes, etc.) as being purely surface poems which leave us with "the certainty that there was nothing to penetrate." There is no question but that Blackmur is sometimes correct. Two of Cummings' tough guy elegies come to mind, "i sing of olaf glad and big" (No. 30), and "rain or hail" (No. 78). Neither poem gives us much more than a surface. Neither poem is likely to demand particularly close attention. Also, sometimes when Cummings is just a fraction away from reaching an important theme, from coming to grips with an important issue, he seems to shy away, content with humor when much more is within reach. "spoke joe to jack" (No. 56) is such a poem. What Cummings gives us is a graphic description of a bar-room fight over a girl. The last two lines, "jesus what blood / darling i said" edge toward the very complicated relationships between violence and sex, but the poem's potential seems abandoned. Also, many of Cummings' satirical poems, such as " 'next to of course god america i' " (No. 24), are watery and thin, eliciting only stock responses. But often Cummings' poems are deceptively simple and we discover that what at first seemed an objective and bare statement involves much more. This is the case, I believe, with "raise the shade" (No. 10).

> raise the shade
> will youse dearie?

rain
wouldn't that

get yer goat but
we don't care do
we dearie we should
worry about the rain

huh
dearie?
yknow
I'm

sorry for awl the
poor girls that
get up god
knows when every

day of their
lives
aint you,

     oo-oo. dearie

not so
hard dear

you're killing me

  If we leave this poem in its own comic world where it seems to stand—and it is, plain and downright, a funny poem—we'll miss its larger importance, its high seriousness, its subtle art that raises it to the first rank of Cummings' poems. Cummings' persona here, probably a mistress or a prostitute on an all-nighter or sleeping with her pimp, speaks much better than she knows, and the poem becomes a wide psychological portrait in a few words and a brilliant example of dramatic irony. Immediately her diction, "youse" and "dearie," gives her away as uneducated, so ignorant that any sort of conscious irony on her part is impossible. But if someone says to us "I'm not a liar, I'm not a liar, I'm not a liar," we know that that person is protesting too much, that he is revealing more than he knows about himself, that he probably is a liar. Listen to our heroine here: "we don't care do / we dearie we should / worry about the rain / huh / dearie?" Her rhetorical questions are dead givaways themselves, and Cummings stands behind her questions. Notice the ends of the lines: "we don't care do / we dearie we should. . . ." And notice the end of the stanza: "worry about the rain. . . ." She is lost, and knows it, even if this knowledge has not reached a conscious level. She also knows, or feels, that "god / knows when" other girls get up to work. She thinks of their routine as hard and dreary, but speaking in Cummings' chosen rhythms she reveals the monotony of her own affairs: "oo-oo, dearie / / not so / hard dear. . . ." In these terms, "you're killing me" becomes a deep statement, the poem's first line becomes a kind of prayer for any light on this waste land. But it is raining, of course, and her partner is not sufficiently interested in her slow death even to say one word.

G. S. Fraser, in a review of Cummings' *Poems: 1923–1954*, argued that what Cummings leaves out of his world is "the complex personal relationships of men and women. What Mr. Cummings seems to me to substitute for this fine traditional theme is, firstly, a celebration of the sexual appetites and achievements of the hearty male animal: and, secondly, the celebration of a kind of mystical attitude toward life in general. . . ." Fraser goes on to say that Cummings' "love poetry is, in a bad sense, impersonal. . . ." In general, I don't think this is true. To Cummings love is a serious and complex matter, difficult to fathom, fraught with darkness as we are reminded in "my father moved through dooms of love" (No. 62). In a poem like "raise the shade," it is the realm of possible love beyond this almost tragic scene that serves as the poem's foil. There are love poems in the Cummings canon as deep as we are likely to find anywhere. Impersonal? Only in the sense that Whitman's poems are impersonal, bulwarked by the faith that if he can truly speak for himself he will be speaking for us all.

I'd like to turn now to something suggested by Fraser's statement that Cummings' poetry celebrates "a kind of mystical attitude toward life." Fraser, by the way, also charges Cummings with "a youthful, not very well-balanced religiousness, a 'reverence for life" combined with a youthful refusal to accept death as a fact." I must admit that this last statement especially puzzles me, since I could argue that all of Cummings begins with the blunt fact of death and attempts to build from there. In any case, this question of Cummings' religiousness, his "mystical attitude toward life," is one that should be examined.

The truth is that Cummings often seems awfully unfashionable. He celebrates and affirms. He cherishes "mystery," one of his very favorite words, and spring and flowers. He prays that his heart be always open to little things, and he gives thanks to God for the grace of each amazing day. He tells us in his *i: six nonlectures* that he loved his parents and that they loved him—how out of step with the times is this?—and tells us that he considers himself no worthy specimen of the so-called lost generation. He insists on individuality. Rather than puzzle over good and evil, he seems to assume that we all know, if we allow our feelings full play, what is right and what is wrong. While Wallace Stevens could say that we need our minds to defend us, Cummings often seems to trust the beneficence of pure emotional Being. "Life, for eternal us, is now; and now," as he says in the introduction to his collected *Poems: 1923–1954*, "is much too busy being a little more than everything to seem anything, catastrophic included. . . ." It is difficult to know what to make of Cummings. Or is it? You know that old adage: if it has feathers like a duck and waddles like a duck and sounds like a duck and eats what a duck eats, it may very well be a duck. Cummings is a Transcendentalist. In *American Poets from the Puritans to the Present* (1968) Hyatt H. Waggoner argues, and to my mind absolutely convincingly, that Cummings' "poetry and prose give us the purest example of undiluted Emersonianism our century has yet provided." We have been slow to recognize this, and I'm not sure why. Perhaps we did not want to equate a writer as seemingly modern as Cummings, with all of his dazzle and virtuosity, with those nineteenth-century sages from Concord. But Cummings is a Transcendentalist, and to call him this, of course, is still not to button-hole him comfortably. He will elude all but general definition, as Whitman claimed to. He will never, as J. Alfred Prufrock, that most non-transcendental of all men, was, be pinned to a lepidopterist's wall.

I will not attempt to summarize the parallels Professor Waggoner draws between Cummings and Emersonian tradition. The point is that given his transcendental assumptions Thoreau, for example, and everything he says in *Walden* and elsewhere is absolutely unassailable. Criticism is beside the point. To complain that Cummings' pacifism, for example, is "not argued out," as Fraser complains, is beside the point. To talk about a "philosophy" or system of thought in regard to a poet who refuses all but illimitable Being is beside the point. Cummings has been speaking a different language from the one so many of his critics have been wanting to yoke him with. We cannot charge a Transcendentalist with unearned joy or sudden irrationality any more than we can charge a mystic. Cummings' transcendentalism explains his poems' tendencies to see society as being in conspiracy against its members, their celebrations of youth and the noble savage like Olaf who only knows that there are some things he will not eat. Cummings' transcendentalism explains his unconcern for consistency, his glorification of intuition, his optimism, even the undercurrent of satirical instruction as in "When serpents bargain for the right to squirm" (No. 89) and "Humanity i love you" (No. 16), poems whose life is rooted in the same love-hate for man and the same desire to lead the townspeople to freedom and happiness that generated *Walden*. Cummings' transcendentalism explains his "not very well-balanced religiousness." If we make the faithful leap and read Cummings in the spirit with which we read an essay by Emerson or Whitman's "Song of Myself," we will find that most of the critical objections seem to melt away. If we do not for any reason see fit to do this, his achievement often seems very thin indeed.

I see that I have made a sort of transcendentalist's circle, one that comes back to where it started but one that may not be entirely round. "Works of art"—this is Cummings quoting Rilke, as you'll recall—"are of an infinite loneliness and with nothing to be so little reached as with criticism. Only love can grasp and hold and fairly judge them." Cummings tilled the soil, as Emerson said every man must, that was given to him to till. To Cummings any poem and the life force that the poem manifested was an ecstasy and an intuition, not an induction. We cannot in any logical way argue with the transcendental assumptions that make Cummings' world what it is and his poems what they are. All we can do is to make a Cummings poem our own, to appreciate its crafts and mysteries as best we can and to come to love it, or we can reject it. His poem No. 96 begins "the great advantage of being alive / (instead of undying) is not so much / that mind no more can disprove than prove / what heart may feel and soul may touch," and ends:

> a billion brains may coax undeath
> from fancied fact and spaceful time—
> no heart can leap,no soul can breathe
> but by the sizeless truth of a dream
> whose sleep is the sky and the earth and the sea.
> For love are in you am in i are in we

"Twin Obsessions": The Poetry and Paintings of E.E. Cummings

Rushworth M. Kidder*

"For more than half a hundred years," wrote E. E. Cummings in 1954, "the oversigned's twin obsessions have been painting and writing." In the article in which this statement appeared,[1] he took some satisfaction in pointing out that his painting—as well as his more experimental poetry, prose, and drama—had been misapprehended, scorned, or ignored by the public. The charge still sticks. A quarter-century later, the public knows Cummings primarily as a lyric poet. Few have ventured into his other literary modes. Fewer still know him as a painter.

Yet he painted, according to his contemporaries, more than he wrote, and he painted with a wholesale devotion. His first serious ventures reflect the impact of the 1913 Armory Show, where Cummings, still an undergraduate at Harvard, drank his first deep draught of the modern painters. Solidifying his impressions of their work with careful readings of such books as Arthur Jerome Eddy's *Cubists and Post-Impressionism* (1914) and Willard Huntington Wright's *Modern Painting: Its Tendency and Meaning* (1915), Cummings soon forged his own alloy of Cubism, Fauvism, and Futurism. By 1918—with Harvard, the war, and the experiences which would produce *The Enormous Room* all behind him—he wrote to his mother: "I have been working very hard indeed on a picture,embodying certain elements of colour and motion which I picked up a week or so ago at Coney Island." Then, apparently in answer to her

*Reprinted from the *Georgia Review*, 32 (1978), 342–68, where the essay was illustrated more fully. Reprinted by permission of the *Georgia Review* and Rushworth M. Kidder.

question about the kind of painting he was doing, he replied: "They are organizations of colour and line,presentative,semi-abstract,& abstract. Figures often are taken in design,more often machinerish elements. There are some 'types.' "[2]

His labors during the early twenties resulted largely in abstractions and "types." Typical of the former is a painting he mentions when writing to his mother on 7 March 1920, commenting that "I think I've got my latest picture,which is 42 x 36", somewhere near where I would like to have it—it's about time,by the way!" Much of his other work in this period was in the same vein and some of it would grow into the several numbered series of paintings he titled *Noise* and *Sound*, of which the best-known appeared in *The Dial* (August 1927) as *Noise Number 13*. Along with the abstractions were the "types"—quick and often small oils and pastels of the characters who haunted the demi-monde of dancehalls, burlesque houses, saloons, and brothels which Cummings found so intriguing. Occasionally these subjects took their places in larger and more formally organized compositions like *Harlem*, and they regularly turned up in his poetry, which is peppered with portraits of such characters as the "Five Americans" of *is 5* ("Liz," "Mame," "Gert," "Marj," and "Fran"), denizens of such cathouses as "Dick Mid's Place."

Towards the end of the twenties, Cummings' predilections turned away from abstraction and towards the more "presentative." From the early thirties onward he did a number of portraits and self-portraits and any number of landscapes. Some of the latter are relentlessly pedestrian: reflecting little of his individual insight, they indulge in a colorful representationalism that lapses into sentimentality and cliché. At their best, however, the landscapes engage his earlier interest in abstract structures of color and line, and allow him to bring to bear on the trees and moon of his favorite New Hampshire settings a curiously expressionistic vision.

The vision was meant to be shared, and Cummings did his best to share it. No mere amateur, he entered his pieces in exhibitions as early as 1919, and continued throughout his career to hold one-man shows in New York, Rochester, and elsewhere. He sold a number of works, gave others away, and left behind in his estate some sixteen hundred more. Long viewed as merely ancillary to his "real" work as a poet, the paintings have recently begun to receive some recognition in their own right. Since his death in 1962 there have been several modest retrospectives in New York (one at the Downtown Gallery in 1963; others at the Gotham Book Mart in 1968 and 1974). A traveling collection of thirty-seven paintings and drawings circulated to various colleges and universities in the New England area in 1975–1976. Most recently, the Hirshhorn Museum in Washington, D.C., mounted a well-documented exhibition consisting largely of his drawings.[3]

These exhibitions, along with an increasing number of scholarly and journalistic pieces on his art,[4] have made several things clear. First, Cummings was entirely self-taught: though he enjoyed the close friendship of the sculptor Gaston Lachaise, the assistance of the painter Walter Pach, the approval of the art critic Henry McBride, and an encouraging endorsement from the painter Albert Léon Gleizes, he never studied with them or with anyone else. Second, he treated his art as profession rather than avocation: he set himself, especially in his early years, to solve problems of composition and color in his canvases, he regularly sought opportunities to exhibit, and he earned some much-needed funds by selling work to *The Dial*. Third, he was drawn to theorize extensively, in his private and largely unpublished notes, on the practice and the aesthetics of the visual arts, ranging in his studies from detailed self-instruction in human anatomy to esoteric investigations into color relationships. Fourth, he constantly probed into the parallels among painting, literature, and music, challenging himself to adapt into literature the principles of the other arts.

This fourth point is of central importance for students of his poetry and for those concerned with the relationships between literature and the other arts. So far, however, the critical terminology in these areas remains rather vague. The term "musical," for example, is not uncommon in discussions of his verse. Yet much remains to be done in analyzing his systematic use of assonance and consonance and in investigating his careful use of musical accents and rests. In a similar way, many readers recognize something they call "visual" in his poetry. They are usually responding to the designs of the words and the space on the page, but these designs, unlike those of Herbert or the concrete poets, are not representational: they are less apt to suggest altars or bottles than such generalized shapes as crescents or squares. The designs grow up out of Cummings' concern for the relationships of the printed words to the spaces around them. For Cummings, it seems, not only thought and heard his poems but saw them as well. Not surprisingly, his best poems tend to be short, of a length readily contained on a single page and easily "seen" in a single glance. In dealing with publishers, in fact, he sometimes referred to his work in visual terms, on one occasion writing his editor that "what I care infinitely is that each poempicture should remain intact. Why? Possibly because,with a few exceptions,my poems are essentially pictures."[5]

The difficulty for the student of literature is in knowing how to respond to such visual dimensions in poetry. When something announces itself to us simply as "poem," we have a seasoned battery of critical concepts to define our responses, and we dispatch it rather handily in terms of imagery, symbolism, irony, rhythm, rhyme, and so forth. So, too, we are aware—even as students of literature—of the proper responses to things which announce themselves as pieces of graphic art: we can speak of color, line, mass, depth, composition, and abstraction. But when an obviously "poetic" object—composed of words, and with at least one unjustified margin—presents itself in a way that insists upon its visual design, we grow uneasy. An ominous clanking of chains in the basements of our thought reminds us that the high tower of our critical vocabulary may also be a dungeon, and that, elevated as we are to a sophisticated disciplinary vantage, we are also sometimes trapped by it. How much more convenient, we sigh, if the poet bothered only with words and left the shapes to the painter!

That urge towards convenience, however, can be pernicious. Quite simply, it can lead us to misapprehend the visually-structured poem by trying to reduce it to an exclusively linguistic statement. Studying in detail its literary aspects, we merely "appreciate" the visual design. The pressure of convenience may also lead us to discount the seriousness with which some poets strive to produce "poempictures." Mustering our forgiveness and condescension, we may try to overlook the use of such a fanciful term on the part of a poet as sober and skillful as Cummings. We sit politely by while he indulges in his hyperbolic talk, patiently waiting for him to stop the nonsense and resume the real business of being a poet.

Such well-mannered skepticism may in fact be the view we ought to take towards many poets. The sea of advertising around us—with its posters and letterheads and television commercials—has spawned some queer birds, and the well-bemoaned preference of recent generations for visual rather than literary stimuli has fed these hybrids rather well. We are not short on poets who, grasping faintly the significance of the artist's métier, have hastened to primp their pages and manhandle their stanzas. Cummings, however, was no tyro. Quite plainly, he knew what he was about in both media. He was, for all his famous lapses in taste and his inability to exercise consistently rigorous self-criticism, an exceptional poet and a masterful painter. So when he says—again and again—that he is both poet *and* painter, and when he makes it plain that he wants his poems to be treated as pictures, we probably ought to listen. At the very least, we should be willing to try his case.

The easiest way to try it is to develop a simple hypothesis and subject it to simple tests. The hypothesis I propose is no more complex than this: there are distinct stylistic relationships between Cummings' paintings and his poetry, and an understanding of them can help us to a sounder sense of his work. The manner of testing it is simply to take three poems, pair them with three paintings, and see what sorts of relationships can—and cannot—be drawn.

Perhaps it will be most useful to begin with a poem and a painting between which there is an evident connection in subject matter. The poem is "Paris;this April sunset completely utters," which was first published in *The Dial* in January, 1923, and later appeared in *&* (1925).[6]

> Paris;this April sunset completely utters
> utters serenely silently a cathedral

before whose upward lean magnificent face
the streets turn young with rain,

spiral acres of bloated rose
coiled within cobalt miles of sky
yield to and heed
the mauve
              of twilight(who slenderly descends,
daintily carrying in her eyes the dangerous first stars)
people move love hurry in a gently

arriving gloom and
see!(the new moon
fills abruptly with sudden silver
these torn pockets of lame and begging colour)while
there and here the lithe indolent prostitute
Night,argues

with certain houses

The poem was first sketched out on the back of an envelope addressed by his mother to Cummings' Paris lodgings and postmarked in Cambridge, Massachusetts, on 29 May 1922. Cummings, then twenty-seven, was making, as he wrote to his father (17 April 1923), "the usual five million drawings a month and now and then a sentence or three,sometimes suitable for 'poetic' consumption that most hideous of diseases." The envelope (now in the Cummings Collection at Harvard's Houghton Library) bears evidence of both arts, for it includes with the poetry some sketches in the Cubist vein.

The poem appeared in the section of & subtitled "Post Impressions," which may suggest that it was done "after" the manner of Impressionist painting, or perhaps in the style of Post-Impressionism. Like such paintings, it is of a specific place (Paris) and time (April evening). It deals, as Impressionism does, with colors ("rose," "cobalt," "mauve," "silver"); it provides detail about shape and movement ("upward," "lean," "spiral," "descends"); it centers upon objects which, although generalized, are nonetheless recognizable commonplaces ("cathedral," "streets," "people," "houses"); and it calls attention to the atmosphere ("rain," "mauve / of twilight," "gently / arriving gloom") as something affecting visual impressions. Its argument—although that is too strong a word for such an essentially imagistic method—is that night is superseding twilight. In the increasing darkness the forms, losing their clearly perceived outlines, are becoming progressively more personified. This dissolving of shape because of the impact or absence of light was a phenomenon much studied by the Impressionists and their followers. Taking their lead, Cummings suggests this dissolving by a dissolution of rigid metrical structure. The first three lines, although more than decasyllabic, are in pentameter. Thereafter the meter, while touching on trimeter and tetrameter for a few more lines, abandons itself to free verse.

It would, however, be unwise to assume that Cummings' intention here was to write a verbal equivalent of a visual image. In fact, the poem goes beyond visual description, articulating ideas which are outside the reach of the painter. A sunset, as Monet presented it, might be said to *illuminate* a cathedral or—given his insistence that light was all the painter had to work with—even to *create* it. Only for a wordsmith, however, does sunlight "utter" a cathedral. And only in literature can stars be depicted as "dangerous" and silver as "sudden": the painter would be hard pressed to present these attributes, just as he would find it difficult to capture the full impact of the final lines ("the lithe indolent prostitute / Night,argues / with certain houses"). The poem, then, can hardly be called a simple translation of visual into literary devices. It is much more accurately viewed as a piece of literature which draws something of its subject and imagery, and one of its strategies (dissolution of form), from the visual arts.

The painting which most readily suggests this poem is an oil of Paris rooftops done in 1933 (*Figure 1*) and now in the collection of Cummings' friend, J. Sibley Watson of Rochester, New York. It is a general view across the city with a cathedral in the distance. Compositionally the piece is not without merit: the balustrade of a balcony in the foreground, set at an angle to the horizon, leads the eye into the painting and parallels the general line of clouds angling downward to the setting sun. The colors, too, are somewhat balanced, with the mass of red rooftops at the lower left balanced by the reddish-purple clouds in the opposite corner. But the buildings themselves, while sketched with some attention to detail, are really rather uninteresting: the light is undirectional, and no shadows break the humdrum recording of the forms. The sky, by contrast, is commanding, as the yellow sun (seen low on the horizon over the shoulder of the cathedral) lights up the clouds with what does indeed, in the language of the poem, suggest "spiral acres" of "coiled" color. Here, after all, is where Cummings' heart is; like Monet's waterlilies and Cézanne's mountains, Cummings' sunsets were to become a preoccupation in his later paintings as well as in some later poems.

Aside from this similarity of place and time, however, the painting and poem are hardly parallel. The movement of the poem from dusk to evening, the image of moon and stars, the allusions to beggars and lovers and prostitutes, and even the general tenor of Impressionist "atmosphere" all drop away in the painting, which, focusing on the sky, makes of central importance something which in the poem was only a few lines of description. Whether or not Cummings had the poem in mind as he painted the scene is immaterial. What is significant is the difference between these two treatments of a common scene. The painting simply

Figure 1. E.E. Cummings: *Paris Roofs with Sunset*, oil on canvas. 22" x 25", 1933. Collection of J. S. Watson, Jr., Rochester, N.Y. © 1978 by Nancy T. Andrews.

represents a landscape, thereby doing what has long been thought proper to paintings. The poem reaches out to incorporate ideas and attitudes from painting; yet, in compelling the visual stuff to subserve literary ends, it becomes more than a mere description of a painting. The painting presents an image. The poem presents a sequence of images suffused with extra-visual attributes. Cummings, it seems, knew that he had two different media on his hands; rather than using them for the same ends, he respected their differences and employed them, even with common subjects, in different ways.

Common subject matter, then, is no guarantee of stylistic relationship. If an individual subject is engaging enough, however, it may determine in the artist's thought a particular mental set that even in different media produces similar results. Such is the case with the painting of burlesque entertainer Jimmy Savo and the poem "so little he is." Nowhere else in his published writings does Cummings mention Savo; and, so far, no other portraits of him have come to light. It seems not unreasonable to conjecture, then, that—whichever of these pieces was done first—Cummings must have had to reckon with the existence of the former while executing the latter. Perhaps he meant them in some ways as companion pieces. Whatever their genesis, they both suggest a common attitude towards their subject.

The poem first appeared in the "New Poems" section of *Collected Poems* (1938).[7]

so little he is
so.
          Little
ness be

(ing)
comes ex
-pert-
Ly expand:grO

w
    i
?n
      g

Is poet iS
(childlost
so;ul
)foundclown a

-live a
,bird
          !O

```
& j &

ji
&
jim,jimm
;jimmy

s:
   A
   V
   o(

        .

        :

        ;

        ,
```

One of the first critics to respond was Lloyd Frankenberg, whose comments in his *Pleasure Dome: On Reading Modern Poetry* (1949) are concise and incisive.

> "So" begins and concludes the poem. The latter "so" encloses "AV" (a root-form for "bird"), thus confirming in Savo's name the birdlike quality expressed in the poem. Savo's "pert" expertness consists in expanding littleness, but not by blowing up its dimensions. He grOws in a series of circular elations, as the miracle ("L . . . O") of a "wi?ng" causes a bird to grow through space. They grow by what their motion encloses. Savo is a "childlost"; yet like a poet recovers original impulses of living: the child, lost to most of us, is found in poet and clown. . . . The trailing punctuation at the end recalls the floating particles of paper Savo can incredibly cause to flutter off from his fingers, with infinite lassitude. And of course Savo began as a juggler; a precisionist at balance.[8]

Frankenberg rightly calls attention to the motion suggested in the poem—a motion arising not so much in the meanings of the words as in their punctuation, spacing, tmesis, and so forth. Cummings includes some of these peculiarities of structure, of course, largely for semantic reasons: the words "be / (ing) / comes," conflating "being" and "becoming," suggests one of his favorite themes, and the isolation of the word *wing* produces overtones unnoticed in the normal arrangement of the word *growing*. Some of these peculiarities can also be justified as aids to oral interpretation: the semicolon in the midst of "so;ul," for example, while isolating yet one more appearance of the word "so," may also suggest the wry preciosity of Savo's pronunciation ("*so*-whul") of the word.

Much of the poem's impact, however, can only be explained in visual terms. In his drawings of stage and ballroom dancers, both male and female, Cummings sometimes suggests motion by catching his figures in the act of landing lightly on one toe. In these drawings, and in many of his paintings, he also seems to favor verticality over horizontality.[9] These two devices come into play in this poem, which is a tall and slender construction of very short lines, balanced precariously on the toe of its last comma. These final punctuation marks move from period to colon to semicolon and finally to comma: they become, in other words, progressively less final. The sequence at the end, however, is only the last of several sequences of these four marks buried earlier in the poem: they first appear in the same order (. : ; ,) in lines 2, 8, 15, and 18, only to reverse themselves (, ; :) in lines 23, 24, and 25 before concluding in lines 29–32. The marks are, in some ways, the major symbol in the poem. Like Savo, they are small, delicate, provocative—and, like any good comedian, possessed of a carefully rational sense of order. While not usually essential to meaning, they permit the addition of worthwhile nuances—just as Savo, hardly an indispensable figure in the world of high or low art, adds to it a "little" but significant grace note. And, in their cyclical movement away from, towards, and away from finality, they suggest the tentative and uncertain nature of this statement, and, by extension, of Savo himself.

The oil painting (*Figure 2*), undated but with a penciled "Jimmy Savo" on the back, is also—even by Cummings' standards—small. He applied the pigment to the 10" x 8" canvasboard in methods ranging from a wash with occasional bare spots all the way to thick impasto, laid on in quick and rather broad strokes of numerous hues. The only unambiguously detailed feature is the face, with bowler above and necktie below. Less defined but still apparent are the outstretched arm (holding some kind of paper or sign), the legs, the feet, and the suggestions of lapels and pocket on his coat. Beyond his body, however, all is conjecture. The foreground may represent the heads of the orchestra in front of the stage, seen from much the same angle Degas so often favored. Or perhaps these shapes are heads of the theater audience, or heads of those seated in a nightclub (with some right angles suggesting table-corners) or dancing in front of the stage. Perhaps they are not heads at all but part of the stage and its footlights. Similarly, the bright vertical bands of color above and behind Savo may be curtains, or the beams of colored stage-lights, or (especially to the right) a hallway leading backstage. The general movement of the line, evident in Savo's body and echoed in the swatches of color in front of and behind him, is from lower right to upper left. It is the same angle produced by the punctuation closing the poem—which is, of course, the angle always produced by progressive indentation.

Like the Paris poem and painting, these two works show a common subject. Unlike the earlier poetry, however, they also exhibit a significant correlation in manner. Each is "little," a central quality (according to the poem) in Savo's appearance. Each is constructed of fragments which need some sort of reassembly to produce the whole figure. Each presents a number of obscurities which, as we stretch ourselves to comprehend

Figure 2. "Jimmy Savo," oil on canvas board, 10" x 8". Collection of Luethi-Peterson Camps, Inc., Barrington, R.I. © 1978 by Nancy T. Andrews.

them, suggest much more than could ever be told by a straightforward ex-actness of visual detail or a prosy precision of descriptive language. Each is "jumpy"—a word Cummings once used in his private notes to describe the effect produced on the viewer by a sequence of unrelated colors.[10] In the poem, the jumpiness results from dislocation, sudden unexpected in-trusions of punctuation, odd spacings, and parenthetical insertions. In the painting, it results partly from the seeming randomness of shapes and more emphatically from the surprising collections of color laid down side by side. Reading across the top of the canvas, for example, we move through major patches of gray, blue-green, chartreuse, rose, beige, gray-green, and ochre—colors which, though they find counterparts elsewhere in the painting and are ultimately coherent, are not calculated to strike us as familiar combinations. Finally, the rhythmic passage on Savo's first name ("& j & / ji / & / jim,jimm / ; jimmy"), with its echoes of a chant or cheer, depends on a technique (familiar to readers of Psalms) known as in-cremental repetition, in which a statement is expanded in restatement un-til it reaches completion. It is a technique corresponding, perhaps, to what Kenneth Burke, in defining the "innate forms of the mind" that underlie thought and art, calls "disclosure."[11] The Savo painting may also suggest a kind of disclosure: it is as though Cummings assembled, around the periphery of his canvas, the raw materials out of which the figure would finally be constructed, knowing that, as we progress from any direction closer to the central point (the face), obscurity would give way to recognizable forms.

This recognition amid obscurity, while it may suggest no more than the visual appearance of a well-lighted figure in a dimly-lit and smoke-filled hall, may also indicate something of the figure's identity. With his body blending imperceptibly into his environment, Savo seems so in-tegrally related to the world in which Cummings finds him that any disengagement of figure from ground—of the sort usually necessary to focus attention in a portrait or a poem—would do him injustice. Separate neither from the raw vigor of his visual background nor, in the poem, from the tangle of letters, syllables, and punctuation marks which are the raw materials of intelligible discourse, Savo remains in a demi-monde of half-formed images struggling towards articulation. It is the milieu that characterizes and identifies him.

Subject matter, then, may give us the impulse to search for more meaningful parallels. If there is a genuine stylistic unity in the works of a poet-painter, however, it ought to show up even in the absence of com-mon subjects. And so it does. The comparison of a third pair demonstrates underlying principles of construction which, even in the absence of blunt similarities of subject, make themselves felt in both media.

The poem "brIght" is the penultimate one in *No Thanks* (1935). Here, progressive disclosure combines with a remarkable symmetry of design.

Cummings, it seems, set himself the challenge of writing a poem with only eleven different words.[12] Each three-letter word ("big," "yes," "who") appears three times; each four-letter word ("soft," "near," "calm," "holy," and "deep," along with "star" in its various incarnations) appears four times; "alone" appears five times; and "bright," in various ways, six times. In addition, capital letters compose additional appearances: a different letter is capitalized each time "yes" appears, assembling materials out of which the reader can construct, by rearrangement, the word "YES." Similar capitalization appears in "who" and "bright."[13]

> brIght
>
> bRight s??? big
> (soft)
>
> soft near calm
> (Bright)
> calm st?? holy
>
> (soft briGht deep)
> yeS near sta? calm star big yEs
> alone
> (wHo
>
> Yes
> near deep whO big alone soft near
> deep calm deep
> ????Ht?????T)
> Who(holy alone)holy(alone holy)alone

The poem is also carefully wrought in its stanzaic pattern. Each of the five stanzas becomes one line longer than the previous one, and—because each stanza extends farther to the right than its predecessor—the layers of stanzas take on the shape of a right triangle. The poem, about the gradual appearance of a bright star, imitates the star's progressive disclosure in the movement from "s???" to "star": the question marks, here and in the last two mentions of "bright," suggest not only the ambiguity of missing letters but also the more provocative question of the nature of this star. Given its description as "big," "calm," and "holy," this may be the Star of Bethlehem—an interpretation not unreasonable in view of the poem's location, in *No Thanks*, among a group of poems on transcendental themes.

The last line—"Who(holy alone)holy(alone holy)alone"—appropriately concludes this poem of balance, a balance perhaps reflecting the halcyon peace of Jesus' appearance, and suggesting the orderliness which a transcendent ethic brings to an otherwise chaotic world. "Who," capitalized in the manner of a name for God, is here "holy" and "alone"—or *all one*, words which, as attributes for Deity, are the etymological roots of "alone." Given Cummings' penchant for fragmenting and recombining words, the letters of "Who(holy" are probably also meant to fuse into *wholly*: God, after all, is "wholly alone." Moreover, this last line embodies a remarkable quasi-visual balance. The central word "holy" is flanked on either side by a parenthesis, then by "alone," and then by "holy." The pattern is not unlike that of traditional paintings and mosaics depicting a central ruler flanked by symmetrical figures. The line can hardly be said to be discursive and rational. Telling us nothing new, the words show us their message by their arrangement and provide a fitting base upon which this triangular poem rests.

Different in subject but related in design is Cummings' large *Autumn Landscape (Figure 3)*. Here the painter sets himself several challenges. He must depict water without the conventional retreat to blues and whites. Further, he must depict it in such a way that it obviously *is* water, flat and glossy, although the pigments he uses must be essentially indistinguishable from those used for the trees on the far shore whose reflections fill the pond. And he must so handle the brushwork that the viewer can distinguish, in all the busy surge and bustle of foliage, just where the foreground bushes leave off and the water behind them begins. To accomplish all this, and still to preserve a sense of depth, is no mean task.

Like the poem, the painting is almost perfectly symmetrical; yet, again like the poem, its symmetry is not obtrusive. The central shape, the pond, is that of a triangle standing on its apex. The rising foreground foliage closes in the pond on either side, providing a self-containment reinforced by the predominantly left-leaning lines in the lower left and right-leaning lines in the lower right. Towards the center foreground, however, the predominant lines shift, and the foliage points inward towards the large red maple on the pond's far shore. These lines, along with the obvious path that opens the near shore's foliage and lets the vision through to the pond, direct the eye inward, across the reflection of the tree, across some whitish lilypads, and on to the tree itself.

That tree, like the word "holy" in the last line of "brIght," focuses the scene. Like Wallace Stevens' famous Tennessee jar, it brings into order the sprawling wilderness by providing a center. At the far left, and at the extreme edge of the pond on the right, it finds an echo in smaller red trees. Between these exact repetitions of color and the central tree there are, on each side, significant patches of the related color orange. Like the last line of "brIght," then, the painting may be "read" horizontally as a central figure flanked by other figures. It has, however, a second dimension. In the advance of the color from the tree towards the viewer something of the same symmetry appears. The large maple is echoed immediately, if briefly, in its reflection just off shore. On the near side of the lilies, the color deepens and combines with some strong oranges. Finally, at the extreme bottom center, come the darker reds on the path. The

Figure 3. E.E. Cummings: *Autumn Landscape*, oil on cardboard. 24″ x 36″. Collection of R. W. Davidson, Lincolnville, Maine. © 1978 by Nancy T. Andrews.

rhythm is similar to that of the horizontal dimension, where reds or oranges alternate with other colors across the line of the background. Reading downward from the central maple, then, we find a straight line of *red* / green / *red and orange* / white / *red and orange* / light blue / *red*. This schematic pattern is not so rigorously applied as to be abstract; Cummings never loses sight of the landscape in his dedication to the principle of symmetry. Nevertheless, the design is clearly here, the evidence of a compositional foundation underlying the painting just as it did the poem.

To touch these three examples is hardly to master Cummings' aesthetic. The examples, nevertheless, should alert us to several things. On the one hand, we do Cummings a disservice if we erect into a principle of parallelism the easy and superficial relations between poetry and painting that are based solely on subject matter. On the other hand, we read only a part of his meaning if we refuse to assess the more complex relations between these arts. Cummings, a restless seeker of unity within or beyond the diversities of human experience, saw so clearly the underlying relations between these arts that he could hardly keep from embodying in one the principles he discovered in the other. Sometimes, as in the Savo pieces, the cross-fertilization may have been a conscious process. At other times, however, it may have operated without direct intention—the result of "intelligence," as he once said of Lachaise, "functioning at intuitional velocity."[14]

That these relations are real and useful—that they are not simply the product of our critical impositions on otherwise innocent pairs of works—should not be surprising. We are accustomed to noticing similar relations in the work of creative talents exercised within a single art: we regularly find that specific identifiable mannerisms hallmark a writer's early and late works, his poems and his plays, his letters as well as his conversations, and we assume that a painter may exhibit individual habits of style throughout a lifetime and across different media. Cummings' individuality resides in his assimilation of the principles of two arts into a single unified aesthetic, an aesthetic which quite naturally gave rise to common devices of style whenever it was put into practice. To underestimate the effects of this aesthetic is to misread a good deal of his poetry.

NOTES

1. *Arts Digest*, 1 Dec. 1954; reprinted in *E.E. Cummings: A Miscellany Revised*, ed. George J. Firmage (New York: October House, 1965), p. 333.

2. Letter to his mother, Rebecca Cummings, 18 June 1918, in the Cummings Collection, Houghton Library, Harvard University. Excerpts quoted from E.E. Cummings' unpublished letters to his parents are printed by permission of Nancy T. Andrews and the Houghton Library, Harvard University, Cambridge, Massachusetts. © 1978 by Nancy T. Andrews.

3. 2 Dec. 1976—6 Feb. 1977; the catalogue—Frank Gettings, *E.E. Cummings: The*

Poet as Artist (Washington, D.C.: Smithsonian Institution Press, 1976)—reproduces sixty-eight of his paintings and drawings.

4. To date, the basic studies of Cummings' work as a painter are Chapter 11 of Charles Norman's *E.E. Cummings: The Magic-Maker* (Indianapolis, Ind.: Bobbs-Merrill, 1972), and Rushworth M. Kidder's "E.E. Cummings, Painter," *Harvard Library Bulletin*, 23 (1975), 117–38. See also, Robert Tucker, "E.E. Cummings as an Artist: *The Dial* Drawings," *Massachusetts Review*, 26 (1975), 329–53; Dagmar Reutlinger, "E.E. Cummings and *The Dial* Collection," *Massachusetts Review*, 26 (1975), 353–56; and Rushworth M. Kidder, " 'Author of Pictures': A Study of Cummings' Line Drawings in *The Dial*," *Contemporary Literature*, 17 (1976), 470–505. Three additional essays on Cummings' art by Kidder have appeared in *The Christian Science Monitor*: "e.e. cummings: American poet and painter," 25 Nov. 1974; "Another line on simplicity," 1 Sept. 1977; and "Precision creating movement," 9 Nov. 1977. Each article cited in this note contains reproductions of Cummings' artwork.

5. Quoted by Norman, pp. 238–39.

6. Quoted here from *E.E. Cummings: Complete Poems 1913–1962* (New York: Harcourt Brace Jovanovich, 1972), p. 93. Reprinted by permission.

7. "so little he is." *E.E. Cummings: Complete Poems 1913–1962* (New York: Harcourt Brace Jovanovich, 1972), p. 471. Reprinted by permission.

8. Reprinted in *EΣTI: eec E.E. Cummings and the Critics*, ed. S.V. Baum (East Lansing: Michigan State Univ. Press, 1962), pp. 157–58.

9. See especially his drawings of dancers in *The Dial*. Cummings' predilection for a vertical format may have been influenced by his literary bent: most book pages, after all, are taller than they are wide. Also, however, he found himself painting many of his works—when money for canvas or canvasboard was scarce—on shirt-cardboards returned from the laundry. These were typically of 18½" x 8" dimensions. Almost always, even in landscapes, he held them upright, the result being the unusual proportions and elongated appearance of many of his paintings.

10. See Kidder, "E.E. Cummings, Painter," p. 130.

11. Kenneth Burke, "The Poetic Process," *Counter-Statement*, 2d ed. (Los Altos, California, 1953), p. 46; quoted in James D. Merriman, "The Parallel of the Arts: Some Misgivings and a Faint Affirmation," *Journal of Aesthetics and Art Criticism*, 21 (1973), 315.

12. Many of the intricacies mentioned here were first pointed out by Robert M. McIlvaine in *The Explicator*, 30 (1971), Item 6.

13. "brIght," *E.E. Cummings: Complete Poems 1913–1962* (New York: Harcourt Brace Jovanovich, 1972), p. 455. Reprinted by permission.

14. "Gaston Lachaise," *The Dial*, Feb. 1920; reprinted in *A Miscellany Revised*, p. 17.

Cummings Posthumous

Norman Friedman*

Apart from *Complete Poems 1913–1962*, which was not published until 1972 but contains nothing except *73 poems* not already in book form within the dates of the title, four Cummings volumes have been published since his death in 1962: *Adventures in Value* (1962), *73 poems* (1963), *Fairy Tales* (1965), and *Selected Letters* (1969). Do these add significantly to his oeuvre? Do they tell us anything about him that we didn't know before?

Before addressing myself to these questions, I want to explain in what order I treat these works, for the order of their posthumous publication does not necessarily reflect the order of their composition. The *Letters*, of course, cover the broadest timespan, running from 1899, when Cummings was just five years old, to 1962, when he was almost sixty-eight. This volume offers, then, a framework for looking at his career as a whole, and it also provides the richest material on the basis of which to speculate about the ultimate meaning of Cummings' life and art and of their relationship, and so I will begin with that.

Fairy Tales contains four tales, three of which were published originally in *Wake* between 1946 and 1950.[1] But they appear to have been written much earlier, as Marion Morehouse Cummings explains on the dedicatory page: "These tales were written for Cummings' daughter, Nancy, when she was a very little girl." Now, since Nancy—the child of Cummings' first marriage, which was to Elaine Orr Thayer—was born in 1919,[2] the tales would have been written sometime before the mid-twenties. Furthermore, as we shall see, they suggest certain very poignant father-child feelings, and an examination of these grows naturally out of a consideration of the letters.

Adventures in Value, containing fifty photographs by Marion Morehouse, with captions by Cummings, was, to the best of my knowledge, the last published work of Cummings for which he saw the proofs. A gap of thirty years, therefore, separates it from the tales, but *Letters* will handily supply the enveloping context, as *Adventures* will provide a convenient bridge to a consideration of *73 poems*.

This last volume contains at least forty-six poems which first appeared in magazines while Cummings was still alive,[3] and it does represent as a whole poems which he regarded as completed. The copyrights go back as far as 1950 but mainly fall between 1958 and 1963. Since the preceding book of verse, *95 poems*, was published in 1958, *73 poems*

*Reprinted from *Journal of Modern Literature*, 7 (1979), 295–322. Copyright © 1979 by Temple University. Reprinted by permission of Norman Friedman and the *Journal of Modern Literature*.

seems to represent work done primarily in his last four years. An analysis of this book, then, will provide a fitting climax for this essay.

I

Although I want to direct attention to certain of Cummings' inner conflicts as they appear in the letters,[4] I will begin by noting a few of their features that seem directly interesting and pertinent in terms of the more public side of the writer.

F. W. Dupee and George Stade, the editors of the letters, say in their Foreword that Cummings "seems not to have regarded letter writing as . . . a conscious art," although "the survival of the first and second drafts of a number of his letters testifies to the care he used when he wanted to" (xv). They mention later that he "normally made and preserved carbons" of his letters from 1947 on (xviii). It seems to me that the latter two remarks are more indicative than the first of what the reader finds in this volume. My impression is that they were very carefully written indeed, for when Cummings sat down to write, he was a writer—no matter what it was he was writing. Dupee and Stade concede the point a bit grudgingly: "Insofar as conscious art is detectible in his letters it is recognizably akin to the art of his verse and prose, since he was as thoroughly all of a piece as any fine and celebrated poet has ever been" (xv).

Cummings generally has three prose styles: the careful and deliberate balance found in "A Foreward to Krazy" or *i: Six Nonlectures*, for example; the zany linguistic hijinks found in *No Title* (1930) and some of the satirical essays, for example; and the ecstatic lyricism of the latter part of the Introduction to the 1938 *Collected Poems* and parts of *Eimi*, for example. And the reader of *Selected Letters* will find elements of the same styles here, but of particular note are the many letters—especially to Ezra Pound—falling into the second category that are so full of surrealistic puns and verbal streams of consciousness that they become well-nigh cryptic. Pound himself, in fact, appears to have had some difficulty in deciphering them (204–5)!

The second public feature is the interesting record of his literary friendships and tastes, and of his remarks about and explications of his own writings—as well as his general comments about art. In addition to Pound, he knew and corresponded with William Carlos Williams, Edmund Wilson, Allen Tate, A. J. Ayer, Archibald MacLeish, Marianne Moore, John Dos Passos, Kenneth Burke, John Peale Bishop, and Robert Graves. He also knew Hart Crane, Malcolm Cowley, and Max Eastman. He makes interesting comments on Gertrude Stein, T. S. Eliot, Céline, Dinesen, Yeats, Dylan Thomas, Santayana, Swinburne, Rilke, Jeffers, Jung, Freud, Thoreau, Blake, Browning, Mann, Joyce, and Lawrence. Of particular value are his reluctant interpretations of his own works when pressed by an importunate reader, and I found of interest his many struggles with printers, editors, publishers, producers, directors, and translators to get his writings before the public properly. Also important are his many comments about art, especially his preference for representational painting and respect for traditional grammar and conventional poetic forms.

These letters are carefully if not deliberately written, then, and they contain a strong public component. As Dupee and Stade reassure us, Cummings "seems not to have regarded letter writing as . . a vehicle for any urgent confessional impulse. . . . he seldom soars to any heights of sustained introspection or plunges into any depths of mere personal scandal, about himself or anyone else" (xv). Furthermore, as they also explain, the letters we have here have been pretty thoroughly winnowed: they have printed only about one-fourth of the total number they recovered (265 out of a thousand or so). Additionally, as the editors inform us, Cummings' first and second wives no longer have any communications that he may have addressed to them. And finally, since this volume was published just before Marion Morehouse, the poet's third wife, died, we can be sure that nothing that might have reflected negatively on Cummings could have possibly gotten through.

None of this is to the point, however, since that kind of privacy is not at issue. I want to deal with the whole problem of conflicts going on inside him which do not find expression in the poetry—or if they do, are pretty well disguised—and which he is only intermittently aware of and only rarely able to integrate, and to trace the course of these conflicts as they work their way through his personal life in the world and leave their mark upon the inner structure of his emotional and intellectual life. The end in view is to place the writings and career in this broader context and, by appreciating what was selected out as well as what was included in, to achieve a greater understanding of their ultimate significance. I once wrote that Cummings (like Whitman) created an artistic persona and then transformed the man into that persona so that they became one, and we could have guessed at what it must have cost. Now we can have a better idea of that price. Indeed, we can have a clearer idea of the slippage which we could have guessed any such attempt must have incurred between man and mask.

First there is an extremely telling ambivalence, as a young man, toward his parents. Between the ages of twenty-three and twenty-nine (1917–1923), when he was in the French prison of *The Enormous Room* and then in an Army camp at Fort Devens, and later when he was settling in New York, Cummings evinced quite a desire to be free of his family's influence and help—even urging Elizabeth, his younger sister, to follow suit. "I see the thing thru, alone, without any monocled Richards, American ambassadors, or anything else," he writes from France in 1917 (40). Apparently his father was offering to wield his considerable influence and obviously did later, as we learn from *The Enormous Room*.

His father also seems to have wondered why Estlin accepted conscription instead of a commission in the Army, and the son answers, "Mine is the perspiration of my own existence, and that's all I give a proper and bloody damn for" (51), and "if my prodigal family wants to keep on best terms with its fatted calf, it will lease the pasture the calf wants to graze in. For even a calf has a will of its own, they say!" (53). Already the self-conscious artist, he affirms the artist's need to know life at first hand (52). After the war, in 1920, Cummings briefly planned a sea voyage (which he never took), and rejected his father's concern once more: "in short, you will let me go my own way in my flannel shirt and my ideas" (72).

But these rebellious sentiments are mild in comparison to his advice, during 1922–23, to his kid sister, who was apparently thinking of moving to New York also. After telling her to be independent and to trust her feelings, he says she won't be able to do these things "until you have KNOCKED DOWN AND CARRIED OUT all the teachable swill of Cambridge etc. And I'm the nigger that knows it and is sympathetic to you for that reason;because my mind has been there too. . . . To hell with everything which tries,no matter how kindly,to prevent me from LIVING MY OWN LIFE—KINDNESS,always,is MORE DANGEROUS than anything else!!" (86). Or again: "to inhabit the amiable and succulent bosom of one's relations not to mention one's family is to—I use Mitchell's momentous words,borrowed from St Paul—'die daily' " (94). And finally: "I am glad you are reading smutty books,living in New York,drinking gasolene coctails [sic], etc. A sister to be proud of" (102).

Cummings, of course, does take a few shots at Cambridge in his published writings, but he never hints at the suffocation he felt in growing up in his family or at the difficulty he felt in breaking free of its influence. He was favored and encouraged by his parents, and this accounts for his public piety and reverence. But he also seems to have felt that along with his parents' approval came a tacit set of values, and that these values interfered with his individuality and growth as an artist. There is, naturally, that normal part of maturing which requires separation and independence, but there is also a suggestion, as we shall see in a moment, that Cummings felt he was *different* from his father and needed to protect that difference. His father, after all, in addition to the vitality and versatility and warmth which Cummings celebrated, was the head and support of a family, a minister, a professor, a social scientist, and reformer—quite a proper, progressive, and intellectual citizen, and as such he must have represented on some level many of the things Cummings felt he had to dissociate himself from.[5] This explains his rebelliousness, but I am not sure why he chose not to deal more explicitly with it in his published writings.

Whatever the answer may be, I do think this dilemma in part underlies his characteristic later stance as the beleaguered New England eccentric, as we shall see below, and is in part accounted for by the unfortunate result that he did not actually succeed in freeing himself from his family's influence after all. He tried, finally, to get a hardship discharge from the Army (55–6), and he characteristically needed and received money from home between 1920 and 1939 (74, 82, 110, 123, 127, 142–3, 147). A very poignant burst of dependency came in 1925 (when he was almost twenty-nine), after his first wife left him: "It seems to me that father's brains(which) I have ever admired,unlike my own) plus the life which he has given to society in the economic sense of the word ought to rise up,here,and somehow . . . magnificantly Save The Day before it's too late—mind you,he may know a Boston lawyer who's a genius;and any-way,he is a famous man whereas I am a small eye poet" (108–9).

I am suggesting that Cummings, having started off in a blaze of youthful vigor and independence, became deeply hurt by the failure of his first marriage and by the fact that he could not make a go of it by himself in his career. Surely such disappointment was sufficient for the develop-ment of a lifelong sense of disparity between himself and most of the rest of the world. And, indeed, he was fortunate in finding in Sibley Watson, who was always a supporter, a substitute for his family during his middle and later years. Having received intermittent moral and financial help from Watson during the 1920s, 30s, and 40s (133, 188, 195), Cummings finally made a formal request at the beginning of 1950: "perhaps you can help me. I cannot see how to go on unless am sure of 5000$ [sic] a year." And then he goes on to spell out his budgetary picture, offering Joy Farm [Cummings' summer place in Silver Lake, New Hampshire, inherited from his parents] as security if need be (202).

There is something rueful in all this, especially in the light of the fact that Cummings *wanted* to be self-supporting. Eleven years previously, in 1939, he had written to Watson, "thank you most kindly for the 300 and am literally American enough to hope I'll be able to 'make my own way' 'some day' 'soon.' Seem to remember mon père telling me the best thing which could happen to you would be that what you want to do most should give you a living;anyhow,feel this is so" (148–9).

And yet, despite his disappointment and the fact that he had infinite difficulty in making his own way, he spoke early and late of self-sufficiency in the face of failure, of his proud independence, of his own defiant scorn of security, and of the virtue of suffering as a gift. Somehow his early need for freedom still had to be fulfilled. How could he do this? Shift the terms of the conflict: not being able to be *economically* indepen-dent, he felt that *spiritual* freedom was a superior virtue. Trying to cheer Stewart Mitchell up in 1920 for the latter's feelings of failure, Cummings says, "only,I quietly insist,my worship of and my confidence in mySelf is unmitigated in the face of these paltry (ourword,Monsieur)Thermopolae" (74). In 1948 he writes to another friend, "concerning uncertainty(alias insecurity,or whatever mostpeople fear)I rather imagine that insofaras an artist is worth his spiritual salt he can never get enough" (186). And in

1956, writing to Mrs. Watson, he mentions some notebooks of his "(whereof 200&some already exist)" and quotes some passages he had written therein nine years before: "all fear is an ignorance of the truth that what we call 'suffering' or 'pain' or 'sorrow' (or 'evil') is a great gift. . . . 'if you turn the other cheek truly', something happens which makes you invulnerable & and your wouldbe foe powerless" (249–50).

Certainly Cummings experienced enough anxiety and deprivation to qualify him for making those statements, and his letters from his fortieth year on speak recurringly of his difficulties, his lack of money, the hostility of the critics, the lack of attention given to his painting, etc. (142, 147, 202, 252, 263). He quotes admiringly, in 1959, near the end of his life, from Isak Dinesen: "and so I learned that,if you have no faith,if you are quite without hope,and if you do just a very little,and then a little more,and again still more,it will all of itself become something" (261). And his letters from age forty-seven on also speak frequently of his arthritis, his thinning hair, his fear of travel, his stage fright, his feelings of tension, and so forth (163, 189, 195, 211, 238, 245).

But without self-pity, blaming, complaining, or bitterness. He could do without these props. Nevertheless, not many can stand naked in the void, and he did need a defense system: the compensatory image he built of himself as taking a lonely stand against a noncomprehending world did the job. Feeling his family's love as an encroachment, and yet needing it, he concluded that his individuality required vigilant protection; launching himself confidently against the world to make a career as an artist and yet finding himself bruised and impoverished, he inferred that he was the champion of values no one else believed in—except himself, fiercely, and a few friends and admirers such as the Watsons. They could give him familial support—both financial and moral—without the importation of well-meaning values to be resisted: "how wonderful! You-&-Sibley understand me:understand that I'm perfectly helpless unless I'm loved by people whom I can respect—understand that such people are very much rarer than rarest," he writes to Mrs. Watson in 1948 (188). Someone with a life-dream may need others to believe in it in order to feel he's real, but that's not the same thing as being independent—it's merely a shift from one sort of family to another to depend on.

The result from his mid-forties on is the pride of the "101% New Englander" (159), the beleaguered eccentric at odds with the world and stubbornly doing his own thing. As he says in the just-quoted letter to Mrs. Watson, "it's that what I'm trying to do,or rather who I'd like to be(the only value which,for me,makes my living worth while)quite incidentally but inexorably unmakes most 'values'; rendering them less than valueless." He feels his paintings have received little recognition (228), that he has fought a twenty-year battle against liberalism and socialism (228), that he opposes the book-distributing and -reviewing marketplace (243), that he deliberately insults "the powersthatseem" (245), that the poet cannot "give a hangnail for social respectability" (256), and that he must refuse an invitation to the White House (275). He must uncompromisingly man his personal barricades: he hates the radio (174–5, 195), the critics (237, 252), the *New Yorker* (230, 245), and he refuses to teach (167, 202, 222, 257) or hold any regular job, to appear on symposia or give autographs, and he disparages automobiles and movies. After years of such energy-consuming battles, it is no wonder that he feels that New York City has deteriorated and turns, as we shall see, to the solace of simple, bucolic virtues.

Indeed, the really significant point is the effect such a life experience and its accompanying defenses had upon the inner structure of his emotional life. Certainly, we know from the published *oeuvre* that Cummings was a hater, but what we get a less clear picture of there is the pain, depression, and self-doubt that inevitably must underlie such hostility. The problem in the published writings is not that he is so naive as to lack a sane and realistic sense of the evil in the world—his innocence needn't be protected against *that* charge. The problem is that he sometimes lacks a sense of any *relation* to that evil, either as it might impinge upon him and get him down, or as it might find a reflection within himself. His desired stance, as I have suggested, is to proclaim he is above being affected by it and is indeed separate from it. But doubts and black moods are precisely what he could not keep out of his letters.[6] Speaking to his mother of his first wife's desertion, he says, "am sitting on a large piece of almost nothing taking my own photograph with a shutterless camera" (108). Many years later, he writes to the daughter whom that ex-wife kept from him and hopes he has had some influence upon her life: "Being myself nearly sans time-sense(except as rhythm)I can only guess when certain still-vivid childhood experiences may have occurred. But shall never forget how my staunch(then as now)friend Sibley Watson,by way of comforting our unhappy nonhero,gently reminded him that the greatly(to me)wise Freud says a child's self('psyche')is already formed at whatever age you were when we lost each other" (269).

In 1948 he writes to a friend,

> it's good to hear that you've outgrown your 'great depressions'. I've the very great honour to inform you that you're way ahead of me! Am possibly emerging from an impossible & v.v. [vice versa] one at the so-called present writing. (186)

He writes to MacLeish about being depressed over his arthritis (189), and to another that he reads Santayana "when an UNworld threatens to get me down" (262). And he has moments of profound self-doubt:

> why doesn't he do this,do that [he imagines people asking]?Why, when he has such&such a talent & could surely score a success there or here,does he renege and refuse;balk,stall,backtrack;hide from,dodge,or even insult those who'd like to help him;put absurd obstacles in his own way,& other-

wise play the neurotic to perfection? . . . Am I wrong about myself? Does my picture of me fail as a likeness? (188)

Or again:

why does little Estlin find it so hard to understand that everything almost(& almost everybody)'s perpetually disintegrating; as well as re-? (203)

And again:

Tell me now,Hildegarde [it is significant that each of these moments is confided to the Watsons], what do you think:am I suffering from what 'the liberals' entitle 'failure of nerve',or from something else most beautifully described by Quintus H as 'nec pietas moram';or may my unending timidities harbour a diminutive amount of truth? (212)

We also know from the published *oeuvre* that Cummings was a transcender, but what is also less specific there, in consequence of what we've been noticing so far, is *what* and *how* he transcends, as well as what it means specifically to him as a person. Counterbalancing the hate, pain, depression, and self-doubt are strong moments in the letters—not merely of acceptance of suffering—but rather of intense self-awareness and inner integration. Here he goes behind his own defensive stance and risks facing the void: I myself am Hell. Writing to his mother in 1941 about their being 101% New Englanders, he remarks that Gilbert Seldes accused him once

of what he called "the egocentric predicament." If Gilbert had been a Catholic he'd have used another phrase—"the sin of pride." For what he meant was that really,underneath everything,I considered myself pretty dam [sic] omniscient.—Well,our hero (being a New Englander)vigorously denied all. But very gradually I began to notice that if something happened which prevented me from doing as I pleased,then (by Jove)I tended to feel downright frustrated:nay, even personally insulted! Talk about "childish"! Maybe,some day,I'll be blessed with a touch of true humility. (159)

Writing to Pound in 1947, he said, "But more & more,as I grow,is the antediluvian undersigned delighted by Doctor Jung's terrafirma riposte when a desperate wouldbe dogooder demanded what can be done to make better the world?quote Jung,make thyself better" (176). He writes to his sister in 1954, "But I feel I'm somehow gradually evolving;despite selfpity narcissism an inferiority complex & possibly several other psychic ailments" (238). In 1955 he writes to Mrs. Watson, "must confess I attribute my physical ills to socalled nervous tension" (245). In explicating "Hello is what a mirror says" for an inquiring reader, he says: "true wars are never won;since they are inward,not outward,and necessitate facing one's self" (247).

The sense that hatred is often a projection outward of what one hates in oneself is also clearly realized several times in the letters. In 1946 he writes, "(may I quote Confucius?)'gentleman blames himself, ungentleman blames others' " (170). Writing to a French friend in 1949, he says, "if only we can transcend the hate which makes us willy-nilly become what we most detest,& somehow achieve the capacity to love . . . then our Selves will survive:no harm can touch Them" (195). He writes to Pound in 1955, "if am not grossly mistaken,'twas David called Thoreau observed he had never met—or hoped to meet—a man worse than himself / talents differ:if heroical thine be cursing swine & ringing nex,our tolerant unhero may only re-mark(vide 6 nonlectures page 70)that 'hatred bounces' " (243). The reference would seem to be to Cummings' 1945 contribution to Oscar Williams' anthology called *The War Poets*: "fear and hate the liar . . . where he should be feared and hated:in yourselves." There is also reference there to Cummings' favorite Bible passage, John, viii, 7, "this masterpoem of human perception, whose seventh verse alone exterminates all conventional morality—'He that is without sin among you, let him first cast a stone at her' " (*i: Six Nonlectures*, 66–7).

Well, then: Fine&Dandy, as Cummings himself might say. But what puzzles is how all this coheres with his own characteristic you-and-me-against-the-world stance, and in particular the many virulent satires where he does more than his own share of "cursing swine & ringing nex," as if he might indeed be without sin and thus free to cast his stone. Then again, I suppose it is not so puzzling after all, for the kind of integration Cummings reached, and under the conditions of his own particular life experience, is extremely rare and difficult to achieve, let alone sustain, and moodswings and ambivalence are inevitably to be expected—as the complicated contexts of many of the above quotes in the letters amply illustrate.

The same divisiveness is to be found in the structure of his intellectual life as well. His antagonism to science is, of course, well-known, and it finds some characteristic expression here in the letters (85, 130, 265). But there is also, surprisingly, an admission of respect for science, and this is not quite so well-known. Working on a poem, which was apparently never published, about the waning moon descending the afternoon sky, he asks his sister in 1956 "whether or not an astronomer would accept this image of mine. . . . If not,shall have to change my poem in deference to science" (253–3). Even more important, however, is his appreciation of Yeats's "equal understanding of perfectly opposed viewpoints—collective & individual, systematic & spontaneous,rational & instinctive" (255).

One could wish that his attitudes toward politics were as clearly integrated.[7] Most characteristically, both in the letters and published writings, his stance is determinedly apolitical, as befits an artist whose vision is transcendental. Politics, after all, deals with the conflicts and polarizations of the material and societal world, whose values are oriented around power and success—everything Cummings realizes he opposes. He rejects joiners, reformers, dogooders, gangs, the tyranny of the majority, Socialism, Communism, Fascism, and liberalism (145, 150, 162, 173, 176, 225, 228, 250, 254). And yet he sympathized with the victims of the May Day fiasco in 1919 (60), excitedly followed the political news from Russia in 1920 (69), called himself a Leninite or Trotskyite (72), and claimed in 1923 that he admired Russia (104). Of course, this was when he was still a fairly young man.

But what happened later was still less apolitical. Writing to his daughter in 1951, he recounts the following puzzling anecdote: "And as for surprise:perhaps the only equally-surprised humanbeing is,or was,my little newyorker pal Morrie Werner;when he demanded pointblank why I called myself 'a good Republican',& I instantly answered 'because the Republicans have an elephant', Morrie looked at our unhero as if Morrie's head would come off;then he moaned that I was kidding him,'no' I said 'I mean it':then he almost fainted from shock(but what better reason could anybody have?) After some terrible moments,Morrie's weak faint trembling voice asked dazedly 'but don't you like donkeys?' 'Yes' I admitted frankly 'but not so well as elephants'. There was a frightening pause. Then he slowly whispered 'je-sus-chr-ist' " (214). Cummings, of course, had early and late a fetish for elephants, but what his Republicanism means will become clearer when we take up *Adventures in Value*. For the nonce it may help to quote from a letter to his sister in 1953: "With every serious anarchist who ever lived,I assume that 'all governments are founded on force' " (223). He opposes, of course, Big Government, but he also opposes Big Business and the Pentagon: his Republicanism was of a rather special kind.

II

Like many of his other writings in prose, Cummings' fairy tales[8] are remarkable for their careful balance—in style and in plot structure. What is equally remarkable is that, in being written openly for children, they are entirely free of coyness and cuteness. And yet they are brilliantly successful, it seems to me, as stories for the young. That is because Cummings takes them absolutely seriously, in that they derive from the same vision which informs his work for adults: an open and receptive attitude toward existence, a lovingness toward individuals, and an emphasis upon spiritual self-dependency. Naturally, we could just as easily turn this argument around and say that his adult vision is remarkable for its emphasis on the child's view of things, but either way we are the gainers, for he takes that with absolute seriousness as well.

"The Old Man Who Said 'Why' " is the most explicitly close to Cummings' other writings. In it, a faerie guru who lives on the farthest star is challenged to investigate a strange old man who has settled on the moon and who is driving all the other denizens of the air crazy by simply saying "why" all the time. So the guru must go and confront this man "with little green eyes and a big white beard and delicate hands like a doll's hands" (12). But every time the guru asks him a question, the man says, simply, "Why?"—until finally, exasperated beyond endurance, the faerie threatens him, saying, "if you say why again, you'll fall from the moon all the way to the earth." And sure enough, of course, "the little very old man smiled;and looking at the faerie,he said 'why?' and he fell millions and millions and millions of deep cool new beautiful miles(with every part of a mile he became a little younger;first he became a not very old man and next a middle-aged man and then a young man and a boy and finally a child)until,just as he gently touched the earth,he was about to be born" (14).

I am reminded of Wordsworth's Immortality Ode and of Cummings' "when god decided to invent," which ends:

> when man determined to destroy
> himself he picked the was
> of shall and finding only why
> smashed it into because (566)[9]

And, of course, there is his conclusion to the Introduction to the 1938 *Collected Poems*: "Always the beautiful answer who asks a more beautiful question" (462). The questioner of this tale is certainly one for whom "birth is a supremely welcome mystery,the mystery of growing" (461), and the image of his turning from an old man into a younger man and then into an infant is exquisite. Recall these lines from "anyone lived in a pretty how town":

> children guessed(but only a few)
> and down they forgot as up they grew (515)

"The Elephant and the Butterfly" and "The House That Ate Mosquito Pie" are both about the pure love of a larger, clumsier creature for a smaller, winged creature, which is happily reciprocated. Probably written a quarter-century later than the others, the first is an almost unmarred idyl, with no threat or obstacle standing in the way except the elephant's lack of adventurousness. But the butterfly (who is, interestingly, also a "he")[10] comes to visit him, and they become friends. Then "the elephant put his arm very gently around the little butterfly and said: 'Do you love me a little?' / And the butterfly smiled and said: 'No, I love you very much' " (19). So the elephant visits the butterfly's house, and the latter asks, "Why didn't you ever before come down into the valley where I live?" And the elephant answered, "Because I did nothing all day." But now he comes to visit every day, "And they loved each other always" (22).

The other story concerns an empty house who is visited by a bird and invites her to stay and live with him. They plan to make mosquito pie for lunch but are interrupted by the arrival of three people who come by and want to move into the house. This threat is only momentary, however, as the house causes all his clocks to strike at once and scares the people away. Then he and his newfound love can enjoy their lunch and their lives alone.

We have seen that Cummings' daughter was taken from him sometime after his first marriage broke up, but that they were later reacquainted. Charles Norman reports, in his memoirs,[11] that Cummings told him the following story just after World War Two: "A year or two before, while at his New Hampshire farm, he passed on the road near his house a young woman he did not know and who did not know him. In the country manner both said 'Good morning'. This occurred several mornings on his walks; he saw that she was a visitor at the farm next to his, which belonged to the family of William James. The young woman was his daughter by his first wife. She had been brought up under another name. She had since learned who her father was, and there had been a reunion at Patchin Place." Norman sees this experience, which seems to me now to have the elements of a Greek tragedy, as being reflected in Cummings' *Santa Claus* (1946), where the girl recognizes Santa Claus even though he has exchanged masks with Death, but without knowing he is also her father.

This seems plausible, and I also think it is quite possible that, when Cummings was writing these fairy tales, he was either losing or had just lost his daughter, and that they therefore reflect his fantasy of being able to be with her and win her back.[12] Certainly these tales are effective enough to stand on their own, but they gain added dimension, poignancy, and significance in the biographical context. And there *is* the recurrent motif of the larger and smaller creature falling in love to be accounted for.

"The Little Girl Named I" carries on this motif in a much more complex and interesting fashion. Here the larger creature is a narrator, and he is telling a story about a little girl to a real little girl. The little girl of the story, of course, is named "I," and the form of the frame is that of a dialogue between the narrator and his listener as he tells his tale. The structure of the story itself consists of a series of encounters between "I" and various creatures, as she looks unsuccessfully for a companion to have for tea. She meets a yellow cow, a white horse, a pink pig, and an elephant, but they are all busy doing something else. She continues on alone after each encounter, until finally she "sees another little girl just like her" (39), who turns out to be just the companion she is seeking.

What the frame accomplishes is to show how the teller and the listener gradually shift roles. During the first two encounters, he asks her what she thinks will happen next and agrees with her answers, but during the third encounter she gets it wrong. Then, during the fourth and fifth encounters, *she* asks the questions and he does the answering. What happens at the end is that they all—the teller, his listener, and the two little girls in the story proper—become one. "And then I said to this other little girl, just like this I said 'Who are you?' / And what did this other little girl say? / 'You. That's who I am' she said 'And You is my name because I'm You'. . . . So then You and I, we went to my house together to have some tea" (39). Recall "Him" and "Me" of Cummings' early play; recall "little you-i" of his poem "o by the by" (593); recall "For love are in you am in i are in we" of "the great advantage of being alive" (664). Doesn't this tale join father and daughter in love through a luncheon, as the house and his bird were joined through their shared mosquito pie, and doesn't it say that you and I, we have only ourselves to count on?

III

Adventures in Value[13] is divided into four sections: EFFIGIES, which contains six photographs; STILL LIFE, which contains eight; NATURE, containing twenty-five; and PEOPLE, with eleven. Three epigraphs stand at the head of the volume: dictionary definitions of "value"; the Emerson quote about society being in conspiracy against the manhood of its members; and the puzzling attribution of a modern-sounding quote to Homer: "I have never tried to do anything but get the proper relationship of values." Marion Morehouse's pictures are for the most part clear, textured closeups, in sharp focus and stark black and white. Her images are hard, shiny, and thick, and characteristically of burlap, wood, porcelain, rock, frond, vegetable, and light and shadow. Curiously, for a collaboration with a poet who celebrates growth, process, and movement, her photographs are generally without motion—and this is as true of NATURE and PEOPLE as it is of EFFIGIES and STILL LIFE.

Cummings' captions are sometimes about the photograph, sometimes reflections triggered by the picture, and sometimes both. When he directs attention to the picture itself, as in II 4, "Composition," a still life of cooking utensils in front of a wooden wall, he will say, "note the nail." When he takes off from the photograph, he explains, comments, interprets, and reminisces. These, of course, will be our primary concern as readers of Cummings. For other pictures he supplies appropriate quotations, and some he simply leaves blank.

For I 4, "The Mountain (Lachaise)," for example, which shows a small statue of a reclining nude, partially obscured by shadow and branches of blossoms issuing from a vase in the back, Cummings writes, "blossoms & sculpture(impermanence incarnate & intrinsic immortality)now fortunately coexist:now the miracle of the alive touches the mystery of the timeless—nothing can add to or subtract from so true a marriage of the multitudinous & the singular;so beautiful a collision of the momentary and the deathless." Seeing the content of the picture and its relationships in almost schematically symbolic terms, he adds movement to a static configuration—"coexist," "touches," "marriage," and even "collision"—and produces thereby a high moment of integration and transcendence of the polarities.

Number I 6, "Monster," shows a maimed statue of a strange animal inside the fence of the Cluny Museum in Paris. Cummings reflects that three mothers, each with a child, were standing behind this statue not long before. Then he recalls an earlier mother and child: "Paris isn't any longer Paris to someone who remembers sitting on the terrace of a diminutive restaurant . . . & gazing with reverential joy at a lady between ladies:very much the loveliest mother,& by far the livingest child." I cannot help but think that this is yet another reference to his first wife and their daughter, and as I look at the "cheerful maimedness" of this statue, I seem to see the baffled spirit of the father in Cummings looking out at us.

"Sunlight As Joy" is the title of III 1, and we are now in the NATURE section. Here we see a translucent shot of forest leaves in the sun, and Cummings' caption is an epigrammatic statement of his transcendent vision: "joy being a mystery at right angles equally to pain & pleasure,as truth is to fact & fiction." I am reminded of the poem, "hate blows a bubble of despair into," whose second stanza is as follows:

> pleasure and pain are merely surfaces
> (one itself showing,itself hiding one)
> life's only and true value neither is
> love makes the little thickness of the coin   (531)

"ΕΛΕΦΑΣ" is the title of III 4, and it is a picture of a large rock in front of a pair of birch trees. In his celebration of this being, Cummings quotes Isak Dinesen: "a being mighty and powerful beyond anyone's attack,attacking no one." Which foreshadows the Tao-like verses accompanying the photograph of Marianne Moore: "in a cruel world—to show mercy / in a hateful world—to forgive" (IV 3). And in III 16 he sees Don Quixote in a pod of milkweed, remarking that here "he's his own Sancho."

But the serenity of these lucidities is crossed, as it is in the letters (and in the published writings), by Cummings' equally characteristic crankiness. In III 8 he manages to move from a picture of a quiet zucchini to yet another attack on the noisy radio. In III 15 he breathes a sigh of relief, over a picture of Patchin Place, that his New York residence has not yet been supplanted by a high-rise and proceeds to lambast the otherwise topsy-turvy world. And in "MOIRA" (III 23), he contrasts the eyes that think with those that feel, and says the former have hands that can cut across a tree trunk with a buzz-saw.

Then, in the PEOPLE section, he writes a series of captions which celebrate—of all things—hard work. Recalling his earlier poem, "old mr ly" (567), in connection with a photograph of Old Mr. Lyman (IV 6), he says, "During fifty years he worked—when loafing wasn't mankind's sole aim—hard & well,on behalf of a railroad." "Minnie (1)" (IV 7) is a portrait of a country woman—"no harder working woman ever lived"—who voted, as Cummings assured her he would too, against FDR. Cummings also admires John Finley (IV 9), the Harvard classicist, who "cheerfully toils in the sweat of his brow under skies which freeze or burn" when working on his New England farm. "Jess" (IV 11), then 75, works harder than the young fellows, "Because work has disappeared from their world." This is in the tradition of "rain or hail" (568), the poem which follows "old mr ly" in *1 X 1*, but which does without the derogation of the rest of the world:

> sam was a man
> grinned his grin
> done his chores
> laid him down.

And so the iconoclastic poet, who celebrated the boulevards, bistros, bordellos, circuses, and burlesque shows of Boston, New York, and Paris as a cosmopolitan young man, and who once proclaimed in a poem that "must's a schoolroom in the month of may" (574), retreats finally into a celebration of the Horatian—not to say Calvinistic—rustic, homely virtues and looks with dismay at the moral deterioration of the world he is leaving behind. His rebellion against the hairless old, thwarted when young, now turns itself against the new.[14] And I think these captions give some further clues to the meaning of his Republicanism. His politics have become a form of agrarian, New England Republicanism, where the industrious and isolated farmer feels in his bones that the government which governs least is indeed the best. He believes in the "character"-laden efforts of the worthy individual, and he will have no truck with government attempts to better the lot of the unworthy—that is, those who don't work hard. Clearly, as I have suggested, these anarchistic planks have only a remote connection with the platform of national Republicanism, with its support of large corporations and a strong military establishment. But since presidential elections are perforce national elections, the confusion of values involved here is noteworthy.

IV

Although *73 poems*[15] is made up of work that Cummings himself considered completed before his death, the *order* of poems in this volume is subject to some question. Charles Norman writes in his memoirs[16] that the poet's widow asked him "to edit the poems Cummings had been putting together before he died." This was in 1963: "I worked on the manuscript from April 19 to April 24. It was arranged in a manner Cummings himself might have followed: three sections comprising 'Portraits', 'Impressions', and 'Sonnets'. Mrs. Cummings sent the manuscript to Harcourt, Brace & World." But then something went wrong. Norman was also working on the second edition of his biography of the poet and offered as a courtesy to let her see the new last chapter. After reading it, "She was furious. She objected violently to it. She objected most of all to the confidential remark Cummings had made to me in 1961 while waiting for the car that was to take them to the airport." He explained that "it was the kind of remark a man would make to his friend, but not to his wife, who might understandably be upset."

The remark in question, as recorded in *E.E. Cummings: The Magic-Maker*,[17] is: "All I ask is one more year." Norman's memoirs continue, "She said that Cummings had not made the remark attributed to him in my chapter, and that I was a liar." She asks him to delete it, but he refuses. "A few days later I received from her, in addition to my manuscript, a note in her own hand: Harcourt, Brace & World had found it 'too difficult' to set up *Last Poems* [Norman's original suggestion for the title] in my arrangement, and the book had been given another format, with the original title [Mrs. Cummings'] restored." (Several interesting additional sidelights might be mentioned here. First is the fact that Norman *did* omit the offending chapter, two or three years after Mrs. Cummings died, in the third edition of his biography.[18] And then there is the curious appearance in *73 poems* of ten poems originally published in *The New Yorker*, indicating that the poet's widow, who arranged for their appearance there, objected less to that magazine than Cummings did.)

I do not know whether Cummings himself might have followed Norman's suggested order (although his poems *are* roughly classifiable along something like those lines, he had not used such divisions for organizing his books since his three earliest volumes, all of which derive from the original *Tulips and Chimneys* manuscript), but there is a useful clue in the letters. Here Cummings says, in writing to Francis Steegmuller in 1959: "all my booksofpoems after the original T&C manuscript . . . start with autumn(downgoing,despair)& pass through winter(mystery, dream)& stop in spring(upcoming,joy). But as I glance over the index of Poems '23–'54,find few hints of this progression;beyond a tendency to begin dirty(world:sordid,satires)& end clean(earth:lyrical,lovepoems)." He sees this as a seasonal metaphor, which he says *95 poems* exemplifies clearly, and interprets it via S. Foster Damon's study of Blake: " 'They' the angels 'descend on the material side . . . and ascend on the spiritual;this is . . . a representation of the greatest Christian mystery,a statement of the secret every mystic tries to tell' " (261).

The story told in a letter to me by George J. Firmage, Cummings' bibliographer, complements and clarifies that related by Norman. It seems that Mrs. Cummings had asked Firmage to take charge of the manuscript (it was actually, Firmage informs me, merely a folder of poems) in early December of 1962—which was *before*, of course, Norman received it. At that time, Firmage was not concerned about its ultimate sequential arrangement. He returned the results of his work to Mrs. Cummings in February of 1963 and did not hear from her again until the last week in April. Apparently she had given the manuscript to Norman and subsequently asked for it back during the interim. Firmage got the manuscript once again during the first week in May, and he "made no attempt to imitate Estlin's previously published booksofpoems in arranging the 73 poems that I had to work with; but merely tried, as best I could, to find a pleasing reading order. There was, if I remember correctly, some attempt to move from sunrise to sunset, from light to dark; but the movement is not, as I see it now, consistent." Mrs. Cummings then approved of Firmage's arrangement—with the exception of four poems, which she rearranged (he recalls that she switched 22 and 27 but does not remember the other two)—and sent it off to the publisher. Manuscript and proofs are now in the Houghton Library collection at Harvard.

It seems strange that Firmage had in mind an order which reverses the one Cummings had in *his* mind, but the fact remains that neither felt very confident about the actual results. And indeed, the book itself shapes up along no very clear sequential lines. It appears to me that the mood in the first fifteen poems is basically positive, that the next three are negative, and that 20–22 are positive again. The next dozen seem mixed, and at the center of the book is a group of very deep sonnets (36–40) dealing with love and death. Following this is a succeeding group of love and mystery poems (41–50), a group of nature poems (51–69), and the final four are mixed but end on a positive note. Except for the central significance of the sonnets, I do not see any other pattern in this order.

But I do see a number of significant developments in these poems, nevertheless, and would like to devote the remainder of this essay to exploring them and relating them to what we have discovered so far about Cummings' life and work from the letters, the tales, and the photographic captions.

Continuing trends in *95 poems* I traced out some years ago, this volume reveals a greater awareness of pain, loss, and emptiness, and a correspondingly greater sense of the difficulty of transcendence.[19] Accepting more of the negative within, the speaker of these poems projects less hatred outward—in accordance with certain trends we have already noticed in the letters—and there are remarkably few out-and-out satires here. As he feels the ominous threat of annihilation, he becomes more and more concerned with Last Things and comes to terms with death on a level he had not as consistently experienced before. And finally, in matters of technique and style, these poems show an increasing movement toward a hard-won and complex regularity after all those years of experimentation, and an absorption of syntactical, grammatical, and typographic deviations into that accomplished presentational fabric.[20] Over two-thirds of the total are written in Cummings' special way of handling regular stanzaic and sonnet patterns, and the rest are written in his characteristically structured free-verse stanzas. And in terms of diction, he uses less of his tough, dialect-colloquial style on the one hand, and less of his unique conceptual vocabulary on the other, depending therefore mainly on his strong and flexible middle range for speaking of the soberly joyous matters herein.

Let us begin at the bottom of Cummings' seasonal metaphor. In no other book do I recall the emphasis I find here on the dark side of nature—which is often far from the cheerful stoicism of *Adventures in Value*. Number 13 shows the speaker going through a spooky, rainy night, until morning stumbles against his forehead. In 23 we find a creepy midnight scene, where animals and people flicker. Number 41 is another night scene indoors, where clocks speak, the moon shines through the rain and the wind. "And i and my love are alone." Anguished trees are seen against the sunset in 50. In 54 another tree withstands the shrieking winds of fall. Number 61 shows a snowflake falling on a gravestone.

Then there are those poems presenting failure and ugliness.[21] We find a dirty sunset over the suburbs in 16, and in 17 dogshit mingling with the snow on city streets. In 70 the poet speaks ruefully of artistic failure, and in 51 of the emptiness of a friend's death. But this is not the end of the story, of course, and we see, in 62, the speaker experiencing a bottomless despair from which he nevertheless rises. And it would not be difficult to find in this book, as well as in the preceding ones, many such characteristically affirmative recoveries, wherein the speaker manages to transcend the negative.

But what is really significant in this volume is that, almost for the first time, the speaker is presented as experiencing moments during which he accepts and *goes into* the negative *before* transcending it. We are shown, uniquely, the *process* involved in transcendence and not just its results. It is not simply a matter, in other words, of experiencing the negative, of being aware of it, of acknowledging it, and of then going on to the positive *despite* that negative; it is rather a question of reaching the positive *because of* having descended into the negative. It is, in effect, a balancing in the void itself. And most of the poems in this group are among those deep sonnets at the center of the book mentioned above. Number 32 begins:

> all which isn't singing is mere talking
> and all talking's talking to oneself
> (whether that oneself be sought or seeking
> master or disciple sheep or wolf)

No matter what or how we say it, the poem continues, it is still you (namely I) and nobody else. Then the poem concludes,

> but the very song of(as mountains
> feel and lovers)singing is silence

The carefully-balanced use of sing-say-silence occurs many times in *73 poems*, and we shall encounter it again before we are done. What is remarkable at this point is the strong note of self-awareness and self-acceptance in relation to negative experience.

In 36 the two lovers are presented as feeling the disappearance of the mortal world at the edge of winter, standing under a star, and experiencing a transcendent acceptance of death: " 'dying' the ghost of you / whispers 'is very pleasant' my ghost to." The speaker is going to sleep on a rainy night, in 44, "feeling that sunlight is / (life and day are)only loaned:whereas / night is given(night and death and the rain." In 49 he hears a "tinying" voice at twilight "of deathless earth's innumerable doom," and feels "acceptance of irrevocable time." The only poem of this kind not a sonnet, number 64 presents a dialogue between the speaker and a purple finch: the former asks why "this summer world . . . must die," and the bird answers, "if i / should tell you anything / . . . i could not sing." Compare the penultimate poem in the book, which reads in its entirety:

> wild(at our first)beasts uttered human words
> —our second coming made stones sing like birds—
> but o the starhushed silence which our third's

But it is in 67 where the full force of experiencing the process of acceptance is felt:

> enter no(silence is the blood whose flesh
> is singing)silence:but unsinging. . . .

The speaker is in the abyss between fall and winter, with the spring far beyond:

> . . . and i breathe-move-and-seem some
> perpetually roaming whylessness—
>
> autumn has gone:will winter never come?

And the speaker utters here one of the most anguished cries to be found in all of Cummings:

> o come,terrible anonymity;enfold
> phantom me with the murdering minus of cold
> —open this ghost with millionary knives of wind—
> scatter his nothing all over what angry skies and . . .

—and—yes, there is a resolution here, but one which gains a hundredfold in intensity from the entering of the pain which has preceded it:

> gently
>   (very whiteness:absolute peace,
>   never imaginable mystery)
>   descend[22]

This is indeed "the secret which every mystic tries to tell," but it is even more than that passing "through winter(mystery,dream)" of which Cummings spoke. It is a staying and not just a passing through—for that is the only way of truly passing through. I have spoken elsewhere of how, in 95 *poems*, Cummings was coming to acknowledge the negative more and learning how to incorporate it into the fabric of his affirmative vision. But what is happening here is that the negative is being gone into, and by virture of its acceptance it becomes part of the affirmation. This, I submit, is a more complex experience and more true to his very concept of transcendence itself. And it does, it seems to me, fulfill certain trends toward true integration we noticed in the letters: more of the life, in other words, is getting into the poetry, and less is being selected out (more of the life, of course, got into *The Enormous Room* and in *Him*, but his directness in dealing with painful material is much less in evidence in the poems—partly because poetry is naturally more selective and partly because for some reason he may not have felt entirely ready to try to deal as explicitly with it there).

Thus, when hostile critics dismiss the concept of transcendence as merely one of Cummings' small store of "ideas," or when friendly critics claim that how he says it is more important than what he says, the basic point is being entirely missed. What such a poem is actually about is neither the concept of transcendence nor the effective artistic embodiment of that concept; it is rather about the *experience* of self-confrontation, the record of a moment of awareness resulting from taking the ultimate emotional risk—loss of the security-seeking self. One goes through the impasse and accepts the death of a part of the self in the never-ending movement toward growth and integration. Cummings' constant preoccupation with this process is not simply a "theme" of his poetry. It is a lifelong struggle, and his poetry is not only the *record* but also the *instrument* of that struggle. Our job, then, is not to talk about his ideas or how he embodies them. What we should be doing instead is following the process of his struggle within himself, and that can never be reduced to a few clichés about joy, love, spring, the individual, children, and so forth. Nor is it simply a matter of tracing his techniques, for art, as he himself said, is only one means toward self-transcendence—although it happened to be *his* way.[23]

As we have been seeing, though, his struggle was never an easy one. It never is. And because he was often less than perfect in his awareness, he often dichotomized—both in relation to his art as well as his mind—where he had every intention of integrating. He wrote poems which were dogmatic statements about the necessity of being undogmatic, and he took positions of exclusion even while he was proclaiming harmony and unity. Some of our failings as readers do derive from some of his failures as a writer. Just as he misleads some into saying that his concept of transcendence resembles the "all you need is love" and "just dream your troubles away" mindlessness of Hollywood and Tin Pan Alley, so too does he mislead others into claiming that it involves a separation between the material and the spiritual and the enlightened and the unenlightened.

It seems to me that the basic problem he had difficulty in resolving was whether transcendence meant for him a rising *from* the material *toward* the spiritual, as the Blake reference implies, or whether it meant a rising above the polarities altogether to where there is no difference between the material and the spiritual.[24] The first is Platonic[25] and lends itself all too well to tension and division, to us against them, and to exclusiveness[26]—although Plato himself varies in his own position, depending upon whether you are reading the "Symposium" or *The Republic*. Cummings' second position, on the other hand, is more truly Oriental and encourages integration, harmony, inclusiveness, and acceptance. And evidence for both views can be found in Cummings' writings, although I myself feel it was the second which represented his true commitment. The trouble is, however, that he rarely seemed to notice this fundamental ambiguity in himself and his work, and if he did, he had the devil's own time in dealing with it. Most of the difficulties of his life and work can be traced, I think, to this self-division.

Further indication of such ambiguity is found in several love poems in which this ghost-like, phantom state, where the self is annihilated by nothingness before acceptance results in resolution, is presented as the result of the absence of the lady, which leaves the lover again facing the void:

> your homecoming will be my homecoming—
>
> my selves go with you,only i remain;
> a shadow phantom effigy or seeming (40)

—whose emptiness can be filled, not by traveling the mystic's way down, but only by the beloved's return. And in 47 the lover tells her of his infinite dependency upon her, saying his selves are to her as birds are to the sun:

> without the mercy of
> your eyes your
> voice your
> ways(o very most my shining love)
>
> how more than dark I am, . . .

Compare the conclusion of number 38:

> yours is the light by which my spirit's born:
> yours is the darkness of my soul's return
> —you are my sun,my moon,and all my stars

These are nicely done and are in that courtly tradition Cummings has always managed to carry on so well. But I am forced to conclude that, if he is wholly serious about this (and I am sure he is), he could not quite have realized how contradictory his image of love is in relation to his mystic's vision. It is one thing to fill your emptiness with your own acceptance of nothingness in whose deserts alone can blossom the flowers of rebirth, but it is quite another to fill it with the presence of your beloved. Perhaps this dependency relates back to that unresolved ambivalence of his early manhood in connection with rebelling against yet needing his family and later to his emotional as well as financial need in connection with the Watsons.

On the other hand, it is quite possible that I am being too "Platonic" myself in seeing these elements as contradictory.[27] As we have seen, Cummings spoke of himself as evolving, and Buddhistic tradition outlines the three essential stages of enlightenment as consisting of materialism, of differentiation, and of reintegration. One who is integrated has achieved a balance between attachment (compassion) and detachment (wisdom): too much of the latter results in quietism and nihilism, while too much of the former leads to sentimentalism and emotionalism. A familiar Zen koan tells the story thus: at first I saw the mountains as mountains and the trees as trees; then I saw that the mountains were not mountains and the trees not trees; now I see that the mountains are mountains and the trees are trees. Although the third stage looks like the first, it is not the same: the first sees nothing spiritual, the second sees the material as symbolizing the spiritual, while the third sees the spiritual *in* the material. The second stage is what happens to people when they first think of enlightenment, distinguishing between good and evil, the enlightened and unenlightened, in order to raise their sights. In the light of this rather brusque and inadequate summary, then, perhaps we may see Cummings' "contradictions" as representing not so much the clash of opposing visions as the necessary phase of growth between the second and third stages, struggling to balance dependency and independency, love and evenmindedness, hostility and acceptance—a struggle which continues perforce through a series of lifetimes.

Yet the final impression left by *73 poems* is of the momentary conclusion of one of those cycles, of intense awareness of Last Things, and of achieved harmony and integration. The speaker reflects in 15 during the early morning between five and six a.m., hearing some birds and thinking at the stroke of six that he hears a bell asking "(of / a world born deaf / 'heaven or hell.' " At this hour and in this mood, "civilization" dwindles in the face of Reality, and the world is seen balancing unknowingly on the edge of eternity. In 37 the lovers experience the presence of the transcendent as a summer night exhibits a falling star: here mystery is revealed, and the intangible is seen as touchable and calculable. Number 39 finds the speaker praying over his sleeping lady that she may encounter the transcendent and return safely:

>   faithfully blossoming beyond to breathe
>   suns of the night,bring this beautiful
>   wanderer home to a dream called time. . . .

And 73, the last poem of the last book, says fittingly, "all worlds have halfsight."[28] They see either with life's eye, which spiritualizes the physical, or with death's, which reduces spirit to materiality. Only love can see the whole, who "strolls the axis of the universe." "Each believing world denies" the halftruth of the other as well as the truth of the whole,

>   whereas
>   your lover(looking through both life and death)
>   timelessly celebrates the merciful
>
>   wonder no world deny may or believe

By now, we are ready to believe *him*, however, for we have a somewhat clearer notion of what it cost him and what he went through in order to achieve such a celebration.

NOTES

1. "The Old Man Who Said 'Why,' " *Harvard Wake*, No. 5 (Spring 1946), pp. 5–8; "A Little Girl Named I," *Wake*, No. 6 (Spring 1948), pp. 3–5; and "The House That Ate Mosquito Pie," *Wake*, No. 9 (Autumn 1950), pp. 5–7. I gather that the "Harvard" was dropped after the editor, Seymour Lawrence, graduated.

2. The story of Cummings' first marriage will be told in Richard S. Kennedy's forthcoming biography of the poet. As for the bare facts relevant to our purpose, Professor Kennedy informs me that Nancy was born December 20, 1919; that Cummings and Elaine were divorced on December 4, 1924; and that he did not see Nancy again after 1926—until the 1940s. Thus she was six years old or so when he saw the last of her as a child. However, the one fairy tale not previously published in *Wake* (or elsewhere), "The Elephant and the Butterfly," appears to have been written much later than the other three, contrary to the dedication, as Cummings was working on it in 1950, sometime after his reunion with his daughter. I want to thank Professor Kennedy for clarifying these matters for me.

3. George J. Firmage was responsible for the manuscript of this volume, and he tells me that it contained twenty-eight as-yet-unpublished poems, plus forty-six which had been previously published in periodicals (one poem was ultimately dropped, on the insistence of the poet's widow). Mrs. Cummings then arranged for the periodical publication of ten more. Grateful thanks are due to Mr. Firmage for providing me with useful information both here and later in this essay.

4. *Selected Letters of E. E. Cummings*, eds. F. W. Dupee and George Stade (Harcourt Brace and World, 1969). My parenthetical references in the body of the essay cite page numbers in this volume.

5. See Richard S. Kennedy, "Edward Cummings, the Father of the Poet," *Bulletin of the New York Public Library*, LXX (1966), 437–39; Peter H. Mott, "E. E. Cummings: Two Texts on the God in Man," Diss. Columbia, 1972; Malcolm Cowley, "Cummings: One Man Alone," *A Second Flowering* (Viking, 1973), pp. 90–113; and Bethany K. Dumas, *E. E. Cummings: A Remembrance of Miracles* (Barnes and Noble, 1974), pp. 16–17.

6. See Anon., review of *Selected Letters*, *Times Literary Supplement*, 17 November 1972, p. 1403.

7. See Karl Shapiro, review of *Selected Letters, Bookworld*, III (6 July 1969), 4.

8. *Fairy Tales*, with pictures by John Eaton (Harcourt Brace and World, 1965).

9. All references to poems (as well as the quote from the Introduction to *Collected Poems* [1938]), except those in *73 poems*, are to page numbers in *Complete Poems 1913-1962* (Harcourt Brace Jovanovich, 1972).

10. Michael Reck points this out in his review of *Fairy Tales, Commonweal*, 11 February 1966, p. 562.

11. *Poets & People* (Bobbs-Merrill, 1972), p. 66.

12. Professor Kennedy writes to me "that Cummings was working on 'The Elephant and the Butterfly' while Nancy was visiting him at Silver Lake, after their reunion; the date seems to be summer 1950."

13. *Adventures in Value*, Fifty Photographs by Marion Morehouse, Text by E. E. Cummings (Harcourt Brace and World, 1962).

14. See Cowley.

15. *73 poems* (Harcourt Brace and World, 1963). Parenthetical references in the body of the essay cite *poem* numbers in this volume (which are the same, of course, in *Complete Poems 1913-1962*).

16. *Poets & People*, pp. 304–06.

17. (Duell, Sloan and Pearce, 1964), p. 236. The first edition is *The Magic-Maker: E. E. Cummings* (Macmillan, 1958).

18. *E. E. Cummings: The Magic Maker* (Bobbs-Merrill, 1972).

19. See J. Jacobsen, "The Legacy of Three Poets," *Commonweal*, LXXVIII (10 May 1963), 189–92; and Eve Triem, *E. E. Cummings*, University of Minnesota Pamphlets on American Writers, No. 87 (University of Minnesota Press, 1969), pp. 42–43.

20. See Horace Gregory, review of *73 poems, Commonweal*, LXXIX (13 March 1964), 725–26.

21. James E. Tanner, Jr., in "The Grammar of Poetry," Diss. University of North Carolina, 1973, Chapter IV, argues by means of stylistic analysis that Cummings' vision is more like William Burroughs', that there is more existential despair and a sense of the absurd in Cummings than we had realized. I agree that it is important to bring out this aspect of the poet, but I feel it is a normal part of the Romantic tradition to experience moments of "dejection" and "melancholy." I also feel that it was a regular part of the 1920s to shock the bourgeoisie (Cummings' prostitutes, for example) and, furthermore and most significantly, that it is an essential part of mysticism to see the way up in terms of the way down. Burroughs, along with Beckett, it seems to me, deals with the negative pretty much apart from its connection with the positive.

22. Lionel Abel comments on this poem in his review of *73 poems, Nation*, CXCVII (14 December 1963), 420–21.

23. *i:Six Nonlectures* (Harvard University Press, 1953), p. 82.

24. In an early essay, Cummings wrote, ". . . language was not always blest with 'opposities.' Quite the contrary. A certain very wise man has pointed out (in connection with the meaning of dreams) that what 'weak' means and what 'strong' means were once upon a time meant *by one word*. . . . in burlesk, we meet an echo of the original phenomenon: 'opposites' occur *together*. For that reason, burlesk enables us to (so to speak) *know around* a thing, character, or situation. To put it a little differently: if the art of common-or-garden painting were like the art of burlesk, we should be able to see—impossibly enough—all the way around a solid tree, instead of merely seeing a little more than half of the tree (thanks to binocular parallax or whatever it is) and imagining the rest." "You Aren't Mad, Am I? Being certain observations anent the extremely modern art of 'burlesk,' " *Vanity Fair* (December 1925); reprinted in *E. E. Cummings: A Miscellany Revised*, ed. George J. Firmage (October

House, 1965), pp. 126–31, especially p, 127. See also Patrick B. Mullen, "E. E. Cummings and Popular Culture," *Journal of Popular Culture*, V (1971), 503–20.

25. See Patricia Tal-Mason Cline, "The Whole E. E. Cummings" (1968), in Norman Friedman, ed., *E. E. Cummings: A Collection of Critical Essays* (Prentice-Hall, 1972), pp. 60–70.

26. Robert G. Tucker, "Cummings the Chivalrous," in R. E. Langford and W. E. Taylor, eds., *The Twenties* (Everett/Edwards, 1966), pp. 25–27.

27. I am deeply indebted to Professor Ellen Nold, of Stanford University, for reading an earlier version of this paper, for calling me into question on this basic issue, and for suggesting the alternative view sketched out in the remainder of my paragraph.

28. See Jane Donahue, "Cummings' Last Poem: An Explication," *Literatur in Wissenschaft und Unterricht*, III (1970), 106–08.

Nature, Time, and Transcendence in Cummings' Later Poems

Guy Rotella*

One way to see what ties together the divergent work of three of New England's important modern poets, Robert Frost, Wallace Stevens, and E. E. Cummings, would be to consider each as responding to a shared native inheritance of transcendentalism. A rough result would be something like this: Frost yearns for the absolutes and absolute knowing transcendentalism offers, but his parallel demand for empirical proof of their existence or non-existence produces ambivalent poetry of believing doubt and doubting belief. Stevens is nostalgic for the ultimate order of transcendentalist faith, but his skeptical sense that every order is a creation separate from or subjectively imposed on unknowable reality precludes his finding ultimates and produces poetry in which the search for order nobly persists but is always subverted by insistent awareness that any order achieved is private, relative, and doomed. Cummings, too, desires transcendent absolutes, and, although he sometimes tests his hopes against the facts of time, loss, and death, his belief that those absolutes exist and that he knows they do produces poetry of confident, assertive affirmation. In Frost, the will to believe is in constant unresolved and unresolvable conflict with the will not to believe; in Stevens the will to believe is just that, an act of will, a necessary, beautiful, useful, but—in any absolute sense—finally futile imposture; in Cummings the will to believe is one with believing. Thus, Frost is a poet of doubt, doubtful even of doubt itself; Stevens, a poet of certain—sometimes jubilant—doubt; Cummings, of certain belief. As these simple oppositions indicate, Frost

*This essay was written specifically for this volume and appears here for the first time by permission of the author.

and Stevens receive their transcendentalist inheritance gingerly when at all; Cummings embraces his. He follows the Emerson of self-reliant witness to truths known with certainty through intuition or mediating nature. Frost and Stevens follow that Emerson, when they do, to revise, testing intuition with fact, nature with science. The same simple oppositions can blur additional similarities, however, for Cummings, too, exposes his hope for transcendence to skeptical challenge. What differs— and the difference is crucial, of course—is the mode of that exposure, its frequency, and its result. Nonetheless, Cummings and Frost and Stevens are joined not only by diverse responses to a shared New England heritage of transcendental thought, but also by their common use of a philosophical "nature poetry" for working out and expressing those responses.

That Cummings' poetry is founded on and fueled by transcendentalist assumptions is the claim, and sometimes charge, of many of his most insightful critics.[1] Norman Friedman has shown that the characteristics and implications of those assumptions are clearest in Cummings' love poems and that over Cummings' career his assumptions grew in depth, pervasiveness, and complexity, particularly in the increasing willingness in his last volumes to confront and include the human limits that threaten those assumptions.[2] Cummings' developing transcendental vision also has a central—and similar—role in his nature poems, principally in those poems in which attention to nature becomes attention to natural process and therefore to time. The response of Cummings' transcendentalism to nature, process, and time illuminates his thought, for despite his (ambivalent) warning to "think twice before you think," Cummings is as much a poet of ideas, however few of them, as of sensations.

It has often been noticed that Cummings' specific interest in transcendence begins with the poems in *ViVa* (1931). Nonetheless, a glance at his responses to process and time in the earlier poems will provide context for a survey of the emerging transcendental vision of the later ones. Furthermore, while poems somehow involving nature make up as much as one-third of Cummings' poetry, only those concern us here in which the observation of nature leads to an awareness of process and, so, to an awareness of time or timelessness. The many poems in which nature is used for comparisons with human behavior or values, for description, for celebration, for praise of a lady, and so on, overlappings aside, are ignored.

It is a critical commonplace that Cummings' early poetry sensuously celebrates sensual process in nature and in man. Yet even in *Tulips and Chimneys, &, XLI Poems*, and *is 5*, time—without which there can be no process—is quite often and conventionally perceived as a threat to lovers and to beauty. A personification from "Puella Mea" puts it bluntly:

> Eater of all things lovely—Time!
> upon whose watering lips the world
> poises a moment(futile,proud,

a costly morsel of sweet tears)
gesticulates,and disappears— [.]³

Of course, the frank assertion of utter transience is softened, as often in the early poems, by a slightly decadent delight in man's precarious position. Nevertheless, here, and in the many early *carpe diem* poems, the power of time is real and final. The poet's typical response to it is a sensual, often sexual hedonism of the here and now, the very stuff of the seize-the-day tradition (although it anticipates Cummings' later concept of a transcendent "now"). Just because of its connection to the *carpe diem* mode it would be a mistake to take the attitude toward time of these poems too seriously as a philosophical position. They are, after all, seduction poems; a despairing sense of time founds their rhetorical equipment.

Nonetheless, a remarkably consistent negativity about time does pervade the early poems. In their context even the apparent celebration of continuity in process of "when god lets my body be" seems, rather, as Rushworth Kidder argues, an attempt to evoke the loved one's pity for the lover's transience⁴ and, in turn, to win for him her present favors.

At any rate, in these Keatsian early poems as throughout his career, Cummings' awareness of time often stems from attention to natural processes. In "as is the sea marvelous" the process is cosmic:

the earth withers
the moon crumbles
one by one
stars flutter into dust

(p. 38).

In "when unto nights of autumn do complain" it is earthly: "the unlovely longness of the year / / droops with things dead athwart the narrowing hours" and drives hope to cower in "dreadful corners." In both poems time's destructive power is immense; in both it is easily, even facilely, resisted by the assertion of a greater power, such as that of memory, or art, or love. Such merely assertive responses to threatening fact earn Cummings his sometimes reputation as a feeble romantic.

Nonetheless, there are early poems in which time is more than a showy opponent in a fixed game. In "Tumbling-hair," for instance, the innocent girl indiscriminately picking flowers is subtly threatened by "Another," whose more discriminate plucking suggests defloration and therefore initiation into timeful adulthood. That this is a matter of both sorrow *and* wonder implies a more complex response to time than seen so far. A companion poem, the famous "in Just-," is similar. The joyous spring celebration of "undifferentiated" youthful innocence ("eddieand-bill"; "bettyandisbel") is qualified by hints of sexual awakening in the figure of the Pan-like, satyric balloon man. A related recognition that the very fact of time permitting spring's return also makes inevitable its loss (as specific season, especially as specific human season) emerges in the dying fall of the final lines (in which the whistle recedes in time as well as distance), and in the chronic emphases of the opening. One thing "in Just- / spring" says is that it is *only* in spring, which is seasonal and can't last, that such delight can be. Even the more primary sense of the phrase, its careful pointing to that single, specific moment when spring begins, implies transience by precise insistence *on* the moment.

Even early on, then, Cummings sometimes responds to time in ways beyond romantic posturing. Moreover, in a very few early poems attitudes toward time and change actually anticipate aspects of the transcendentalist response to them he later developed. This occurs when Cummings perceives that not resistance but nature's very acceptance of time and death is what permits the growth he so desires and so often finds implied in cyclical recurrence. For example, "a wind has blown the rain away and blown" implies that waiting as "suddenly" and patiently as time-shorn trees against the changeful moon might permit man, too, to share "doom's integration," the returning spring and summer that fall and winter prepare for. Still, the attitude toward time expressed in the poem is at best ambiguous: death is personified as paternal (fathering), but also as crazy and cruel, and the trees do stand *against* the moon.

Acceptance is more complete in "the glory is fallen out of." There, when

> the last immortal
>
> leaf
> is
>
> dead and the gold
> year
> a formal spasm
> in the
>
> dust
>
> (p. 41),

the poet preaches or prays for a shared "passing" (without "lingering" or "backward- / wondering") that will

> lead us
> into the
> serious
> steep
>
> darkness
>
> (p. 41).

General reminders of Shelley's "Ode to the West Wind" (wind-driven leaves, a tone of exalted invocation) strongly imply that the promise of spring rebirth is what makes the dying feet and faces "glad" and "glorygirded," and what ruins fear.

The clearest statement in the early poems that nature's acceptance of time and death is creative appears in "O sweet spontaneous": earth conceives spring precisely by being

> true
>
> to the incomparable
> couch of death thy
> rhythmic
> lover

(p. 46).

The joining here of this theme to Cummings' habitual critique of analytic philosophy and science and of institutional religion underscores the argument that man might better ensure his own growth by following nature's yielding example than by demanding that nature be more or less than it is. Such ideas are infrequent in Cummings' early work, and implications of transcendence are slight if present at all; nonetheless, the few poems discussed point toward things to come. It is, again, in the poems of *ViVa* that Cummings' specific interest in transcendence begins.

However, in *ViVa*, Cummings' explicit transcendentalism is only on occasion connected to attention to natural process. Furthermore, in at least one poem, "because i love you)last night," time and death are as threatening as anywhere earlier, although perhaps only in nightmare. On the other hand, "n(o)w" nearly inverts "because i love you)last night" in its own typographically experimental celebration—and imitation—of the growth achieved through natural violence. More to the point, and not surprisingly in a volume dominated by satires of perverted or failed awareness, the few poems in *ViVa* that do touch on themes of nature, time, and transcendence concern the ways in which attitudes toward natural process condition us to deny or affirm the hope of growth. In "you," for example, falsely distanced perception (seeing through "un / washed panes") produces false judgments. The observer, viewing urban passersby in winter, sees only ugliness, defeat, and death. His categorization of people and seasons obscures for him the speaker's insight—applied implicitly to persons as well as trees; knowledge of natural process permits the speaker to glimpse rebirth incipient in superficial death:

> i
> have seen trees(in
> whose black bod
> ies leaves
> hide

(p. 354).

Similar ideas inform "when hair falls off and eyes blur. And." In a world where "minds / shrivel" and "hearts grow brittler," a world with anodynes against the "Ills" of "Laughing Virginity Death," nature's eternal cycle offers no hope against loss. However, because such a world, resisting timeful facts, is wholly false, so, too, is such a conclusion. More direct is "speaking of love(of," in which a grassblade's (or poem's) power to think "beyond or / around" "Our picking it," can signify that "life's only half" and give us confidence to feel "through / / deep weather then / or none"[5] the "all" of transcendence. Cummings' strongest assertion so far that a proper ("natural") awareness and acceptance of process, time, and death assures a world beyond them appears in "when rain whom fear." Children (and lovers)—unlike men—are unafraid of rain; they know that the rain, predicting doom, thus predicates "forever." So knowing, they assume "the laughter of afterwards." This *belief* that accepting loss and death as part of natural process is the way to transcendent growth is what Cummings' later poems concerned with nature, time, and transcendence consistently return to: to assert, to question, to assert again. The spirit-matter dualism such belief implies is what a few of his last poems try to reach beyond.

There is, then, a distinct progression from the often callow early poems to the more philosophical and religious work that begins in *ViVa*. Of course, many critics deny such growth; and there are certainly weak, weak-minded and weak-spirited, poems in every Cummings' volume. However, most of the critical denials rest not on the poetry itself but on a rejection of what informs it—transcendental belief, and of what produces such belief, an epistemology of intuitively known, not empirically measurable, fact. Against the frequent charge that such a mode of knowing cannot be proved, the believer, like any transcendentalist, can offer only witness. This formulation does less than full justice to the later Cummings, who often tests belief against material fact in ways not wholly inconsistent with the high modernist mode. Nonetheless, even such testing results less often in ironic ambiguity than in affirmation, an affirmation that finally rests on Cummings' self-reliant faith that he knows what he knows.

The appropriate places to look for the roots of Cummings' growth in the poems beginning with *ViVa* are in Richard S. Kennedy's detailed life of the poet, *Dreams in the Mirror*, and in the enormous collection of Cummings' papers in Harvard's Houghton Library. For present purposes, though, a very brief biographical foray, drawn in part from Kidder's *E. E. Cummings*,[6] will serve to make a few suggestions. The rapid publication of Cummings' early poems—four books in less than three years, the fourth in 1926—calls attention to the five-year hiatus before the appearance of *ViVa*. Cummings' notable productivity did persist throughout the period; he published a play, a collection of stories, and a book of reproductions of his art work; he sketched, painted, and took part in several exhibitions; he took the month-long trip to Soviet Russia, the diary of which later became *Eimi*. However, the period was also one of drastic change in his personal life. In 1925, at her insistence and to his confusion and distress, Cummings divorced Elaine Orr Thayer; his ineffectual struggle to secure rights to see their daughter Nancy dragged on into the late twenties. An often troubled affair with and marriage to Anne Barton followed. In 1926 Cummings' father was killed and his mother seriously injured in an automobile accident. Concurrent changes mark Cummings' art. He shifted from abstract to representational painting (often of natural settings, such as Mount Chocorua or his nearby New Hampshire summer place, Joy Farm). In his writing this was paralleled by his beginning in *ViVa* to write a transcendental nature poetry which is often profoundly religious. That his altered aesthetic views and deepened thematic concerns in fact stemmed from personal suffering is difficult to say for sure. It seems likely. In any case, the development intensifies in succeeding volumes.

No Thanks appeared in 1935. Its burgeoning attention to natural process as indicating not only time but also possible transcendence intensifies that of *ViVa*. Several poems take up the theme; see, for instance, "snow)says!Says," "at dusk," and "Do.," in the last of which surrender ("relaxing / / -ly") to "Do. / omful" process permits an ego-erasing oneness with nature and a human other. Three poems in *No Thanks* treat Cummings' transcendent vision of nature with special clarity and fullness. In "here's to opening and upward,to leaf and to sap" transcendence is present by implication. The poem may seem at first a pure celebration of nature's "upward" growth, yet one more example of Cummings' supposed obsession with spring. In fact, it celebrates the entire process of nature, morning and twilight, flowers and snow, birth and death. This inclusive awareness becomes explicit in the recognition of the final line that the "fatal songs" of any carnate world "are moving in the moon." The moon, of course, is an ancient sign of change, but if it signals mutability it does so changelessly. Thus, the speaker's embrace of all of process permits (against doubt and fear, necessity and fate) the intuited promise of "one undiscoverable guess." Two other poems discover what that guess might be.

"[C]onceive a man,should he have anything" defines the ideal man, what he isn't and what he is. He is not analytical, consumed by "howish time"; he is not a "rotting scholar" seeking to generalize from life abstract rules to apply like a grid to living. He is, or if he existed would be, attuned to both nature's stability ("mountains for friends") and mutability ("bedfellows for moons"). This holistic acceptance (another form of the generosity that defines him: "should he have anything / would give a little more than it away"), allows the ideal man an insight into nature's chronic cycle that orders and unites time precisely by perceiving its intricate interpenetrations: "(His autumn's winter being summer's spring / who moved by standing in november's may)." That insight, in turn, permits him to lift from material roots to the realm of spirit: "dark beginnings are his luminous ends." Thus, the time and death implied by natural process, when properly seen as essential parts of a larger, coherent, and constant whole also implied by natural process, become entrances to a transcendent world of timelessness and life renewed.

"sonnet entitled how to run the world)" makes parallel points. As Gary Lane has shown in a reading to which this one is much indebted, the octave warns against the dangers of imposing neat but dead generalizations on a messy but living world, and against the several related dangers of analytical intellect ("feel opens but shuts understand"), possessiveness ("gladly forget little having less"), and allegiance to abstraction ("highest fly only the flag that's furled"). The sestet recalls once more nature's permanent interpenetrations (reversing Isaiah's "All flesh is grass" to "grass is flesh") and concludes with the speaker's bequeathing his "rest" (not "eternal rest" or his remains, but rather the spirit that lives on after his flesh pays to dying the one life it owes), to "these / / children building this rainman out of snow." Yielding to the cyclical entirety of process (gain, loss, gain; flesh, grass, flesh; snow, rain, snow) is again the key to transcendent growth. The children build their snowman knowing it will melt, but knowing, too, that its melting is part of a process that will surely create new snow. Like the figure of "conceive a man," they are ideal, and the rightful heirs to the speaker's deathless spirit.[7]

Clearly, Cummings has turned sharply away from the early poetry's typical and assertive resistance to time and death and toward calm acceptance of them. Nevertheless, the assertion that transcendent growth is the result of such acceptance remains an assertion, however ancient and honored its underlying pattern of dying into life. Although such a claim takes time into account—indeed, proceeds by turning it to account, by converting it—it provides no skeptical testing of hope by threat. That is yet to come. Nevertheless, Cummings' stance in these poems is hardly naive. "sonnet entitled how to run the world)," for instance, claims no persistence for the specific self and perhaps hints that its entire project is an act of "will." This, and Cummings' approving quotation, in a letter to Matti Meged, of Plato's reminder that a man must live for the transcendent ideal whether or not it actually exists,[8] may even recall the differing "as if" faiths of Stevens and Frost. In any case, before examining further developments in Cummings' concern with nature, time, and transcendence, an additional point should be made. Cummings is often caught up in the transcendentalist paradox of using nature as a model for getting beyond nature and its built-in limits. Although it need not, this paradox can lead to an attention to natural fact that ends in devaluing nature or even in contempt for it.

Cummings' next new volume, after the *Collected Poems* of 1938, with its relatively few new pieces, was *50 Poems* (1940). There, as in the next two books, *1 x 1* (1944) and *Xaipe* (1950) (for convenience the three are treated together), natural process as a reminder of time and teacher of timelessness remains a constant theme. The familiar idea that time in nature, like social conformity and abstraction, can destroy nature (assassinate "whole grassblades") is the subject of the syntactical dislocations of "am was. are leaves few this. is this a or," in which the natural process of autumn turns "am" into "was," life into death.[9] Equally familiar is its insistence that, unlike the "murders" of society and intellection, those of nature are not only not final but even assure us that "only dying makes us grow." This is the transcendental vision, based in a holistic view of natural process, that evolved in the nature poems of *ViVa* and *No Thanks*. It is re-expressed in several such poems in *50 Poems, 1 x 1*, and *Xaipe*. A few examples will suffice.

In "('fire stop thief help murder save the world," man's socialized panic in reaction to the onset of fall is wholly out of tune with nature. In contrast, the mountain yields calmly to coming winter sleep, despite the frightening blood-red turning of its maples' leaves. Its acceptance promises both present persistence, in the continuing green of the pines, and the future return of spring. This is exemplary, and not only mountains so behave. Three human characters in these volumes share the mountain's "giving" response. Two in a country, one in an urban setting, they agree that earth is a " 'big / thing,' " " 'made'bout / right' " (see p. 567) and that acceptance of the whole of it is essential. The "ice / / coal wood / man" speaker of "goo-dmore-ning(en" puts it this way:

> nic
> he like
> wint-air
>
> nic like ot-am
>
> sum-air(young
> old nic
> like spring yoo
>
> un-air-stan?me
>
> crazy
> me like
>
> evry-ting

(p. 618).

The transcendental implications of such acceptance are made explicit in the third of the three, "noone' autumnal this great lady's gaze," in which "time [is] turned to dream," limits are erased, and " 'growing is . . . was and will always remain.' "

The best known poem on this theme in these volumes is "when serpents bargain for the right to squirm." Its finely absurd conditionals mock man's commercial and bureaucratic categorizing as "unkind" in the full Elizabethan sense of "unnatural." The satirized perverseness of "march / denounces april as a saboteur" is vintage Cummings, and it suggests no simple-minded elevation of spring over other seasons. March, and for that matter November or February, are as integral to April as squirming to snakes, thorns to roses, altitude to mountains. Acceding to the entire complex of living-dying-living is what assures rebirth, as is also asserted by the necessary failure of a man who "would have from madame death / neverless now and without winter spring" in "hate blows a bubble of despair into,"[10] and by "this(let's remember)day died again and."

These poems are consistent with those examined from *ViVa* and *No Thanks*. However, many of the nature poems of *50, Poems, 1 x 1,* and *Xaipe* move in new directions. Cummings' promise of transcendent growth as the result of yielding to timeful process raises some difficult questions of logic—to use a word one uses nervously in proximity to Cummings. How, for instance, does nature's time-bound and -driven, however constant, cycle leap out of time to timelessness? And what can nature's subjugation of individual to general continuity mean to specific human selves? One response to such questions is to say that they do not matter, that the poet's self-reliant witness to intuited transcendental truths, precisely because beyond proving, renders them immaterial. Nevertheless, in some poems in these volumes Cummings recognizes that a transcendental vision with nature as its model has intrinsic limits which make it less than sufficient to his needs. One reaction to this recognition is to supplant nature as model with a "higher" transcending power, that of love. Of course, the transforming power of love is hardly a new theme for Cummings; it has been his ethical center at least since *ViVa*, and perhaps, if in different ways, from the beginning. What *is* new in these volumes is the contrast in the same poems of nature and love as means to transcendence.

One version of that contrast appears in "love is the every only god." Its syntax at first seems to permit the roles of love and nature, as creator and created, to be interchanged ("love" "spoke this earth"; "this earth" "spoke" "love"). Further, natural objects—seas, skies, and stars—are presented as appropriate equivalents for love's truth that "beginning means return." However, the poem's conclusion dissolves this apparently equal partnership: the primacy of love is certain in the syntax of "the skies / by merciful love whispered were." Moreover, nature, although some specific aspect of it might seem "illimitable," is incomplete without the addition of love: "completes its brightness with your eyes / / any illimitable star."[11] In such poems, nature becomes secondary; if not quite devalued, it is certainly revalued, and at times can seem no more than a convenient source of fleshly metaphor for a world of spirit beyond mere flesh. For a further instance, see "love is more thicker than forget."

That the displacement of nature by love is urged by an awareness of nature's limits is perhaps most explicit in "darling!because my blood can sing." In it, not only social institutions ("armies") but also nature's own timefulness ("every isn't that's under the spring") can cloud man's vision. Nature is not to be blamed for this; human perception of nature is what makes for "pitiless fear" or "perfect hope." But this is precisely the point. The significant power here is not nature's but man's (a view earlier implicit, now explicit). The greatest power, the affirming power, is love. The images of rebirth in the poem *are* natural images, the familiar ones of nature's cycle turning the dead world of winter to living spring. However, what drives that cycle is not nature itself but the creative force of love: only if a lover's "look should april me" is "death . . . killed dead" and the hills made to "jump with brooks," trees to "tumble out of twigs and sticks." Such a poem implicitly rejects the physical world of nature for another believed to be more "real."

The same is true of "what if a much of a which of a wind," in which the apocalyptic destruction of universal nature is welcomed as an entrance to the "all nothing" that is "our hugest home." The final assertion is familiar: "the most who die, the more we live," but it is grounded now in a faith beyond one founded on a promise of cyclical rebirth based in observation of natural process. On the other hand, a good index of Cummings' paradoxical thought in such poems is that, in this one, persons marked for rebirth are recognized by their very relation to nature: "whose hearts are mountains, roots are trees." At any rate, the tendency to affirm a spiritual world by denying the physical one also appears in other poems, among them, "as any(men's hells having wrestled with)," as Norman Friedman has pointed out,[12] and "quick i the death of thing."

Cummings' most direct treatment of several matters traced so far in *50 Poems*, *1 x 1*, and *Xaipe* is the last volume's " 'summer is over." Three aspects of the human self (hierarchically, from least to greatest, mind, heart, and soul) respond to the facts of time and death arising from attention to natural process. Mind is cynically sure that time erases all. Human hope is either mere "demanding" or foolish "pretending," "for all / sweet things are until." In response, the optimistic but tentative heart uncertainly offers the now typical hope that as nature signals time it also signals saving cycle:

> "spring follows winter:
> as clover knows,maybe"
> (heart makes the suggestion)
> "or even a daisy—
> your thorniest question
> my roses will answer"
>
> (p. 625).

Mind interrupts this, reasserting the inevitability of death and perhaps suggesting that if nature's cycle is real enough it in no way solves the problem of individual death fundamental to that cycle. Now the poet interrupts to judge mind's "wisdom": mind is clever, but a "fool." But heart's response is not accepted either; however attractive, here it lacks force. The right response is soul's. Crying and smiling at once, soul posits a realm beyond mere contraries, beyond nature and time, a transcendent eternal "now":

> "truth would prove truthless
> and life a mere pastime
> —each joy a deceiver,
> and sorrow a system—
> if now than forever
> could never(by breathless
> one breathing be" . . .
> "more"

(p. 625).

Other matters here demand comment, but for now let it suffice to say that the poem once more asserts Cummings' belief in a realm beyond nature by leaving nature behind.

These poems, then, react to time quite differently from those offering natural cycle as solution, model, or proof. At their extreme, they render nature irrelevant, a Platonic veil of illusion. Nonetheless, they occur within the larger context of others with greater faith in the promise implied in natural process. Furthermore, some poems in these volumes lyrically celebrate actual nature both for its own sake and for its beauty's power to release moments of intensity and transcendence (see, for instance, "might these be thrushes climbing through almost(do they," "life is more true than reason will deceive," and "(nothing whichful about").

One further matter, more or less absent in *50 Poems*, but important in *1 x 1* and *Xaipe*, merits attention here. Most of the poems examined so far are poems of belief. They respond to the threats of time and death by assertively leaping through or beyond them. But Cummings was not always so confident. Just as he often faces the darker facts of this world in more "social" poems, so, too, in a few of the nature poems here his idealistic hopes fully confront his realistic doubts.

A hint of this can be shown by returning to "summer is over," discussed above. The soul in that poem asserts that life in time has meaning because there is "more" than time, an eternal "now" beyond it. However, the assertion is conditional, governed by an "if" convertible to "yes" only by the assumptions of belief. The "evidence" for such belief is, at best, negative: for things to be otherwise would be too much to bear: truth would be truthless; sorrow, a system; life, but a pastime. The very mention of such possible results, unwilled or unwanted though they may be, implies that—whatever their final proportions—hope is here chastened by doubt.

Doubt also qualifies Cummings' revisions of the Eden story in "it's over a(see just." The speaker asserts that it is foolish to obey constricting rules, here society's, and stay out of the tempting orchard, since the apples (and we) are doomed, anyhow, to fall, an idea that fits well enough the common image of Cummings as liberating rascal. However, the speaker also asserts that the apples ("nature") are "as red as to lose / and as round as to find." As man contains both life and death, the "who" of spirit and the "which" of flesh ("you're who as to grow"; "you're which as to die"), so, too, does his world. Furthermore, despite the possibility of growth, no transcendence of a dual or cyclical condition is claimed. Indeed, the tone of the whole is richly ambivalent, as Kidder's quite different reading of it shows.[13]

The major poem of hope confronted by doubt in these volumes is "nonsun blob a." It forecasts much that occurs in Cummings' last two books.

> nonsun blob a
> cold to
> skylessness
> sticking fire
>
> my are your
> are birds our all
> and one gone
> away the they
>
> leaf of ghosts some
> few creep there
> here or on
> unearth

(p. 541).

A masterpiece of the elliptical modernist mode, the poem has been given a thorough interpretation by Barry Marks.[14] Here it will do to note that it sustains two opposed responses to the awareness of erasing time that, as so often in Cummings, results from attention to natural process, here late fall. The sun is faded and faint; all the summer birds have gone; a last few leaves "creep." As we by now expect, one reaction to such loss is hope, both for cyclical return and for transcending mere cycle. Although pale, the sun persists, "sticking fire." The memory of a world made one by an intimate response to nature and by the inspiring vision of love (see the pronouns and pun of the second stanza) renders the remnant leaves reminders ("ghosts") of either the spirit that will return with spring or of the continuing presence of spirit in a realm ("unearth") beyond any "there" or "here," where or when. Yielding to dying again permits growth. However, the poem's syntax (or lack of it) enforces attention to an opposite reaction. The late fall sun is shapeless and cold, too weak to transform "skylessness" to sky. Unifying love and identification with nature are mere memories. The creeping "ghosts" of leaves lend a desolate atmosphere. The world ("unearth") is as little itself as the sun ("nonsun"). What is important is that neither the hopeful nor despairing view is clearly chosen (even the unexpected "and" of stanza two—which, as Marks rightly says, asserts continuous growth—has a qualifying counterpart in the doubtful "or" of stanza three). Of course, such poems of even nearly balanced ambiguity are rare in Cummings' work. His usual stance affirms. Nevertheless, in refusing to easily override doubt, "nonsun blob a" prepares for a shift in Cummings' treatment of nature, time, and transcendence in his final volumes, 95 *Poems* and 73 *Poems*.

Norman Friedman has defined the change this way, writing of 95 *Poems*: more transcendental than ever, Cummings' "affirmation is now frequently accompanied by an acknowledgement of the absolutely real existence of failure, suffering, time, death and mortality."[15] Elsewhere Friedman finds 73 *Poems* to disclose a similar pattern: "this volume reveals greater awareness of pain, loss, and emptiness, and a correspondingly greater sense of the difficulty of transcendence." Transcendence is, nonetheless, still typically achieved, but now with that "greater awareness" presented as part of the (also presented) process of achievement.[16] As we will see, these general remarks apply well to some of the nature poems in the last two books. However, others in them treat nature, time, and transcendence in more familiar ways.

Some use awareness and acceptance of process as the means to leave process behind. For instance, in "if in beginning twilight of winter will stand" acceptance of daily and seasonal change, of the deprivations of twilight and winter, "reveals" a world beyond time, beyond the "nonexistence" of merely physical being, a world where loving spirits approvingly whisper " 'dying . . . is very pleasant.' " Similarly, in "all nearness pauses,while a star can grow," nature's cyclical pattern asserts a timeless beyond. The generalizing conclusion claims once more that we fall to rise, that we die into life:

> Time's a strange fellow;
> more he gives than takes
> (and he takes all)nor any marvel finds
> quite disappearance but some keener makes
> losing,gaining
> —love!if a world ends
>
> more than all worlds begin to(see?)begin
>
> (p. 750).

Also familiar are poems which more directly leap to transcendent realms, annihilating the timeful world of seasons and cycles as they go. In "let's,from some loud unworld's most rightful wrong" the lovers climb not only from bruising society into healing nature ("a cloverish silence of thrushsong" where "mountains speak truth"), but also beyond nature (here at best a mediating stage) to "ultimate / earth" where they are "shrived" of "nonexistence" and time is dissolved: "illimitable day," "immeasurable night." Familiar, too, are poems, including the preceding one, in which nature's status is lowered by the primacy of love. In "Song" ("but we've the may") affirming love has power to conflate (and therefore control) the seasons: "our summer in fall / and in winter our spring / is the yes of yes." In "over us if(as what was dusk becomes," actual process as a model for persistence or transcendent rebirth, even as represented in Cummings' beloved stars, is reduced to mere abstraction (agreed to "with nothing deeper than our minds") by the insistence that "love(and only love / / comprehends huger easily beyonds."

These themes are united in a poem reminiscent of " 'summer is over,'" the parable-like "the first of all my dreams was of." Its original dream is of ideally intimate lovers "strolling . . . (mind in mind)" in a natural paradise. However, nature's implicitly seasonal facts soon impinge, and in the second dream comes a threatening fall: "the sky is wild with leaves; which dance / and dancing swoop(and swooping whirl / over a frightened boy and girl)." The cycle proceeds, though, and soon it is calm and "magical" winter. Given the view of process frequent in Cummings, this fact itself might generate hope, but not for this dreamer, who "wept," until his *lover* dreamed for both of them a vision of spring. It is love transforming nature, not transforming nature, that has the power to save.

The counters of these poems, then, are typical of those in the nature poems from *ViVa* onward. Nevertheless, hints of the darker and more inclusive vision Friedman describes appear in them (see, for example, these ambivalent lines from "if in beginning twilight of winter will stand," discussed above: "mute each inch of their murdered planet grows / more and enormously more less"). Even so, however, faith in transcendence prevails. In striking contrast are a few poems in *95 Poems* and *73 Poems* in which nothing at all avails against the threats of time, death, and emptiness. The bleakest of these is not one of the nature poems, but does relate to new directions in them. It responds to the death of a friend. These are its anguished final lines:

> Feeling
>
> only
> (jesus)every(god)
>
> where
>
> (chr
> ist)
>
> what absolute nothing
>
> (p. 823).

Such feelings invade some of the nature poems as well. "joys faces friends" makes a Frostian statement of nature's indifferent and wholesale dismantling of man's constructions. Even the cellar hole is engulfed. There is no escape or resistance:

> rapidly this
>
> (a

forest has slowly
Murdered the House)
hole swallows it
     self

while nobody

(and stars moon
sun fall rise come
go rain snow)

remembers

(p. 693).

In other poems natural signs even of resistance to nothingness promise no more than momentary stays. The chickadee of the jaunty "spirit
colossal" is undaunted by winter's void, but all the speaker can hope to
take from its example is a lesson of courage in facing the silent "nowheres"
of his own coming winter. In "faithfully tinying at twilight voice" the accepting patience of insects and non-migrating birds at day's and season's
end is equally limited. Their "whisper's whisper" merits gratitude, but
the speaker's sense of overwhelming time permits no transcendent belief.
He knows that even nature's remaining few persistent sounds will soon be
"subtracted from . . . hope's own hope."

Founded, no doubt, on increasing awareness of his own coming
death, there are few such poems in Cummings' canon. The few there are
indicate the deepening respect for natural fact and the refusal to leap too
easily beyond it that mark the final development in his career-long treatment of the relationships of nature, time, and transcendence: poems in
which affirmations rise from a thorough testing against what resists them,
in which difficulties are not overwhelmed but recognized as persistent
parts of a complex whole. One of these is "to stand(alone)in some." The
time is fall. The speaker is witness to the world's being "never by never
robbed of / day" as the sun tracks south. His attention reveals the
"patient" earth's acceptance of this loss: its response is to put on dream,
implying returning spring. Taken as a model, this provides him, in turn, a
"taste" of "not . . . imaginable mysteries." All this is familiar. The threat
of process is observed; properly accepted, the cyclical facts of process
point to transcendent hope. Here, though, these matters are not straightforward. For the speaker, to witness earth's acceptance is to

taste
not(beyond
death and

life)imaginable mysteries

(p. 674).

The placement of the parenthesis allows, of course, the paraphrase
already given: what's tasted are unimaginable mysteries beyond life and

death, in a word, transcendence. However, the parenthesis (a device Cummings typically employs to multiply rather than to restrict potential readings) also gives an alternative: perhaps the mysteries are imaginable (even imagined?) ones not beyond death and life but only of this world. They are lovely, even comforting, but limited in fact and application. The not quite balanced suspension of these alternate readings leaves open questions Cummings often ignored, was often able to ignore: how far can we with conviction extrapolate from natural fact; where does knowing leave off and believing begin? The complicating parenthesis shows Cummings' common assumption that believing *is* knowing to be far less sure than before.

Related complexities characterize a companion piece, "now air is air and thing is thing:no bliss." The sonnet's octave celebrates the recognition that this world is just that, this world, not a clue to or metaphor or symbol of some other. The recognition exhilarates: "such a sharpening freedom lifts our blood / as if whole supreme this complete doubtless / / universe we'd(and we alone had)made." The sestet carries out the octave's implications: put simply, there is no realm for spirit beyond the realms of flesh. Not surprisingly, Cummings is far from prepared to accept such a view. The sestet more strenuously implies that man's "creative" pride is hubris, that his real courage is to see that this world is but a "green trance," to accept his limits, and to yield humbly to death as the entrance to that eternity beyond imagining that man is made for. Nevertheless, this view, too, is qualified. The sestet begins with a "yes" that affirms the octave, and not *all* ironically; it is governed by "or," by possibility, not certainty; and its hope, like man's creative boast, is conditioned by "as if." The point is not that materialist and idealist views are held in a sort of perfect New Critical balance. They are not. In fact, the oppositions of this poem are even more displaced toward transcendental faith than those of "to stand(alone) in some." The point is that what resists belief and will is not annihilated by them. The obstacles to affirming remain within the argument for affirming and lend that argument conviction.

One last example of such a poem, this from Cummings' final book. In one sense, "enter no(silence is the blood whose flesh" is an anthem of transcendental faith. At first, the speaker is anguished, his meaning lost in a shadowy limbo between fall and winter that might predict April: "i breathe-move-and-seem some / perpetually roaming whylessness." However, his prayer for winter (again with potent references to Shelley's "Ode to the West Wind") suggests confidence that the loss of mere physical self ("scatter his nothing") will give spirit "absolute peace." The ground of this is, again, familiar. Natural process, the seasonal descent to winter permitting ascending spring, is the paradigm for man's more transcendental process: yielding to death gives dying into life. In this poem, though, the poet is careful not to push his conclusions quite so far. Winter's (time's) power is awesome:

o come,terrible anonymity;enfold
phantom me with the murdering minus of cold
—open this ghost with millionary knives of wind—
scatter his nothing all over what angry skies . . .

(p. 839).

Moreover, although storm can turn gentle, there is no insistence here that
this proves for individual man a transcendent spring to parallel nature's
real one. The poem ends in descent and whether to the peace of death or
the promise of spiritual life is left unanswered.

The attention given such poems ought not to assert too much. It
would falsify Cummings' career to suggest that it ended with affirmation
in doubt. Poems like those just examined are few and surrounded by many
in which affirmation rises with confidence even from desolate threats of
despair, as, for example, in "now does our world descend." It would be
false, too, to suggest that Cummings moved toward some modernist norm
of ironic ambivalence. The presence of such poems in his final books is
better explained by the deepening sense of man's condition that began in
the poems of *ViVa* and continued throughout Cummings' life, a deepening that moved him slowly—perhaps too slowly—away from reductive
dualism and toward a fuller vision of limited man in a limited world.
Sensing the weakness in Cummings' dualistic view Norman Friedman has
put this in more philosophical terms:

> It seems to me that the basic problem [Cummings] had difficulty in re-
> solving was whether transcendence meant for him a rising *from* the
> material *toward* the spiritual . . . or whether it meant a rising above the
> polarities altogether to where there is no difference between the material
> and the spiritual. The first is Platonic and lends itself all too well to ten-
> sion and division. . . . Cummings' second position, on the other hand, is
> more truly Oriental and encourages integration, harmony, inclusiveness
> and acceptance. And evidence for both can be found in Cummings'
> writings. . . . The trouble is, however, that he rarely seemed to notice
> this fundamental ambiguity in himself and his work, and if he did, he had
> the devil's own time in dealing with it. Most of the difficulties of his life
> and work can be traced, I think, to this self-division.[17]

One way to extend and apply this insight is to note that Cummings'
problems with dualism arise from intractable difficulties at the core of
transcendentalist thought, the difficulties that generate the skeptical
poetries of Stevens and Frost: the tendency, when using nature as a model
for escaping nature's limits, to devalue the model itself, replacing matter
with spirit; the problem of moving, except by assertive belief, from the
timebound model to the timeless parallel desired; the questionable relation of individual consciousness to a cycle which continues life in general
by sacrificing specifics; the dilemma posed by using repetitive cycles as a
metaphor for continuous growth. In his later poems (concurrent perhaps
with his increasing care for actual nature at Joy Farm) Cummings seems

more and more alert to those difficulties, and although they almost never overwhelm or convert him, the greater inclusiveness of the later poems, their more common refusal to escape through faith from natural fact, reflects the larger attention such problems came to demand from him. One certain example of Cummings' awareness of these matters is the last poem of *73 Poems*, and of *Complete Poems 1913–1962*.

"[A]ll worlds have halfsight,seeing either with" exposes the constricting exclusiveness of any dualistic view, whether its emphasis falls on matter or on spirit. The only resolution is still believing love, by which we might climb up from time into the "beauty of the truth." However, believing and knowing are not now so easily made one. Both matter and spirit are real; doubt *and* faith are this world's counters. The "merciful / / wonder" of transcendence is what "no world deny may or believe." This is faith of a deeper and more complex and qualified kind than before: the uncertain faith of mystery, not the certain one of knowing. Even so, there are persistent problems of clarity and coherence in Cummings' vision, problems perhaps inevitable when a fundamentally psychological concept of self-development[18] is grafted onto the already engrafted natural supernaturalism of transcendental belief. Nevertheless, even a narrowly focused look at Cummings' work reveals his development as a religious poet well beyond the naive singer of Cummings legend. At last, he attended to both "dark beginnings" and "luminous ends" and found in nature's "eminent fragility" and in himself that "disappearing poet of always" he once called the snow.

NOTES

1. Among them, Rushworth M. Kidder, *E. E. Cummings: An Introduction to the Poetry* (New York: Columbia Univ. Press, 1979); Richard S. Kennedy, *Dreams in the Mirror: A Biography of E. E. Cummings* (New York: Liveright, 1980); Gary Lane, *I Am: A Study of E. E. Cummings' Poems* (Lawrence: The University Press of Kansas, 1976); Hyatt H. Waggoner, *American Poets from the Puritans to the Present* (Boston: Houghton-Mifflin, 1968), pp. 512–24; Eve Triem, *E. E. Cummings* (Minneapolis: Univ. of Minnesota Press, 1969); Patricia Buchanan Tal-Mason [Cline], "The Whole E. E. Cummings," *Twentieth Century Literature*, 14, No. 2 (1968), 90–97; Edith A. Everson, "E. E. Cummings' Concept of Death," *Journal of Modern Literature*, 7 (1979), 243–54; and especially, Norman Friedman, *e. e. cummings: the art of his poetry* (Baltimore: The Johns Hopkins Press, 1960); *e. e. cummings: The Growth of a Writer* (Carbondale: Southern Illinois Univ. Press, 1964); and "Cummings Posthumous," *Journal of Modern Literature*, 7 (1979), 295–322.

2. Friedman, *e. e. cummings: the art of his poetry*, pp. 178–83 and "Cummings Posthumous," pp. 313–22.

3. *Complete Poems 1913–1962* (New York: Harcourt Brace Jovanovich, 1972), p. 23. All subsequent quotations are from this edition and are referenced by page numbers in the text.

4. Kidder, p. 23; for an alternative reading, see Lane, pp. 56–59.

5. Compare "steep / / darkness" above.

6. Kidder, pp. 83–84.

7. Lane, p. 49.

8. *Selected Letters of E. E. Cummings*, ed. F. W. Dupee and George Stade (New York: Harcourt, Brace & World, 1969), p. 275.

9. See Friedman, *e. e. cummings: The Growth of a Writer*, pp. 128, 130–131.

10. It should be added, though, that in this poem at least man may be saved from the dangers of such willful demands if he converts them to song.

11. Compare Kidder, pp. 152–53.

12. Friedman, *e. e. cummings: the art of his poetry*, pp. 178–79.

13. Kidder, pp. 157–58.

14. Barry A. Marks, *E. E. Cummings* (New York: Twayne, 1964), pp. 26–33.

15. Friedman, *e. e. cummings: the art of his poetry*, p. 179.

16. Friedman, "Cummings Posthumous," pp. 315, 316–17.

17. Friedman, "Cummings Posthumous," pp. 319–20.

18. Compare Roy Harvey Pearce, *The Continuity of American Poetry* (Princeton: Princeton Univ. Press, 1961), p. 360.

INDEX

A Note to the Index: The usual practice of displacing initial articles to the ends of entries is followed throughout with one exception: titles of Cummings' poems follow the index of first lines in *Complete Poems 1913–1962* in leaving articles in place. Titles of secondary works that are not identified by an author's name in parentheses are direcly concerned with Cummings and his works and are fully identified in the text.

DATE		
APR 2 9 1985 AUG. 23 1993		
MAY 2 0 1985 NOV 17 '93		
NOV.05.1996		
MAY 05 86 APR 05 '94 NOV.26.1996		
APR.16.1997		
DEC 0 1 '86 APR 05 '94 DEC 1 9 2001		
APR 13 '8 MAY 09 94		
DEC 23 8 JUN 2 7 2005		
MAY 15 '89 NOV 22 '94 MAY 2 0 2008		
AUG 19 '92 MAY 17.1995		
NOV 18 '92 MAY 26 1995		
APR 21 '93		